DATE DUE

Under Five Shahs

GENERAL HASSAN ARFA

WILLIAM MORROW & CO.

New York, 1965

Contents

Illustrations

Foreword

The decision to write this book was taken on the advice of an old and valued friend who has himself recently published an autobiography in which he tells of certain events in Iran in which we both participated, but which he sees from a point of view entirely different from mine. After reading his book I told him the true story of other and more recent happenings in Iran about which he had heard quite a different version and he then suggested that I should render a service to my country by writing my reminiscences and making known the truth about certain events in which I had taken part. As my parents were of different nationalities with completely dissimilar backgrounds, I have had the opportunity of meeting many interesting personalities and of being concerned in one way or another in much of the recent history of my country. Others had also urged me to write the story of my life, and so this book has been written. In it I have tried to set down what I remember of the events in which I have taken part in a dispassionate and impartial way, from the point of view of an Iranian army officer which I was for thirty-three years and which I remain in spite of my subsequent political and diplomatic career.

I hope that none of the persons whose names have been mentioned in this book or their relatives will be hurt by anything I may have said in my efforts to give a true account of things as I remember them.

I should like to express here my deep gratitude to my wife without whose encouragement, help and advice this book would certainly never have been written and who for forty years has given me her unfailing moral support.

As I have been not only the spectator but one of the actors in the tremendous evolution of my country from the position of a mediaeval oriental state to that of a modern progressive one, this national renaissance being entirely due to the untiring efforts of the late Reza Shah the Great and of his son and heir His Imperial Majesty Mohammad Reza Shah, I wish here to offer my humble tribute to the Imperial House of Pahlavi, to which the Iranian nation owes the preservation of its independence and in which it places its hopes for the future.

Acknowledgment

This book, which is my first attempt to write in English, although it was written in a very short time, was so stuffed with memories which directly or indirectly influenced my life, and were woven into the history of my country, that it was shapeless and sometimes confused. Thanks to her energy, intelligence and understanding, Mrs. Osyth Leeston of John Murray, so shaped and reduced this production of my inexpert pen, as to render it, I hope, readable to the British Public, and I am deeply grateful to her.

In the last century

The structure and political institutions of Iran at the beginning of the nineteenth century did not differ much from what they had been under the Safavi dynasty which reigned from 1502 to 1736, and there was little change up to the First World War and the appearance of Reza Shah.

Administration did not exist, the towns and provinces were ruled by Governors, some hereditary, some sent from the capital, whose absolute and arbitrary power was only limited by that, more absolute and more arbitrary, of the Shah in Teheran. In particular most of the border regions were under local hereditary chiefs who, although acknowledging allegiance to the Shahinshah, were practically independent, and had their courts, their armed forces, regular and irregular, who more often opposed the Shah's forces than marauding tribes of robbers. These chiefs even conducted correspondence with foreign powers and the Central Government as if they were truly independent. They were the Khans, the Amirs, the Sardars, the Valis in Azerbaijan, Kordestan, Lorestan, Khuzestan, Fars, Baluchistan, Khorasan and Mazenderan, and in that part of the Caucasus which belonged to Iran, before it was annexed by Russia after prolonged wars.

The region to the north of the Aras river was sometimes called Arran, and sometimes Moghan and Shirvan and comprised nine semi-independent Khanates: Kuba, Baku, Sheki, Shirvan, Talish, Ganja, Qarabagh, Nakhchevan and Erivan. The first seven were lost by Iran in 1813, the last two in 1828. Since the revolution of 1917 this region is known as Russian (today Soviet) Azerbaijan, although the real Azerbaijan has always been limited to the province to the south of the Aras.

During the war of 1826–8, the Khan of Erivan, loyal to the Shah, resisted for a long time, but finally was defeated and obliged to surrender. His chief Vazir, or Minister, was Mirza Ibrahim, a man renowned for his wisdom piety and kindness, who died in Erivan shortly after the coming of the Russians. His son Hassan, not wishing to remain in a country occupied by foreigners, emigrated to what had remained Iranian soil and by doing so forfeited all his properties and estates, according to the rule of the Russian authorities, and established himself in Tabriz where he married and had seven children, three boys and four girls. The eldest boy was Reza, my father, who was born about 1846.

At first, Hassan, who was later called Sheikh because he was learned in the Qoran and other holy books, started a modest commerce in silk and cotton materials. He made money and bought a plot of land in the town on the banks of the river Aji Chai and built a house there and also a public bath and a shop. He went to Mecca and became a Haji and married three of his daughters to merchants; one of these went to trade in Rasht, another to Constantinople, the third remaining in Tabriz.

Then luck deserted him. In 1864 a particularly bad flood of the Aji Chai destroyed his house, shop and bath and without the aid of his sons-in-law the family would have become destitute.

Reza meanwhile had grown up and his father decided to send him to a religious school in order that he should become a mollah. This, however, was contrary to Reza's ideas, as he had always dreamed of becoming a Government servant. Being an obedient son he could not oppose his father's wishes, but the disaster which had wrecked the family fortunes was to influence his life and allow him to follow the career that he wished.

Sheikh Hassan went to Rasht to try to restore his business with the help of one of his sons-in-law, and Reza, who could not continue his religious studies, accepted the offer of his brother-in-law Haji Agha Reza Salmassi to go to Constantinople to assist him in his commercial business there. So one day he gathered together his modest belongings and with the blessing of his mother, Kulsum Khanum, who gave him a prayer from the Qoran contained in a little wrapper of Kashmir cloth to hang on a chain round his neck, he joined a caravan which was going to Russia and set out on his journey.

He had to ride to Erivan as at that time there was neither railway nor carriage road and once arrived there he stayed with his grandfather's relatives. He was presented to Haji Molla Baba the Qazi, or Shiah religious chief of Erivan, who took a liking to him. When the Molla received an appointment as Qazi in Tiflis, the young Reza went with him. He spent two weeks in Tiflis, before going to Istanbul to his brother-in-law, and while working at his shop, took French and Turkish lessons at a Greek school. After a few years in Istanbul, Reza fell ill, and decided to return to Tabriz, but on arrival in Tiflis, Haji Molla Baba insisted on his remaining there, and sent him to a Russian school where for two years he studied Russian. He was endowed with good looks, a modest demeanour, was amiable, gay and sociable with a keen intelligence and he won the affection and esteem of the old Haji Molla Baba, who treated him as a son. He gave lessons to Haji Molla Baba's nephews in Persian calligraphy and Arabic, a knowledge of which he had acquired during his studies at the religious school in Tabriz, and in return received board and lodging and 8 roubles a month.

It happened that an epidemic of cholera was raging in Tiflis at a time when Nasr-ed-Din Shah, accompanied by a numerous suite, was about to leave for a tour in Europe by way of Russia. An interpreter was needed and the Iranian Consul-General in Tiflis, Ala-ol-Molk Diba, was instructed to send one to Jolfa to accompany the Shah's party during their journey to Tiflis and to remain with them during their stay there. The only person speaking Russian on the Consulate Staff had fallen a victim to cholera and Haji Molla Baba proposed Reza as a substitute, praising him so highly that Ala-ol-Molk asked to see him and liking his manners and bearing accepted him as temporary interpreter and sent him to Jolfa.

I do not think that my father's knowledge of Russian was too extensive, but as no member of the suite was in a position to realise this, and as his manners were faultless, and he was pleasant and entertaining, the Shah when leaving Tiflis congratulated the Consul-General on his interpreter. And as a result Reza was appointed Third Secretary of the Consulate General, his salary being 25 roubles a month.

During the Russo-Turkish war of 1876–8 the Turkish Government asked through the International Red Cross for a neutral person to be appointed to visit the Turkish prisoners of war in Russia. Mirza Reza was designated by the Iranian Government, on account of his knowledge of both Russian and Turkish, and acquitted himself with such zeal that he earned the gratitude of the Turkish Government which accorded him the Order of

Mejidiye, Fourth Class. This was the first of the very many decorations from all countries of the world that he was destined to receive during his long career.

Mirza Reza invented a reformed alphabet which he called 'Rushdiye', and presented to his chief, Ala-ol-Molk. The Arabic alphabet, which was also used in Persian, was singularly deficient in vowels. Ala-ol-Molk sent it to the Crown Prince Mozaffer ed Din Mirza who resided at Tabriz as Governor-General and the Prince praised this work and conferred on my father the rank of Khan, and the honorary function of adjutant to the Crown Prince, besides the order of the Lion and the Sun, Fifth Class. In 1881, having become First Secretary of the Consulate General, he accompanied the mission sent to congratulate the Emperor Alexander III on the occasion of his coronation.

In 1883 Mirza Reza Khan was appointed interpreter to the Iranian party on the mixed Commission for the delimitation of the Irano-Russian frontier that had become necessary by reason of the Russian conquest of the Khanate of Khiva and of the Emirate of Bukhara, as formerly the frontier between these two states and Iran had never been properly delimited. The work of this Commission lasted for five years, as in 1885 Merv had also been occupied by Russia which necessitated complementary work on the eastern frontier of Iran, up to Afghanistan. While there, Mirza Reza Khan succeeded in preventing the inclusion by Russia of a stretch of land that was vital to the inhabitants of the little frontier town of Lotfabad, thanks to his friendship with the family of a Russian General whom he knew in Tiflis, and his chief having reported this fact to the Shah in Teheran, the latter appointed him his General A.D.C.

A few months later his former chief Ala-ol-Molk was sent to St. Petersburg as Minister, and asked for my father as his counsellor, and the Shah readily agreed to this nomination.

During my father's time in Teheran, he acquired the protection and friendship of the then Grand Vizir, Atabek Azam, and this friendship lasted until Atabek's assassination in 1907.

In 1889 my father was included in the suite of Nasr-ed-Din Shah during his third and last journey to Europe and the Shah showed his appreciation of my father's services by appointing him Consul-General for all the Caucasian region with residence at Tiflis. It was here as Consul-General that he met and fell in

love with Mlle Ludmilla Jervis. My mother had the most extraordinary family background, which certainly contributed to the
forming of her personality, and to some extent to that of her son,
myself. Her father was a British engineer, the son of a retired
Commodore of the British Navy, who had been a midshipman
at the battle of Trafalgar. After retiring from the Navy, Commodore Jervis settled in the U.S.A., for reasons unknown to his
great-grandson. His son, Charles, decided to become an engineer,
went to France and entered the Ecole Polytechnique in 1848.
In order to do this he had been obliged to accept French citizen-
ship, and having taken part in manifestations by students against
the 1851 *coup d'état* by Prince-President Louis Napoleon Bonaparte, the future Napoleon III, he was arrested, and together with
his comrades jailed and deported to Noumea, in French New
Caledonia, used at that time as a penitential colony.

Luckily for him his ship had a mishap and he managed to
escape. History does not mention how, and when he had completed his engineering studies he went to Russia to build railways.
Then in a Moscow shop he met a young girl whom he overheard
speaking English to the governess who accompanied her.
Foreigners were rare in the Russia of those days and making the
excuse of their common language the young man introduced
himself and a conversation started. Probably the two had a few
subsequent meetings, thanks to the complicity of the English
governess: in any case they fell in love with one another, and the
young engineer put on his best frock-coat, top hat and yellow
gloves and presented himself at the imposing mansion of the
Demidoffs, the millionaire owners of the famous Ural gold mines
who since their forebear Demid, the founder of Russian industry
and close friend of Peter the Great, had become one of the great
boyar families of Russia. A serf footman ushered him into the
presence of Major-General Piotr Pietrovich Demidoff, the father
of his beloved, who was sitting in his drawing-room playing
patience.

Major-General Demidoff was born in the early seventeen-
eighties, his career followed the usual course for a young nobleman of those days. As an officer in the Guards he distinguished
himself in 1825 during the unsuccessful military rising against
Nicholas I by taking the side of the young Emperor whose aide-de-
camp he later became. He retired after the Hungarian campaign,

in which he took part with the forces that the Russian Tsar had sent to help the Emperor Francis Joseph against the Hungarian rebels in 1849.

Demidoff's elder brother, Anatole, who was a General in the Russian Army, had been so hurt that General Prince Wittgenstein had been preferred to him as commander of the vanguard of Kutusoff's army during the pursuit of Napoleon's Grand Army in 1812, that he left Russia for good and settled in Paris. Later his son bought the Principality of San Donato in Italy, thus acquiring the title of Prince San Donato Demidoff for that branch of the family, and married Princess Mathilde, the daughter of Lucien Bonaparte and the niece of Napoleon I.

Perhaps Piotr Pietrovich Demidoff was by nature no worse than most men of his class at that time, but when he became angry there was no limit to his fury, and as he was as strong as an ox and in such moments apt to lose all reason, the results were appalling as these two examples will show.

One day he asked for his carriage and was told that the coachman was lying drunk in the attics. He mounted the stairs, took the man by the neck, hurling him down into the cobbled courtyard so that he was killed instantly.

When his only son had completed his studies at the military academy his father awaited his return to the Demidoff country estate, but the boy failed to arrive at the time he was expected. Demidoff became furious and imagining that instead of coming home the young cornet was having a gay time in town, ordered his serfs to flog him on his arrival until their master should stop them. Later he fell asleep, but as the serfs were mortally afraid of him they did not dare awaken him when the boy arrived early in the morning, having been delayed by a snowstorm, so they flogged him to death.

After this appalling action he got rid of his wife by forcing her into a convent and then in a fit of remorse ordered a church to be built on one of his estates. When, however, he presented himself for communion the priest, a conscientious man, although trembling with fear refused to give it to him on account of his monstrous sins. Beside himself with rage, Demidoff nearly strangled the miserable priest and then had him transferred to one of his estates in the Ural.

All these crimes were disguised as accidents and protection in high places prevented them from reaching the ears of the Tsar. A Russian proverb says 'Tsar is too far and God is too high'.

He was nearly sixty when he married Miss Claxton, the daughter of the British Consul in Moscow. When about to give birth to her first child the doctor despaired of saving both mother and child, but my great-grandfather unhesitatingly ordered him to sacrifice his wife, and so in 1838 my grandmother was born at the price of her mother's life. All these fearful tales were told to me by my grandmother, who is my only source, and I fervently hope they were exaggerated, but in any case these show that the Russian nineteenth-century liberal had reason to be dissatisfied with things as they were.

Having delivered his formal request to General Demidoff for his daughter Anastasia's hand in marriage with true British assurance the young man hopefully awaited the boyar's reply, but the huge Russian, incensed by what he considered the impertinence of this unknown Englishman asking to marry his daughter, without uttering a word seized him with his great bear-like paws and threw him out of the window from the second floor of the house on to the pavement.

The unfortunate suitor was taken to hospital where he remained for several weeks. While there he managed to see Anastasia and when he finally recovered carried her off, returning to her father the clothes she had worn with a note saying it was the girl he had wanted and not her fortune. The furious General disinherited his daughter and never saw her again as long as he lived.

Charles Jervis and Anastasia had seven children, but all died in their childhood except Ludmilla, my mother, who was born in 1870. Shortly after that my grandfather went to the U.S.A., to take part in a building project. My grandmother told me that it was the Brooklyn Bridge, but she was not quite sure about it. Then came the news that he had been murdered in a hotel room and robbed, presumably by his valet who had afterwards disappeared.

My grandmother at once departed to New York in order to trace her husband's presumed murderer and recover the money he had stolen, leaving her four-year-old daughter with her father-in-law, the ninety-year-old Commodore who was living in Baden-Baden.

My mother used to tell me how well she remembered her British grandfather who, after dinner, often used to describe the battle of Trafalgar in such a vivid way, that glasses and china felt the impact of it as if they had been French vessels subjected to British broadsides. When her mother returned from America empty-handed and embittered, the little Ludmilla was so attached to her naval grandfather that she was loth to leave him and unfortunately showed it. My grandmother was so indignant that her child should prefer staying with her grandfather to returning to her mother that her feelings of resentment towards her lasted throughout her life and poisoned for ever the relations between mother and daughter.

As her husband had left her nothing and her father, who had disinherited her, had died and she was too proud to accept any help from her Demidoff relatives, she resolved to give lessons to the children of the Russian nobility in order to keep herself and her small daughter. She was well qualified to do this, as thanks to her lavish upbringing she had a perfect knowledge of English and French as well as being an excellent pianist. All these accomplishments she passed on to her daughter who, after completing her studies as a pianist at the Conservatoire, became also a composer.

When my mother was fourteen years old, influenced by the liberal ideas of the youth of that period and much affected by social injustice, she wrote a poem criticising absolutism and the arbitrary ways of the administration, and sent it to a liberal weekly. The paper published this expression of youthful liberal enthusiasm and was at once suspended. The authorities ordered the arrest of the editor as well as that of the author of the poem. When it was discovered that the delinquent was a fourteen-year-old girl, the authorities were disconcerted and decided to keep her not in jail, but in a room at police headquarters. She did not remain there for long as her mother went to St. Petersburg, petitioned the Tsar, and obtained her release. I do not know what happened to the editor of the too hospitable weekly, who was not a girl, was older than fourteen, and whose mother was not Anastasia Jervis *née* Demidoff.

In 1887, having heard that a man thought to be the valet who had murdered her husband had been traced to Constantinople, my grandmother decided to go there to continue her search for him, taking her daughter. She failed to find her quarry, but was engaged by a Pasha to teach music and French to his children.

From what my mother used to tell me, they had a wonderful time. The Pasha was most courteous and his wife (he had only one) and the other Turkish ladies with whom they came in contact were amiable and cultivated. Turkey was still quite oriental, and appeared extremely picturesque to foreigners. The hundreds of slender minarets towering above the grey cupolas of the mosques and dominating the narrow cobbled lanes bordered by wooden houses with lattice-covered windows, the crowds of people from all parts of the then extensive Ottoman Empire in their special and widely different national clothes, and the veiled women, all presented a bewildering spectacle and fascinated the newcomers to that extraordinary 2500-year-old metropolis.

In the night, policemen were not to be seen, but each district had several *bekchis*, or night-watchmen, paid by the people living there. These men walked the whole night banging the ground with their iron-tipped canes so that the inhabitants of the houses should know that they were awake and watching, and in consequence sleep in security.

When there was a fire, which was often, as nearly all houses were built of wood, a red light appeared on the top of the Galata tower and the watchmen immediately announced what district was affected. Then all the *bekchis* repeated a special long-drawn-out cry '*Yangin var*' in such and such a district. The fire brigade consisted of half-naked men carrying on their shoulders long hose-pipes. Their duty was to run on foot all the way to the place of the fire. Of course with such primitive and ineffectual means of fighting it the fire consumed scores and sometimes hundreds of wooden houses in a few hours, and where there had been a well-built district, an empty space appeared where grass grew up and sheep and goats grazed.

Sometimes a sudden heart-rending cry would be heard, but instead of rushing to see what had happened and offering help, people would shut their windows and refrain from any kind of interference. They knew it was probably due to the summary execution of some politically undesirable person by the redoubtable *hafiyes*, as Sultan Abdul Hamid's secret police were called, disguised as robbers, and it was unwise to have seen or heard anything unusual.

On Fridays, the holiday of Moslem countries, my mother used to drive with lightly veiled Turkish ladies in a landau to the then fashionable promenade at Kiatkhane with smart Turkish officers riding beautiful Arab horses following the carriage and exchanging glances and even compliments with the pretty *désenchantées*.

After two years in Turkey my grandmother decided to return to Russia, and they settled for a while in Tiflis, in what is now Soviet Georgia. Being the capital of the Caucasus and the headquarters of the Viceroy, Tiflis did not give the impression of a provincial town. It was aristocratic and at the same time popular and cosmopolitan, with a mixed population of Georgians, Armenians, Azerbaijanis, Persians, Circassians, Lezghis and Russians. Being a frontier town, both with Turkey and Iran, it had an important military garrison and officers of the Imperial Army in brilliant uniforms mixed on the boulevards and public squares with civilians in *cherkesskas* (known by foreigners as cossack tunics) and astrakhan caps and beautiful black-eyed Georgian ladies. There were also several foreign Consuls, and one of them, a handsome oriental who always wore military uniform, attracted much attention from the fair sex. This was the Iranian Consul-General, Mirza Reza Khan, my father.

The Georgian aristocratic families, all of them bearing the title of princes, and many of them related to the former royal houses of Georgia, Imeretia and Mingrelia, dispossessed by Russia at the beginning of the nineteenth century, formed a fair proportion of the officers' corps of the Russian army in the Caucasus. The soldiers were Russians from Russia proper, Georgian recruits being sent to serve in the purely Russian provinces. In this way, the former Georgian governing class stayed in Georgia, without the security of Russian rule being endangered by the possibility of a military rising by local army units. These Georgian princes, the Shirvashidzes, Chavchavadzes, Tseretelli, Orbeliani and others of gay exuberant character and hospitable habits, used to keep open house and give parties at which young and old enjoyed drinking sparkling kakhetian wine, singing old Caucasian ballads and dancing the celebrated *lezginka*.

It was at such a party that my father saw and fell in love with my mother, then a slender girl of twenty. She did not fail to fall under the charm of the handsome heart-breaker and besides longed to escape from the harsh rule of her mother who, on being asked to consent to her daughter's marriage, replied by breaking an umbrella over her head! The poor girl then left her home and took refuge in the house of a Russian General's widow where she stayed until my father bore her off through Baku to Enzeli (now Pahlavi) on the Iranian shore of the Caspian Sea, where the marriage ceremony took place according to Moslem usage, my mother having first become a Moslem and an Iranian subject. This procedure was necessary, as in Russia it was illegal for a member of the Orthodox Church to marry anyone not a member of that church and thus the difficulty was overcome, at any rate in my father's opinion.

After their return to Tiflis my mother had to lead the secluded life of a Moslem woman of that time, staying at home, never going out with her husband and never receiving any male visitors. My father had bought a fine house in Tiflis for the ornamentation of which he brought special skilled workers from Iran who decorated several of the rooms with inlaid mirror work and scenes from Firdausi's *Shahname* painted on the ceilings. He then built a large villa in Borjom, a place celebrated for its mineral waters, which he called Firouze (Turquoise) on account of the beautiful blue tiles with which it was adorned. He also built a smaller one in a garden of roses above Borjom which had been given to my mother as a wedding present by the grand Duke Michael Alexandrovitch.

It was in the Tiflis home that on 10th May 1895 I opened my eyes on the still stable and secure nineteenth-century world all unconscious of the crises, wars and revolutions which were to happen in my lifetime, changing not only the political maps of the world but the social and economic structure of every country.

PART I

Before the First World War
in Europe and Iran.
Under the last Qajar Shahs
1895–1919

Childhood and youth

When I was born my father had already left Tiflis, having been appointed Iranian Minister in St. Petersburg and also in Norway and Sweden, which countries were at that time united under King Oscar II. Two months after his arrival in St. Petersburg my father assisted at the gorgeous ceremonies of the Tsar Nicholas and the Empress Alexandra's coronation. He was a horrified witness of the terrible Khodianka catastrophe when hundreds of people were killed in a panic during a distribution of gifts on behalf of the Emperor, considered by many people to have been a bad omen for the reign, and later happenings certainly justified these forebodings.

When I was a few months old my mother brought me from Tiflis to St. Petersburg where my father resided in the splendid mansion of Prince Bieloselski-Bielozorski on the Krestovski Island. My mother continued to lead a secluded life, never accompanying my father to parties and never appearing at the Legation, but she was allowed to drive out in our victoria and even sometimes to drive her favourite trotter herself in a dogcart on the famous Strielka promenade bordering the Neva river.

From that time I was in the constant care of a young man called Mirza Mohammad, who was the son of my father's agent in Tiflis and the grandson of Haji Molla Baba and who stayed with us from my second to my ninth year. He was modest, good-tempered and diligent and had a passion for history which even at that age influenced me, and I never remember his being harsh with me. My very real affection for him continues today, but neither he nor I could have imagined then that he would rise to be several times Foreign Minister and three times Prime Minister. This remarkable career was entirely due to his capacity, honesty and intelligence.

I remember when I was four years old being taken by train to Hapsal with my parents and Mirza Mohammad. In Hapsal I went to a kindergarten and fell in love for the first time with a rosy-cheeked blonde little girl four years old like myself. When I came home it appears that I sat for a long time gazing into space, and when asked what I was thinking about replied, 'Let me alone—I am thinking of my love'. This produced much laughter at my expense and I retired red in the face to sulk in a corner.

It was at about this time that Mozaffar-ed-Din Shah, who had succeeded his father Nasr-ed-Din Shah, came to Russia on his first visit to Europe accompanied by a retinue of sixty persons, ranging in rank from Grand Vizir to *kalyan* (hookah) bearer. The Shah was much pleased by Europe and wished to repeat his visits, but those journeys were such a drain on the Iranian exchequer that a loan of 2,000,000 roubles on very onerous conditions had to be negotiated with Russia to finance them.

On his arrival in St. Petersburg he was met by the Tsar Nicholas II, my father being also present at the station. When the Shah alighted from his carriage before the Legation all the staff, including myself in a Persian frock-coat and a black cap, were standing at the door. Everybody bowed low, but I remained erect staring at the Shah and when remonstrated with, announced in a loud voice—'That is not the Shah—I have seen the Shah's picture and he has black moustaches whilst this man has white ones'.

The Shah, who used to dye his moustaches, had neglected to do so on the journey; instead of being angry he laughed and pinched my cheek and I received the appointment of First Secretary to the Iranian Legation, and the title of Arfa-os-Soltan (highest near the Sultan), my father's title being Arfa-ed-Dovleh (highest in the State).

The giving of titles of this sort which were purely honorary dates from the time of the Abbassid Khalifs who accorded them to great vassals and dignitaries and even to kings. In Iran this practice was followed and many government officials and their families had such resounding titles bestowed on them, but the custom was discontinued by Reza Shah in 1925, and all the previously given titles and honorary military ranks suppressed.

Thanks to his social gifts and unfailing presence of mind, my father was a success at the brilliant Court of St. Petersburg, and became a great favourite, especially with the wives of the high dignitaries to whom he presented flattering verses in Persian, translating them himself into French or Russian. He even dedicated a poem to the Empress Alexandra Feodorovna, and won her favour as well as the Emperor's consideration by his clever repartee and dignified manners. In consequence, the Emperor complimented the Shah on his Minister, and such appreciation was naturally very gratifying to His Majesty.

After coming back from The Hague, my father was entrusted with a very important mission. The Russian Government, taking as pretext the fact that cholera and other epidemics were endemic in India, established a quarantine station in Sistan in Iranian territory. After a while they decided to send a squadron of Cossacks as a protection against any eventual tribal disturbance, although no such disturbance was expected; this being a move in the Russian forward policy. The *mollas* of the Holy City of Mashad where the Shrine of Imam Reza, the eighth Imam, is situated, provoked a mass demonstration of the people to protest against the Russian intrusion into this holy region and the Iranian Government was in a difficult situation. My father was instructed to try to dissuade the Russian Government, and as he succeeded in doing this directly through the Emperor, the Shah was much pleased and accorded him the personal title of Prince in recognition of his services.

At the end of 1899 my mother was obliged to have a serious operation and the doctors advised her to go abroad. There was another reason for my mother taking me away from Russia, which finally brought about the separation and then the divorce of my parents. My grandmother had been unceasing in her efforts to bring about the separation of my parents in order to punish her daughter for her disobedience in marrying a Moslem. Up to this time my grandmother had not succeeded, but she finally sent a petition to the Tsar stating that the marriage of her daughter was illegal according to Russian law and asking that I should be taken from my mother and given to her to be brought up in accordance with the Orthodox faith.

In this way an impossible situation arose for my father, his diplomatic career was in danger of being ruined and he decided to send us away from Russia, so in May 1900 my mother, Mirza Mohammad and I left St. Petersburg for Paris where we arrived just in time for the 1900 Universal Exhibition.

From Paris we went to Dresden, where my mother rented an

apartment. The honorary Consul-General of Iran was a rich industrialist called Wunderlich and having heard from my father of our arrival, he at once called on my mother and soon she became well known in Dresden society. It was at this time that the free manners and unprotocolaire behaviour of the Crown Princess Louise of Saxe were provoking much comment and criticism among my mother's acquaintances, and I remember their indignant exclamations when somebody, forgetting the presence of a child, began to tell of her latest *frasques*. Shortly after that she eloped with her children's French tutor, and finally married the Italian composer Toselli, who composed for her his celebrated serenade.

In 1900 my father was appointed Ambassador at Constantinople, the only Embassy we had, all our other representations being Legations. Just before taking up his post my father was sent to The Hague to represent Iran at the first Peace Conference and this Conference produced such a deep impression on him that he became a convinced pacifist and was inspired to narrate its proceedings in a poem composed in Persian which was translated into twelve languages.

The Peace Conference had been assembled through the initiative of the Russian Emperor Nicholas II, who had proposed that all powers should agree not to increase their armaments for a specified period. But as this proposal was opposed by the German representative, the Conference ended in failure. At the last meeting my father made a speech warmly supporting the Russian proposal and praising the Tsar's initiative. Nicholas II was so pleased by this that on my father's return to St. Petersburg he presented him with a malachite box with his enamelled portrait in miniature surrounded by small diamonds with four large diamonds at each corner. This precious Imperial gift is still in my possession. Then in 1902 my father was sent from Constantinople to Spain to represent Iran at the coronation of the eighteen-year-old King Alphonse XIII.

In the summer we used to go to the seaside resort of Blankenberge near Ostend, in Belgium, or to Caux in Switzerland. During a holiday in Blankenberge in 1902 I saw Mozaffar-ed-Din Shah for the second time when he visited Ostend. My father was not in attendance, but the Shah hearing that Arfa-ed-Dovleh's son was in the neighbourhood, sent for me and I was presented to His Imperial Majesty, who greeted me very kindly. As it was past noon, the Shah's party then adjourned to the hotel's dining-room, His Majesty sitting at a small table and the rest of the party of about thirty people taking their places at a long table close by. I was placed at the right of the Grand Vizir, Atabek Azam.

During the lunch, as I noticed that wine was being served to all the persons of the suite, I said in Azeri Turkish, the dialect of the north-western province of Iran, addressing myself to the Grand Vizir: 'Is wine not forbidden to Moslems according to the Qoran?' With a smile he answered: 'Yes, of course, but sick persons who need wine to restore themselves are authorised to drink wine.' This answer did not satisfy me, and looking around the table, I said again in my high child's voice: 'Are you all sick, then?' This question provoked general laughter and the Shah inquired its cause, and being told by the Grand Vizir, was much amused. After lunch, the Grand Vizir gave me a gold pencil holder as a souvenir, which I still have.

My father wished me to enter the famous Theresianum College in Vienna, where several Iranian boys were studying, so my mother took me to Vienna, but apparently the doctors considered that the cold and damp climate of that town would not suit me, so after one week in Vienna we visited Semmering, and Gratz, where my grandmother who had been searching for us finally ran us to earth, and my earliest memories of her date from that time. In October of that year we went to Lausanne, where my mother rented a villa and I began to attend a private school.

Early in 1904 my beloved Mirza Mohammad received a letter saying that his mother was very ill (in reality she had died, but in Iran deaths are never announced brutally to near relatives, and it is considered proper to prepare them for the sad news), and he was recalled to Tiflis. After a few weeks my cousin Abdul Rahim Khan, son of Haji Agha Reza Salmassi with whom my father had stayed in Istanbul in the late sixties, arrived from there sent by my father to replace Mirza Mohammad and to learn French. He was eighteen years old, gay and amusing, and I liked him very much. But unlike the chaste Mirza Mohammad, he had a great liking for the fair sex, and not being accustomed to the ways of the country often ran into trouble, to the great annoyance of my mother, who had Victorian ideas as to how people should behave.

In 1905 my mother took me to Vittel near Contrexeville in France, where Mozaffar-ed-din Shah accompanied by his numerous suite was undergoing a cure during this, his third and last journey to Europe. I had my two last meetings with him, and have kept a vivid memory of them. I was walking one day in the country with my cousin, when a cavalcade appeared on the road in a cloud of dust, and stopped in front of us, the Shah having noticed my Iranian black cloth cap. When the dust subsided I saw the Shah sitting in a carriage landau *à la* Daumont, with outriders, the new Grand Vizir Eyn-ed-Dovleh, an old prince with snow-white drooping mustachios sitting on his left, and my father and the War Minister Amir Bahador Jang sitting opposite. The Shah's landau was preceded by a troop of French Hussars in light blue dolmans and red breeches, who were responsible for the dust, and followed by several other carriages, a second troop of Hussars ending the cavalcade.

My cousin lost his head and fled behind some trees, but I stood at attention and with hands joined on my stomach bowed deeply according to Iranian Court etiquette.

'Who is this boy?' asked the Shah. 'It is my son, Your Majesty's slave,' said my father. The Shah ordered the door of the landau to be opened and I was helped by a footman into the carriage. The Shah pinched my ear and talked to me in Azeri Turkish which he knew very well, the Qajar dynasty being descended from a Turkoman tribe. I was praised for my little black cloth Persian hat, making my father very proud of me. After that I was allowed to go, and the cavalcade disappeared in a new dust cloud. Two days afterwards I was summoned by the Shah to his hotel at Contrexeville, my uncle Ali Akbar Khan telling me that when ushered into the Presence, I should kneel and kiss His Majesty's feet. I duly attempted to perform this ceremony, but the Shah kindly raised me up and gave me a chain composed of alternate gold and platinum links, telling me that it was a souvenir from his father, Nasr-ed-Din Shah. Overwhelmed with pride I was allowed then to kiss the Shah's hand.

Shortly after this my cousin went back to Istanbul, where he was employed at the Embassy, as also was my former tutor Mirza Mohammad after his return from Tiflis, and I was left alone with my mother. We went to Paris on our way home, where I enjoyed watching the varied and colourful uniforms of the French Army.

In 1906 we left Lausanne and went to live in Geneva, where my grandmother was already living. During a summer holiday spent in Beatenberg in the Bernese Alps we made friends with an old Geneva family who advised my mother to send me to a private school in Geneva which was organised on military lines like a cadet school, the schoolboys wearing Swiss army uniforms with miniature rifles which were the exact copies of Swiss Army regulation rifles and here I spent a very happy year. In winter we went to the winter sports resorts in the mountains, such as Arosa, Caux and Chateau-d'Oex, and I particularly enjoyed the last-named place, where we went in 1907–8 and 1908–9, renting a picturesque chalet built with pine-wood, warm and cosy. I learned to ski and with my dog, a collie called Castor, I used to wander in the snow-covered pine woods imagining I was a trapper in Canada or Siberia.

My mother gave me lessons in Russian and a teacher came in the afternoon to teach me Latin, mathematics and French literature. It was during this year that we learned for the first time that after his divorce from my mother my father had married the daughter of a Swedish professor and that I had a brother Ibrahim and a sister Fatimah.

On the occasion of my twelfth birthday my mother gave me toy soldiers, and I had a huge table made for me on which I used to stage battles in accordance with the history of Napoleon's wars that I was reading at the time. In this way my passion for everything military developed and drove me towards a military career.

In spite of the strained relations between my mother and my grandmother, we used to visit her from time to time, remaining with her for the night, and although I knew of the old lady's hostility towards my mother I enjoyed these visits, because she lived in the country. I liked to be wakened in the morning by the crowing of cocks, the cackle of hens and the mooing of cows. I was very fond of reading Russian books like Turgienief's *A Hunter's Sketches* and had a romantic feeling for country life.

In 1908 my mother took a delightful old country house at Troinex near Geneva with a big barn separated from the house by a cobbled yard. There was a large garden, and with an air-gun and my dog Castor I used to wander in the woods looking for birds and rabbits.

I was at this time attending the Collège de Genève, where I was often in trouble for my wild ways, but I was already passionately interested in history and geography and had begun to devour the French and Russian classics.

While at Troinex I kept pedigree hens, pigeons and rabbits and my taste for country life developed so that for a time I hesitated whether to become a soldier or a farmer. In the end I became both!

In the summer of 1909 my mother sent me to a boarding-school at Coppet on the Lake of Geneva, and one day at luncheon the headmaster excitedly announced that Blériot had successfully flown the Channel. But still only a few people believed at that time that 'heavier than air' machines had a practical future, and would completely displace airships.

In the autumn, according to my father's wish, my mother took me to Paris, and I was sent to a private school in the Passy district not far from the Bois de Boulogne, where several Iranian students were already studying so that I met young Iranians of my own age for the first time.

The Paris of 1909 was very different from that of today. True, the famous Parisian cabs with the cabmen in beige or grey shining top hats were only rarely seen, but the two-decked horse-drawn omnibuses were still in use and many tram-cars were steam powered. Electric private motor-cars with footmen drove in the Bois de Boulogne, and on Sunday mornings young bloods in morning coats, grey top hats and carrying gold-headed canes, and elderly gentlemen in light grey frock-coats, strolled about appraising the *élégantes* in wide-brimmed hats through black beribboned monocles. I was sent to a tailor and put into grown-up clothes for the first time, and suddenly, without any transition, I passed from childhood to adolescence.

The Avenue des Champs-Elysées was bordered by private mansions belonging to aristocratic families and surrounded by gardens, and no shops or large buildings interfered with the green beauty of that marvellous thoroughfare. Sometimes we went to the theatre, and I saw one of the early performances of Edmond Rostand's famous and controversial play *Chantecler* with

Lucien Guitry in the leading role. I had already seen Edmond Rostand's *L'Aiglon* and *Les Bouffons* in Geneva with Sarah Bernhardt. On Sundays we were sent to visit the museums, and of course the Carnavalet and Invalides attracted me because I was tremendously interested in contemporary history and the Napoleonic wars.

It was at this time that my father, after having served for ten years as Ambassador in Turkey, decided to retire to a villa he had built in the Principality of Monaco on the lower slopes of Mont Turbie on a site dominating the whole Principality and the coast of the Riviera to Bordighera in Italy. Before settling there he visited America on the invitation of an old flame who had married a millionaire, but before leaving Europe he came to Paris to see me and gave me and my Iranian class-mates gold fountain pens which were still a great novelty.

After spending some two months in America and attending the funeral of Edward VII in London he went to see my mother in a château she had rented at Labbeville-Frouville near Valmondois north of Paris, where I was recovering from an attack of scarlet fever. The Château de Briecourt was an old seventeenth-century mansion surrounded by 50 acres of woodland and fields, where I wandered for hours, watching squirrels, foxes, badgers, pheasants and wood pigeons. My mother had rented this place with the idea of starting a farm. Her staff consisted of a woman cook, an old coachman and cowman, who remembered having seen the Prussians in occupation of the château in 1871, and a former bluejacket of the Imperial Russian Navy, who was a kind of jack-of-all-trades. This man stood at attention while talking to my mother and used to tell me how he took part in the mutiny in the Russian battleship *Potemkin* in the Black Sea in 1905 during the first unsuccessful Russian Revolution. He told me in the most natural way in the world, how the men threw their officers overboard, hoisted the red flag and wandered about in their ship in the Black Sea until they were finally interned in the Rumanian port of Constantza. Here they were released to go wherever they wished as, being considered political refugees, their extradition was refused. Many years afterwards I saw this episode in a Soviet film, and recognised the accuracy of my naval friend's narrative.

I still thought of becoming a farmer, but at school I was

considered rather difficult and so for the summer vacation of 1910 I was sent to Montargis, to stay with a schoolmaster who was a strict disciplinarian. However, after a few weeks I eloped with the professor's wife who left her husband and two children. The incensed husband informed the Iranian Minister in Paris and the police. The Minister wired my father and my mother who both arrived in Montargis, and the police having traced us to the town of Nevers, we were arrested. The unfaithful wife returned to her home and I to my father, who took me to Liège where he was a member of a Masonic Lodge. He wanted me to become an apprentice mason, but I firmly refused, saying that masons were always on the side of revolutionary movements and that I was by principle royalist and on the side of authority. As my father imagined that all young men ought automatically to be radical minded, he was rather taken aback by my answer, but did not insist.

After that I was sent to the Lycée Michelet in Paris, but after a few days I disappeared from there and for a week lived in a small hotel on the Place Ste-Geneviève with a Lettish student who had fled from Russia on account of some terrorist outrages committed during the Revolution of 1905 and whose acquaintance I had made through Alexis, the deserter from the *Potemkin*.* Then I drifted again to Brécourt and after these *intermezzi* my father decided to take me to Monaco. In December 1910 I arrived at Villa Danishgah, which means the house of Danish, this being the pen-name of my father, and made the acquaintance of my stepmother, my eight-year-old brother and my four-year-old sister. My stepmother, Elsa Lindberg, was a tall handsome woman some thirty-five years old, gay, dynamic and cultured, with an artistic temperament. I liked her and she did not dislike me, as we always joked and laughed together about everything. My brother fell at once under his big brother's influence, but my sister was rather scared of me and remained aloof under the protection of her mother.

I entered the Monaco College, situated on the rock in the old town between the Prince's palace and the Oceanographic museum, to which I had to walk twice a day from our villa down the steep steps to the low-lying district of la Condamine and then climbing

* I learned later that after the Russian Revolution of 1917, this man, called Purin, had been a Minister in the first revolutionary Government of Latvia.

up the rock and back. I was young and it was good exercise.

During the winter every week there were performances of opera, comedy and ballet at the Casino theatre, and twice a week classical and symphony concerts. I never missed one of them and became a confirmed lover of opera, ballet and music. I saw Puccini's *Tosca* and many Italian and French operas with Battistini, Tito Schipa and once even Caruso, who came from the United States and sang in *Don Quichotte*.

I liked to stroll on the terraces behind the Casino and sit at the Café de Paris, listening to Franz Lehar's Viennese waltzes played by tziganes and watching the endless procession of people of all nationalities and the gorgeously dressed, beautiful ladies. At that time the visitors to Monte Carlo were chiefly Russian Grand Dukes and aristocrats, petty German rulers, Britons and a few Americans. The German Emperor and King Gustav of Sweden were frequent visitors and played baccarat at the Sporting Club. This kind of atmosphere was not very suitable for a schoolboy, and I often missed classes under one pretext or another, and sometimes without any pretext at all. My father was not very strict nor did he take much notice of me. He kept open house, and usually we had Iranian or Turkish house guests from Istanbul, Iran or Tiflis staying at the villa.

I was already interested in politics and followed with keen interest the news about the Chinese revolution of Sun-Yat-Sen and Yuan-Shi-Kai, and the conquest of Morocco by the French. I was strongly Pan-Islamic as a result of my tutor Mirza Mohammad's influence when I was still a child. He used to tell me how the Afghans had defeated the British in 1842 so that not one of the British Army escaped, and how the Lezghian chief Shamyl defied the Russians in the Caucasus for thirty years, and of the wars of Abd-el-Qader with the French in Algeria, always taking the side of the Moslem warriors against the European colonialists.

Of course I resented Russia's and Great Britain's interference in Iran and the manner in which they had divided my country into spheres of influence in 1907, and still more the brutal Russian aggression followed by the occupation of the Northern Provinces of Iran in 1911. On the 7th October the Italian aggression against the Ottoman province of Tripoli took place (today's Libya) and this so moved me that I asked my father to allow me to go to Tripoli to fight with the Turkish Army against the Italians. My father praised my sentiments and shared in my indignation, but refused absolutely to allow me to go, saying that it was folly for a boy of sixteen to go to an unknown country on such an adventure. I retired to my room, disappointed but decided, and next day I took the train to Marseilles where I presented myself to the Turkish Consul, asking for a permit to enter Tripolitania, as I wanted to enlist in the Turkish Army as a volunteer.

The Consul was taken aback and tried to persuade me not to embark on such a venture, but I stood firm, and finally he gave me a permit and I took a ticket on a steamer for Tunis, from where I hoped to be able to reach the Tripolitanian frontier; but the next day, just as I was boarding the steamer, two policemen who were standing by the gangway told me to follow them. They took me to the police station for identification, and then put me in a train and accompanied me to Monaco where I was duly delivered to my father who had sent telegrams to Marseilles asking the police to look for me and bring me home. From this moment I decided to enter the Military Academy in Turkey in order to be able to fight for Islam and my country.

As my studies at the Monaco College had not been satisfactory, my father decided to send me to the Lycée in Nice. Of course, after the free life I had led in Monte Carlo, I did not like being in a boarding-school, so I managed to leave the school every evening and returned only in the small hours, until the Director of the Lycée respectfully asked my father to remove me. I returned to Monaco, spending my time in the cafés, and at the Beausoleil and Cannes casinos, where young people under twenty were allowed to gamble. I continued going to the opera and the ballet and had the luck to see Nijinski and Karsavina in *Les Sylphides* and Pavlova, who had come with a small company, in the ballet of the opera *Ivan the Terrible*.

In February 1912 my uncle Ali Akbar Khan came from Istanbul with a Mr. Beyiklian, the Armenian director of a branch of the Ottoman Bank. I asked them to intervene with my father to allow me to go to Istanbul and enter the military academy there and my father finally agreed, so it was arranged that I should accompany Mr. Beyiklian when he returned, and I left Monaco on the 10th of March for the East, where I was afterwards destined to spend most of my life.

The Ottoman Empire

Thanks to the tales I had been told in my childhood by Mirza Mohammad, the Ottoman Empire represented for me the chief Moslem state, heir of the Arab Khalifates and the champion of Islam facing the encroaching European powers. I was deeply grieved by the plight of that Empire and its continuous recession and decline since the eighteenth century, losing, as it had done, one after the other of its European provinces and now despoiled of its last African possessions in Libya. I dreamed of an alliance between Iran and Turkey and of the subsequent rehabilitation of other Moslem states and burned with the desire to be able to do something myself towards this. I was young, and, in spite of the life I had led in Monte Carlo and Paris, full of idealism, and although I had never been in a Moslem country, knew nothing of Islam and its rites and had been educated by a mother who, though outwardly converted to Islam, had kept her Christian sentiments, I considered myself a member of the Moslem nation, comprising as it did then the three hundred million Moslems of the world.

Arrived in Vienna, as Mr. Beyiklian had to stay some days there on business for his bank, I had time to see this beautiful city, which was then, as the capital of a vast empire and the seat of the Hapsburg emperors, at the height of its glory. The brilliant uniforms of the 'Kayserlich und Königliche' army, the elegant officers and chic amazones riding on the Prater, the gypsy musicians and the ladies' orchestras playing the waltzes of Strauss and Lehar in the cafés and bierhälles, the Wienerwald, all these have left with me a memory of something wonderful that has disappeared for ever—gone with the wind.

After four or five days we started for the south. Soon after Pressburg the landscape became a desolate one of plains traversed by muddy roads leading to isolated villages. All the women had coloured kerchiefs on their heads and short very full skirts and both men and women wore high boots. As the train stopped for a few hours in Budapest, I was able to leave the station and wander about in the streets, and here, suddenly I realised that I was at the gate of the Orient. Many of the people were in white embroidered Magyar costumes. In the square in front of the station there were dozens of high-wheeled carts, and even the big Magyar horses which drew them looked quite different from their Western brothers.

After crossing the Puszta, or Hungarian steppe, our train stopped at Semlin, the last Austro-Hungarian station. Then, after slowly crossing the Save, it entered Serbia and stopped at Belgrade. We were in the Balkans, in a territory that thirty-five years earlier had been part of the Ottoman Empire.

Beyond Sofia, I saw the first Turkish peasants in the province of Eastern Rumelia where two-fifths of the population are Moslem Turks. These peasants wore baggy trousers with short coats and fezes with turban and broad cloth belts; the women dressed in the same way but with the head covered by a white veil. On the following morning we reached Mustafa Pasha, then the Turkish frontier station. By the Peace Treaty of 1913—which ended the Balkan War—this place was included in Bulgaria and is now known as Slivengrad. At the sight of the Turkish soldiers mounting guard in front of the station my heart nearly burst with enthusiasm. The Turkish inscriptions in Arabic characters enchanted me, although I was unable to decipher them. At last, after a rather dreary journey through the treeless steppes of Thrace, we arrived at the Sirkeji station in Istanbul.

My cousin's husband, Mirza Abdul Rezzaq, who had been employed by my father as superintendent when he was Ambassador, and Haji Reza, our cook from St. Petersburg, who had been brought by my father to Istanbul, were waiting for me at the station and took me to my cousin's house in the old part of Istanbul not far from the At Meidan or Hippodrome. My cousin, Qamar Khanum, was the daughter of Haji Agha Reza Salmassi, my father's brother-in-law, in whose house he had lived in his early youth in Istanbul in the sixties. She had a very big family of whom one son, Yusuf, was head of all the three Turkish military schools he attended during seven years, and one daughter, Marzie, who after studying medicine in Istanbul and joining the Iranian Army, became a Brigadier-General, the first woman in the Middle East to reach this rank. Their home was a typical

Turkish house of that period, very much like the house where Atatürk was born in Salonika, now preserved as a museum. It proved an excellent base from which to explore the town.

I spent nearly three months at this house, having lessons in Turkish every day in order to master the Arabic script. I had great difficulty in learning Osmanli Turkish and the Arabic script in which it was written, but as I wanted to enter the Military Academy as soon as possible, I worked really hard.

In 1908 a secret committee of young (and also a few elderly) officers, called the Committee of Union and Progress, had launched a military revolution. After occupying Istanbul they forced Sultan Abdul-Hamid to concede a Constitution, but in July 1909 some of the soldiers of the Sultan's guards, chiefly composed of Arabs and Albanians, rebelled against their officers, many of whom they killed, in an attempt to re-establish the Sultan's absolute rule. The Revolutionary Army of the Committee of Union and Progress had then marched from Salonika and Edirne, and after a fierce battle reoccupied the town whilst Abdul-Hamid, suspected of having encouraged the guardsmen to revolt, was deposed and sent to Salonika. His aged brother, Mohammad V, who until then had been kept in seclusion by Abdul-Hamid, was brought to the throne, completely bewildered at finding himself Sultan and Commander of the Faithful.

After the promulgation of the Constitution all the inhabitants of the Empire had been proclaimed equal and brothers, but alas this brotherhood did not last very long. Already in 1908, just after the first revolution, a number of Armenians had been massacred in Silicia, and revolts in the Yemen and in the Albanian provinces as well as the endemic warfare of the Macedonian chetes, or bands, against the Turkish forces and amongst themselves were destroying the short-lived harmony. When I arrived in Istanbul, the halcyon days were already over, and feelings of distrust and veiled hostility between the Turks and the Greeks were apparent. At that time the population of the Ottoman Empire amounted to: Turks and Turkomans 11 million; Arabs 9; Greeks 2; Kurds 2; Albanians 1·5; Armenians 1·5; Serbo-Macedonians 1; Bulgars and Bulgaro-Macedonians 1; Circassians 0·8; Kutso-Vlakhs 0·2; Lazes 0·2; Assyrians 0·2; Jews 0·2; Foreigners 0·2. Total 30·8 million, of these 23·5 Moslems, 7·1 Christians and 0·2 Jews.

Most of the non-Turks were asking for secession and independence, and not only the neighbouring Balkan States but also the Great Powers, Russia, Great Britain and France, who considered themselves as having special interests in the Ottoman Empire and had views on the outlying Turkish provinces, encouraged these sentiments by more or less veiled propaganda, so the task of keeping their extensive and straggling Empire together was very arduous for the Turks.

The Italian superiority at sea prevented the Turks, with whom they were still at war, from sending any reinforcements to Libya, and although Egypt was officially under the Ottoman Sultan's suzerainty, the British occupying power prevented any Turkish force from crossing through that country. Only small parties of officers disguised as Arabs managed to reach the fighting zone, among whom was Mustafa Kemal, the future Atatürk. The Italian fleet kept the sea clear and Italian forces were disembarked in Rhodes and the Dodecanese islands near the Turkish coast. Finally the Ottoman Government was forced to abandon both Libya and these islands and thus lost their last possessions in Africa.

Inside the country, the Union and Progress Party, who represented the ultra-nationalist side of Turkish public opinion, was opposed by the Etelaf-ve-Hurriyet or Entente Libérale, a more moderate group which was more inclined towards collaboration with the Great Powers.

The attitude of the Christian minorities in Istanbul towards the Turks was compounded of a feeling of superiority through having a common religion with the Great Powers, which were at that time politically dominating and economically exploiting the Ottoman Empire, and of fear because the Turks were still the masters. The 1895 massacre of 10,000 Armenians by the Kurdish hammals of Istanbul, whilst the police remained aloof, was not forgotten. The feelings of the Turks towards the Christian minorities, and at that time principally towards the Greeks, was one of distrust and barely concealed hostility because they knew that these people nurtured the secret hope of an ultimate union with an independent Greece. The Jews were better tolerated because they had no ties with Turkey's hostile and expanding neighbours, and indeed conversions of Jews to Islam were not rare and after two or three generations these converts were indistinguishable from other Turks.

I was not fluent in Turkish, nor advanced enough in mathematics, so I could not enter the Military Academy at once, but had to pass some months at a military secondary school situated at Chenguelkoï on the Bosphorus. I was given a khaki uniform and ordered to provide myself with a full-dress uniform of dark blue cloth with red facings and black astrakhan cap. The discipline was harsh not to say savage, the food so indifferent that even the patient Turkish cadets twice organised a hunger strike to protest against it (for which they were severely punished), and the work, both in the classrooms and in the field, hard and exhausting. This was a great change for me from my leisured life in Monte Carlo, but I was happy there and took a special pride in being one of the khaki-clad youths who represented the might of Islam. After two weeks, as my full-dress uniform was not yet ready, I was ordered to remain at school on holidays until it should be available. When Thursday came, all the cadets in full-dress uniform were aligned ready to go out but I, with two others, remained outside the line in our khaki fatigue dress, and after the others left, feeling very sorry for ourselves we resolved to escape and return on the Friday night by the hospital door as if we were coming from there.

After our evening meal when we retired for the night, we tied together four or five sheets, fastened them to an upper floor window, which was not protected by iron bars like those on the ground floor, climbed down, and as Chenguelkoï was on the Asiatic shore of the Bosphorus, had to hire a rowing-boat which took us to Beshiktash, before we could reach town. Unfortunately, being new to school we did not realise that on Friday there would be a roll-call of the cadets deprived of leave, and that we would be found missing.

The result was that we were punished by twenty-five lashes each, administered to us by two sturdy Anatolian soldiers, the officer on duty counting the strokes in a loud voice before the 1500 cadets of the school. According to the school's tradition, not a groan or even a sigh was to be heard during this operation, the cadets jumping quickly to attention after the punishment and after a smart salute to the officer on duty, rejoining their place in the ranks. Although for two or three days it was painful to sit on a chair, I did not feel humiliated, considering this punishment as soldierly and taking it in the spirit in which corporal punishment is accepted by public schoolboys in England. The following week, the tailor having sent me my full-dress uniform, I could go on leave and parade in all my new glory in the Beyoglu street of Pera.

In October 1912, after a period of tension between Turkey and the four Balkan States, the armies of Bulgaria, Serbia, Greece and Montenegro simultaneously crossed the frontiers of the Ottoman Empire and started the invasion of the last remains of the Turks' European possessions. The news created an extraordinary moral upheaval at the Cadet School. Our officers were mobilised and sent to the front. More than 200 cadets (including me) volunteered for service as privates in the operational units, this application being rejected on the ground that we were too young, and that it was considered wasteful to send future officers to the front as private soldiers.

During the first days of the war, fantastic news of resounding Turkish successes circulated in the capital, and the local newspapers refrained from giving true information about what was happening. In order to get more information, on our leave day I bought the Paris newspaper *Le Temps*, where the events were presented quite differently. When back at school I was foolish enough to impart this information to the other cadets. This provoked in them such fury, that, calling me traitor, they rushed at me and gave me such a beating that I refrained from commenting on the news from the Front.

We were about 750 cadets in my class, organised in companies of about 80 to 100 in each, but otherwise, we grouped ourselves by races; the Turks forming several groups according to the regions from whence they came, and the Arabs. There were Albanian and Kurdish groups also, and, though I do not know why, I joined the Albanian group. Sometimes feuds arose between groups, when champions were chosen who engaged in single combat in the presence of their respective followers, who encouraged them vocally but never interfered in the fight. When it became clear who was the victor, his group was declared victorious and received the apologies of the defeated champion's group. These competitions used to take place in the vast lavatories' courtyard, one cadet being posted at the entrance in order to give the alarm if an officer appeared in the vicinity. If this happened all the cadets disappeared into the lavatories and the courtyard was left empty. I happened to be chosen one day by the Albanian group as champion to fight against the Yemeni Arab group's champion, a sturdy Bedouin who knocked my two front teeth out and then disappeared with the rest of the cadets at the approach of the officer on duty to whom I told a tale about having had an accident slipping on the stairs and falling on my face. The officer looked incredulously at me, but as I was bleeding and my face was swollen, I was taken to the school's infirmary where I stayed two days.

I had an Arab friend from Tripoli who had a string of dry objects I thought to be mushrooms hanging by his bed. Once I asked him when he intended to serve us a dish of these as an extra to our rather poor meal. He laughed and told me that what I had taken for mushrooms were Italian soldiers' ears that he had cut off during the Tripoli war from dead Italian soldiers on the battlefield, and he was keeping them as souvenirs!

From the first days of the war, the Turkish Army, insufficiently supplied, suffered reverses and sustained heavy losses, especially among the officers, and the Government decided to transfer our class from Chenguelkoïy to the Military Academy of Harbiye in Pera in order to speed up our promotion to officer's rank. At the end of October the Turkish Armies in the Balkans had been completely defeated and the Thrace Army, which had been thrown back to the Chatalja defence lines some thirty miles from Istanbul, lost a great part of its war material. A garrison had been left in Edirne, this town being later completely encircled by the Bulgarian Army.

As so often happens in wartime an epidemic of cholera broke out in Istanbul among the soldiers and the Moslem refugees who poured in from Thrace. The big mosques were transformed into hospitals, and the upper floor of the Military Academy was also taken over for cholera patients, whilst we were moved downstairs into our classrooms. One wing of the building was transformed into a surgical ward, and put at the disposal of a Swedish Red Cross ambulance to which I was attached, at first as interpreter, but after a few days as anaesthetist during operations. Turkish soldiers were very patient and bore great pain without uttering a word. I remember an Anatolian N.C.O. whose leg had to be amputated who obstinately refused to be given chloroform during the whole operation, which lasted at least half an hour. This man smoked cigarettes, and only after his leg had been carried off in a basket, did he sigh, saying: 'My leg is gone'.

After the front-line had moved close to Istanbul, the cadets began to feel restless and by twos and threes left the Academy with rifles and ammunition, deserting to the units at the front, where they were incorporated as privates or corporals. My best friend, whom I admired very much, was a boy called Husein Aouny from Aleppo. One day he told me that he intended to join the battalion commanded by his father which was stationed in the northern sector of the defence line near the Black Sea coast. I decided to go with him, and taking with us our rifles and field equipment we reached the Belgrade forest on the northern fringe of which my friend's father's battalion was occupying a defensive position. We were both good walkers and in spite of the darkness we managed to keep our direction with the help of a compass. It was about midnight when we saw the light from a fire gleaming through the trees and as we were very cold in the drizzling rain, we welcomed the idea of warming ourselves by it. Coming nearer we were very astonished to see sitting around the fire a party of thirty or forty men in military uniforms, most of whom were well past the age of military service, and all of whom were bearded in a most unsoldierlike manner.

As we noticed an N.C.O., who looked more normal, sitting amongst them we approached and asked to be given a place by the fire. Without a word the strange people made room for us, and the N.C.O., after asking from where we came and where we intended to go, offered us a hard ball of bread and a bowl of hot tea, which were most welcome. Being tired after our night march, we dozed until the morning and when we woke the strange party was preparing to break camp. Taking the N.C.O. aside, we asked him about his peculiar companions and he told us that these people were mostly murderers condemned to perpetual imprisonment, who had petitioned to be allowed to fight for their country. The Government had ordered them to be taken to a small fishing port on the Black Sea, there to embark in small boats and be taken to the Bulgarian coast, where they would be set on shore and sent to the interior of the country to wage partisan warfare. The N.C.O. was in charge of them until they reached the port, after which they would be left to take care of themselves, none of them being expected to escape from that venture alive.

We walked the whole day and towards the evening reached the headquarters of the 8th Infantry regiment to which belonged the battalion of Aouny's father. The commander of the regiment said that we were too young and not strong enough to serve as soldiers at the front. 'But our souls are strong,' answered my friend, who was even thinner than I was. The Colonel laughed, and allowed us to be incorporated in the battalion with the rank of corporal, being Harbiye cadets. I was only seventeen and Aouny nineteen, but the soldiers refrained from any kind of chaffing because of Aouny's father being their battalion commander. We had to live with them in tents, the floors of which were covered with tree branches, because the ground was damp through the continual rain. I slept under a tent with seven Anatolian soldiers, and in the night when the tent was closed the smell of the unwashed bodies was so strong that I had to lift the canvas and put my head outside on the wet ground not to be suffocated.

The battalion was in the first line, but the trenches and defence works were situated nearly a mile and a quarter from the tents, which were among the trees on the edge of the forest. The Bulgars occupied some heights at about one mile and a half in front of us on the shore of the Derkos lake, but their forward line was in some places as close as 200 or 300 yards from our front trenches, to which we were soon moved.

One day the battalion received the order to attack a position that had been occupied by the Bulgarian infantry during the night and from which they could fire on the right flank of our position. The attack had to be executed by two companies in three waves. The first wave was constituted by one platoon, destined to reveal the enemy's fire. Then, under the protection of an artillery barrage, the two other platoons of the 1st company were to follow. Behind these, the 2nd company had to attack in one line and to drive the assault up to the Bulgars' position, the 3rd company being in reserve. Just before coming into the open, I felt frightened and uneasy, with a strange feeling of emptiness in the lower part of my stomach and a feeling of unreality about everything that was happening around me. I confess I thought it had been foolish on my part to have come here of my free will to face the danger of being killed or wounded in an ugly way, but looking around I saw the confident and impassive faces of soldiers preparing their arms for the assault and pulled myself together.

'*Süngü Tak!*' Fix bayonets! rang the command. That was better; the handling of the short Mauser bayonet gave me courage. Then started the concentrated artillery preparation, the shells bursting in front of us. '*Yashasin*, it's our guns,' the soldiers were saying gaily. Then came the command: '*Birinji Takim, ileri!*' 'Allah, Allah,' shouted the soldiers, jumping out of their trenches. '*Ikinji Bölük!*' Now it was our turn. No time to think. We jumped up and ran over the open ground. 'Allah, Allah', shouts, cries, shrieks, foul abuse, machine-gun fire, shrapnel bursting over our heads, a soldier next to me fell to the ground.

I was in the 2nd company, that is in the 3rd line, but when we had covered 200 yards, all these lines were mixed together on account of the Bulgarian fire. At about 50 yards from the enemy's trenches, a Bulgarian officer rose up and shouted in a stentorian voice in Turkish: 'Go back, donkeys, sons of donkeys, go back.' The effect of this forceful intervention was such that the whole attacking line wavered and stopped dead for a few instants. Then a Turkish officer brought him down with his pistol, and the line moved forward and jumped into the Bulgarian trenches. Tossed about by the soldiers around me I was quite bewildered to find myself in the trench. A few Bulgarians lay dead on the ground, a dozen, mostly wounded, were taken prisoner, the rest had fled. My bayonet was clean and shiny. We destroyed the trenches, artillery fire levelled the ground and in the night we returned to our lines.

Twenty-five days after our arrival at the front, the belligerents had signed a truce in London under the auspices of the Concert of European Powers, and we were sent back to Harbiye, where we were incarcerated for fifteen days for having left the Academy against orders.

According to the terms of the Armistice, Edirne had to surrender, but the old commander of the garrison, Shukri Pasha, insisted on surrendering to Serbs and not to the much more hated Bulgarians. The provisional demarcation line was to run in a direct line from Midia, on the Black Sea, to Enos on the

Tribal map of Iran

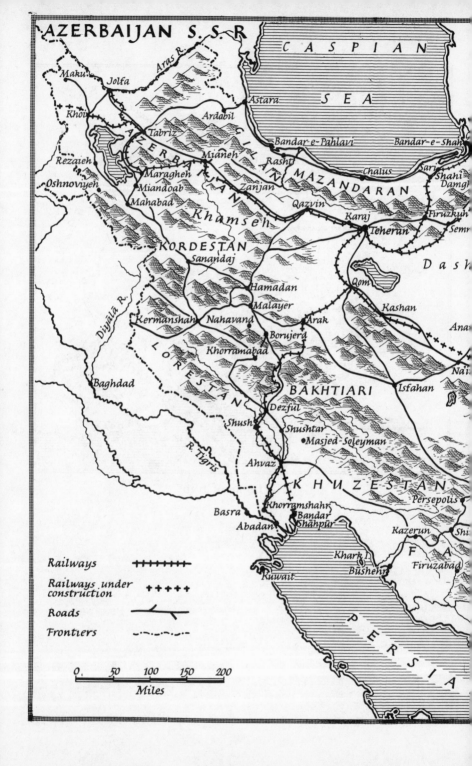

AZERBAIJAN S.S.R

CASPIAN
SEA

Maku
Jolfa
Astara
Khoi
Ardabil
Aras R.
Bandar-e-Pahlavi
Bandar-e-Shah
Tabriz
GILAN
Chalus
Sari
Mianeh
Rashti
MAZANDARAN
Shahi
Damgl
Rezaieh
Zanjan
Firuzkuh
Oshnoviyeh
Maragheh
Qazvin
Semr
Miandoab
Mahabad
Khamseh
Karaj
Teheran
Dash
KORDESTAN
Sanandaj
Qom
Hamadan
Malayer
Kashan
Kermanshah
Nahavand
Arak
Ana
Diyala R.
Borujerd
Khorramabad
Nai
LORESTAN
BAKHTIARI
Isfahan
Baghdad
Dezful
Shush
Shushtar
Masjed-Soleyman
R. Tigris
Ahvaz
KHUZESTAN
Khorramshahr
Persepolis
Basra
Bandar
Shahpur
Abadan
Kazerun
Shi
Kuwait
Khark I.
F   A
Büshehr
Firuzabad
PERSIA

Railways   +++++++
Railways under   +++++
construction
Roads   ╱
Frontiers   ─·─·─

0   50   100   150   200
Miles

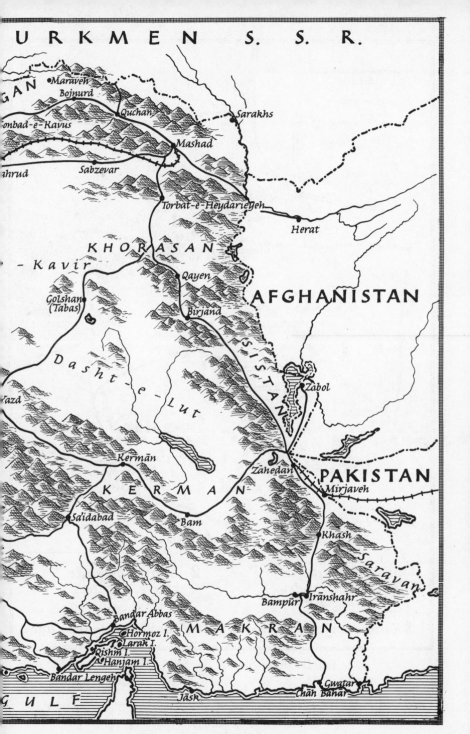

General map of Iran

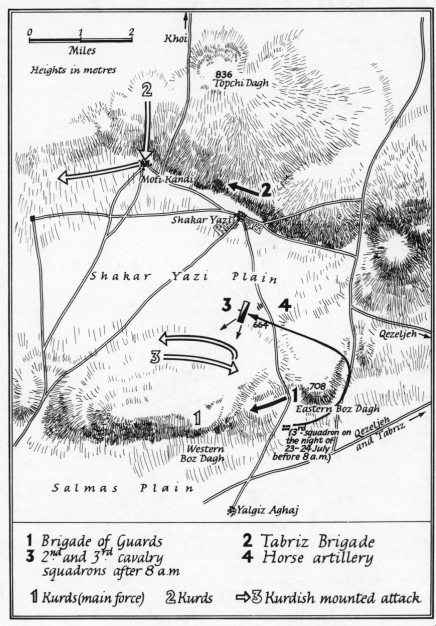

The Battle of Shakar Yazi, 24 July 1922

Aegean, leaving nearly all the European possessions of the Empire including most of the Thrace Vilayet to the victors. Italy and Austria–Hungary insisted on Albania being independent, and not divided between Greece and Serbia, as it had been planned by the last States. These terms provoked general indignation in Turkey, the Government of Kiamil Pasha being accused of criminal negligence in the preparation of the war, incompetence in waging it and supineness in accepting such impossible terms.

One day while walking on the Bab-Aali Jaddesi I saw a crowd surrounding an officer on horseback, and shouting 'Long live Enver bey, long live. the Ottomans, curses on the traitors!' Curious to see what it all was about I joined the crowd. The officer dismounted from his horse and was carried on the shoulders of the people towards the Sublime Porte, where it appeared that a cabinet meeting was in progress. I recognised Enver bey, the handsome and popular young Lieutenant-Colonel, hero of the 1908–9 revolution and of the Tripoli war against the Italians. In front of the Sublime Porte building he was lowered from the shoulders of his admirers and mounted the few steps in front of the entrance. An officer—the War Minister's aide-de-camp—came to the door and tried to prevent him from entering; a shot rang out, and the officer fell dead. After that Enver, followed by others, entered the building and I heard several more shots from inside. I learned afterwards that Enver bey killed the War Minister, General Nazim Pasha, who had left the Council room to inquire about the pistol shots. Subsequently the crowd entered the building, manhandled several Ministers, but respected the old Kiamil Pasha who was allowed to get into his carriage and drive home. The next day he left Istanbul for Europe.

After a while the crowd dispersed and I returned to the Academy where I noticed a feeling of exhilaration and of hope among the cadets, all of whom were for the Union and Progress and the denunciation of the Armistice with the Balkan States. The next day, a pro-Union and Progress Government came to power, and Enver bey was promoted Colonel and after a few days Brigadier-General. Turkey's chance came soon when the Balkan States quarrelled over the spoils, Bulgaria wishing to annex most of Macedonia which was also coveted by Serbia and

Greece. These two countries joined together and their armies attacked the Bulgars at Bregalnitza. The Bulgars were beaten, and profiting by this, the Turkish Army sallied from the Chatalja lines and throwing back the Bulgarians reoccupied the Edirne Vilayet, known as Eastern Thrace, including the town.

At the end of the war, things returned to normal, our officers came back, the cholera patients mostly died and after a thorough disinfecting of the rooms we moved upstairs again.

The defeat of the Ottoman Empire at the hands of its former subjects, without the help of a European power, was at the same time humiliating and instructive, demonstrating to the authorities that a politics-ridden army cannot fight properly. The Union and Progress Government started a reorganisation of the armed forces at once, and individual German officers were to be replaced by an important military mission under General Liman von Sanders, with full powers. Nationalist and pan-Islamic sentiments were exalted, and I discovered that the 'Ettehad Islam', or Pan-Islamic Union, had ramifications in the Academy. I was invited to become affiliated to it, and as I knew Russian and French and a little English and German, I was given the job of addressing envelopes to members of that Union scattered all over the world, especially in the Caucasus, Central Asia, Crimea and Volga regions of Russia, as also in India, Africa and Netherlands East Indies. I was not told what was written to these people, but noticed that many of them, especially in Russia, were school teachers, and in India Government civil servants.

This year the fasting month of Ramazan occurred in summer. We had different working hours because fasting, as also prayers five times a day at the Academy's mosque, was obligatory.

It was forbidden for a Moslem to eat, drink or smoke in public places or in the streets, but as sunset approached many people kept their cigarette and matches in their hands ready to light them at the sound of the gun announcing the end of the fast. In the evenings crowds swarmed in the Divan Yolu and Shah-zadebashi streets and filled the theatres where Turkish plays were produced. Turkish women were all veiled then, the women's roles at the theatres being played by Greeks or Armenians.

During the year 1913, Turkey's relations with Russia and Great Britain were becoming more and more strained. Turkey had occupied the district of El Hasa on the Persian Gulf south of

Kuwait, and considered Kuwait as subject to its sovereignty. The Sheikh Mobarak of Kuwait had other ideas about his status, and Great Britain supported him and sent a cruiser to impress the Turkish Government. At that date, the Sheikh entered into special treaty relations with Britain, and received protection against Ottoman encroachments.

From all this it became clear that British policy was more and more interested in Mesopotamia, and the international political situation showed that this interest was destined to take more definite shape in the future. One day, talking about these problems with a cadet friend, I told him I was sure that before ten years, Baghdad would· be under the British. He became very angry, and offered to bet, that if after ten years I should prove wrong, he would find me wherever I was and kill me, and if I should be right, he was ready to be killed by me. He appeared quite in earnest, and I accepted the bet, but after Baghdad was occupied by General Maude's Army in 1917, I did not think of trying to find my friend in order to exact the price of our bet.'

In the autumn of 1913 my father was called to Teheran, where he was offered the post of Minister of Justice, which he accepted. Although I had not finished my studies at the Military Academy he wrote to his brother to send me to Teheran, as he knew that he would not remain long in Iran and he wished to settle me in Government service while he was there. I learned afterwards that he still cherished the hope of putting me into the Diplomatic Service.

I was thrilled beyond words at the thought of seeing Iran for the first time and also of travelling through Russia, which was for me a kind of sentimental motherland, although I disliked very much the Russian Government's aggressive policy towards Iran.

First contact with Iran

It was in January 1914 that I embarked in a Lloyd Triestino boat bound for Batum on my way to Iran. The sea was calm, and it was amusing to see the dolphins following the ship, plunging and reappearing again.

On the morning of the fourth day we anchored in Batum, the first Russian port taken from the Turks in 1878. The ship was moored to the quay, but before we were allowed to land, Russian gendarmes and health officers came on board. Our luggage was taken to the customs and to my great annoyance all the Russian books I had in my suit-case were removed for inquiry, although they were classical literature having nothing revolutionary about them.

Early in the morning of the next day I arrived at Tiflis, the town where I was born. I took a droshky to a hotel in the main street not far from the Dvortzonaya Ploshchad where the Viceroy's palace was situated. The coachman wore an enormous padded overcoat reaching to his feet and tightly belted in at the waist so as to present a colossal behind to his passengers. This was the traditional costume for cabbies throughout Russia.

I found Tiflis an enchanting place with its Russian atmosphere augmented by the Caucasian and Georgian element. I went at once to our Consulate General where I explained about the confiscation of my books to the Vice-Consul. Suddenly after looking at my passport he took me in his arms and I recognised Mirza Mohammad, my former tutor! I stayed with him at the Consulate until it closed, and then he took me to his home where I lunched with him and his beautiful bride, a girl from Riga. After visiting the town I returned to Mirza Mohammad's home where a family party was gathered, all very much interested to hear about my adventures in Turkey and especially about the Chatalja Front. The following day Mirza Mohammad took me to visit the Consul-General. In the evening I saw Rubinstein's opera

Demon produced on an extraordinarily lavish scale with gorgeous costumes and scenery with complicated moonlight effects and live camels among the performers. The house was crowded with elegant ladies and officers in full-dress uniforms, whilst any cadets who were in the audience would rise and stand with their backs to the boxes during the intervals as it would not have been permissible for them to be seated in the presence of an officer, except during the performance when the house was in darkness.

A few days later, the Consul's efforts to secure the return of my books having completely failed, I took the train to Baku where I arrived early in the morning to be thrilled by the sight of the Caspian Sea, whose waters lapped the shores of Iran and of fabulous Central Asia.

In Baku I already felt myself in Iran as more Azeri Turkish was heard in the streets than Russian. The town was dusty and completely lacking in the aristocratic charm of Tiflis, the air being permeated by the smell from the oilfields. Apart from the mixed indigenous population of Shiah Moslems (wrongly called Tartars by the Russians but who do not differ from Azeris), and the Armenians and Russians, there were some fifty to sixty thousand Iranians who came every year from the neighbouring districts of Ardebil, Ahar and Serab in Iranian Azerbaijan to work in the oilfields and in the docks of the port, returning to Iran after six or seven months. Some of these labourers remained permanently in Baku but kept their Iranian passports and remitted a part of their earnings to their own country. They were clearly distinguished from the rest of the population by their costume—a coat with a pleated skirt, called a *sardari*, a felt waistcoat open in front, called an *arkhaluk*, and a brown felt cap.

Before embarking for Enzeli (*Pahlavi*) I changed my civilian clothes for my full-dress Turkish cadet's uniform and greatcoat to which I added a Caucasian sheepskin cap and an enormous cuirassier's sword, both of which I had purchased in Baku. No doubt taking me for an officer in a newly created Russian Guards regiment, the gendarme on duty at the gangway gave me a smart salute and did not trouble to look at my passport.

I noticed an imposing gentleman with upturned moustaches and two young men in European clothes who looked obviously Iranian and I started to converse with them in Azeri. Two of them knew that dialect and one of them was the son of the late

Grand Vizir Atabek Azam. I made friends with the moustachioed gentleman, Sardar Saed, and his companions and we travelled together to Teheran.

Late in the evening, a dark line of high mountains appeared far on our right which Sardar Saed told me were the Talesh Mountains, running from north to south along the coast from Russia to Iran; the part visible to us was probably in Iran. I was profoundly moved as I tried to pierce the darkness and look for the first time on the land of my forefathers. When I awoke the next day the steamer had stopped. I looked out of the porthole and saw a low-lying coast bordered by trees and bushes. The sky was grey and a drizzle was falling. Terribly excited, I put on my fancy military get-up and went on deck.

After some formalities we disembarked and were rowed across the lagoon, landing at Qazian, on the opposite shore. Here we took a small bus that brought us to Rasht. On the road we met a platoon of Russian Cossacks, to the great anger of Sardar Saed, who was a fiery patriot and disliked seeing foreign military forces in occupation of Iranian territory. We also saw a troop of Persian Cossacks escorting the mail-carriage.

Sardar Saed explained to me that the Persian Cossacks were a military organisation of about the strength of a brigade organised in 1882 by Russian instructors, Nasr-ed-Din Shah having been so impressed by the Russian Cossacks escort that had been given to him in Russia during his second journey to Europe in 1878, that he had asked the Tsar to lend him a few Cossack officers to organise a similar force in Teheran, to serve as his guard. The Tsar was only too glad to oblige and to expand Russian influence in Iran in this way, and first a cavalry regiment, then a mixed brigade were formed in which now more than twenty officers and the same number of N.C.O.s were serving as instructors. This brigade was paid on order of the Imperial Russian Embassy by the Russian Banque d'Escompte, and accredited to the Iranian Government. The commanding officer being a Russian officer appointed by the Imperial General Staff in St. Petersburg he corresponded directly with that Staff. In this manner, although being an Iranian military unit paid by the Iranian Treasury, this Brigade was entirely under Russian influence, its Iranian officers holding only subordinate positions. Several units of the Persian Cossack Brigade were stationed in the Russian occupied region, to the exclusion of the Governmental Gendarmerie, newly organised (in 1911) by the Constitutionalist Government with the aid of Swedish instructors, much to the displeasure of the Tsarist Government, which saw in this move a challenge to their influence and authority in Northern Iran.

The revolution of 1906 and the promulgation of the Constitution by Mozaffar-ed-Din Shah a few days before his death had certainly been influenced by the Russian revolution of 1905, and was highly obnoxious to the Tsarist Government whose encroachments on Iran's sovereignty were opposed by the Iranian nationalists who supported the Constitution. For that reason, the reactionaries who had been grouped around Mohammad Ali Shah, the absolutist son of Mozaffar-ed-Din Shah, were supported by Russia, and the Iranian Cossack Brigade under Colonel Liakhoff by order of the Shah and with the tacit approval of the Russian Embassy actually bombarded the Majles, or Parliament, in 1908.

When the Nationalist Forces marched on Teheran from Rasht and from Isfahan in 1909, Mohammad Ali Shah was forced to fly to the Russian Legation, from whence he fled to Russia in exile. In 1911 Russia tried to restore him to power and sent him on a Russian ship to the port of Bender Guez, near Asterabad (Gorgan), providing him with money and arms. Mohammad Ali Shah then marched on Teheran with a force of Turkomans and a handful of reactionaries, but his lieutenant, Arshad-ed-Dovleh, was met near Khar by Government forces, defeated, seized and executed, the Turkomans flying to their homes and the ex-Shah re-embarking for an indefinite exile in Russia.

In 1911 in order to be liberated from foreign pressure the Iranian Government had invited an American financial expert, Mr. Morgan Schuster, to reorganise its finances, but as that was contrary to Russia's wishes, a flimsy pretext was seized upon to demand the dismissal of that conscientious official and the dissolution of the Majles, and Russian military forces were sent to Iran in order to ensure the execution of these demands. Unfortunately, to the disappointment of the Iranian liberals, Great Britain not only abstained from remonstrating against Russia's high-handed action, but advised the Iranian Government to comply with Russian demands. *

* *The Strangling of Persia*, by W. Morgan Schuster. New York, 1920.

I was passionately interested in all that Sardar Saed told me and as a result conceived a great dislike for the Russian-led Cossacks and a sympathy for the national-minded Gendarmerie.

We hired a carriage to Teheran. The road from Rasht to Qazvin and Hamadan was then the only carriage road existing in Iran. It had been built by a Russian company about ten years before. This company had also rendered more or less passable for wheeled traffic the caravan track from Qazvin to Teheran, that road being part of the famous silk road between Baghdad and Samarkand in the Middle Ages. The company was allowed to take tolls along this road, and toll gates were established at a distance of every twenty to thirty miles, with pleasant little houses adjoining them where the Russian road employees lived with their families. Every 50 or 60 miles there were post stations or *chaparkhanes* where horses could be changed and where one could find rooms of a sort and some kind of simple food. Sometimes these *chaparkhanes* were established in old caravanserais most of which had been built by Shah Abbas in the late sixteenth century.

For the first 50 miles the road from Rasht to Teheran runs through dense forest and after that follows the course of the Safid Rud river through a defile in the Alborz Mountains which separate the Caspian provinces of Gilan and Mazandaran from the plateau, the slopes of the mountains becoming gradually barer. After Rudbar, a mountain village near an extensive plantation of olive trees, the road passes through a narrow defile to a wide plain where the rivers Qezel Owzan coming from the north-west and Shahrud coming from the south-east join and pursue their course to the north under the name of Safid Rud. The road then lay in a narrow valley, crossing and recrossing a mountain torrent, up and up through a second mountain-chain running east-west. Here the slopes were barren and there was vegetation, chiefly poplars and willows, only in the valley bordering the torrent, especially around the few villages that we passed. The reason for the contrast between the luxuriant vegetation of the Caspian provinces and the bareness of the inland plateau is due to the fact that the moisture brought by the north wind from the sea, forming the rain clouds, is stopped by the high coastal mountains, and although the rainfall in these regions is from 3 to 6 feet per year, it is only 10 to 12 inches on the plateau immediately to the south of the mountains.

The higher we went, the loftier were the rugged mountains towering above us, until we reached the summit of the pass where a bitterly cold wind was blowing and we found ourselves not on a ridge but on a high plateau subsiding gradually towards the Qazvin Plain. Here I saw for the first time a sight that I have since seen many times, and always with feelings of romantic pleasure—a camel caravan. First we heard the grave and hollow sound of the big bells, 1 to 3 for each camel, clanging in time to its slow and regular steps, and then the silvery tinkling of the smaller bells hanging from the necks of horses and mules. The caravan people were silent, the padded feet of the camels made no noise, and the caravan emerged from the darkness a ghostly procession preceded by the rhythmic music of the bells.

In Qazvin we spent the night at the port relay station, and the next day started for Teheran, where we arrived in the evening, after having changed horses three times. To enter the town we drove over a bridge through gates ornamented by decadent mosaic work, and after having left my companions at their homes, the carriage took me to my father's garden. Arfaieh was on the northern fringe of the town, just inside the Yusufabad gate, in a deserted district, and after passing through a gateway inside which four soldiers in khaki uniform were standing, the carriage stopped in front of a low one-storeyed house from which my father and my cousin Abdul Rahim Khan, my old friend from Lausanne days, came out to greet me. Arfaieh was a large garden covering about 6 acres. It had a round swimming-pool and a number of pine, poplar, chenar, acacia and pomegranate trees. I shared a small house of three rooms with my cousin, one room was occupied by Bahram, our Zoroastrian gardener, and his family, the third being reserved for my father's confidential political interviews.

Iran in 1914 was completely different from everything that I had seen before in Europe, even in Turkey, and I was enchanted to discover the oriental way of life. Teheran is a comparatively new city, becoming the capital of Iran in 1795 before which it was little more than a village. In ancient times there was an important town near the present site called Rhages and afterwards

Rey, but this town was several times destroyed by various invaders. Finally the Mongols of Chengiz Khan levelled it to the ground.

In the year 1870 the town was surrounded by a wall protected by a moat which could be flooded on the model of the Paris fortifications, as they still were in 1909 when I was there. This wall increased the area of the city particularly to the north-west which until then had been limited by a wall passing south of the present Meidan Sepah, then known as Topkhane or Artillery Square because the guns of the Imperial artillery were kept there in covered buildings. The new wall took in a number of gardens belonging to the Shah and to various grandees, including that of my father, and in 1914 when I arrived in Teheran this region was still very sparsely inhabited, sheep and goats grazing there on the scanty grass. The only buildings of any importance in the town were the Sepah Salar Mosque on the Baharistan Square, which had been built by a former Grand Vizir who had been Ambassador in Turkey and who had drawn his architectural inspiration from the Istanbul mosques; the Masjid Shah in the bazaar and the Golestan Palace, most of which was built between 1797 and 1834 during the reign of Fath Ali Shah. This building now houses a museum but is still used as a palace on important State occasions.

The most interesting feature of Teheran was, and still is, the covered bazaar. It is the biggest in the world, much more extensive than the famous bazaar of Istanbul, and covers several square miles of the town's area, including a maze of narrow and tortuous lanes, and comprising not only shops, but numerous caravanserais, mosques, public baths and private habitations. The whole economic and even political life of Teheran was concentrated there, and whenever the people were dissatisfied with the Government they would close the shops, an action usually upheld by the influential *mollas*, so that the whole economic life of the capital was paralysed. In the northern part of the city the avenues were wide and planted with trees, but unpaved and very muddy in winter.

One day when I was walking in town with my cousin there was a sound of galloping horses and shouts and we had just time to throw ourselves into a doorway before a carriage in which an old gentleman was sitting passed at a gallop, preceded, surrounded and followed by a number of horsemen. Abdul Rahim Khan told me that it was Vali Khan Sepah Salar Aazam, a wealthy landowner of Mazandaran, who had headed the force which had come from Rasht in 1909 to re-establish the Constitution threatened by Mohammad Ali Shah. Having succeeded in this with the help of Bakhtiari tribesmen under their chief, Sardar Assad, he now refused to pay any taxes, considering himself above the laws of the Constitution he had helped to revive. The Government had ordered his arrest, but as he was living at Zargandeh village 7 miles to the north of Teheran, which had been given by the Shah to the Russian Legation as a summer resort, and therefore considered as Russian territory, it was impossible to arrest him there. Every time he wished to visit his house in Teheran he had himself escorted by some two hundred armed retainers, knowing that the Government could not dispose of such a force at short notice.

The village of Golhak had been given to the British Legation at the same time as Zargandeh to the Russians and the extra-territoriality of both villages was preserved until 1928 when under Reza Shah all special rights of foreigners were abolished together with the capitulations.

Another day, while walking on Naderi Street, which borders the British Embassy to the south, I heard the sound of guns coming from the next street. When I reached the corner I saw gendarmes firing a machine-gun in a southerly direction. I was told that they were shooting at Sardar Asad's Bakhtiari tribesmen who were occupying a block of houses where the Bank Melli is now on Firdowsi Avenue, and not having received the allocation due to them since they occupied the town in 1909 were demonstrating against the Government. These incidents go to prove how shaky the Government was and that it had no reliable security forces at its disposal to uphold its prestige or to control unruly elements.

During the reign of Nasr-ed-Din Shah, the Central Government had a kind of loose control over the provinces, many of which were administered by hereditary governors whose degree of obedience to the Government varied according to the distance of their provinces from Teheran. After the 1906–9 revolution and the 1911 civil war between the Government and the forces of reaction, this system collapsed, most governors freeing themselves from all kinds of governmental authority except a purely nominal one. The provinces of Azerbaijan had been occupied by the Russians after fierce fighting with the constitutionalists, and the patriotic Olema who had protested against the Russian aggression were hanged without trial.* The Russians then appointed a reactionary landowner of Maragha, Haji Samad Khan, Shoja-ed-Dovleh as Governor of the province and this worthy refused to acknowledge the Central Government of Teheran, taking his orders directly from the Russian Consul. The officials from Teheran were cowed or expelled and anyone mentioning the Constitution was seized and murdered in the most barbarous fashion. Outside Teheran the Government had no real influence except along the roads where the newly organised Gendarmerie had its posts and garrisons.

Ahmad Shah was at that time a boy of seventeen and the country was governed by a regent, who was then Nasr-ol-Molk Qaragozlu of Hamadan, a senior statesman educated at Oxford. He had escaped being hanged by Mohammad Ali Shah for his liberal views in 1908 only through the intervention of the British Legation. The cabinet was headed by Ala-os-Saltaneh, a nice old gentleman who had been my father's chief in Tiflis after Ala-ol-Molk, the other Ministers being Vossuq ed-Dovleh (Foreign Affairs), his brother Qavam-os-Saltaneh (Finance), Hakim-ol-Molk (Public Instruction), Mostofi-el-Memalek, a patriotic liberal (War), my father (Justice) and several others whose names I have forgotten.

Most of the Ministers were honourable and of good will, but the finances of the State were in a sad plight as nobody was willing to pay taxes and the Government had no power to induce them to do so. The foreign governments, chiefly those of Russia and Great Britain, interfered in all the details of the administration. The Government had tried to negotiate a foreign loan from some countries other than Russia and Great Britain, but as these two powers had divided Iran in 1907 into spheres of influence, they opposed any outside influence and sought to force on Iran a loan that would subject her even further to their domination. The patriotic finance minister Sani-ed-Dowleh was assassinated by two Caucasians in the pay of the Russian Legation for opposing this project. The two assassins were arrested on the spot by the

* *The Persian Crisis of December 1911*, by L. G. Browne. Cambridge, 1912.

Iranian police who were obliged to hand them to the Russian Legation which sent them to Russia ostensibly to be tried, but as soon as they reached Baku they were freed and proceeded to spend the money they had received for their deed. After that the British and Russian loans were forced on us, the revenues of the customs serving as guarantees for them, those of the Persian Gulf ports for the British and those from the northern frontier for the Russians and the stranglehold on Iran was thus completed.

One day my father told me that he had decided to transfer me to the Foreign Ministry, and that he had already talked the matter over with the Foreign Minister, Vossuq-ed-Dovleh, who was expecting me that very morning. I did not dare to protest, but donned my fancy uniform with the cuirassier's sword and enormous spurs and went to the Foreign Ministry which at that time occupied one of the numerous wings of the Golestan Palace. Mounting the stone steps noisily, my sword strapped on purpose very low in order to bang on my spurs and the steps, I made such a stir that many doors opened, the officials intrigued by the noise and even more by my peculiar appearance. I asked one of them to take me to the Minister's office, which he did without daring to argue, probably taking me for a newly arrived Russian officer.

I entered the office and introduced myself to the astonished Minister. He asked me to sit down, offered me tea, and after nearly half an hour's pleasant conversation during which I told him of my adventures in Turkey and particularly on the Bulgarian Front, told me that he understood that I was much more suited to a military than to a diplomatic career. I left, enchanted by the result of the interview. I suppose that Vossuq-ed-Dovleh let my father know of his views about me during the next cabinet meeting, and thus ended my father's last endeavour to put me into a diplomatic career. He never imagined then, nor for that matter did I, that forty-four years later I would be sent as Ambassador to Turkey to the very post he had occupied himself.

Finally I entered the Imperial Guards detachment with the rank of sub-lieutenant, and exchanged my fancy uniform for that of the Guards. The Iranian Army was then composed of several branches differing in leadership, uniforms, organisation, regulations, words of command and armament, according to the nationality of the foreign instructors who had presided at their

U.F.S.——E

formation or still commanded them. In order that the meaning
and the causes of certain events may be understood I will give a
brief explanation of the situation of the army as it was in 1914
just before the First World War.

The army nominally consisted of 72 infantry regiments of
about 600 men each. The men were recruited only from the
country, the towns being exempted from military service.
According to the conscription laws each village was obliged to
provide a certain number of soldiers according to its importance
at the time. The duration of service was anything between five
and twenty years but after a few months the enlisted man could
go on indefinite leave if he had enough money to soften the
heart of his colonel. Those who were not so fortunate used to
work as labourers in their garrison town in order to provide
themselves with food, as they were neither fed nor paid by the
authorities and usually clothed only every two or three years.
Their arms were kept in arsenals and they were summoned for
drill not more than half a dozen times in a month. The N.C.O.s
were promoted from the ranks without any kind of rules, their
chief role being to provide their officers with any small sums
they could squeeze out of the soldiers who were allowed to work
outside on payment of a monthly sum for that privilege—keeping
of course something for themselves.

The officers were usually small local landowners or relatives
of the C.O. and had not the slightest military or any other
kind of instruction, many of them not being able to read or
write. They had learned some rudiments of drill, but shooting
instruction was given very seldom, and there were soldiers who
had never fired a shot from their rifles. The officers also sometimes worked in town, mostly as shop-keepers—I remember once
in Teheran seeing a captain of one of the foot regiments in a
sort of uniform acting as a butcher.

There was a military school in Teheran, but it was really a
secondary school where some military instruction was given,
and the cadets were not boarded at the school. The ten or twelve
young officers commissioned each year from that school were
employed at the War Ministry and once or twice a year sent to
the provinces to inspect the regiments. There were never more
than 100 to 300 men present in the vicinity of the garrison.
When information about the impending arrival of the inspectors

was received by the commander of the regiment he rounded up all the soldiers he could lay his hands on, and completed his units by hiring for a few *shahis* (pence) a number of labourers or even loafers for the day. These men were given uniforms and rifles, which were kept for the occasion in the regimental depot, drawn up in line and told to stand without moving during the inspection. When the inspectors arrived, a command was given and the men stood at attention. The inspectors, who were aware of the situation, reviewed the line, acknowledging the presence of the men according to the roll-call, and then went to the C.O.'s home from where they departed quite satisfied.

Besides the infantry there were 16 detachments of artillery, with about 60 Austrian Ohacius breech-loading guns. During his last journey to Europe, Mozaffar-ed-Din Shah had bought some thirty 75-mm. quick-firing Schneider-Creuzot guns, but the artillery men were quite incapable of handling them and they were kept in the buildings on the Topkhane Square, except for a few that had been given to the Gendarmerie. The artillery had no horses, and even in Teheran, when an artillery exercise was contemplated, carriage horses from the Imperial stables were borrowed for the guns.

This army was quite incapable of fighting against the numerous and much better armed tribes, and when some of these became unruly the matter had to be settled by negotiation, or by mobilising against them the forces of rival tribes which were induced to take the field by a prospect of loot or in order to settle their private feuds.

The Shah's Guards, to which I was appointed, about 200 strong, was officered by Military School commissioned officers, the men being fed and quartered in barracks, but very seldom paid. The drill was better, and they had some shooting instruction.

The Persian Cossacks consisted in all of 3000 men. Although the Cossacks' instruction left much to be desired, it was much better than that of the 'Army' and they could be used in tribal operations.

The Gendarmerie comprised at that time about 6000 men in all. It was by far the most efficient force. It had been organised in 1911 by a mission of Swedish officers engaged by the Constitutional Government. As these officers had full powers, discipline was strictly enforced and the young officers commissioned after training at a special Gendarmerie school directed by the Swedes, were keen and conscious of their standing and prestige as officers. The relations between the Gendarmes, considered to be the backbone of the new Iranian Constitutionalist Regime, and the Cossacks, tools of the Tsarist Russian Legation and supporters of reaction, were very strained, and every day an outburst was to be expected.

On the 21st of March, Nowruz, the first day of the Iranian New Year 1293, was celebrated after a particularly cold winter, Teheran having been under snow for several weeks. Nowruz is probably the oldest feast in the world, dating from long before Islam and Christianity. It has been celebrated in all countries of Europe and the Middle East and has been adopted by the Christian Church as Easter. The Iranian New Year is now dated from the Hegira or flight of the prophet from Mecca to Medina in 622, but unlike the lunar Hegira year which consists of $354\frac{1}{3}$ days, is a solar year with 365 days. For this reason, at the time of writing, although the official Iranian Hegira date is 1341 the lunar Hegira date is 1382.

Nowruz has always been and still is the most important feast in Iran. Everyone prepares for the festivities weeks beforehand. The houses are cleaned, the carpets washed, new clothes provided for the whole family even in the poorest homes, and sweets of all kinds prepared. Wheat or lentil grains are put on plates and watered so as to produce miniature green fields ready for the New Year celebrations. Nowruz begins at the exact moment when the sun passes from the sign of the Fish into that of the Ram and this passage varies every year by a few hours and minutes, occurring sometimes at night time and sometimes by day— usually on the 21st and rarely on the 20t 1 of March. The family gathers together in a room where a cloth has been spread on the floor or on a table on which certain traditional things must find a place: a Qoran, a mirror, symbol of life, candles, the growing wheat, a bowl of goldfish symbolising the Zodiac Sign of the Fish, sweets and seven objects whose names begin with an S, the symbolical meaning of which I have so far been unable to discover.

Nowadays the birth of the year is announced on the radio as well as by cannon shot and at that moment incense is thrown on a brazier, the candles are lighted and the family exchange greetings and 'sweeten their mouths' with sweetmeats, after which the happiest person in the family (usually a small child) goes out of the house and returns to bring in happiness for the year. At the same moment an orchestra of ancient instruments begins to play an extraordinary melody which has not changed from time immemorial and is probably the oldest form of music known today. This used to be performed on the roof of the Golestan Palace, but is now played more prosaically, in the Teheran Radio Studio. Immediately after that the Shah congratulates the nation and afterwards the radio relays a speech by the Empress.

The New Year holidays used to last for thirteen days but have now been reduced to five for the administration and seven for the schools. During this time people must call on all their friends and relatives, and visits must be returned before the thirteenth day. On this day everybody leaves the town to picnic in gardens or fields and the growing wheat or lentils must be taken from their receptacles and thrown into running water—an ancient rain charm to secure a good harvest.

It was the first time that I was introduced to Nowruz with all its pageantry, having known the feast so far only as an occasion on which I received handsome presents from my parents. On the first day there was a military parade in the Golestan Palace—Ahmad Shah was seated on a throne surrounded by standing courtiers. He was clad in a black frock-coat on the front of which shining diamonds were sewn symmetrically on both sides of the chest. He had a black astrakhan cap surmounted by a diamond aigrette on his head and at his girdle hung an enormous jewel-studded sword. He was short and very fat, and his smooth round face wore an expression of submissive boredom. The courtiers and ministers wore long cashmere robes with woollen girdles, cashmere turbans on their heads and red morocco leather boots. Beneath the window stood the generals, in every kind of fancy uniform, some of Russian, some of Austrian and some of Prussian style but all covered with decorations and ribbons.

As soon as the Shah was seated, guns started to fire every half-minute. One of the high officials then pronounced a congratulatory speech, after which a court poet chanted a suitable poem in a high-pitched voice. The different military formations in full-dress uniforms massed in an outer courtyard, called the

Takht-i-Marmar Court, entered the palace garden by a narrow gate, re-forming afterwards inside the garden. Every formation had its own band. First came the Guards. Our band struck up a march, but as at the same time the bands of the Cossacks and the Gendarmerie were playing in the outer courtyard, I had great difficulty in making the men keep step. We passed somehow, not very brilliantly. Then came the Silakhor infantry regiment, 200 men in all. The soldiers of this regiment, coming from the Silakhor district near Lorestan, garrisoned in Teheran, were chiefly employed to guard the houses of high dignitaries (we had four of them in our house, Arfaieh), and their march past was deplorable. After them came the Cossacks dressed in Caucasian-style *cherkesskas*, led by their Iranian officers, the Russian instructors being in the group of high officers under the window. They marched past tolerably well, in spite of the Gendarmerie band playing waltz tunes outside in order to drown the sounds of the Cossacks' band and so confuse and spoil the effects of their march past. Last came the gendarmes. They looked smart and efficient, and their Swedish officers were rightly proud of them.

Before this show, during the morning, the Shah received the clergy, the Ministers, the high dignitaries and the foreign counsellors, all dressed in traditional Persian robes like the Ministers, the generals and the Diplomatic Corps, who presented their congratulations for the New Year. This ceremony was called the Salam and still takes place today.

Shortly after Nowruz, my aunt Khadija Khanum, who had not seen her brother since 1889, arrived from Tabriz in order to visit him. The fact that she had come first by carriage from Tabriz to Jolfa, then by train through Tiflis to Baku, then from Baku by boat to Enzeli and finally again by carriage to Teheran, illustrates the state of insecurity of the country as it was then. The direct road from Tabriz to Qazvin could not be used for wheeled vehicles, but the chief obstacles to using this road between Tabriz and Mianeh were the raids by Shahsevan tribesmen. The Shahsevans were nomad tribes very unruly and predatory but at the same time intensely patriotic and loyal to the throne as their name indicates, Shahsevan meaning in Turki 'lovers of the Shah'. They used to make raids not only in Iran, but also sometimes in the Russian part of the Moghan steppe in the loop formed by the Aras and Kura rivers. They had fought fiercely against the Russian occupation forces in 1911, and although they sustained heavy losses, had never been subdued by the considerable Russian forces sent against them.

Khadija Khanum was a very neat old lady who must have been very pretty in her youth. I was glad to know my father's family from Tabriz and to hear the many stories about life there that my aunt told me. She stayed three months in Teheran, but was obliged to abandon the idea of making the pilgrimage to Imam Reza, the eighth Imam's shrine at Mashad, because the Teheran-Mashad road was as insecure as the Tabriz-Teheran road on account of the Turkomans who came from the Turko-man plain, known today as Dasht-i-Gorgan, to loot travellers and the villages of the Shahrud and Sabzevar plain. They used to carry off any of the hapless inhabitants they could lay their hands on to slavery, especially girls and young women who were added to their harems, and young boys who were used as labourers. From the time of Nader Shah, before 1747 until 1925, this region, though nominally Iranian territory, had never been under the Central Government's control or administration and Government forces never penetrated further than Aq Qal'e (now Pahlavi Dezh) inside the Turkoman territory extending from the Gorgan river to the frontier of Transcaspian Russian territory.

Instead of going to Mashad my aunt decided to make a pil-grimage to Qom, 98 miles to the south of Teheran, to visit the tomb of Fatmeh, Imam Reza's sister, commonly called Hazrat Masume or the Exalted Innocent.

In the summer of 1914 came the news of the assassination of the Archduke Franz-Ferdinand, but few people realised the implications of this political murder. A few weeks later, when the Austro-Hungarian Government adopted a strong attitude towards Serbia, still nobody believed in the possibility of world-wide complications. People in Iran were much more concerned about the impending changes which would result from the coming of age of Ahmad Shah, and the retirement of the Regent Nasr-ol-Molk. The young Shah was crowned in the throne-room of the Golestan. The audience consisted of the Cabinet Ministers, the heads of missions, a few Olema, a few generals and the top foreign advisers, altogether not more than some 120 persons. I was on duty in the throne-room and saw the ceremony, which was far from sumptuous. When all the persons present had taken their places, the Shah appeared and after acknowledging the greetings of the audience, he who bowed, went straight to the throne and sat down on it. The military band which was in the garden played the National Anthem. Then two religious dignitaries approached, one from each side, and a Court official tendered to them the Imperial Crown on a velvet cushion. The Qajar Crown was rather high, entirely covered with pearls and surmounted by a diamond aigrette. The two Olema took the crown together and put it on the Shah's head after he had removed his black astrakhan cap with the big diamond in front and a more modest aigrette, and had handed it to a Court dignitary. The crown was heavy, and when the Olema removed their hands it nearly fell off, the Shah being obliged to seize it and to hold it for a few minutes until protocol allowed him to remove it and give it back to the courtier. After that he again put on his black cap and listened to speeches and poems recited by Court dignitaries, the cannon firing 101 shots. The whole ceremony lasted about forty minutes, after which the Shah came down from his throne and disappeared through the small door, while the military band again played the National Anthem.

The oath-taking ceremony was performed at the Majles or Parliament. The newly elected deputies were in *Sardaris* (pleated frock-coats), or in religious garb, as about a quarter of the 120 deputies were *mollas*. There was one box for the high officials, one for the diplomatic corps, one for the military, into which I managed to squeeze myself although I was only a lieutenant, and one for the press. The Shah arrived in the state carriage preceded and followed by troops of Cossacks and gendarmes, and by farrashes on foot. The crowd massed on the Baharistan square in front of the Majles greeted the Sovereign by clapping their hands. When he mounted the rostrum, all present rose to their feet, the guns began firing and the Shah read the oath formula, swearing on the Qoran to respect the Constitution and to work for his people, after which he departed and the ceremony was over.

I cannot describe what took place at the Sepah Salar Mosque as I was not present. If the ceremony of the Coronation and the Oath-taking had been lacking in pomp and majesty, the reception at the Saltanatabad Summer Palace left nothing to be desired. The oriental palace with its mirrored rooms, lofty vaulted ceilings, priceless Persian carpets and blue-tiled pools with fountains fed by running streams, the romantic charm of the moonlit park and the soft strains of Viennese waltzes alternating with Russian and Tzigane airs played by the Cossack orchestra, was a wonderful background for the party which was organised according to European Court etiquette. The great pool in front of the palace was surrounded by candles burning in coloured glass shades, the light from them being reflected in the water. There was a miniature ship, also lighted with candles, and the evening ended with a firework display. Seeing the foreign military attachés in their brilliant pre-First World War uniforms talking gaily with each other, no one could have imagined that a few weeks later these same officers clad in khaki, *feldgrau* or *bleu horizon* would be at each other's throats fighting in a pitiless, protracted war which would result in the world's ruin and misery!

I was promoted on the occasion of the Coronation with other officers of the Guards and with a second gold star on my collar became a first lieutenant. I was attracted by the idea of becoming a cavalry officer and I therefore applied to the War Ministry asking to be sent to the Cavalry School of Saumur in France. After the assumption of power by the Shah, the cabinet had to resign and my father was appointed to head a mission to the Courts of Europe to announce the Shah's Coronation and I was to accompany him, when the unexpected declaration of war changed all our plans. This declaration certainly caused great surprise, but the general opinion was that the German Army was so much superior in armament, organisation and efficiency to those of Russia and France that the war would probably be over in a few months if not weeks. Except for a few Paris-educated Francophiles in the upper classes and fewer genuine Russophiles—the majority of these being so only by opportunism—the great majority of Iranians of all classes were pro-German, not for Germany's sake, but from hostility to Russia, and were rejoicing, thinking that with the defeat of Russia, that country's intolerable pressure on Iran would be removed.

The entry of Great Britain into the war against Germany provoked second thoughts among certain sections of public opinion and some of the small number of intellectuals existing then in Iran still had friendly feelings towards Great Britain on account of the help given to the liberals during the 1906–7 revolution. Although afterwards the British Government had concluded a treaty with Russia dividing Iran into spheres of influence and the British Legation had supported the Russians against the Constitutional Government on several occasions, notably for the dismissal of Mr. Morgan Schuster, it was considered that Great Britain had been forced by the world situation and the dangerous strength of Germany to adopt a policy of co-operation with her erstwhile rival, Russia.

In opposition to this minority, the majority of Iranians were on the side of the Central Powers, considering that in the case of an Allied victory Russia would become even more aggressive and dominating and that Great Britain would not be able to restrain her ally's expansionist policy towards the Persian Gulf's seaports.

As soon as the war started the Iranian Government addressed to all the Legations a note proclaiming its neutrality and requesting the Powers whose armies were in occupation of parts of Iranian territory to evacuate them. Russian military forces were stationed in Azerbaijan, Gilan, Asterabad and Khorasan provinces, the British had military units in some of the Persian Gulf ports, in Khuzestan and a cavalry detachment in Shiraz, and the Turks since 1910 had troops in some of the border districts of Western Azerbaijan. This declaration was met with scorn by the Russian Legation, which returned it to the Foreign Office. The British were more polite, but refused to contemplate the possibility of recalling their forces; as to the Turks, they declared that they were ready to recall their units if the Russians would evacuate Azerbaijan. As a result of this situation the declaration of the neutrality of Iran was rendered meaningless, as was proved by ensuing events.

Because of the war, my father's mission abroad was cancelled; he decided to return to Monaco and took me with him with the intention of sending me afterwards to the Saumur Cavalry School. On the 3rd October we left Teheran in a small bus, in company with two ladies from the French Legation whose husbands had been mobilised in the first days of August and who were going back to France. Our journey from Teheran to Enzeli was uneventful: we arrived at Enzeli and on the same afternoon our boat started for Baku. I thought about the war going on all over Europe, about the fate of Iran that we were leaving, and Turkey which was drifting towards war. I wanted to fight for Iran, and for Islam, and I went to my cabin well after midnight, leaving with regret the starlit sky, the sparkling sea, the moonlight and my thoughts and dreams.

The War Years

On our arrival in Baku we were met by the Iranian Consul and lunched at the Consulate. Then we drove to the station, where the special rooms reserved for the Emperor, which existed at all important railway stations in Russia, were opened for us by an attendant wearing the livery of the Imperial Court. It was at this railway station that we saw the first signs of the war.

The main lines were completely occupied by military trains taking troops and war material to the front, and the train which was to take us to Odessa had to follow along branch lines. Sometimes it was stopped at a station for several hours to allow troop trains to pass and we only reached Odessa six days after leaving Baku. I passed the time in the dining-car talking to Russian officers going to the front. On the whole their morale was good, 'We lost the battle of Tannenberg, but by drawing the Germans to our front, we saved our allies and allowed them to beat the Germans on the Marne'; that was the general attitude of the Russian officers. One of them told me that he had been in Iran since 1909.

The Russian Government, on the pretext that the disturbances following the 1906–7 revolution threatened their interests, had occupied Tabriz and afterwards, as they had met with opposition in other districts and particularly in the Ardabil region inhabited by the war-like Shahsevan tribes, sent a division into the country. According to this officer who had been there, the Shahsevans, who knew the region well, inflicted heavy losses on the Russians and as they were nomads living under tents and moving all the time it was difficult to retaliate. The Russians occupied the town of Ardebil and looted the tombs of Shah Esma'il and his ancestors, carrying off priceless old carpets, manuscript Qorans and other books. Of course, the Russian officer did not say that they 'looted' them, but that they 're-moved' these objects, which are now at the Hermitage Museum in Leningrad.

The operations against the Shahsevans had to be suspended on account of the war, but a Russian garrison remained for a time in Ardebil, as also in Tabriz and Urmia (now Rezaiyeh).

In Istanbul I noticed a great change in the political and moral atmosphere of the population. The feeling of fatalistic submission to defeat that was general eight months earlier had completely disappeared. The town was full of soldiers, and the officers walked proudly in the streets, looking with cold assurance on the Greeks, Armenians and foreigners.

The Government had proclaimed general mobilisation, 'not for war-like reasons', said their speakers, 'but to be able to uphold their neutrality'.

I understood that this moral upheaval was due to the work of the German Military Mission, headed by General Liman von Sanders and comprising some two-score officers, who had taken the reorganisation of the Turkish Army seriously in hand. I noticed a great feeling of hostility on the part of the Turks towards the British. This was due to the fact that two dreadnoughts which had been ordered by the Turkish Government in England and already paid for by public subscription had been requisitioned by the British Government at the beginning of the war, the Turkish crews who were undergoing instruction being sent back to Turkey. The protest of the Ottoman Government was of no avail, but the British naval mission which was in charge of the instruction of the Ottoman navy under Rear-Admiral Limpus was dismissed and sent back to England.

I saw the *Goeben*, renamed *Yavuz Sultan Selim*, under the Turkish flag and was told of the extraordinary adventures of that ship, which, together with the cruiser *Breslau*, after a lively pursuit by British ships in the Mediterranean, had taken refuge in the Dardanelles, closed to the pursuing British men-o'-war, and the ships declared purchased by the Turkish Government in lieu of the battleships requisitioned by the British. The crews of the German ships donned fezes to show that they had entered the Turkish service.

On the 29th October, news came as a thunderbolt that the Ottoman navy, including the two newly acquired German ships, had bombarded several Russian Black Sea ports and sunk a number of ships. As a result of this action on the part of Turkey the British and French Ambassadors, after having transmitted to the Porte their Governments' declarations of war, were given a special train to take them to Dedeagach, then belonging to Bulgaria, and my father decided to leave Istanbul by the same train. We left on the 1st November, after passing through eastern and western Thrace, where the signs of the Balkan War were still visible—burned railway stations and other buildings. We reached Dedeagach and embarked on a ship bound for Marseilles. This had been specially sent from France to bring the French and British Embassy staffs and nationals who had left Turkey after the declaration of war, my father and I being the only neutrals on board. We reached Malta without adventure and my father and I visited the town. Seeing an old church which we thought would be interesting, we entered it. At once we had a shock: the walls of the church were covered with black cloth and ranged along them were skeletons, standing erect and glaring at us from their black eye sockets. The effect of the white bones against the black-covered walls was extraordinary.

I asked one of the two black-robed priests whose skeletons they were. He said that they were the remains of the Knights of Malta who had defended the island against the French in 1798 and whom Napoleon, on his way to Egypt, had ordered to be shot.

We arrived at Marseilles and went to Monaco, before I left for Paris to enter the Saumur Cavalry School. After the battle of the Marne the situation on the Western Front had become stabilised, and the bloody battle at Ypres was dragging to its end, dashing the hopes of the Germans to make a break-through in the coastal region. Life in Paris was quite normal. Gold coins were still in use alongside bank-notes. Soldiers wore a light grey-blue uniform called *bleu horizon*, which was not very visible in the autumnal morning fog, but many officers were still to be seen wearing their red trousers and breeches.

In Paris I was told by our Minister that the Saumur Cavalry School had been transformed into a centre of instruction for artillery, but that he had talked with the Swiss Minister in Paris who thought that it would be possible for me to follow a cavalry instruction course in the Swiss Army. I was pleased with the idea, because I liked Switzerland, and the Minister undertook to try and obtain the Swiss Government's consent to the plan. It would be some time before the result would be known and I decided to go to Geneva where my mother was living and await the answer of the Swiss Government there.

In April I heard that the Swiss Military Department had accepted my application, and that I should go to Berne to present myself to the Chief of the Cavalry Service. Introduced into the Chef d'Arme's office I found myself in the presence of a tall, athletically built handsome man in the Swiss Army uniform. He greeted me courteously, asked about my situation in the Iranian Army, and then directed me to go that afternoon in uniform to the cavalry barracks and present myself to the Commander of the Cavalry recruits regiment, Lieutenant-Colonel Poudret.

In my uniform, with my sword and black astrakhan cap, I made a sensation in the hall of the hotel, but trying to look unconcerned I took a taxi to the barracks. Lieutenant-Colonel Poudret met me in his office in a brisk military manner, saying that as he was just about to take the officers of the regiment for a ride in the country I should accompany them. He ordered a horse to be saddled for me. I felt myself quite unprepared to accompany these cavalry officers, but having no excuse ready I dared not refuse.

The colonel took me with him to the riding school where a dozen officers were waiting. He introduced me, saying: 'This is First Lieutenant Hassan Khan, of the Iranian Army; he will be with us during our courses, and he is welcome amongst us.' We all saluted. Then he introduced the officers one by one by name, every one clicking his heels and giving a stiff Prussian-style salute. I did the same. A soldier brought me a horse, I mounted it, but did not know how to hold the four reins. We started two by two behind the colonel. He was a slight, wiry man in the middle forties, with a black moustache and severe eyes. All the officers were extremely chic and I had the feeling that they looked at me very critically. My horse was tall and broad and much bigger than the Turkish and Iranian horses and I felt rather uncomfortable on it. But it was when we began to trot that my real sufferings began.

In Iran the horses are taught to amble and not to trot, and it was only in the new Gendarmerie that the Swedish instructors had introduced the rising trot. I was tossed about and felt relieved only when we started to gallop. Although the colonel was in front of me, he understood, I do not know how, that something was wrong with my riding, and when we came back and I alighted exhausted, he ordered a tall, good-looking first lieutenant to look after me and 'enlighten me about Swiss riding methods'. I was grateful for his tact and at once made friends with Lieutenant Vogel, as also with the other young officers who were friendly and helpful. The great majority of Swiss are extremely patriotic, considering military service as an honour and a sacred duty to their country, and in spite of only two to three months' presence with the colours, acquire a soldierly appearance and are subject to a strict discipline. I was amazed at the perfection of the exercises and the enthusiasm of the men and cadres in performing their military duties.

The cavalry officers were all well-off and belonged to aristocratic families, called in Berne patricians, and they spent freely, drank much and behaved generally very much according to the pattern of German or Austrian officers. Although they were really civilians in uniform spending a very short time in the army, as soon as they had put on their uniforms, they adopted a haughty and arrogant manner towards civilians, copied from the Prussians. On the other hand a feeling of class distinction did not exist, as I had the occasion to witness a few days after my arrival.

I was crossing the square between the railway station and my hotel when I was saluted by a very smart young infantry officer followed by a batman carrying his suit-case, who also saluted me. At first I did not recollect who these people were, and then suddenly recognised the officer as being the hotel porter, and his batman as the hotel's director. Both had been mobilised on account of the war and were going to join their units at the frontier. The porter having passed through the officers' school had been mobilised as an officer, and the director, not having done so, as a private, and both found it natural that the director should act as batman to his porter and carry his luggage.

I was attached to the 1st squadron, as a supernumerary officer, and wore my Iranian Guards uniform. We did a lot of riding, obstacle-jumping, riding-school work, reconnoitring and manœuvring in the country around Berne. Every fortnight the colonel organised a regimental dinner at the Burgerhaus, where a special room was reserved for us. The meal was ordered with great care by Colonel Poudret himself, who, besides being a well-known rider at horse shows, was a great gourmet. Ladies were not invited because he considered that their presence at table prevented proper appreciation of the quality of the food, but after dessert officers were allowed to invite their girl friends and sometimes the adjutant was sent to bring a car full of chorus girls. The party lasted until the small hours of the morning, but the colonel retired after midnight.

I learned to drink heavily without showing it, to appear drunk being considered unworthy of an officer. These gay evenings never prevented our attending the six-thirty morning drill punctually, although sometimes after a late party we had only just time to have a bath and a shave and to change our clothes without going to bed at all. As we were young and healthy we did not suffer unduly from this kind of life, but my purse lacked my physical resilience, and I had hard work composing convincing letters to my parents to induce them to give an adequate allowance to 'a young cavalry officer who had to uphold the prestige of his Army in a foreign land'.

The Chef d'Arme Colonel Vogel was a bachelor and a sybarite and lived in a fine old house on the Aar, where he used occasionally to invite us for dinner. I liked these parties as besides getting a good meal he used to play us delicate melodies on his violin, while we gazed at the starlit sky through the open window, smoking excellent Havana cigars.

At that time a troupe of artists came from Vienna and gave a few performances of operettas at the local theatre. We met the artists after the show and invited them to the Casino of Berne for supper. The Austrian Assistant Military Attaché, with whom we became acquainted, came also and triumphantly announced the fall of Lemberg (now Lvov) to the Austro-Hungarian Army. We ordered champagne and drank to the Emperor Francis Joseph and the *Kaiserlich und Königliche Armee, drei mal hoch!* The next day we were put under arrest for twenty-four hours for having violated Swiss neutrality, the Austrian major being rebuked by his Legation to which the Swiss Foreign Department had sent a formal protest. At the beginning of August I joined another recruits regiment at Aarau, after which I joined the cavalry officers' school in Berne, where we worked ten hours a day. In November we went to Basle and then to Rheinfelden, on the Rhine, opposite the German town of the same name.

In order to protect the north-western frontier, the Swiss cavalry was organised in three brigades, to one of which I was attached and sent to the region of Delemont and Porrentruy, on the Alsatian frontier. From this place the artillery duel between the French and the Germans could be clearly heard. Later I returned to Berne where Colonel Vogel gave a dinner in my honour, and then I left for Monaco as my time with the Swiss Army was finished.

In Monaco, life was almost at a standstill. The Casino, which had been closed during the first months of the war, had timidly reopened and concerts were being given twice a week at the Monte Carlo theatre, but tourists were few and many of the luxury shops were closed.

At home my family was divided into two camps: my father, my brother, then thirteen years old, and I were pro-Turk and consequently pro-German; my stepmother and my nine-year-old sister were pro-French, but did not dare say so openly before my father.

I wanted my father to allow me to enter the Turkish Army as a volunteer to fight against the Russians. At first he resisted this suggestion, considering it crazy, but finally he gave me the necessary money to go to Istanbul, and I started my journey by going to Switzerland to visit my mother, so as to be able to leave France.

I stayed about one week in Geneva, taking visas from the Turkish, Austro-Hungarian and Bulgarian consulates, and then took a train to Zürich, and from there went on to Vienna. I had to stay for a few days to get the necessary permission to use the Balkanzug, running between Berlin, Vienna and Istanbul through newly occupied Serbia. The Balkanzug was an official military train, but a few other people were allowed to use it. I went several times to the Polizei-Amt to get such an authorisation without success and finally, as I gave the reason for my journey my wish to join the Turkish Army in the war, was directed to the War Ministry. After all kinds of security investigations and after signing a great many papers, I was accompanied by an N.C.O. to the proper office. A black-whiskered uniformed functionary sitting under Emperor Francis Joseph's picture ponderously examined my passport, and told me that it was not possible to allow me to board the special train because although I was an officer of the Iranian Army, Iran was officially a neutral country, and only the officers of the Central Powers were allowed to use it. I went back to my hotel in despair and told the manager. He smiled and advised me to go again and to slip unobtrusively a 50-krone bank-note amongst my papers and await the result. I said that such an important personage would never accept a bribe and would probably have me arrested. The manager smiled and said: 'I do not think so, but if he objects, tell him that this bank-note just slipped by mistake into your papers'. To my great astonishment the official dexterously removed the bank-note from my passport without my noticing it, and told me that having consulted higher authorities, he had come to the conclusion that he could authorise me to use the Balkanzug after all! I was dumbfounded, but tried not to show it, and received a duly stamped authorisation to travel to Istanbul 'for official reasons'.

In February 1916, Vienna had not yet been very much affected by the war, although the Russian Front was not far away, having reached the Carpathian Mountains between Galizia and Hungary. The restaurants and *bierhalles* were full of officers, some in *feldgrau* on leave from the Front, and others in their pre-war dark blue or brown uniforms.

The first signs of war were seen at the Belgrade station, which had been completely destroyed by Austrian artillery. Afterwards, all the stations in Serbia were surrounded by trenches and barbed wire, because Serb guerrillas were still scattered over the country, and I even heard during the night the sound of shots obviously directed at our train. Beyond Nish the Austro-Hungarian soldiers guarding the line were replaced by Bulgars, and two days later I reached Istanbul. From the Sirkeji station I took a carriage to the Tokatlian Hotel in Pera, and went to the restaurant to dine. As soon as I sat down, a loud and familiar voice called me. Looking back I saw my uncle, Ali Akbar Khan, sitting alone at a table and looking at me with an air of angry surprise. 'How and why did you arrive here without letting me know, and why did you come to this hotel instead of to my house,' he shouted, attracting the attention of the other diners. He ordered me to come to his table, and while I tried to explain my hopes of enlisting in the Turkish Army, he abused me for my folly and my father for his weakness, and after dinner paid my bill and took me to his house.

I stayed two weeks in Istanbul, trying, through the War Ministry, to enter the Ottoman service and be sent to the Caucasian or the Mesopotamian Front. I had counted on my friend Husein Aouny of Chatalja days, as his uncle was an influential General, Zeki Pasha. Unfortunately Aouny was at the Dardanelles Front and Zeki Pasha was representing the Turkish Army at German headquarters in Berlin, and as my uncle was a close friend of Enver Pasha, the War Minister and Vice-Generalissimo of the Ottoman Armies (the Generalissimo being nominally the Sultan), he was able to prevent my efforts from succeeding.

During my stay in Istanbul I tried to contact my Harbiye friends, but nearly all of them had been commissioned and sent to the different fronts, my cousin Yusuf to the Dardanelles, his brothers to the Russian Front, and I was sad to learn that several of them had been killed.

The political atmosphere was heavy. After a bloody battle the Turkish Army had had to abandon the fortress of Erzurum, which was the strategic key to Eastern Turkey. The Ottoman Crown Prince Yusuf Izzeddin had committed suicide, but people hostile to the Union and Progress Government were insinuating that he had been dispatched by order of Talaat Pasha the Prime Minister and Enver Pasha because he had been opposed to the war against the Allies, favouring a separate peace while there was still time. All men had been mobilised and for the first time women were to be seen driving the tramcars and sweeping the streets, clad in the uniforms of the Municipality.

Seeing that I had nothing to gain by remaining in Istanbul, I consented to be sent home to Monaco, and I boarded the train to Vienna, to the great relief of my uncle.

While I was travelling through Thrace feeling depressed and frustrated at having failed in my endeavour to fight and ashamed to go back to Monaco having achieved nothing, I suddenly had what I thought to be a brilliant idea: instead of going back to Vienna I would quit the train at Sofia and go through Rumania and Russia to Iran, where I would join the Gendarmerie which was helping the Turks in the region of Kermanshah and was now fighting against the Russian forces operating in the Hamadan-Baghdad direction. After counting my money I thought I should be able to get as far as Teheran, and so at Sofia I took the train to Bucarest. Then taking the train to Galatz, I crossed the Danube frontier successfully but arrived at Reni, on the Russian side, where the customs officials, discovering in my suit-cases military uniforms, an automatic pistol, a sword and binoculars, turned me back, saying that I was probably going to Iran to join the Gendarmerie, which was indeed the case. This time, I had to return to Monaco for good, as I had no wish to volunteer in the German or Austro-Hungarian armies fighting in France or Poland.

In Vienna I went to see our Minister, Safa-ol-Memalek, who had been my father's Counsellor in Istanbul and was very kind to me, and bought a set of large-scale war maps of the Eastern, Western and Balkan Fronts.

I then took the train for Switzerland, but at Feldkirch in the Vorarlberg, near the Swiss frontier, my passport was examined, and to my astonishment I was told that they were obliged to send it to Vienna to be checked, and that I would have to wait in Feldkirch. After a week my passport was returned but when I had paid my hotel bill I was left with only a very few francs. I thought that, having my ticket to Geneva where I could go to my mother, I should not need more money and taking the next train to Zürich, I arrived at the Swiss frontier of Buchs. I went to the passport control, and suddenly saw an announcement saying that no foreigners having with them less than 200 Swiss francs in cash could enter Switzerland. My statement that my mother was in Geneva and that I was not a pauper was of no avail, and I went back to my carriage to take my luggage out. I intended sending a telegram to my mother asking her to wire me a money transfer to Buchs, when an elderly Armenian couple, whose acquaintance I had made on the train, inquired what had happened. When I explained the situation they told me not to worry, and in ten minutes' time brought me 200 francs which they had borrowed from several passengers! When I showed this sum to the official he looked rather suspicious, asking me how was it that I had not shown it before. I muttered something, and he did not insist. I must say, it was a relief when the train left Buchs for Zürich.

After a month in Geneva with my mother I took a train for

Marseilles, but another trial was in store for me at the French frontier. Arrived at Bellegarde I passed the passport control smoothly, notwithstanding the Austrian, Bulgarian and Turkish visas gracing my passport, and was going towards my carriage with a clear conscience when a tough-looking man, obviously a police officer in plain clothes, accompanied by two uniformed gendarmes stopped me and took me into an empty room. '*Aha, mon coco, nous vous tenons!*' he said, brandishing a thick, ominous-looking file. I protested vehemently, but the man asked me to look at it. What I read was not comforting: 'Between the 28th March and the 2nd April, an enemy spy with a Persian passport bearing the name of Hassan Khan will try to pass the frontier into France either at Frasne-Vallorbe or at Bellegarde. Have him arrested and send him under escort to the Ministry of the Interior in Paris.'

The date was 31st of March, and my name on the passport was Hassan Khan. I was at a loss how to convince the man that it was a mistake, when lifting the page I saw under it the picture of the presumed spy. He was a thick-set man, heavily mustachioed, about forty years old. 'Look at this picture,' I said to the policeman. 'Do I look like him?' The policeman gazed at the photograph and admitted that I had certainly changed in appearance. He reluctantly consented to send a telegram to the French Consul in Monaco inquiring about my identity. I had to stay at the station under police surveillance until a satisfactory answer came back and I was released, with the minimum of apologies.

After all these adventures I was glad to get back to Monaco but not to a comparatively idle life which was to last for more than three years. With the tremendous events of the war rocking the world, I found this life in the Monte Carlo backwater very tedious. Many Allied officers came to spend their one-week leave in the luxurious atmosphere of the Riviera. Others, who had been severely wounded, came for a longer time, enjoying the mild climate and the easy life before returning to the hell of trench warfare on the Somme, or in Flanders or Verdun. I became a permanent member of the much-sought-after International Sporting Club of Monte Carlo, as the son of Prince Arfa, princes becoming automatically members of that Club. I was interested in tennis tournaments and became a member of the

Monte Carlo Tennis Club, where I made the acquaintance of an English woman with whom I often played tennis. She was tall and slim, with a narrow aristocratic face and very intelligent eyes. Her name was Mrs. Nicolson, and I learnt much later that she was the famous poet and author, Victoria Sackville-West.

In March 1917 came the news of the revolution in Russia, and of the abdication of the Tsar. Being a convinced monarchist and having an ingrained respect towards all sovereigns, I was shocked by these happenings. On the other hand, as Iran had always been subjected to aggression from Russia and was actually under the threat of losing its independence at the hands of that Power, anything that might enfeeble Russia was welcome to us. Certainly a revolution, which would doubtless result in chaos and disorganisation, would have that effect.

The news from Iran was scanty and unreliable, but we knew that early in 1915 a Turkish detachment had penetrated from Baghdad and Khanegin towards Kermanshah, trying to induce the Iranian tribes of that region to join them and fight with the Russians. At that time the British Army, which had disembarked in Basra and advanced as far as Ctesiphon near Baghdad, had been defeated there and retreated to Kut-el-Amara on the Tigris, where it had been surrounded by the Turks. The Supreme Allied Council and the British Ambassador in Petrograd had asked the Russians to send an important force through Iran to attack Baghdad from the north-east and co-operate with the British Army in Mesopotamia and with this request in mind the Russians disembarked a substantial force in Enzeli and concentrated it in Qazvin. This force later formed the 1st Caucasian Cavalry Corps, commanded by General Baratof, whilst another Russian Army Corps was concentrated in Tabriz, after this town had been temporarily occupied by a small Turkish force supported by local anti-Russian elements in December 1914. These forces were expelled by the Russians after a few days.

Wishing to secure his left flank, General Baratof sent a Cossack regiment from Qazvin to Karaj, 25 miles from Teheran. This move provoked a panic in the capital. The Majles proclaimed that the neutrality and independence of the Government of Iran could not be enforced under the military occupation of one of the belligerents and suggested that the Shah and the Government should leave Teheran and go to Isfahan. At first

the Shah agreed to this and orders were given to the Gendarmerie to start towards Qom, most of the deputies leaving at
the same time, but just as the Shah was about to start and the
Imperial carriages were ready, the Allied Ministers prevailed on
him to stay.

The Government, headed by the nationalist leader of the
Democratic party, Mostofi-el-Memalek, then resigned and was
replaced by a pro-Ally Cabinet, but the representatives of the
Central Powers as well as the gendarmes and the majority of the
deputies went to Qom where a Committee of National Defence
was formed, and from there to Hamadan, where it was joined
by other Gendarmerie units from Isfahan, Burujird and Qazvin.
After some fighting with the Russian advance guard, it finally
arrived in Kermanshah where it took the name of the Free
Iranian Government, headed by Nezam-os-Saltaneh Mafi, the
Governor of that province. Later he concluded a treaty of alliance
with the German Minister, Prince Reuss, and received from the
Germans a substantial subsidy.

In Shiraz the commander of the Gendarmerie regiment had
announced his adherence to the Free Iranian Government and
had arrested the British Consul and all the members of the
British colony, but after a time, as the gendarmes and the
N.C.O.s did not get any pay, they were secretly approached
by the emissaries of Qavam-ol-Molk, a pro-British grandee of
Shiraz, and revolted against their commander, who shot himself.
The regiment was then disbanded.

Meanwhile, the Baratof Cavalry Corps opened an offensive
against the Free Iranian forces supported by the Turks, and
threw them back to Khanegin in Turkish territory. Here the
Cavalry Corps was counter-attacked by the Turkish General Ali
Ehsan Pasha, who drove them back to Kermanshah and afterwards beyond Hamadan, where the Front became stabilised for
six months (1916), and General Townshend, who was not relieved either from the south by the British or from the north
by the Russians, was forced to capitulate.

In Teheran, the Russian and British Legations forced the
Iranian Government, then headed by Sepah Salar Aazam, to
agree to the organisation of two divisions recruited in Iran, one
in the Russian sphere of influence under the command of Russian
officers and one in the southern part of the country under British

command, to ensure the internal security of the country and allow the Russian and British forces to concentrate against the Turks. In view of the impossibility of resisting the foreign forces occupying the country, the Iranian Government announced its readiness to enter the war on the side of the Allies, but the latter refused this offer, which fact was considered in Iran to mean that the Allies had already decided to divide the country and to end its independence. What happened afterwards proved this assumption to have been true.

In the north the Russians expanded the already existing Persian Cossack Brigade into a division, increasing the number of Russian officers and N.C.O.s and providing it with a few more guns and machine-guns.

In the south the British had to organise something from scratch and Brigadier-General Sir Percy Sykes, who had long experience of Iran having been British Consul in Kerman and Mashad, was charged with this task, and how he acquitted himself has been narrated in great detail in his *History of Persia*. After many adventures and much fighting with the Qashqai and other tribes in the Fars provinces he was able to organise one brigade in Shiraz and another in Kerman, but the road from Shiraz to Bushire remained in the hands of hostile tribesmen until the end of the war. The German agent Wassmuss, whose pluck and daring became proverbial, was very active in this region and caused much annoyance to the British.

Early in 1917, the Baratof Corps moved from near Qazvin towards Baghdad, which was occupied by General Maude, obliging the Turkish General Ali Ehsan Pasha to evacuate Iran in order not to be taken between the British and the Russians. Baratof followed the Turks across the frontier up to the Diala river, but was repulsed there with heavy loss. The revolution and the subsequent disintegration of the Russian Army prevented him from further operations, and shortly after this he was recalled to Petrograd. At the end of 1917, after the Bolsheviks had seized power, the Russian Army at war ceased to exist as such. In Azerbaijan the soldiers killed many of their officers and went back to Russia, abandoning part of their armaments. The officers of the Baratof Corps were luckier, as they managed to reach Teheran, and as this town was not under Russian occupation, they escaped massacre and were able to go into exile through

India. The Grand Dukes Boris Vladimirovich and Dimitri Pavlovich were among them.

The British High Command hoped to be able to bolster up the few remaining Russian detachments under Colonels Bicherakhof and Shkuro with a few British officers including General Dunsterville and to re-form a defensive front against the Turks, but Shkuro's men rebelled and returned to Russia, while Shkuro himself managed to join Denikin.

Dunsterville managed to induce Colonel Bicherakhof, who had assembled some one thousand Cossacks from different units, to open the way from Qazvin to Enzeli. The road had been cut by an Iranian leftist political leader, Mirza Kuchik Khan, who had taken the field with a force of partisans to oppose the foreign occupation of Iran. Bicherakhof threw Mirza Kuchik Khan back into the forest of Gilan, but on reaching Enzeli he embarked for Baku, eventually joining the White Russian Armies of Denikin fighting the Red Army in the Northern Caucasus.

In January 1918, I was shocked to read in the papers the terms of the secret Anglo-Russian treaty of 1915 which had been published by the Soviet Government. This treaty stipulated the division of Iran: Great Britain to receive the central part of the country which had been considered 'neutral' under the 1907 Anglo-Russian Agreement but which comprised the Anglo-Iranian Oil Company's concession area, whilst Russia was allowed to annex all the North of Iran including Teheran. The Soviet Government emphasised by this publication the duplicity of Great Britain and of the former Tsarist Government, and solemnly cancelled the 1907 treaty, which they called 'a glaring example of predatory imperialistic policy'. The final defeat and disintegration of the Ottoman Empire made me sad, but for the time being Iran seemed to be saved by the Russian revolution.

In June 1919 my father went to Paris, taking me with him, to settle his financial affairs with the Crédit Lyonnais Bank, three-quarters of his fortune having been placed in the Imperial Russian State Bank which with all its assets had been nationalised by the Soviet Government without any compensation to the shareholders.

Our houses in Tiflis and Borjom had not been taken over as the region to the south of the Caucasian Mountains had separated from Russia and a Transcaucasian Republic organised there early in 1918. The population of this Republic was composed of Georgians, Armenians and Moslems who were all at daggers-drawn with one another and split after a short time into three independent states: Georgia, Armenia and Azerbaijan with Tiflis, Erivan and Baku as their respective capitals. Azerbaijan in 1918 took this name with the hidden purpose of annexing the Iranian Province of Azerbaijan, situated to the south of the Aras river.

The population of Nakhchevan had wished to join Iran and had sent a deputation to Teheran, but the Allies were not sympathetic to the idea, having promised Nakhchevan to the Armenians, in spite of the fact that the majority of the population of that district were Moslems. In Iran, the situation as a result of the war was appalling, for though not a belligerent, 2 million out of her population of 12 million had succumbed to the famine with its attendant epidemics, caused by the destruction of crops and foodstuffs by the opposing armies.

After the Russians vanished from the Iranian scene as a result of the revolution and the secession of the Caucasian States, the British Government occupied Iraq and wished to fill the vacuum by including the whole of Iran in its sphere of influence so as to constitute a British-dominated zone from India to Palestine. The former Russophile Vossuq-ed-Dovleh who was Minister of Foreign Affairs, a clever and ambitious man, fell in at once with this plan but in the summer of 1918, the Prime Minister was a Bakhtiari chief, Samsam-os-Saltaneh, whose nationalistic out-look did not fit in with these ideas. The chief of the Gendarmerie was then the Swedish Colonel Lundberg, who saw eye to eye with the Prime Minister, but another of the handful of Swedish officers who had remained in Iran was a Major Gleerup, who commanded the 2nd Gendarmerie regiment, and he was induced to take his regiment to Hazrat Abdul Azim. After taking sanc-tuary there he demanded the resignation of Samsam-os-Saltaneh and the appointment of Vossuq-ed-Dovleh, threatening to use force. Political pressure was also exercised on the Shah and Samsam-os-Saltaneh resigned, Vossuq-ed-Dovleh became Prime Minister and Gleerup was promoted Colonel and replaced Lundberg at the head of the Gendarmerie.

At once negotiations began between the Iranian and British

Governments, the latter represented by its Minister Sir Percy
Cox, former Resident in the Persian Gulf, acting on behalf of
Lord Curzon who was then Foreign Secretary in the Lloyd
George Cabinet. The aim of these negotiations was the conclusion
of a treaty by which Great Britain would give a loan to Iran
and undertake the rehabilitation of the Iranian Army and
finances under conditions which would place the Iranian
Government under the practical control of Great Britain. The
Finance Minister, Prince Firuz Nosrat-ed-Dovleh, and the
Minister of the Interior, Sarem-ed-Dovleh, supported the Prime
Minister, but Moshaver-ol-Memalek Ansari, the Foreign Minister, was opposed to this scheme, saying that it was contrary to
Iranian independence, that the eclipse of Russia was certainly
only momentary, and that should such a treaty be signed, her
reappearance on the frontiers of Iran would result in a dangerous
situation which would affect Iran adversely.

In order to have his hands free, Vossuq-ed-Dovleh sent
Moshaver-el-Memalek to Paris, to try to gain admittance to the
Peace Conference. Iran he considered was entitled to receive
substantial compensation, although he knew that Lord Curzon
would never consent to this.

My father tried to influence the U.S. delegates to accept
Iranian participation in the Conference, but British opposition
prevented it and Moshaver-el-Memalek was then appointed
Ambassador in Turkey, where he spent a few months before
going to Moscow, where he negotiated the famous Irano-Soviet
treaty of 1921.

I had the luck to assist on the Place de l'Etoile at the great
parade at the end of the war, when units of the French Army,
with token forces from all the Allied Armies, marched past under
the Arc-de-Triomphe where the Unknown Soldier had not yet
been buried, with Marshals Joffre and Foch riding at their head.
The enthusiasm of the crowds was indescribable: people waited
all night in the streets and even perched in the trees of the
Avenue des Champs-Elysées to be able to see this unforgettable
pageant.

A few days earlier, I had seen President Wilson, Mr. Lloyd
George, Clemenceau and others driving from Versailles where
the treaty had been signed. That night Paris was illuminated
and huge crowds roamed about the town. I saw the façade of the

Opera flood-lit and the famous singer Marthe Chenal appeared on the balcony in a flowing Greek robe carrying the French flag and singing the 'Marseillaise', the crowd accompanying her.

A few days after this my father went back to Monaco and I took the train to Switzerland where I expected to stay for a couple of months with my mother, but after six weeks my father wrote to me that he was leaving for Teheran and that he wanted me to accompany him.

PART II

Iran under Reza Shah Pahlavi—
Modernisation 1919–1941

After the War to the Coup d'Etat

It was not possible to reach Iran by the usual route through Russia, and so my father decided to follow the newly reopened route through Istanbul (which had just been occupied by the Allies), Batum, which was also under Allied occupation, Tiflis, Baku and Enzeli. The whole of this region was still under Allied military supervision and special permission had to be obtained for the journey.

Batum was under British military occupation, but was administered by a council composed of White Russians and Georgians not dependent either on the Georgian Republic or on the White Russian Government headed by General Denikin, who was fighting in South Russia against the Red Army.

The British Commander, Brigadier-General Cooke-Collis, called on my father, as well as a handsome colonel of the Russian Army, Prince Qajar, of Iranian origin, whose grandfather, Bahman Mirza, a son of Fath Ali Shah, had emigrated to Russia in the early thirties. The Prince, who was wearing a military *cherkeska* covered with Imperial Russian crosses and medals, had been in command of a regiment of the famous 'Wild Division' of the Caucasus, entirely composed of Moslems, but officered by both Russian and Caucasian officers. The Caucasian Moslems being exempt from military service, this division was composed entirely of volunteers, and was organised in six cavalry regiments, according to the races and tribes of the soldiers forming them. These were the Tatar, the Daghestan, the Chechen, the Ingush, the Osset and Kabarda regiments, all of whom had served with great gallantry throughout the war in Galizia. Back in Transcaucasia, the Tatar regiment formed the nucleus of the Azerbaijan Republic's Army, but after the occupation of that Republic by the Soviet Army in 1920, part of it passed into Iran, its officers joining the Iranian Army, in which they served loyally.

In Tiflis we were met by the Iranian Consul and by Mirza

Faraj Khan, my father's bailiff, a tall thin man of about seventy, with a beard dyed flaming red with henna. My father took me to visit friends of his Consulate General days twenty-five years before. At the house of General Tamansheff I felt rather awkward when one of my father's former belles looked at me critically through her lorgnette observing: 'The father was better!'

At that time Georgia was menaced from the north by the White Russian Army of General Denikin, who committed the fatal error of fighting at the same time the Soviet Red Army in the north and north-east, the Poles, the Ukrainians, the Caucasians and even the Kuban and Terek Cossacks. In the south there were latent hostilities between Georgia and the Armenian Republic, but on the east, the relations with the Azerbaijan Republic were friendly, as both were hostile to Denikin and to the Armenians.

I was told that when Tiflis was under German occupation many young Georgian girls became engaged to German officers and N.C.O.s, but that after their hurried departure and the arrival of the British many of them had married British officers. When the latter also departed by train to Batum, they insisted on taking their new wives with them and all these ladies were put in the rearmost carriage of the train, but at the first station after Tiflis the British authorities, not wishing to be encumbered with them, had the carriage detached, and they were left behind. I do not know if any of them managed to join their husbands in England or their fiancés in Germany.

We left Tiflis for Baku and I was astonished to see two of Faraj Khan's sons in military uniform, accompanied by some fifty youths also in uniform and carrying army rifles with bayonets and literally covered with ammunition belts, awaiting us at the station. When we appeared, Jamshid issued a command in Russian and the young soldiers presented arms. When I inquired who these people were, I was told that they were the military escort of His Highness Prince Arfa whom they were to guard on the train, as the country between Tiflis and Baku was not secure. I was astonished next morning to find that they had vanished in the night. I heard afterwards that it had been a trick to smuggle arms from Georgia into Azerbaijan, the Georgian authorities not allowing the export of arms to that country, where they would be used against the Armenians.

Baku was the capital of the Azerbaijan Republic which had come into being after the disruption of the Transcaucasian Republic formed early in 1918. The unwillingness of the Moslems to fight the Turkish Moslems and the lukewarmness of the Georgians to do so had caused the speedy conclusion of peace; the Armenians being defeated by the Turkish Army and repulsed from Erzurum and Kars to Erivan.

In March 1918, when the Baku Moslems had started to organise their Government, the Armenians, with the aid of Russian Army units who had become Bolshevik, seized power in that town and massacred some 18,000 Moslems. The Moslem Azerbaijan Government took refuge in Ganja (Elisabethpol during the Tsars and Kirovabad today), half-way between Baku and Tiflis, and called the Turks to their aid. The Turkish commander on the Caucasus front, deciding to help the Azerbaijanis, sent them Nuri Pasha, Enver's younger brother, and a division. The Moslem General of the former Tsarist Army, Samad Bey Mehmandarof, organised a local division with the help of the Turks, and in August, after two more Turkish divisions had joined them, the whole force under the command of Nuri Pasha moved against Baku.

After having defeated the Armenians in the region of Kurdamir, they came close to the city, where a short time before that General Dunsterville had brought two British battalions from Enzeli to help the Armenians resist the Turks and prevent the Baku oilfields from falling into their hands. In this way Baku was defended by British, Armenian and Communist forces, the last being local Communists, cut off from the Red Army of the newly created R.S.F.S.R. (Soviet Russia), the Soviet Union not yet having come into existence. Dunsterville had utilised part of the Russian Caspian Fleet, which had been put under the command of Commodore Norris, to move his troops from Enzeli, where he had come from Qazvin, following in the steps of Bicherakhof. The latter was also in the Baku region, to the north of that town, but had adopted a more or less independent attitude, not wishing to collaborate with the Communists.

Early in September the Turko-Azerbaijanis began their attack. After several days of fierce fighting the sector occupied by the British gave way and an infantry company was overwhelmed and taken prisoner. Then the centre, where the Armenians were holding the hills to the west of Baku about the Balajari station, was pierced, and a debacle followed, everybody flying towards the port. The British embarked on their ships and sailed to Enzeli, and the Communists surrendered, but the Armenians, knowing that there would be no quarter for them, dispersed in panic in the city, only a few of them being able to find boats to take them to Petrovsk or to Krasnovodsk. Complete chaos reigned in the town, nobody being in authority, while the Turks were advancing, firing indiscriminately on anyone they saw.

Meanwhile a few Moslem merchants assembled at the Iranian Consulate, the Consul being then my former tutor Mirza Mohammad Khan, and implored him to go to the Turkish commander to arrange a cease fire and to discuss the modalities of the surrender of Baku, in order to stop the advance of the attacking forces into the town and to prevent the indiscriminate slaughter of the peaceful inhabitants. Mirza Mohammad Khan, a courageous and conscientious man, accepted and placed an Iranian flag on one side of his car and a white flag on the other and started towards the Turks in company with the merchants, bullets whizzing past them. On the outskirts of the town they met the first advancing Turkish soldiers who stopped their car, and after much palavering, took them to Nuri Pasha. The Turkish General received them courteously and consented to halt the advance of the Turks into the town, but General Mehmandarof, considering himself in his own country, refused to give orders to the Azerbaijan division not to enter the town. Many of the relatives of the Azerbaijani soldiers had been massacred in March by the Armenians, and in order to avenge them the Azerbaijani massacred in their turn all the Armenians they could lay hands on, about thirty thousand persons losing their lives during the first three days. Nevertheless, many Armenians were saved by Moslem families in whose houses they had taken refuge.

After that, the Azerbaijan Government was installed under the leadership of M. Topchibashef, with Mehmandarof as War Minister. The Turkish Army retired, partly to Kars, leaving one division protecting the Daghestan region where a mixed Chechen-Lezghi Provisional Government had been formed against the White Russians, but the Turks were later obliged to evacuate the country altogether according to the terms of the Moudros Armistice of 31st October 1918.

Diplomatic representatives for Azerbaijan were appointed in several countries, including Iran, and Mirza Mohammad Khan, who had adopted the name of Saed, had been promoted to the rank of Diplomatic Representative. Like that of the other regions of the former Russian Empire which had proclaimed their independence after the revolution, the existence of Azerbaijan as a separate independent entity was precarious, both the White Russians and the Bolsheviks being opposed to its independent existence, and in the case of the ultimate victory of either, these countries would have to sustain a struggle to remain free. For this reason all strove to be officially recognised by the Allies, but the latter, considering themselves still bound by alliance to Russia, were not ready to subscribe to the partition of its territory.

In Baku all the Ministers came to call on my father and treated him with great respect. After a few days they offered him the Presidency of the Azerbaijan Republic, on condition that he would do all he could to bring about the inclusion in the Republic of the Iranian province of Azerbaijan with its chief town of Tabriz. Of course my father refused even to consider such a proposition, telling them that on the contrary, they ought to unite with Iran, their mother country from which they had been torn by Russia in 1813 and 1828. Unfortunately, the situation in Iran was such that the Azerbaijan leaders would not accept this proposal since they considered themselves stronger and more advanced industrially and politically than Iran.

We had been in Baku a few days when a delegation arrived from Teheran, headed by Seyid Zia-ed-Din Tabatabai, a former prominent journalist, whom I had met five years before in Teheran in a *molla*'s garb, but who was now wearing a frock-coat. He was accompanied by several other persons, including Captain Kazem Sayah, a Gendarmerie officer whom I had known when he was in the Military Academy in Turkey. This delegation had been sent by the Iranian Government to establish friendly relations with the three new republics, Azerbaijan, Georgia and Armenia. Afterwards it was said that it was also instructed to open negotiations with the Azerbaijan Ministry of Industry and Mines on behalf of the Anglo-Persian Oil Company, to try to bring the Baku Oil Industry into the A.P.O.C.'s sphere of interest. These negotiations if they took place were very secret, but when the Soviet Army occupied Baku in 1920 the former Azerbaijan Government's Industry and Mines Minister, Tlekhas, was accused of having negotiated with the Iranian delegation 'the cession of Baku Oil to the British Imperialists' and he was shot.

The Azerbaijan Government invited the members of the delegation and also my father and myself to a gala performance at the Municipal Theatre, where the popular Azerbaijani operette *Arshin mal alan* was performed. My father, Seyid Zia-ed-Din, and Mirza Mohammad Khan occupied the box of honour, while Captain Sayah and I were in the opposite box. We were astonished to see that a good proportion of the public, both civilians and soldiers, entered the house carrying daggers, swords and firearms of every description, and took their seats holding their rifles between their knees. There was an interval after the first act during which a dispute arose between a man who went to have a drink outside and another who had occupied the former's seat while he was away. Suddenly, a dagger blade flashed, a shot rang out, and pandemonium started. Every spectator armed with rifle or pistol began to shoot in every direction. After a few minutes police intervened, calm returned, half a dozen dead and wounded were taken out on stretchers, and the manager came on the stage to announce that 'the direction regrets the little disturbance, but it is now over and the play will continue', which it did.

On the 12th December we left Baku by boat and next morning arrived in Enzeli, then still under British occupation under Brigadier-General Champain, who had replaced Generals Thompson and Dunsterville in command of the British Brigade and reduced them to one British and one Indian battalion. After an interview with the General, we were given an open Ford car with an Indian military driver and started towards Teheran. The weather was bitterly cold, the Ford having probably served through several campaigns, threatened to fall to pieces. One of the headlights was broken and the light of the other very weak, but the driver was jolly and knew his job. We knew ours and did not complain, glad as we were to have found any means of transport at all, and one which had been graciously put at our disposal by the British General, only the petrol consumed being paid for by us. On our way, near Molla Ali we saw lying in a ravine several British Ford cars wrecked by Mirza Kuchik Khan's partisans, who were quite active in the dense forests of the Gilan province.

We were nearing Teheran when the second headlight went out and the driver borrowed a storm lantern from a roadside tea-shop and hung it on the front of the car. Unfortunately it started to rain, the wind blew out the lantern, and a few instants later we felt a crash, and found ourselves lying in cold water with our car on top of us. I was not hurt or even bruised, but was very much concerned for my father. Luckily the river-bed into which our car had fallen after having crashed into the brick wall of a bridge was not deep, and there was only a trickle of water in it. I helped the driver to extricate himself from behind the wheel and saw that although not badly hurt he was shocked. Then I brought all our suit-cases from inside the overturned car, with the help of a few peasants who had gathered in the road.

The traffic on the Qazvin-Teheran road was then far from what it is today and motor-cars were a rarity. We were at least ten miles from the town, but I remembered having passed a *gari*, or cart drawn by four horses. Eventually the cart appeared, I made it stop and climbed on to the sacks of merchandise covered with rugs on which half a dozen peasants were sitting. My father declared that he would stay in a nearby tea-shop and await a means of transport which I was to find in Teheran and send to him. The horses walked slowly in the mud and it took us more than two hours to reach the Qazvin Gate, which was closed for the night. We banged on the door a long time before it was finally opened by soldiers after I had shouted that I was an officer. I telephoned to the Prime Minister Vossuq-ed-Dovleh's house, explaining the situation, and he at once sent his carriage in which I drove back to bring my father and our luggage. It was half-past ten when we arrived at Arfaieh, drenched and dead tired.

Teheran was plunged in a controversy about the Anglo-Iranian Treaty which had been signed a few months earlier but which had not so far been ratified by the Majles, although several of its provisions were already being put into operation. A financial mission under the direction of Mr. Armitage-Smith was already in Teheran preparing a plan of reorganisation for the financial system. A military mission with General Dickson, who had been in command of the East Persia Cordon, stretching from Dozdab (now Zahedan) to Birjand and after the Russian revolution to Mashad with the purpose of preventing German agents or missions from reaching Afghanistan through Iran, and Lieutenant-Colonel William Fraser, were discussing with the Iranian officers Sardar Moktader and Lieutenant-Colonel Fazlollah Khan the organisation of a new Iranian Army. British engineers were surveying the Teheran-Khanegin route for the building of a railway line to Baghdad. Prince Firuz Nosrat-ed-Dovleh, the Finance Minister, was in London negotiating the loan which would be advanced under the treaty. It was considered that the ratification of the treaty was a foregone conclusion, although the Majles which had to ratify it was not yet elected.

The Iranians are a political-minded people, and always very suspicious and critical of their Government and it must be recognised that public opinion was against this treaty, which was considered as destined to bring about a kind of protectorate over Iran. Several foreign Legations were supporting these views. The Americans were dissatisfied with the clause stipulating that foreign experts engaged by the Iranian Government had to be British. The French, whose professors were teaching in Iranian high schools, did not wish them replaced by the British. The U.S.S.R., which had hoped to use Iran as a springboard to spread their revolutionary ideas all over the East, although not yet represented in Teheran, were actively agitating against the treaty, having themselves solemnly renounced their capitulatory rights in Iran, beside other 'Imperialistic' concessions which had been enjoyed by them. The Soviet Government had even sent a diplomatic representative named Kolomitzef, to establish friendly relations with Iran, but he was seized in Mazanderan by Persian Cossacks under Russian officers and shot by order of Colonel Staroselsky, the then Cossack Division Commander, who considered himself under the authority of General Denikin. This high-handed action was executed without the knowledge of the Iranian Government.

Most of my father's friends were opposed to the treaty, and several of them had been arrested by Vossuq-ed-Dovleh and exiled to Kashan, where they were kept under police supervision. My father was also against the treaty, and did not conceal his feelings, but at the same time had normal social intercourse with

Sir Percy Cox, the British Minister, and the members of the Government.

A few days after our arrival, Colonel Staroselsky called on my father and proposed to take me into the Cossack Division, my Guards detachment having been suppressed during the war for budgetary reasons. As I was present during the talks, I asked for time to consider this and after Staroselsky had gone, told my father that I preferred to enter the Gendarmerie, which was a national force. I was enrolled with the rank of first lieutenant in the 2nd Gendarmerie regiment quartered at Bagh-e-Shah, on the outskirts of Teheran, and put in command of the 1st platoon of the 2nd squadron of that regiment.

The Gendarmerie was in process of reorganisation because out of its six regiments five had joined the Turks in the war and had been disbanded after that, only a few hundred men having remained in Teheran. Most of the Swedish officers had returned to Sweden, only three having remained in Iran—Colonel Gleerup, Colonel Lundberg and a Captain Lassen, a Russian officer of Danish origin who had happened to be in Iran during the war and had miraculously escaped being massacred by his soldiers in Rezaieh at the time of the revolution. Other forces composing the Teheran garrison at that time were the Cossacks, and a newly formed Central Brigade, numbering some 600 men. The Cossack division's Russian officers, about seventy in number, were loyal to Tsarist Russia and consequently to the White Army Organisation headed by General Denikin and later by General Wrangel, and hoped that the ultimate defeat of the Reds and the re-establishment of a unified non-Communist Russia would restore Russian influence in Iran. Their policy then was to try to oppose the encroachments of Great Britain on what they still considered to be Russian rights, but they had to be careful in so doing, because after the war the Iranian Government was bankrupt and subsisted only through the financial aid they received from the British Government. Therefore the pay of the Cossacks, as also of the other military formations, as well as that of the handful of civil servants in Teheran, depended entirely on the goodwill of the British. On the other hand large sums were owing to the Iranian Government to whom they had paid none of the oil royalties due to them since the beginning of the war, although important deliveries of oil had been made to the

British Navy throughout this period. This debt was finally settled for one million pounds sterling which sum was considered in Iran as entirely inadequate.

In order to understand what happened later and radically influenced the trend of events in Iran, it is necessary to follow the Cossack Division during these last years. In the spring of 1917, during the first phase of the Russian revolution, Kerenski's War Minister, Guchkof, recalled the Russian Colonel who commanded the Persian Cossacks, and replaced him by a liberal-minded officer, Colonel Clergé. Passing through Tiflis on his way to Teheran, he met there an old friend, Colonel Staroselsky, who had formerly commanded the Tatar regiment of the 'Wild Division' and was without a job as a result of its dissolution. This officer asked Clergé to arrange his transfer to Teheran as his second in command, which was easily done. A short time after this, Staroselsky began intriguing against his chief, spreading the rumour that Clergé was a Communist and was preaching dangerous ideas to the Iranian officers. In reality, Clergé was telling the Iranians that they were in their own country, that the Cossack division belonged to Iran, and that the duty of the Russian instructors was only to train them and afterwards to return to Russia. In order to get rid of Clergé, Staroselsky had either to act himself with the aid of the Russian officers, who were all dissatisfied with Clergé's attitude which they considered contrary to their interests, or bring the Shah to order his removal. The Shah did not make a decision, and Staroselsky thought rightly that his direct intervention would create discontent among the Iranians.

There was then among the Iranian officers a Colonel Reza Khan, who had risen from the ranks and was renowned for his strong personality, iron will and extraordinary capacity for leadership, and who was clever and ambitious. Reza Khan belonged to a traditionally military family of the Bavand clan of the upper Mazanderan region of Savadkuh. His father, Abbas Ali Khan, had been a Colonel in the local regiment, and his grandfather, Major Murad Ali Khan, had been killed in 1856 at the siege of Herat. After the death of Colonel Abbas Ali Khan, a family quarrel started on account of his succession, and the young Reza's mother had to leave the family property and came with her son to Teheran. Being physically unusually vigorous and endowed with a strong and virile character, he enlisted at the age of fourteen in the Cossack Brigade and owing to his remarkable military qualities rose very soon from private to N.C.O., and then from N.C.O. to officer rank. It was to this man that Staroselsky turned to organise a *coup d'état* inside the Cossack Division and Reza Khan accepted. While the unsuspecting Clergé was having his evening tea in his house the premises were surrounded by Iranian Cossacks, Reza Khan entered the room and quite politely invited him to take his place in a carriage waiting at the gate. This carriage took the Russian under escort to Enzeli, from there he sailed for Russia.

Reza Khan was promoted to Brigadier and received the command of the Cossacks Guard infantry regiment. This operation made him think how easy it would be to change the Iranian Army by transferring power from the hands of a few foreign officers to those of a strong and enterprising Iranian. He began to gather together the Iranian officers and to talk to them of the sad plight of their country and of the possibility of its regeneration through union and strength.

All this did not escape the attention of Staroselsky, who showed his displeasure by dismissing Reza Khan from the command of his regiment. From that date, Reza Khan became friendly with General Dickson, who liked Reza Khan and held him in great esteem.

Meanwhile the Government of Vossuq-ed-Dovleh was preparing elections destined to bring into existence a docile Majles which would ratify without demur the Anglo-Persian Treaty. Every kind of pressure was used but very soon those in power realised that when individually approached the prospective deputies seemed yielding and submissive, but when brought together they were likely to have quite different and sometimes contrary views.

The day of Nowruz 1299 (21st March 1920) was marred by a very sad happening which illustrates the deep dissatisfaction felt with the Anglo-Iranian Treaty. One of the Iranian members of the mixed military commission, Lieutenant-Colonel Fazlollah Khan, was found dead in his room, in full parade uniform with a revolver in his hand. In front of him on the desk was a letter written by him stating that as it was against his conscience, being a patriotic Iranian, to agree to the subordination of the Iranian

Army to a British command, he preferred to quit this world. Although this letter, after being shown to Vossuq-ed-Dovleh, was destroyed, the news of it spread in Teheran and produced a deep impression, which was certainly not favourable to the application of the treaty.

Meanwhile I was enjoying my work in the regiment. My platoon comprised thirty veteran gendarmes, all volunteers, two sergeants and one warrant officer, with thirty-three horses, our work starting at 7 a.m. in winter and 6.30 a.m. in summer. My squadron commander introduced me to his coterie of friends who happened to be young Cossack officers who had graduated from the Cossack school or had studied in Russia. Many of them played important parts in events in Iran afterwards, and I have kept up my friendship with the few who are still alive. At the head of this group was Major Morteza Khan Yazdanpanah, a very brilliant young officer with a strong personality, who used to be drill instructor at the Cossack school and had great authority with the others. He afterwards became Chief of the General Staff, War Minister and H.M.'s General A.D.C.

From the beginning of spring there were rumours of trouble in the Mazanderan province, where a local nobleman of Savadkuh, who had great influence in the province, revolted against the Central Government, refusing to pay taxes. It was decided to send a Gendarmerie detachment there comprising a cavalry squadron and infantry battalion and a machine-gun section under the command of Major Habibollah Khan Sheibani, an officer who had collaborated with the Turks on the Kermansheh front during the war and had just returned to Iran after a two years' absence in Berlin. The first squadron of my regiment was chosen and was ordered to Firuzkuh, 95 miles east of Teheran, to proceed thence to Mazanderan. I was very disappointed that my squadron was not to go, and at once applied for transfer to the 1st, this being accepted. I also transferred to my new unit my orderly, Rustem Qaragozlu, a Turkish-speaking little fellow from Avaj, near Hamadan, who was a good rider and a diligent soldier. It was my first operational expedition and I was very excited about it. I packed a few things which I needed in my saddle-bags and having bound my great-coat on my saddle we started on the afternoon of the 31st May through the Dovlet Gate.

At sunset we arrived at Sorkh Hessar, a hunting-pavilion of Nasr-ed-Din Shah's which had been abandoned for many years, and was situated in a garden surrounded by half-ruined mud walls. The tents were pitched, the horses tethered, the squadron cook lighted a fire under his cauldron, and after they had groomed their horses, the men lighted individual fires to prepare tea in the small kettles they carried in their saddle-bags. The officers spent the night in the pavilion, sleeping on the floor.

All this appealed to my sense of romance and I imagined the Armies of Nader Shah, of Teimur and Chengiz Khan camping in the same way in these same surroundings. After leaving Teheran, we no longer saw any sign of twentieth-century civilisation. No roads—just a track—no modern bridges, not even a telegraph line was to be seen. There were only pack transport caravans of camels, mules, horses and donkeys and it took us three days to reach Firuzkuh, where the infantry battalion was awaiting us, Major Sheibani arriving there two days later. Firuzkah is a very ancient and picturesque little town situated in a narrow gorge with high mountains towering above it and an old ruined fort dating from Sassanian times. To the east, the gorge opens into a plain where there is now a new town, which did not exist in 1920, and the railway station on the Teheran-Bender Shah line, built in 1932.

On the third day after our arrival, my squadron started its march to the north under my command, as the two officers senior to me were sick. We followed a track bordered by meadows where innumerable flocks of sheep and goats were grazing. Our route was straight and we went up and up until towards the evening we came near to the Abbasabad Pass. Here my advance pickets met with enemy fire coming from the crest of the ridge, which was occupied after a short skirmish. Early the next morning we continued our progress to the north. The track was abominable, mostly following the bed of the Talar river, and the horses stumbled on the boulders. The slopes of the mountains became covered with vegetation, until after Pol-i-Safid, where we crossed the river over the first (and last) bridge we saw during this expedition, dating from the time of Shah Abbas, the great builder, as did also the paved road, traces of which we also saw, we entered the dense primeval forest carpeted with ferns and moss.

After two days we arrived at Shirgah, between Zirab and Aliabad (now called Shahi) where we had to pitch our camp to await the arrival of the rest of the column from Firuzkah. We learned here that a Bolshevik Russian force coming from Baku had disembarked at Mashad-i-Sar and moved to Barfrush (now Babol), some 12 miles to the south of the coast, and that the rebel Amir Moayyid had joined them with his followers. After the defeat of the Denikin Army in the Northern Caucasus, the elements of this army fled by sea to the Crimea and partly to the east towards the Caspian Sea and thence by boat to Enzeli. The advancing Red Army, having disposed of the Whites, found itself in contact with the Turkish forces which were supporting the Daghestan Moslems against the White Russians.

Turkey was then fighting desperately against the British-supported Greeks, and needed the moral and to some extent material support of Soviet Russia in order to withstand the Greek onslaught. A secret agreement was arrived at between the Turkish commander in the Caucasus, Kazem Qarabekir Pasha, and the Red Army, according to which the Turkish forces were to abandon the Caucasus to the Bolsheviks who occupied the Daghestan region up to the Azerbaijan Republic's frontier on the Yalama river north of Baku. Then, one day without any warning, armoured trains crossed the frontier and the Red Army occupied Baku practically without fighting. Many of the Azerbaijan Government officials were executed, a small number managed to escape to Iran, some rallied to the Soviets and the Azerbaijan Republic was incorporated into the Soviet Union. After a few weeks of fighting against elements of the Azerbaijan Army dispersed in the provinces, the Red Army occupied the whole of the country up to the frontiers of Iran, Armenia and Georgia, the last two countries continuing to enjoy independence for a few more months.

In March 1920, on pretence of pursuing the remnants of Denikin's forces who had earlier taken refuge in Iran, a Russian fleet appeared off Enzeli, demanding the surrender of the few hundred White refugees. These had left Enzeli several weeks before and most of them had already passed through Iran on their way to other countries. Enzeli was then still under British occupation and Brigadier-General Champain refused to consider the Russian commander's request. The latter disembarked a force to the east of Enzeli, cutting the only line of communication of the British force, and delivered an ultimatum to the effect that unless Enzeli and its eastern suburb of Qazian were immediately evacuated and the British force withdrawn they would be bombarded from the sea and attacked from the land. Champain had to comply, and the two British battalions evacuated Enzeli, passing between the lines of the Bolsheviks with great loss of prestige. The Red Army pushed on to the south, occupying Rasht where it was joined by the rebel force of Mirza Kuchik Khan.

A Soviet Republic of Iran was now proclaimed in Rasht, the object of the Soviets being to conquer and communise the whole of the country before proceeding to other Middle Eastern countries. It was in order to apply this policy that a Bolshevik force was disembarked in Mazanderan, and instead of having to fight only a group of rebels we were faced with a foreign enemy whose aims were much more important than the refusal to pay taxes to the Central Government. We learned also then that these events, together with the dissatisfaction of the majority of the Iranian nation, proved to Vossuq-ed-Dovleh the impossibility of having the Anglo-Iranian Treaty ratified, and convinced the British Government that the matter must be dropped. Vossuq-ed-Dovleh resigned and departed for Europe, and Sir Percy Cox was later transferred as High Commissioner to Baghdad, where the Arab revolt had started, and where he presided over the enthronment of King Faisal, who had just been expelled by the French from Syria.

The Government decided to send more forces to Mazanderan and Gilan, where the Red Army supported by Mirza Kuchik Khan and Amir Moayyid was operating, but meanwhile our detachment was ordered to push forward and to contact the enemy forces in the Barfroush region. The squadron moved first, and we reached Aliabad the next day. We were joined there by a Gendarmerie company of about sixty men who had evacuated the town of Sari, administrative centre of the Mazanderan province, which had been occupied by Red forces from Babol-Sar and Barfrush.

The next day the column was concentrated in Aliabad, this village having a strategic position at the opening of the Talar valley into the Mazanderan coastal plain, where the south to north track which we were following in the narrow valley bifurcated to the west towards Barfrush, and to the east towards Sari. The hills densely covered with forest ended here, and we reached the plain of Mazanderan with green rice fields and other crops, interspersed with woods and thick bush tracks. I was ordered to take four horsemen to reconnoitre the direction of Barfrush, reporting on the activities of enemy forces in that region. I chose four seasoned gendarmes from my platoon, including my orderly Rustem, and started at four o'clock in the morning. Unfortunately it began to rain, which added to the difficulty of moving fast in an unknown region without any map. Shortly after leaving Shahi, we had to cross the river Talar, swollen by the rain and with a swift current. There was no bridge and no ford could be found, so we had to swim part of the way. One of our horses with its rider was carried away for some distance but we were able to pull them out of the water, bruised and soaked but still able to proceed.

We were drenched by the rain and one of the soldiers having a sudden attack of malaria, I was forced to leave him in a peasant's cottage, threatening the village elder with a thousand deaths if anything happened to the man. We were proceeding at a fast pace, walking, trotting, galloping until towards noon we reached the open plain to the east of Barfrush. We dismounted and leaving two men with the horses under a clump of trees I went on foot with Rustem, hiding behind trees and bushes and using a half-dry canal towards the outskirts of the town. Through my field-glasses I could clearly see a group of Red Army soldiers mounting a machine-gun on an earthwork. I could even distinguish the characteristic beribboned caps of several Russian blue-jackets. We then retreated towards the horses, crawling most of the way. I was lucky enough to meet with two pedlars who told me that there were about 300 Reds, but that Amir Moayyid was in a nearby village with 700 men and that he had come two days before to Barfrush and had had a meeting with the Russian commander. I took some bearings of our route, and returned to Aliabad to report, after having recovered the sick man from the village where we had left him.

Major Sheibani then ordered me to take twenty-five men and two sergeants, and go to the enemy-occupied region and raid their line of communication between Barfrush and Sari. I was to remain there for a week, buying food and fodder from the villages. Of course, I was enchanted, and left with my platoon. I was to take up positions in the thickets close to the Barfrush-Sari track after leaving our horses about a mile away hidden in the woods, and then ambush the Red detachments as they passed, as it was not possible for them to detach flank-guards in the thick jungle bordering the road. In this way we managed to inflict on them casualties and to take many rifles.

One day, I decided to attack a fish-drying factory where according to my information a Red Army post had been established. Having left the horses in a thicket, I crawled with fifteen men along a ditch full of water quite close to the building. Looking from behind a bush I saw a party of Russians sitting outside around a table, on which was a samovar, drinking tea. There was a sentry on the roof, but his attention was concentrated on the road, and he did not see what was happening in the ditch. I told my men that I would fire a shot from my revolver and rush out of the ditch, and that they were to follow me. When I fired and jumped into the open, I realised that none of the men were following me, but it was too late to return, so I rushed towards the table firing and shouting abuse in Russian. The tea-drinking party were so surprised that they ran, abandoning their rifles and samovar, and I made for the factory door. After this instant of hesitation, the gendarmes jumped out of the ditch and followed me into the building. The Russians having escaped into the jungle, we did not take any prisoners, and nobody was killed, but five or six rifles were taken as booty.

After a few days I was recalled to Aliabad, where Major Sheibani, to whom I had presented a sketch-map of the region which I had drawn in the past ten days, charged me with the vanguard duty, to reward me for my work behind the Reds. We started in the morning, and Sari being at a distance of some 15 miles in a straight line from Shahi, arrived there before noon. The town was empty of the enemy, who had evacuated it two hours previously. I assembled the population on the Central Square, in front of the Governor's House, and hoisted the Iranian flag, my platoon giving three cheers for the Shah. The rest of the column arrived there and we were assigned our camping ground in the meadows outside the town. We remained several days in Sari, awaiting the arrival of reinforcements before moving against the bulk of the Bolsheviks concentrated in Barfrush. This operation was to be executed by surprise. In order to prevent any Red elements from escaping from Barfrush to the north, I was instructed to take the squadron (the command of which had now been entrusted to me) first from Sari to the sea, and then following the shore to the west, to cut the road between Barfrush and Mashad-i-Sar, and so prevent the retreating Reds from reaching the sea and embarking on their ships. I received this order at eleven in the evening of the 21st July, and started out at three in the morning with forty gendarmes and two N.C.O.s. Our horses were in good shape and although we had to cover about 45 miles in a partly wooded and difficult terrain, cross country, and only halting for a few minutes at a time, we reached the outskirts of a village called Rostamkola close to the Barfrush–Mashad-i-Sar road at midday. Here, as a villager told me the place had been occupied just an hour earlier by a Red detachment of unknown strength, I ordered the horses to be concealed in a wood under the guard of fifteen men with Sergeant Abbas Qoli Beg, and taking twenty-five dismounted men with Sergeant Mohammad Ali Beg and my faithful Rustem, crawled towards the village along a ditch knee-deep in water, emerging from it some 100 yards from the first walled garden.

We rushed through the gate, and caught three men who were having their lunch inside. They were completely surprised, not expecting any attack from that direction, and had not time to use their arms. They were regular soldiers of the Azerbaijan Republic who had been incorporated in the Red Army after the occupation of that Republic by the Soviet Army, and were Turki-speaking Moslems. We made them prisoners and I sped to the next house with Rustem, followed by the other gendarmes. Entering through the open door into a courtyard I was faced by a Red soldier armed with a rifle, standing just inside the gate. Before he could use his gun, I struck him on the head with the butt of a rifle I was carrying (one of those I had taken from the Russians), and as he fell without a groan I saw seven men sitting on a terrace in front of the house, opposite the door, eating their lunch, with their arms lying about.

'*Teslim ol!*' (surrender) I shouted in Turki, covering them with my rifle. Dumbfounded, they raised their arms in silence, and under the protection of my rifle, Rustem collected their arms, which were handed, together with the prisoners, to my gendarmes who appeared at that moment.

From there I proceeded along the wide village street bordered by wooden cottages on the right and by a ditch on the left, intending to enter the next house, when suddenly I heard a loud bang and felt a shock which brought me to the ground. I heard Sergeant Mohammad Ali Beg cry in anguish: 'Oh! mother', and then a gurgling noise and looking to my right saw him lying on the ground two steps from me, blood pouring out of his wounded neck. He was dead, his rifle had been thrown against me and this had caused my fall. I tried to get up, but could not do so, feeling a strange paralysis in my body. I then put my hand on my side and saw that it was covered with blood, although I did not feel any pain. I realised that I was wounded, probably by the same bullet which had killed the poor sergeant, as I had heard only one report. To see if my lung was affected I put my right hand before my mouth, coughed and spat on it, and seeing that there was no blood felt reassured.

Then I heard another shot and a cry coming from the house on my right. I saw a Red soldier, who had tried to come out of the window, huddled on the window-sill, apparently dead. Then shooting began from everywhere, and somebody lifted me from the ground, took me on his back and carried me away towards a house. It was Rustem, my orderly. He was following behind me when he saw us hit; he jumped into the ditch, and seeing the man who probably had shot us emerging from the window, shot him dead, and then jumped out of the ditch and rescued me from under the enemy's fire. I could never have imagined that this little fellow would be strong enough to carry me on his back for nearly 100 yards.

After depositing me in the house he disappeared, leaving me bleeding freely on to the carpet. I wondered what had happened to him. I could not believe that he had abandoned me like the other gendarmes who had all fled after seeing me fall. He reappeared after a few minutes, bringing back my cap, and my rifle as well as the dead sergeant's. I told him to tie up my wound, as I felt rather faint through loss of blood. He asked an old woman who was in the house for a bandage, but she did not understand and Rustem seized a dirty piece of cotton cloth and bound it tightly round me.

During this time, the Reds came close to the house, and were shooting through the wooden walls, bullets whizzing across the room with a frightful noise when hitting the wood. Rustem took his rifle and ran from one window to the other, shooting in all directions. It was clear that one man, however brave, could not withstand such an assault for long and we would soon be overwhelmed. Then I heard the sound of renewed shooting and shouts indicating new arrivals on the scene of the fighting. The Reds were driven back and my gendarmes reappeared with Sergeant Abbas Qoli Beg at their head. It seemed that the gendarmes who saw me fall, thinking I was dead like Mohammad Ali Beg, retreated towards the horses. Arrived there, Abbas Qoli Beg asked them what had happened to the lieutenant and the sergeant. They answered that both were dead. But Abbas Qoli Beg was made of sterner stuff, and telling them that it was shameful to abandon the corpses ordered them to counter-attack, joining them himself with five more gendarmes, leaving the others to guard the horses and the prisoners. We were rescued, but the village had to be abandoned because contrary to expectations the Bolsheviks had evacuated Barfrush, where our three converging columns found only some thirty stragglers who had remained behind in order to surrender, whilst the whole enemy force of nearly 300 men was in Rustemkola on its way to Mashed-i-Sar, where they embarked the next day for Enzeli, then also under Soviet occupation.

I was put on my horse and taken to a village in the forest, the prisoners holding me up from both sides, loudly expressing their gratitude at not having been shot. Every step the horse took caused me great pain, but after what seemed to me a very long time we reached a village where I was left with Rustem and a squad to guard me, the rest of the squadron joining the detachment. I was still in considerable pain and was unable to lie down, so Rustem put a wall of bolsters around me and told me long Turki fairy stories to help me to sleep.

The next morning, Captain Lassen came to see me and announced that Major Sheibani had telegraphed to Teheran recommending me for the rank of Captain, and being sure that this would be accepted, he gave me two stars from his uniform to be fixed on my shoulder straps. I was taken to Sari, and remained there in the local hospital about twenty days. My wound refused to heal, the local doctors were unwilling to undertake the necessary operation so it was decided to send me to Teheran on muleback, the mule being supposed to have a more level pace than the horse. I started with Rustem and a hospital attendant, my wound needing to be dressed every day, as it was suppurating. I passed through Barfrush, where the men of my squadron gave me a very moving send-off, and after passing Amol began the steep ascent along the Heraz valley to the Alborz Mountains. As soon as we left the plain, the track became even worse than the one by which we had come from Firuzkah to Aliabad. Most of the time the narrow path was bordered by a perpendicular stone wall on one side and a precipice on the other, and the mules having the habit of walking on the outside part of the path one expected at any moment to be precipitated into the torrent below. After emerging from the forest we were faced by towering mountains cut by deep gorges with tumultuous torrents.

We had to cross a 9000-foot pass and it took me some five days to reach the little town of Damavand, near the mountain of the same name which is the highest peak in Iran with an altitude of 18,934 feet. From there two days more brought us to Teheran where I was welcomed with much relief by my father who, having heard I had been wounded, had been very anxious.

The next day he took me to the military hospital where the Chief of the Gendarmerie medical service, Colonel Dr. Saed Khan Malek, told my father that he would examine my wound and decide when to operate. As soon as my father left, I insisted that the Doctor should operate without delay, so that everything would be finished when my father returned. He objected, saying that nothing was ready and the anaesthetist was not available. 'Do it without them,' I said, and Dr. Saed Khan performed the operation very neatly, extracting the bullet which was deep in the flesh, and drawing a basin full of my blood. He told me that as my wound was nearly one month old it would have become gangrenous if the operation had been delayed much longer. When my father arrived I was able to present him with the bullet, but when he saw the basin full of blood on the floor he nearly fainted.

After a few days my father took me to the Sahibgranieh Summer Palace to be presented to the Shah who was to give me the gold military medal. Before the audience we sat in the park under the shade of the ancient elms with the Shah's chief eunuch, Aziz Khan Khaje, talking about the situation in Iran. Aziz Khan impressed me as being an intelligent man well informed about world events and politics.

'If a strong and patriotic man should appear and succeed in pulling Iran out of the political and economic morass it is in, I would leave him my whole fortune,' said he. I knew that this fortune was considerable, and recalled his words after his death several years later when he left everything he had to Reza Shah.

Presently a palace official came to fetch me and conducted me through a series of halls and corridors to a room on the upper floor. In a few minutes the new Prime Minister, Moshir-ed-Dovleh, came into the room and told me to tell the Shah about the situation in Mazanderan, as it would interest His Majesty. The Prime Minister left and then returned, announcing His Majesty the Shahinshah. Ahmad Shah appeared. He was short and fat, with a half-bored and half-apprehensive expression on his clean-shaved face. For a few moments we stood facing each other in silence. Then Moshir-ed-Dovleh leaned towards the Shah and whispered: 'Ask him about what happened.'

'What happened,' repeated the Shah mechanically, looking at me.

I began describing the operations against Amir Moayyid and the Red forces, but noticed that the Shah was completely uninterested, his thoughts far from me and farther still from Mazanderan. I finished somehow, and the Shah gave me the gold medal and allowed me to depart. In spite of my loyalty to the throne I felt rather sad and dispirited after this interview, as Ahmad Shah did not impress me as a worthy representative of royalty.

After the interview, my father and I were invited to lunch in the garden with the Ministers, who had had a meeting in the morning at the palace. During the lunch the Prime Minister made a complimentary speech and the War Minister, Vossuq-es-Saltaneh Dadvar, presented me with the Imperial Farman of the gold medal.

In the Gilan province a detachment of the Cossacks Division under Russian officers had been sent from Qazvin and after retaking Rasht, which had been occupied by Red forces co-operating with Kuchik Khan, had pursued the retreating

Bolsheviks nearly to Qazian (the eastern part of Enzeli). Here they met the cross-fire of the Soviet fleet from the sea and of Red forces operating from a flotilla of small craft which had penetrated into the Enzeli lagoon and were attacking the Cossacks' left flank and rear. This force suffered heavy casualties and its remnant had great difficulty in extricating itself from the narrow peninsula on the east of Enzeli.

The Reds then reoccupied Rasht together with the whole Gilan province, the Cossacks retreating to Imamzade Hashem, on the Qazvin road.

Meanwhile the British brigade which had previously evacuated Enzeli and had been concentrated in Qazvin moved forward and took up a position at the head of the Safid rud valley, in order to stop the advance of the Bolsheviks and allow the Iranian Cossacks to be reorganised.

The blame for this defeat fell on the Russian officers of the Cossack Division and the British Legation demanded their dismissal, the Shah being obliged, against his will, to agree to this, as the British were threatening to cut their subsidies.

An Iranian Cossack General, Sardar Homayun, was appointed commander of the Cossack Division, and several British officers were attached to his staff to advise him on the reorganisation of that force, which had been badly shaken by its losses and retreat in Gilan.

After the resignation of Vossuq-ed-Dovleh, the anti-treaty opposition leaders came to power, with Moshir-ed-Dovleh at their head, and my father was appointed Iran's first delegate at the League of Nations. The Imperial Farman confirming this appointment failed to appear for a long time until finally my father was told to prepare two purses filled with gold, which he should send to the palace. The ultimate destination of those purses remained unknown, but the Farman promptly appeared and my father was able to start.

My father decided to go by the southern route passing through Isfahan, Shiraz and Bushehr and then by sea to Marseilles. Three young men whose parents asked my father to take them with him to Europe where they were going to study were to accompany him. One of them was the son of the Zoroastrian deputy at the Majles, Arbab Keikhosrow, who intended to go to England. They started from Arfaieh in a carriage and would have to change horses along the route. I accompanied my father on horseback as far as Hazrat Abdul Azim, and then rode back to Arfaieh.

I then received the command of the 3rd squadron of my regiment, which did not yet exist except on paper, with the mission to organise it. This appealed to me and I started to hunt for officers, N.C.O.s, privates, horses, arms, equipment and last, but not least, barracks and stables.

A few days after my father's departure I heard that the Iranian representative to the League of Nations, on his way to Geneva, had been attacked and robbed by brigands between Isfahan and Shiraz, and that one of his travelling companions had been killed. I went at once to the Foreign Ministry to inquire but received only confused information and long afterwards my father told me what had happened.

My father and his three young companions had started from the village of Yazd-e-Khvast towards Shiraz, with an escort of half a dozen mounted irregular local road guards. The chief of these braves, armed to the teeth, was trotting beside the carriage boasting of his prowess against robbers and highwaymen, when some armed tribesmen on horseback were sighted on the nearby hills. My father asked the man who these horsemen were, but he looked rather worried and did not answer. A few minutes later, shots were fired at the carriage. The road guards with their heroic chief disappeared at once, the coachman was wounded, the horses stopped and Shahrokh the young Zardoshti who was sitting beside my father fell across my father's knees crying: 'I'm hit, I'm dying!' My father was covered with the blood of the poor young man and thought that he too was wounded.

The brigands ceased firing and approached the carriage. They removed the corpse of Shahrokh and forced my father and his two companions to get out. Then they stripped them of their clothes, took all their belongings, and forced them to walk barefoot in the hills covered with thorns and sharp stones. After a few hundred yards my father sat on the ground and said: 'I am wounded, I will not go further, let me die here.' There was an argument between the two brigands as to the necessity of killing my father, and finally one of them said: 'We are short of cartridges, let the old man die by himself.'

The brigands then put the dead man back into the carriage,

took away the horses and the luggage and disappeared. After a while, my father realised that he was not wounded, and he and the two young boys retraced their steps towards the road until they came to a watch-tower built with mud bricks with a wooden door on the upper floor. They were challenged by a watchman from the roof, and after making themselves known, were admitted into the tower, having to climb up a ladder which was lowered from above. The watch-tower was occupied by several road guards—not those of the escort who had fled—who gave my father and his young friends hot tea. The next day, a carriage with an important escort of *real* gendarmes arrived from Abadeh and my father was taken to Shiraz, where he was the guest of the Governor, Dr. Mosaddeq, who thirty years later was to gain such controversial notoriety as Prime Minister.

In Shiraz, my father was promised by Ibrahim Khan Qavam-ol-Molk, the son of the Qavam-ol-Molk who had been mentioned on the occasion of the Shiraz Gendarmerie revolt in 1915, that his stolen effects would be recovered and the brigands punished. My father was invited, together with Governor Mosaddeq to a place outside the town where he saw more than one thousand fully armed men ready to start on an expedition. Qavam told them that these men were all his retainers, and that they were to chase the brigands, who belonged to the Qashqai tribe, arrest the robbers and bring them to Shiraz together with the stolen property. Apparently these men were tribesmen from the Khamseh Tribal Confederation, who regarded Qavam as their overlord, but were, most of the time, in open hostility with the Qashqais.

A few days later this force returned with several prisoners laden with chains, and the greater part of the stolen effects, which were solemnly given back to my father in the Governor's house by Qavam in the presence of Mosaddeq.

Qavam afterwards explained to my father that the Government having recalled Prince Farman Farma, the Governor-General of Fars province, on account of the discontent of the population, and appointed Dr. Mosaddeq, Farman Farma's friends in Shiraz had devised a plan to make trouble to show that only Farman Farma had been able to enforce security in that region, and for this purpose had incited the tribes to attack travellers and create disturbances.

Although outwardly in Teheran the situation was calm, the general feeling was that a storm was approaching from the north. The Congress of Oriental Nations convened in Baku under the auspices of the Soviet Government in September 1920 with the participation of unofficial leftist and nationalist delegates from Iran, Turkey, India, Afghanistan, the Arab countries and, of course, from the Caucasian and Central Asian Republics of the U.S.S.R., stressed the need to start a strong propaganda campaign in the Middle East and especially in Iran, and the prospect for this part of the world looked gloomy. The British Government had recalled the detachment they had sent to Khorasan after the Russians had evacuated that province during the revolution, and the weak force stationed at Qazvin with a covering detachment on the Rasht road could certainly not constitute a serious deterrent to the so-called Persian Communist forces, reinforced as they were by the Red Army. These forces, being unwilling to commit themselves to open warfare against the British, were operating now to the east of Gilan, trying to infiltrate through the Alborz mountains into the Qazvin plain so as to turn the defences concentrated on the main road between Qazvin and Rasht through Alamut and the Salambar pass on the track from Shahsavar to Qazvin. Brigadier General Reza Khan was appointed to the command of the Hamadan detachment.

In Teheran, the Moshir-ed-Dovleh had resigned after the dismissal of the Russian Cossack officers as a result of British pressure on the Shah, considering this to be an intolerable intervention in Iranian internal affairs, and had been replaced by Sepahdar Aazam Akbar, a nobleman from Rasht, who was more malleable.

On the morning of the 20th February 1921, Major Sheibani called me and announced that about 1000 Cossacks had rebelled at Qazvin, as they had not received their pay for several months, and were marching on Teheran to get their money. They would probably reach the town in the evening and he ordered me to take command of the regiment for that evening, and to occupy the western approaches of the town, from the Qazvin Gate to the Bagh-e-shah Gate inclusive. I had to prevent the Cossacks from entering the town and see that the Bolshevik prisoners, who numbered several hundred men, and had been kept in a camp behind Bagh-e-Shah, did not escape. I was astonished on receiving these instructions, and remarked that there were four other captains senior to me in the regiment, and this being so how could I take command. Major Sheibani replied that he had already disposed of this difficulty by giving two days' leave to the other captains. I asked him if I had to open fire on the Cossacks if they tried to force my barrage. 'You can fire on them if they open fire on you,' he answered.

I was perplexed by these extraordinary instructions, but felt proud to be entrusted with such an important mission, not understanding why the Major himself should not command his regiment in such an emergency. After making the necessary dispositions I went to the Commander's office, with an advanced command post at Shahr-Nô, the distance between these two places being 1¼ miles. On my left, south of the Qazvin Gate, was disposed the Central Brigade, with about 300 men. My right flank was unprotected.

At 8 o'clock the telephone rang: 'I am captain Arfa-os-Soltan, in temporary command of the 2nd regiment at Baghe-Shah,' I said. 'I am the Shah,' said the voice. 'How is the situation?' I reported to him. 'I am at Farakhabad' (a hunting lodge five miles east of the town) 'do not let the telephone line be cut, and report anything that happens.' I promised to report any change and sent a mounted patrol to guard the telephone line which passed to the north of the town. Afterwards I rode to Shahr-Nô.

Half an hour later, at 9 o'clock, my advanced post's picket challenged shadows moving in the darkness on the road. The shadows stopped, and a disturbance started. I went forward on foot to see what was happening. A big man on a horse, surrounded by mounted Cossacks, was abusing the gendarmes. 'Let us pass, sons of dogs,' and then a whole string of unspeakable abuse. 'What do you want?' I asked, my hand on my half-drawn pistol. 'Who is the commander?' barked the man. 'I am the commander.' Another stream of abuse and then the Cossack Colonel turned back and vanished into the night, followed by his horsemen. I afterwards learned that he was Lieutenant-Colonel Hoseyn Aga, who in 1924, as commander of an infantry regiment, was dismissed by Reza Shah for not having actively intervened to prevent the murder of the American Consul Imbrie by a fanatical crowd.

I telephoned to the Shah and to Major Sheibani, but did not

get an answer. Then I went back to Bagh-e-Shah. At '11 o'clock I heard the report of gun shots coming from the middle of the town. I telephoned again. This time Sheibani answered me saying that the Cossacks, numbering perhaps 1500 men, had entered the town through the Gomrok Gate, guarded by the Central Brigade, which had surrendered, and after reaching the Topkhane Square (Sepah Square of today) had fired on the police headquarters, the policemen having refused to surrender, and killed three of them.

'All is over,' said the Major. 'Take your people back to Bagh-e-Shah, except the guard in the prisoners' camp, shut yourself in, and do not allow the Cossacks to enter inside the walls. If they try, you may shoot, but do not take any notice if they pass in front of the barracks, going to the town through the Bagh-e-Shah gate, or coming out of it, and stay shut in the barracks until I come.'

I passed the night in my office, and the whole of the next day watched from the roof of the stables what was happening on the road and on the earth-works behind the moat. I neither saw nor heard anything unusual, and nobody came near the barracks. The next day Major Sheibani came to Bagh-e-Shah and told me that the Cossacks had occupied the town and installed a new Government headed by Seyid Zia-ed-Din Tabatabai, that the military commander was General Reza Khan of the Cossacks Division, that many important people had been arrested and that I could go home and have a rest for 24 hours.

General Reza Khan received the title of Sardar Sepah and a jewel-studded golden sword, whilst all the officers and soldiers who had taken part in the *coup d'état* had received a pecuniary reward, the officers being promoted, but it was not until much later that I heard the whole story of the *coup d'état* from people who had taken part in it.

Besides being a statesman with a great personality and original ideas linked to a rigidly conservative outlook, Lord Curzon was endowed with an extraordinary capacity for work and a keen and intelligent interest in problems which he considered important for the British Empire and the maintenance of the *Pax Britannica*. This interest led him to undertake two journeys in Asiatic Russia and in Iran, the outcome of which were his monumental works *Russia in Central Asia* and *Persia and the Persian Question*. He was deeply influenced by these travels, both from the point of view of the Russian Empire's position in the newly conquered regions of Central Asia and the Caucasus, and its policy of conquest directed towards the warm waters of the Persian Gulf and the Arabian Sea, and ultimately towards India, and the possibility of making Iran into an effective buffer, bolstering its administration, finances and military potential, and using the outstanding qualities of its people under British guidance. His term as Viceroy of India strengthened this point of view and his tour in the Persian Gulf confirmed him in his convictions.

At the time of the Russian collapse after the First World War he was at the head of the Foreign Office and this gave him the opportunity to put his long-cherished ideas into operation. In Vossuq-ed-Dovleh and his group of Iranian statesmen he found people responsive to his ideas, and with certain timely pressures and inducements the treaty of 1919 was signed. There was a talk of £132,000 given to the Iranian Government without any trace in the records of the Iranian Finance Ministry of the way it was spent.* Then occurred the unforeseen events of 1920—the reappearance of Russia under the guise of the Soviet Union as a great power on Iran's northern frontiers and the quasi-general opposition of the Iranian Nation to the treaty; the last fact precluding any possibility of having it ratified by any Majles. On the other hand it was obvious that if Iran was abandoned to its own devices, without money or military force and with a weak Central Government, it would become the prey of anarchic forces represented by well-armed predatory tribes and leftist revolutionary elements, and would drift towards Bolshevism and eventually become engulfed in the wave of the Communist advance towards India and the Arab Middle East.

These considerations led Lord Curzon—whose hands the Prime Minister, Mr. Lloyd George, had left free in this matter—to envisage the coming to power in Iran of a strong Government, friendly to Great Britain but not compromised by the 1919 treaty negotiations, which could be helped to apply piecemeal certain of the stipulations of the treaty after they had been watered down.

* Balfour, *Recent Happenings in Persia*, 1920 (before it was expurgated). Vincent Shean, *The New Persia*. New York, 1927.

Prince Firuz Mirza Nosrat-ed-Dovleh, one of the negotiators of the treaty and former Finance Minister in Vossuq-ed-Dovleh's cabinet, who was in London at the time, was willing to undertake this task and went to Iran with others, including Mohammed Ali Khan Foroghi and Colonel Prince Amanollah Mirza Jahanbani. It was a particularly cold winter and the day they arrived in Hamadan a heavy snowfall blocked all the roads. The snow continued to fall, preventing any traffic over the high mountain passes, and Prince Firuz's party was marooned in Hamadan while things were happening in Teheran and London.

The British authorities in Teheran, the new Minister Mr. Norman, General Dickson and a few others, considered that Prince Firuz was too much compromised in the 1919 treaty business to be able to appear with a new policy. They proposed to give their support to an active and dynamic ex-journalist, Seyid Zia-ed-Din Tabatabai, who had already been entrusted with important missions, notably in the Caucasus in 1919, and was known for his pro-British sentiments. In order to be able to establish its authority notwithstanding the conflicting views and interests of older politicians, and enforce a progressive policy which would certainly be opposed by the wealthy landowners, semi-independent chiefs of tribes and all other privileged persons, Seyid Zia-ed-Dun's Government needed the support of a military force. Seyid Zia-ed-Din approached General Reza Khan whose strong personality made him suitable for such a venture. He saw his opportunity and with the instinct of the true field commander, seized it. In great secrecy half a dozen high-ranking Cossack officers were approached by Reza Khan and swore to follow and obey him. Reza Khan knew very little about Seyid Zia-ed-Din, and cared less about his aims. His extraordinarily acute and realistic sense of political expediency made Reza Khan realise that, with the reappearance on the northern frontiers of Iran of a Russia which had abrogated all the treaties with Great Britain and had again assumed the role of a rival, the position of Great Britain, rendered unpopular in Iran by endeavours to impose the 1919 treaty, had been substantially weakened. A homogeneous disciplined military force under his command, acting on a proclaimed platform of independence, nationalism, non-engagement towards Iran's two powerful neighbours and the assertion of national dignity and reforms, might create a strong Central Government capable of withstanding external and internal intrigues.

On the 16th February the Cossacks started their march on Teheran, which they reached on the night of 20th February 1921. Reza Khan at once issued a proclamation to the Army, explaining that the intention was to save the country from traitors and to establish a strong Central Government which would uphold the independence and dignity of Iran and work for the prosperity of the nation. Reza Khan did not lose time in concentrating the command of all armed forces into his hands.

An incident took place at the Salam which brought home to everybody that foreigners were to lose their privileged positions and changed overnight their behaviour towards their Iranian subordinates and collaborators.

All the units which had to march past the Shah were massed in the Marble Throne courtyard, before entering the Golestan Palace gardens. I was with my squadron's gendarmes on foot when Sardar Sepah entered the courtyard. He wore a black Cossack *cherkesska* with the ribbon and jewel-studded sword which had been given him by the Shah. He passed in front of the senior officers and stopped in front of the Swedish Chief of Police, General Westdahl, an enormously fat pink-faced man the tips of whose fingers were not quite touching his sheepskin cap. 'You are a General, but you do not know how to salute,' he said, and seizing the stupefied Swede's hand he pushed it towards his cap with such violence that the cap fell to the ground. Westdahl nearly had a heart attack.

Under the command of Lieutenant-Colonel Sheibani the 2nd regiment gained enormously in efficiency. The Colonel was one of the most brilliant officers I have had the privilege to meet. He was calm, severe, just, brave and meticulous, a good administrator and a good chief, taking care of his subordinates, but expecting them to work to their utmost capacity. He had studied in France, at Saint-Cyr, before the First World War. He also brought to his regiment Lieutenant-Colonel Shahab, who took command of the three cavalry squadrons.

At the beginning of May, Reza Khan became Minister of War keeping the command of the Army, in which the Gendarmerie had now been incorporated as a separate entity. One of the first acts of Seyid Zia-ed-Din was to denounce the 1919

Anglo-Persian Treaty. Then on the 26th February 1921 he signed the Irano-Soviet Treaty which had been negotiated by Ali Qoli Khan Ansari and Chicherin. By this the Soviet relinquished all the concessions and rights which had been acquired by Imperial Russia in Iran, except the Caspian Sea fisheries concession, but received the right to bring its military forces into Iran in the event of hostile organisations using Iranian territory as a springboard to attack Soviet territory; this clause being intended to apply to White Russian or anti-Soviet Caucasian forces, as was explicitly stated in a letter attached to the treaty.

The Iranian Government was trying to induce the British Government to transfer the South Persian Rifles, counting two brigades with about 6000 men, to them in accordance with the arrangement made in 1916 between the two Governments. The British replied that they did not know of any Iranian high-ranking officer who could assume command of this important force and that should the S.P.R. be disorganised its armament would fall into the hands of the robber-tribes of Fars, which would endanger the British interests. When the Iranian Government proposed to send one of the Swedish Gendarmerie instructors to take command of the force, the British replied that they had no confidence in these officers and insisted on the S.P.R. keeping its organisation under the command of British officers. The Iranian Government refused to accept this and the British disbanded the S.P.R., part of its arms and equipment being taken to India and part being destroyed in Shiraz and Kerman. Most of the Iranian officers and N.C.O.s later joined the local forces of the Iranian Army.

Meanwhile, in spite of some reforms effected by Seyid Zia's Ministry, a growing opposition began to manifest itself against him. Following the *coup d'état*, he had ordered the arrest of former statesmen and grandees, including Prince Farman Farma, and levied important contributions from them. He had also ordered the arrest of Qavam-os-Saltaneh, Governor-General of the Khorasan province, a brother of Vossuq-ed-Dovleh and a former Minister. Lieutenant-Colonel Mohammad Taqi Khan sent him to Teheran under an escort of gendarmes. As a result all the relatives and friends of these people were agitating against Seyid Zia. Reza Khan realised that Seyid Zia was becoming a dead weight, even the British were less partial to him, and the necessary pressure was exercised to induce him to resign (25/5/21). Seyid Zia left Iran and those persons who had been arrested were freed, including Qavam-os-Saltaneh who became Prime Minister. His first act was to recall Lieutenant-Colonel Mohammad Taqi Khan, whom he thought had humiliated him at the time of his arrest. Considering that he had only executed the orders of the Prime Minister and that his recall was a flagrant injustice, Mohammad Taqi Khan refused to come to Teheran and openly proclaimed the rebellion of his force. He began enrolling local irregulars and soon was at the head of some 4000 men. The Government had not the necessary military force to send to Khorasan, more than 600 miles away, and for the time being the Colonel remained in occupation of that province.

CHAPTER SIX

Campaigning against the Tribes

Reza Khan Sardar Sepah, Minister of War, and to some extent already the determining factor in Iranian politics, knew that in order to be able to rehabilitate the country he needed money, and money must be taken from people under the guise of taxes, custom duties, etc. But people had never been accustomed to paying equably administered dues to the Central Government regularly and since the revolution of 1906–9 and the war very few had paid any taxes at all. In order to make them pay force was necessary, but the Government disposed of a minimum of military forces which were poorly armed and equipped, and whose pay was generally months in arrear. In this huge country, there were in 1921 about 12,000 gendarmes, dispersed all over Iran, and 7000 Cossacks, including the newly incorporated Central Brigade Troops. The armament, comprising rifles and a limited number of machine-guns with a few artillery pieces, was of every make, and the stock of ammunition was restricted. These Government forces controlled only the capital and its immediate surroundings, all the rest of the country was in the hands of tribes and other unruly elements.

During the war the belligerents had used the tribes as auxiliaries to fight their battles and had armed them accordingly. Many thousands of British rifles too, which had fallen into the hands of the Turks at Kut-el-Amara and had been given by them to the Arab irregulars to use in fighting the British, had been sold by the Arabs and acquired by the tribes of Southern Iran. Besides this, more than 100,000 rifles, many machine-guns and even several mountain guns, together with all kinds of other war material had been left by the Russians in the depots of Tabriz and Sharafkhaneh or sold by the disbanded soldiers to the population before leaving for Russia. Most of Iran was then in the hands of war lords of varying importance under the name of governors, chiefs of tribes and warders of the marches who were ruling large tracts of the country in a completely independent manner, ignoring the Central Government and sometimes having direct relations with foreign powers.*

This then was the situation of the country immediately after the *coup d'état* of 1921, when Sardar Sepah was to tackle the colossal task of bringing order out of this chaos. He began his great work, calculating all the elements of the enterprise, preparing methodically the details necessary for the execution of his grandiose schemes, disclosing his plans to nobody, using, with the skill and clairvoyance inherent to genius, factors which fate had put into his hand.

Early in May 1921 a Gendarmerie column was sent to the Khamseh province against Jan Shah Khan Amir Afshar. After several weeks of skirmishing he was defeated and had to surrender. In the beginning of June another detachment, comprising an infantry company, a machine-gun company and two squadrons, started from Teheran towards Zanjan, the ultimate destination being probably Azerbaijan, but nothing was said about it.

I was commanding one of the squadrons, while Captain Mikeladze, a White Russian officer who had fled to Iran after Denikin's defeat and was serving with the Gendarmerie, commanded the other. We became close friends. It was at Yengi-Imam, just half-way between Teheran and Qazvin, that I had my first interview with the man who was to become the Great Shahinshah of Iran. We were camping in the garden of the Imamzade (shrine of a saint) close to the road, when a rather dilapidated ex-British Army open Ford car driving from the Qazvin direction stopped in front of the gate apparently for repair. Besides the Cossack driver, who got busy with the carburettor, a single person was sitting in the back of the car. I recognised him at once: it was Sardar Sepah, the Minister of War and Commander in Chief! He was dressed in a simple khaki Cossack's Russian blouse with a full General's insignia on his shoulder straps, dark-blue breeches, high boots without spurs and a black sheepskin cap worn on the back of the head and showing his high, domed forehead. His complexion was rather dark and his eyes of a strange golden hue were large with a searching look which it took courage to meet. He had a small

* See Appendix.

black moustache slightly turned up at the ends, and altogether
his appearance was extremely virile and soldierly.

I reported about my unit. He took my report with his hand
to his cap, but without getting up and coming out of his car.
Then, for nearly an hour, while his car was repaired, he spoke
of our duty to the country, the necessity of putting an end to the
lawlessness and anarchy of the tribes and troublemakers and of
asserting the control of the Central Government. How all the
different military organisations of the country must work together and finally be unified, and so on. . . . I kept my hand at my
cap in the Cossack fashion during all this speech and was deeply
impressed by what he said, spoken in a low voice full of conviction. When the car was ready he departed, refusing the tea I
offered him.

We reached Qazvin, where we remained for two days before
starting towards Zanjan. After three days' march, we came to
the outskirts of Zanjan. Several officers of the units which were
in occupation of that town rode out to greet us. I was friendly
with one of them, whose name was Captain Turaj Amin who,
seeing me, approached at a smart trot. Then, something went
wrong. For no apparent reason his horse suddenly reared and
rushed at my horse and myself. Then his horse seized my right
arm with his teeth and in spite of my hammering on his nose
with my left hand, dragged me off my horse. As I fell the two
brutes galloped twice over me, trampling on me with their
hooves. This happened in a narrow lane bordered by walled
gardens, and the horses, pursuing each other in a terrible battle,
were about to rush over me a third time, probably with fatal
results as I was so bruised that I could not move, when a colonel
ordered a soldier of the infantry company to thrust his bayonet
into the attacking horse's belly. Turaj had also been thrown from
his horse, but was not wounded. The horse stopped, his intestines
bulging out of his belly, and I was transported on a stretcher to
a field hospital. I had three ribs broken, and my right arm torn
and I breathed with difficulty on account of my broken ribs.
They put me in a waistcoat of plaster of paris and dressed my
wounded arm. I had to remain in hospital for three weeks, after
which I left for Mianeh, which was the first locality in the
Azerbaijan province.

After spending a night in the Shah Abbasi caravanserai of

Jemalabad we crossed the Qezel Owzan by an old brick bridge and climbed the steep slopes of the Qaplan Kuh mountain, considered to be the geographical boundary of Azerbaijan. From the top of the pass we saw the green valley of the Qarangu river, and on the other side the little town of Mianeh, part of which was hidden behind a low hill. To the north, the high and continuous chain of the Bozgush Dagh grimly barred the horizon as though concealing the menace of the Shahsevan robber hordes ready at any moment to come down on the peaceful dwellers of the plain. Here we were met by the famous 'Mianeh wind', blowing gently all the time from the north. We crossed the wooden bridge on the Qarangu and pitched our camp in a poplar plantation on the bank of the river. Mianeh was a dirty little town, looking more like a village, and all the houses were of mud bricks.

After a week, we again took to the road, I passed one night at the little town of Torkmanchai (now Torkaman), the scene of the fateful treaty of 1828 after the Russo-Persian War when we lost the Erivan and Nakhchevan Khanates to Russia, and next day proceeded towards Tabriz. All the villages were fortified and watch-towers were erected in the fields to allow the peasants in case of a Shahsevan raid to take refuge inside them. Many peasants carried rifles or shot-guns while working in the fields. I was told that in order to take the villagers unaware, the raiders resorted to all sorts of stratagems. For instance, once the villagers saw on the road a marriage procession preceded by musicians, with the bride under a veil on a horse, and surrounded by merrymakers. This kind of spectacle always draws onlookers, and the procession on entering the village was met by the unsuspecting villagers, when suddenly the musicians and 'relatives' of the bride produced arms. The 'bride', discarding her veil, sprang from 'her' horse and proved to be a brigand chief and the whole party fell to pillaging the village and departed with considerable booty. Another time it was a funeral, the corpse jumped from his stretcher and together with the mourners robbed the bystanders before disappearing behind the hills.

Several times we were challenged by people firing at us from the watch-towers, thinking we were Shahsevans, and I had to order my trumpeter to sound signals to make them understand that we were a military force. Half-way to Kara Chaman my advance guard came into contact with a party of Shahsevan horsemen some forty strong. I deployed my squadron and attacked them at once. They fled after firing a few shots from horseback.

Four miles from Tabriz I was informed that many notables were waiting to greet us two miles from the town. I gave the order to halt, dismount, clean the equipment and arms, brush the uniforms and wash, to make a good impression on my father's compatriots, and we approached the waiting citizens with as warlike and formidable a countenance as we could muster for the occasion. Two men emerged from the group of notables and greeted me warmly, calling me by my name, saying: 'We are your cousins, and have come to take you to your house.' They were the sons of my aunt Khadije Khanum, whom I had known in Teheran in 1914. We were to camp in an extensive park outside the town, called Bagh-e-Shamal, which was then an enormous orchard with every kind of fruit tree. The horses were tethered to ropes fixed on the ground and the men pitched their tents, all very spick and span. After seeing that everything was in order, I went with my cousins to their house. It was really our house because it was built by my grandfather, Sheikh Hassan, on the site of the house which had been destroyed by the floods in 1864 and had never been divided between his three sons and four daughters. Tabriz was a town of some 250,000 inhabitants, all Turki-speaking. It had a few large avenues and an infinity of narrow lanes, in one of which our house was situated.

In mid-September I was ordered to go with my squadron to Saujbolagh (now Mahabad) to the south of the Urmia lake, where I was to join Major Malekzade who with a detachment of 550 gendarmes was watching the Kurds, with orders to prevent any extension of Simko's rebellion to the south.

After leaving Tabriz I arrived at Ajab Shir. I tried to telephone from there to Saujbolagh, to inform Major Malekzade of my coming, but the telephonist in Miandoab told me that the communication with Saujbolagh was interrupted, and that apparently fighting was going on. I arrived at noon in Bonab and telephoned again. This time the telephonist told me that Major Malekzade's detachment had been attacked by Simko himself with several thousand men and practically destroyed, and that a few men who had managed to escape had already arrived in Miandoab.

I pushed on and towards evening arrived at Malek Kandi, a big village on the intersection of the Tabriz-Saqqez and Maragheh-Saujbolagh roads where I met some of the refugees from Sauj-bolagh, amongst whom was Captain Azertash, a Caucasian officer of the Azerbaijan Republic's army who had come to Iran the year before, after the occupation of Baku by the Red Army, and who told me the whole story.

Malekzade had heard that an attack by Simko was imminent, but had not given credit to these rumours. Suddenly, the Kurds had come from the north, throwing back all the outposts of the gendarmes. They were several thousand strong and attacked from all sides, throwing the defence line back into the town. The fight lasted late into the night, some 200 gendarmes being killed and 150 taken prisoner. Major Malekzade with Captain Taqi Alp and a handful of men resisted the whole of the next day in their headquarters, and only surrendered when promised that prisoners would not be killed. This was not respected, as nearly all prisoners had been shot after being stripped and their corpses left to rot near the town, only Malekzade, Alp and the few men who had been with them were spared and afterwards released and sent to Teheran. A few prisoners managed to escape, throwing themselves on the ground among the corpses of their comrades and lying there without moving until dark, when they fled towards Miandoab. This was the case of Azertash, who after being stripped completely naked and machine-gunned, threw himself among the dead where he was badly wounded in the buttocks by machine-gun bullets. In spite of his wound he started after dark and marched the whole night, avoiding the Kurdish villages. About 200 men escaped unharmed, but they were in such a state of demoralisation that I could not think of using them and sent them to Tabriz, after providing them with some money and food. I did not see any officers among them, nearly all had been killed in Saujbolagh.

Early the next day we continued towards Miandoab, which was at that time a big village, owing its name Mian do ab— between two rivers—to the fact that it has the Jaghatu on the east and the Tatavi on the west. The sergeant whom I had sent on ahead of the squadron to prepare our lodging reported to me that there were 500 irregulars from the Afshar and Moqaddam tribes there under Sardar Nasser Moqaddam. These tribesmen

had been brought to Miandoab at the request of the Governor-
General of Azerbaijan, in order to protect their own district
against a Kurdish invasion from the left bank of the Tatavi, this
river forming the racial and linguistic frontier between the Kurds
and the Turki-speaking Azeris. I realised that these tribesmen
would remain in Miandoab only until the first Kurd appeared
on the horizon, and would then carry out a strategic retreat
towards the eastern hills.

I asked my man where he had prepared our camp and the
billet for the officers, including myself. He told me that all good
camping sites had been occupied by the tribesmen and that the
only proper lodgings for me and the officers had been requisitioned by Sardar Nasser. I realised that if the Kurds attacked
Miandoab I should not be able to resist them with only 100 men
and that I should have to organise the defence with the help of
the tribesmen who would certainly disappear at the first sight of
the enemy as always happens with irregulars, and I had therefore
to establish my authority. When dealing with tribes authority
is inseparable from prestige and to maintain mine I could not
accept a position of inferiority. I ordered the N.C.O. to show me
the best camping site, and taking my squadron there, ordered a
tribal group of some one hundred horsemen to evacuate it without delay. Then I sent a circular order to the chiefs of the tribal
detachments, ordering them to come to a meeting with me at
5 p.m. There were half a dozen of them and they all came, a
little ruffled but awed and impressed by the smart appearance of
the gendarmes.

'The situation is dangerous,' I told them. 'The Kurds may
appear at any moment and I have orders from High Authorities
to take command of all the forces in the region. I intend to
resist on the Tatavi's right bank without any thought of retreat,
and I will court-martial and shoot any man, including a chief,
who retreats without my special order. From today, I will take
command of the 500 tribesmen and organise them in five
squadrons, each squadron under the command of one of my
platoon commanders, the platoons commanded by my N.C.O.s
and corporals, and each squad commanded by a gendarme. The
chiefs will form a military council and nobody will be entitled to
give orders except me.'

They listened to me in gloomy silence and I distributed to

them copies of an order embodying these points, duly signed and sealed, and gave the necessary orders to my officers.

The next day, the Tatavi position was occupied by 400 men, 200 being kept in reserve on the western outskirts of the town; all the units were mixed and my gendarmes very proud to be each of them in command of five armed mounted tribesmen. After that I did my best to be pleasant to the chiefs and especially to Sardar Nasser, emphasising to them that we were protecting their estates from plunder by the Kurds. I think that our display of force was not without effect, the Kurds did not approach our positions. Besides, the Tatavi position, with an open plain extending for miles without any cover and a hostile Azeri population backing that position, offered much less favourable conditions for the Kurds' attack than a garrison encircled by high commanding hills in the midst of a hostile and armed population. We only saw a few reconnoitring parties of twenty to thirty horsemen, who never came within a mile of us.

I did not remain for long in Miandoab, and was ordered to proceed with my squadron to Khoi to join the other units of the expeditionary corps from Teheran. These were concentrated there under Colonel Lundberg, with the idea of attacking Simko from the north-east while the Qarajadagh chief Amir Arshad with two thousand irregulars attacked him from the east, passing to the north of the Urmia lake.

We arrived at Khoi after marching through a desolate stretch of land where the water was brackish. Khoi is a very picturesque little town, surrounded by a double line of fortified walls and a moat. Most of the walls were in ruins and the moat was dry. Antiquated as they were, Khoi's fortifications had been useful in 1918. At that time, General Andranik, self-promoted irregular Armenian forces commander on the Turkish front, repulsed by the Turkish Army, crossed the Iranian frontier and appeared before Khoi. The population shut the gates and refused to let him in, and a few old soldiers finding a brass gun dating from the time of the Russo-Persian war of 1826–8, mounted it on the wall, above the gate.

The Armenians did not imagine that there could be artillery in Khoi, and brought a mountain gun close to the wall, hoping to smash the gate and to enter the town. Just when they were about to fire, the ancient gunners fired a shot from their muzzle-loading cannon. By extraordinary chance, the ball struck the men standing by the mountain gun, killing two of them. Rendered more careful, the Armenians decided to move their gun out of reach of the Iranians' fire. While they were doing so one of their scouts announced that a Turkish battalion was approaching Khoi. Andranik at once abandoned his attack on Khoi and retreated towards Shahtakhti.

When I was told this story in Khoi I remembered having seen in 1919 in Paris on the Champs-Elysées a swarthy, slim, clean-shaven man in a snow-white *cherkesska* with a dagger hanging from his belt, accompanied by two huge men in black *cherkesskas*, with daggers and pistols, apparently his bodyguards. I read in the papers the next day that General Andranik had come to attend the Paris Peace Conference on behalf of Armenia. After his return to Armenia, he rebelled against his Government and was killed in the fighting.

There were only a few troops in Khoi, the bulk of the detachment having been sent to the south, to the village of Seyid Tajeddin, to join Amir Arshad, who was advancing on Salmas from the direction of Sharafkhaneh. Simko did not wait for us to execute this manœuvre. He attacked Amir Arshad at once with three to four thousand men, and Amir Arshad's 'Army' lost 200 killed including himself, the rest flying in disorder towards Qarajedagh, after which the Kurds attacked us along the ridge from west to east in the direction of the Seyid Tajeddin Pass. Our infantry, in spite of the superior numbers of the Kurds, resisted stubbornly. Unfortunately they were short of ammunition and none was available in Khoi nor even in Tabriz, as our rifles were British Lee-Enfields and the country was flooded with Russian Mossines and French Lebels which had been brought at the end of the war by a French military mission to arm the Christian Assyrians against the advancing Turks.

The infantry was ordered to retreat towards Khoi under the protection of my squadron. The Kurds did not pursue us and the infantry retreated to Khoi, 15 miles from there. In Khoi, the whole Gendarmerie detachment, numbering about 700 men, were rearmed with French Lebels taken from the local population in exchange for our Lee-Enfields, as there was plenty of ammunition for these rifles around Khoi. We had been informed that Lee-Enfield ammunition had been sent from Teheran, but with horse-drawn transport from Teheran to Qazvin and then pack transport from Qazvin to Tabriz and eventually to Khoi, at least three weeks would elapse before it would be available. We promised the population of Khoi to give them back their Lebel rifles as soon as our ammunition should arrive, and to pay them for the Lebel ammunition which had been expended.

Shortly after I was recalled to Khoi and ordered to proceed to Reyhan, a village some 12 miles to the south-west of Khoi at the entrance of the Kotur valley, to protect this village together with three other villages in its vicinity, at the request of an influential local landowner called Sartip Khan Makui (related to the Khan of Maku), to whom they belonged. I occupied the village, which was fortified.

The next day, Makui came to visit me and told me that the Kurds were in a village called Ezdikan at a distance of fifteen miles. As he knew all the mountain paths leading towards it, with the aid of his guides it would be easy to take them by surprise in the early morning if we marched by night and he would himself accompany us. Once in Ezdikan, we should command the entrance to the Salmas plain from the north, which would greatly facilitate further operations against Simko. I was tempted by this proposal, and asking Colonel Lundberg for permission to come to Khoi, rode there and told him Makui's plan. Lundberg convened a War Council, with Lieutenant-Colonel Puladin, Major Lassen and the Governor of Khoi, Bayat Makui. There was also present another Makui, who had been sent by Eqbal-os-Saltaneh with 100 armed mounted irregulars, to help us against the Kurds. The Makuis said that we could have full confidence in Sartip Khan, who was their cousin, and I was authorised to execute this operation.

I returned to Reyhan and at midnight started towards Ezdikan by mountain tracks which were at this season (mid November) already covered by a thick layer of snow. First we had to climb along a narrow track up the hills to the west of Reyhan, then coming down in a valley, go towards Ezdikan village between two chains of hills. I posted a lieutenant with seventeen men on the top of the hill, to protect our left flank, and cover our retreat if necessary. It was then that I noticed the disappearance in the dark of Makui and his men. I did not like this, but could not believe that they had betrayed us. We continued and at daybreak arrived on a hill from where we could see the village of Ezdikan. Then suddenly a fusillade began from all sides. I realised that the Kurds had been warned of our intention to attack them, and that they had occupied all the snow-covered hills commanding the valley, encircling us from three sides.

I tried to resist, taking the village under machine-gun fire, but after an hour's fighting, being under the Kurds' fire from the high hills which surrounded us, decided to retire towards a hill which dominated the one we were on. I ordered a platoon commander to take two platoons and occupy this hill, whilst I held on to the lower hill. They were to signal us with a red flag and protect our retreat by their fire, until we should reach the hill in our turn. I saw him reach the top of the hill trotting and galloping, but I never saw any signal and decided to retreat towards the hill. We did this without protection, the two platoons having proceeded at a fast pace towards Khoi, leaving us in the lurch on the lower hill. In this way, we had to climb the second hill under the heavy concentrated fire of the Kurds: all the men of my platoon except three had been killed, and my horse suddenly reared and fell to the ground, kicking wildly and staining the snow with its blood. I' fell clear and the horse died at once. I had bought a very good saddle with saddle bags from a Russian officer who had arrived in Tabriz after the revolution, and did not want to abandon it. So I removed it from the dead horse and putting it on my head continued to advance with great difficulty in knee-deep snow, the bullets whizzing around me. I finally reached the top of the hill, where I found only my orderly, Mohammad Hadi, who had caught a horse without a saddle, and with his help I saddled and mounted it. Just then Mohammad Hadi was struck by a bullet and fell dead without uttering a word. I saw Rustem emerging from behind some rocks, limping and using his carbine as a walking stick. He had been wounded in the foot. I helped him to climb on poor Mohammad Hadi's horse and we followed the tracks of the two platoons, with Sergeant Mansur Khan who had also miraculously escaped.

The seventeen men I had posted on a hill with Mohammad Hoseyn Khan had been wiped out by the Kurds and when we arrived at Khoi the platoon commander had announced that I had been killed with the others. It appeared that out of 100, I had lost forty men killed or missing; nine of these, including the sergeant-major in command of the machine-gun section, had been taken prisoner and on being released after a few days told their story.

The sergeant-major was taken while defending his jammed machine-guns with his sword, and the others after their horses had been killed and they remained on foot. They were all taken before Simko together with the machine-guns and Simko asked the sergeant-major to explain their mechanism to him. The sergeant-major took some time to de-jam one of the machine-guns, and then, seizing a cartridge band, pushed it into the gun and swiftly turned it towards Simko, intending to fire on him. Simko grasped at once what was to happen, and leaping on the gun, seized the hands of the sergeant-major, saying: 'Thank you, I understand now how to use it.'

He was so pleased by the courage of the man, who had wanted to shoot at him in the midst of all the Kurdish chiefs who certainly would have killed him afterwards, that he released all the prisoners, giving them one gold pound each and an escort to take them safely to our lines.

At the beginning of December the Gendarmerie expeditionary corps, reinforced by the 100 horsemen from Maku, started an offensive towards Dilman. This detachment was attacked at Qara Tappeh, both in front and from the flank by 2000 Kurds lead by Simko. After three hours' fighting the gendarmes lost about sixty killed, including Kostia Mikeladze who displayed great bravery under fire. The Maku contingent did not take any part in the fighting, having disappeared as soon as firing began. Their commander afterwards said that they had been protecting the right flank and rear of the column, and that without them the Kurds would have surrounded the gendarmes and annihilated them all, as they had done at Saujbolagh. As usual with the tribes, the Kurds did not follow up their success, and the detachment returned to Khoi, having suffered two heavy defeats in less than a fortnight.

The next day we evacuated Khoi, and while the Gendarmerie detachment moved through Marand and Sofian to Sharafkhaneh, I accompanied Lundberg and Lassen to Tabriz. In Tabriz, the news we received from Teheran was confused and irregular, but we heard of the failure of Colonel Mohammad Taqi Khan, who had been killed in a fight against the Zafaranlu Kurdish tribe of

Kuchan, which was on the side of the Government. Meanwhile the Communist chief Ehsanollah Khan had started an offensive against Teheran. The Government forces under Colonel Zahedi (the future Prime Minister) and Sheibani counter-attacked and after several temporary reverses and successes, finally defeated them.

Amir Moayyid who had joined the Red forces was left alone, his partisans having surrendered to the Government, and had gone to Samnan to ask for Sardar Sepah's pardon, which had been granted. In Gilan a split occurred between Kuchik Khan and Ehsanollah Khan, the former declaring against Communism as contrary to Islam. Ehsanollah Khan, left with only a few men, was defeated by the Government forces, and Kuchik Khan was in his turn abandoned by a chieftain called Halu Qorban and several hundred men who were at once incorporated into the army, Halu Qorban becoming an honorary colonel. After his defeat Ehsanollah Khan left Iran for Baku and Kuchik Khan tried to escape towards the Khalkhal district, but while crossing the high mountain pass of Masuleh covered with snow he froze to death.

The collapse of the Communist movement in Gilan and Mazanderan was due to three causes. First, the local population and the discontented chiefs came to realise that Communist ideology clashed with the spirit of Islam, and that the Soviet Government, heir to Tsarist Russia, was after all continuing the old policy of expansion and domination in another guise. Secondly, for the first time the operations of the Central Government's forces were conducted according to a prepared plan, with a unity of command which was badly lacking in the rebels. Thirdly, having realised that a sweeping ideological Communist victory was not possible in Iran, and that an open intervention in that country would provoke the hostility of all the people of the Middle East and so jeopardise the work of Communist propaganda in that region, the Soviet Government concluded the 1921 treaty with Iran and decided to withhold all military and material help to the Gilan insurgents, at least for the time being.

On the 5th December Reza Khan announced by Army Order No. 1 the organisation of the Imperial Army, unifying the Cossacks, Gendarmerie and provincial troops. The army to be composed of five divisions: 1st (Teheran), 2nd (Tabriz), 3rd

(Hamadan), 4th (Isfahan) and 5th (Mashad) and the Northern Independent Brigade (Rasht). In addition a special Gendarmerie force was organised under the name of Amnieh for the security of the roads.

After having finished with the rebellion in the Caspian provinces, which would, if successful, have endangered the very existence of the Iranian State, Reza Khan decided to pursue his plan of bringing all the tribes to submit to the Central Government by disarming them and breaking the power and influence of their chiefs. As always, the policy of sending military forces by small detachments which were defeated one after the other had failed in the operations against Simko, who after each success against Government troops became stronger and bolder. Reza Khan realised this and decided, against the opinion of several other Ministers who favoured negotiations, to send to Azerbaijan enough forces to liquidate not only Simko, but also other troublemakers. He began to concentrate in Qazvin military forces which had been liberated by the ending of operations in Gilan, and to send them towards Tabriz.

Preceding these reinforcements, General Sheibani, accompanied by a few officers and a mounted escort, arrived from Teheran, having covered 450 miles in thirteen days. After a few days the General left to inspect the Gendarmerie detachment renamed 14th regiment in Sharafkhaneh, which was then under the command of Lieutenant-Colonel Puladin, as Colonel Lundberg and Major Lassen were at that time in Tabriz. After that he went to Miandoab to inspect the Cossacks detachment of Moqaddam.

I had just begun my duties as A.D.C. to the new Tabriz divisional commander when news came from Sharafkhaneh that the Gendarmerie detachment had rebelled against its commander, that Major Lahoty lately transferred to this regiment was at the head of the rebels, and that he was marching on Tabriz with the regiment. (1st February 1922.) The situation was serious as there were practically no troops in Tabriz, the Cossacks being in Miandoab five days' march away, and the gendarmes being all with the mutineers.

I learned of their arrival early on the 3rd and at once went to Colonel Shahab's house to put myself at his disposal. He was not there. In the street I met a Caucasian officer who had fled the year before from the Azerbaijan Republic, after it had been occupied by Soviet forces.

'Come with me,' he said, 'I am going to the barracks in the town where the gendarmes are.'

'But they are rebels,' I said.

'Well,' he said, 'let's go and see what they say, we are not obliged to join them,' and thinking that I would perhaps find Seifollah Khan there, I accompanied him on foot to the centre of the town where the old barracks were situated.

The big square was full of gendarmes and in the commandant's office about twenty Gendarmerie officers were gathered, all talking at the same time, laughing and congratulating each other. I was greeted by them. 'Join us,' they were saying. 'We are going to march on Teheran.'

I sat in a corner listening and observing, when suddenly the door opened and Seifollah Khan, a stick under his arm, entered the room. Everybody got up and stood at attention.

'What are you doing here?' he asked in his calm and polished voice.

'We have been put under the command of ignorant Cossack chiefs and the Cossack Colonel Mohammad Ali Puria came to Sharafkhaneh to take over the 14th regiment, so we have arrested him as well as Colonel Puladin who refused to join us. Our chief is Major Lahoty who will be here presently,' said one of the officers.

Shahab's features hardened, and his voice took on a metallic tone. 'You acted in a most irresponsible way,' he said. 'Your duty is to obey the commanders who are appointed by the Government, and to execute their orders, not to plunge the country into wild and dangerous adventures. If you are dissatisfied, you can resign your commissions and go home, but not rebel against the constituted authorities. I advise you to think this over and to desist from following this mad course before it is too late.' Having said this, he turned on his heel and went out, followed by me.

'Let's go to the Governor's house,' he said; 'we will confer with Mokhber-os-Saltaneh.'

The Governor's house, or Ala Qapu, was surrounded by two encircling forces, the rebellious gendarmes forming the outer and the Cossack guards the inner ring, watching each other with fingers on the triggers of their rifles. Being in gendarme uniform,

the rebels let us pass, and telling the Cossacks we had been summoned by the Governor, we were allowed to enter the building.
Mokhber-os-Saltaneh, a tall gaunt man, was pacing to and fro in
the big drawing-room. We told him what we had seen.

It was decided that I would try to get to the Nezamieh, report
the situation to the divisional commander and ask him to make a
raid into the town to rescue the Governor. Shahab stayed with
the Governor and I proceeded on foot towards the Nezamieh.
It was a long march, and when I came close to Bagh-e-Shamal,
I saw some gendarmes looting a house. When I inquired from
an N.C.O. what they were doing he answered that they were
'removing things from. General Esma'il Aqa's house'.

I finally reached the Bagh, but all the approaches to the
Nezamieh were guarded by gendarmes who threatened to fire
on me if I advanced further. I went back, but on approaching the
Ala Qapu I learned that in the meantime the rebels had disarmed the Cossack guard and arrested both Mokhber-os-Saltaneh
and Shahab. I was already a staunch admirer of Reza Khan and I
had decided not to join the rebellion and if possible to oppose it.
I went home to await developments.

Next day many N.C.O.s and men of my squadron asked me
to join the rebellion. Afterwards my squadron's sergeant-major
came and told me that he had been sent by order of Lahoty to
fetch me. I told him to say that I was ill. He came back next day,
saying that Lahoty had ordered him to bring me in a carriage
and that I must go. I went on foot and was told at the office
that the *Rais* (chief) was in conference. There were several
officers there, one of whom, a first lieutenant, was obviously a
foreigner. He was blond with a pink face, upturned nose, and
a slim waist. He saluted, asking in Russian if I were Captain
Arfa-os-Soltan. Then he introduced himself: First Lieutenant
Prince Grigori Mikeladze, Kostia's brother. He had emigrated
from Russia to Iran and his brother having been killed on
Iranian service he had been accepted with his Russian rank in
the Iranian Army.

A lieutenant then entered the room and told me that the *Rais*
was ready to receive me. Major Lahoty rose, shook hands and
asking me to be seated sat down beside me on the sofa. He began
to praise me and to criticise the senior officers of the
Gendarmerie detachment, and in rather a pompous manner

declared that the country needed real reforms, that the people who had the power now were incompetent, corrupt and devoted to foreign interests, and that he had decided to mobilise all the patriotic forces of Azerbaijan and march on Teheran.

'I appoint you chief of staff of the Iranian Army and commander of the cavalry. I will give the necessary orders,' he said, rising and stretching out his hand to signify that the interview was over.

'I am sorry,' I said, 'but I cannot associate myself with your enterprise.'

'Why not?'

'Because I have sworn loyalty to Ahmad Shah my sovereign.'

'Who told you that Ahmad Shah is opposed to us?'

'He has not said he is for you.'

'What about the *coup d'état* of Reza Khan?'

'The Shah approved it as soon as it was executed which was in one night, but you will have to cross 450 miles on foot before reaching Teheran and you will be defeated. Then no real opposing forces were in existence, but now there is an organised army fresh from a victorious Northern Campaign and concentrated in Qazvin. There will be a bloody civil war which will end in catastrophe for you and those who have followed you.'

Lahoty became angry, and said that he had already arrested and imprisoned in the Ark (citadel) half a dozen colonels, and it would be easy for him to imprison me also. 'Do so, then,' I said, 'but you say that you fight for freedom and yet you are not ready to leave me free to act as I choose.'

He paced in silence for a minute, and then turning towards me, said again quite amiably: 'I shall not arrest you, and I will tell you why: some years ago I had to leave Iran after a political misunderstanding and I went to Istanbul where I was in great difficulties. Your uncle Ali Akbar Khan helped me by giving me money to rent a book-shop on which I lived for five years. So I let you go.'

We shook hands and I departed, glad to have got off so easily. There were no newspapers and we were in the dark about what was happening.

After several days my cousin Mahmud Khan came from the bazaar and told me that General Sheibani had arrived with important forces and relieved the Nezamieh from the rebels' pressure.

The next day there was heavy fighting and several bullets entered the courtyard. After four o'clock cannon fire ceased and small-arms fire became sporadic. I had three orderlies with me, Rustem, Hoseyn Aqa and Aqa Hoseyn. The two last had slipped away without my authority to fight with their comrades against the Cossacks and I had great difficulty in preventing Rustem from doing the same. At five o'clock I heard hurried steps approach and then a discreet knocking on the street door. Rustem went to open it and came back with Aqa Hoseyn, looking very dejected. He told me what had happened.

After a whole day's fighting, the Cossacks who had come from Miandoab with General Sheibani had attacked first from the south then the west, and having occupied the Nezamieh and joined with the Cossacks who were defending it against the gendarmes, penetrated into the town through Bagh-i-Shemal. Captain Turaj Amin, who was the real military commander of the rebellion, was wounded and the gendarmes fell back. Thereupon Lahoty abandoned his partisans and fled with some 200 mounted gendarmes to the north, eventually taking refuge in Soviet territory.

My two orderlies returned and, so that they should not be suspected of collaboration with the rebels, I threw their rifles in the frozen pond through a hole in the ice. Many gendarmes caught with their rifles were summarily shot that night and more than a hundred men, mostly rebel gendarmes, were killed during the fighting.

In the morning my cousin told me that suspicious-looking Cossacks had been seen in our street, looking inquiringly at our house and asking about the gendarme officers who were living there. In order to prevent any unpleasant incident I asked Reza Khan, my other cousin, to go to the Governor's house to see General Sheibani or someone else in authority and report where I was and ask for a Cossack officer to be sent to my house to accompany me to headquarters. If I went alone, the Cossacks who were roaming the town might take me for one of the rebels. After an hour Reza Khan came back with a Cossack lieutenant and two Cossack privates. The officer accompanied me to the Tabriz police headquarters and the soldiers were left at my door to prevent any intrusion by the Cossacks. This precaution was very necessary as I saw, while walking in the streets, many

Cossacks looting houses and shops without any interference from the police, who had completely disappeared.

Afterwards I went to see General Sheibani and Shahab, who had just been released from arrest, and I was appointed chief of the operational section of the Division's Staff of which Shahab was chief.

The two Cossack soldiers remained for two days at my door, bitterly complaining that they had lost hundreds of tomans as all their comrades were engaged in looting while they had to sit there and look on. Their tune changed the third day, when order was re-established and all the loot confiscated and given back to its owners and the looters arrested and punished. The mutinous gendarmes were all reincorporated in the army, but their officers, including my friend Turaj Amin, were tried and condemned to terms of imprisonment. Eventually they were pardoned by Reza Khan and reinstated in the army, with loss of one grade.

I then asked for and obtained the command of a squadron in the newly organised Layemot Tabriz cavalry regiment. At my request I received as platoon commanders Prince Mikeladze and another Caucasian, Selim Soltanof, a former first lieutenant of the Tatar regiment of the 'Wild Division'. The second in command of the regiment was Colonel Kalb Ali Khan Nakhchevan, a former Lieutenant-Colonel of Her Majesty the Empress's Uhlan regiment. Lieutenant Mikeladze was a typical Georgian, always gay, a mine of anecdotes and funny stories and extremely sociable. He lived in the same house as Colonels Lundberg and Shahab, Lassen having left for Teheran. Thanks to Mikeladze I became acquainted with most of the Russian, Armenian and Moslem Caucasian officers who had come to Tabriz after their countries had been occupied by the Soviet Army. We also made friends with two members of the Soviet Consulate, who joined us in our nightly revels. We went freely to the Consulate to visit them, entering without anybody stopping us. It was the time of Lenin's NEP (new economic policy), when private enterprise was partly re-established and social relations were eased. All that changed in 1924 with Lenin's death and the coming of Stalin.

In April a detachment of 500 former rebels under the command of Halu Qorban was brought from Gilan and concentrated in Miandoab. From there they marched on Saujbolagh to retake it from Simko's Kurds. There they met the same fate as Malekzade with 200 killed, including Halu Qorban himself. After this operation they were disbanded and sent back to their province.

A few days later Sheibani was recalled to Teheran and Jahanbani was entrusted with the forthcoming operations against Simko's Kurds. General Jahanbani had been educated in Russia, and was there when he heard of the death of his father, Zia-ed-Dovleh, who in 1911 was commander of the Government forces in Tabriz and had taken refuge at the British Consulate when the Russian Forces entered the town and installed Shoja-ed-Dovleh Governor of Azerbaijan. When the British Consul told Zia-ed-Dovleh that he must quit the Consulate he shot himself, not wishing to surrender to the Russians or to the Governor appointed by them. But first he spread a small Persian carpet under his feet so that although in the British Consulate he might die in Iran.

Reinforcements began pouring in from Teheran and these forces formed the Guards' Brigade under the command of General Zahedi. The Azerbaijan Division units were organised in an operational 'Tabriz Brigade' under General Moqaddam. A volunteer Armenian battalion was organised with the Armenian refugees who had come from Russia, under the command of Colonel Begzurabof, a former Russian Army Guards' officer. All these forces, numbering a little more than 8000 men, were concentrated in the region on the north of the Urmia lake. The cavalry regiment was encamped at Chahragan and we underwent three weeks' intensive training.

On the 23rd July an order came from headquarters directing the advance of the Operational Corps on Salmas, our regiment being on advance guard. We began our march to the sound of massed trumpeters, to a village half-way between Chahragan and Alma Sarai. Here the forward supply centre of the armed forces, including a bakery, had been established by General Jahanbani; this centre being protected by the Armenian volunteer battalion. After that we deployed our defences, one squadron being in advance guard and another forming the flank guards.

We passed through Qezeljeh which was deserted, entering the no-man's-land between us and the region occupied by the Kurds. After Qezeljeh we left the coastal plain and climbed up the hills.

We bivouacked by a small village, where General Jahanbani joined us with his staff. To the west of this village the mountain chain separating the plain of Khoi in the north from the coastal plain and the Salmas plain in the south divides into two branches forming a horse-shoe, with a large valley in the middle. The northern branch joins the Zagros north-south chain by the pass of Qara Tappeh. The southern branch is formed by two elongated hills, separated by a chasm, rocky and abrupt on the southern side and sloping gently to the north. This branch, Boz Dagh, was not joined to the Zagros, being separated from it by a north-south valley with a stream. On the 24th July I was ordered with my squadron to the south of Boz Dagh, in the plain, facing the village of Yalgiz Aghaj in Kurdish hands. The Armenian battalion was one mile in front of us, on the south slopes of the Boz Dagh.

During the night the Guards' Brigade of Zahedi had progressed along the eastern Boz Dagh and occupied it with his Pahlavi regiment, one battalion facing the western Boz Dagh, occupied by the Kurds, and the other in second line. They had the support of two mountain batteries. The Ahmadi regiment was in reserve. The Tabriz Brigade was on the hills of the northern branch, above the Shakar Yazi village, the heights dominating Mofi Kandi being in the hands of the Kurds.

At seven o'clock, firing began on my right, the Kurds attacking the forward battalion of the Pahlavi regiment. At nine o'clock I was recalled and after marching to the rear, brought my squadron behind a little hill situated in the plain near the bifurcation of the two mountain branches and ordered the men to dismount in a ravine at the foot of the hill. The 2nd squadron was already there and a section of the horse battery was in position a little above and behind us. On the summit of the hill, about 100 yards from us, I saw General Zahedi looking through field-glasses towards the south-west, where fighting was going on between the soldiers and the Kurds.

At about twelve o'clock I received from Kalb Ali Khan the order to take both squadrons and to move forward to protect the right flank of the Guards' Brigade and the left flank of the Tabriz Brigade and to establish a liaison between them. The horse-artillery section was also put under my command, giving me, if required, the support of its fire. I deployed my group in double column, and moved forward. We were in a completely flat valley, some six miles wide. I could clearly distinguish the Pahlavi battalion on the western side of the eastern Boz Dagh on my left and the Kurds on the northern side of the western Boz Dagh, and heard unceasing machine-gun and rifle fire, but neither side appeared to be making progress. On my right, the high hill above the village of Mofi Kandi, concealed behind a mass of trees, was covered with little black specks which were the Kurds and by the speed of their movements I saw that they were all on horseback. Opposite, the hills above Shakar Yazi, which I knew to be occupied by the elements of the Tabriz Brigade, seemed empty, the men being probably concealed in the ground.

At 2 p.m. I saw a dark mass of swiftly moving enemy cavalry appearing from behind the western Boz Dagh evidently with the intention of enveloping the right flank of the Pahlavi regiment from the north. I ordered the 2nd squadron to execute a movement to the left, in order to bring the attacking Kurds under its fire. Taken between the machine-gun fire of the Pahlavi regiment and our rifle fire, the Kurdish attack collapsed and they turned back as quickly as they had come, leaving half a dozen horses and several men on the ground. I noticed the gradual decongestion of the hill above Mofi Kandi, the Kurds coming down the slope by twos and threes and disappearing in the village behind the trees of Mofi Kandi. I realised that they intended to attack our thin line, and pushing towards the centre of our disposition, reach our artillery position and drive a wedge between the two brigades.

I ordered the artillery section commander to open fire on the Mofi Kandi village; the first shells passed over our heads, and then others followed in quick succession, hitting the village. Then I saw the Kurds coming out of the village and galloping to the west, like a flight of sparrows out of a tree when one throws a stone at it.

At four o'clock I received the order to be ready for the pursuit, and soon after that Kalb Ali Khan arrived with four squadrons and we pushed towards the west. We saw the Kurdish mountain-guns pack and disappear in the distance, but they were too far for us to reach and capture them. I learned then that after a whole day of close fighting, with bayonets, hand- and rifle-grenades, losing and regaining their positions at least four times, with nearly 80 men killed and wounded, the Pahlavi Regiment had pushed back the Kurds and reached the western Boz Dagh hill. Here the Ahmadi Regiment attacked the retreating Kurds who were trying to take the position on the top of the hill, but were driven back towards the Salmas plain.

This was the signal for a general retreat of the Kurds, all our units taking part in the pursuit, and the town of Dilman was occupied that same evening. The Kurds retreated towards Kohne Shahr and their stronghold of Chahrik, where Simko had his fort and his confederates from the other tribes returned to the north, west and south of the Salmas plain. We learned afterwards that Simko had employed more than 10,000 well-armed Kurdish warriors with three mountain-guns and forty-five heavy and light machine-guns with plenty of ammunition in the Shakar Yazi operation.

The success of our force was due to the considerable effectives engaged and also to the fact that our troops advanced along the crest of the hills and not in the valleys and that their flanks had been protected by security dispositions. Also, for the first time in this kind of mountain warfare, the supply of foodstuffs, forage, ammunition and sanitary equipment was well organised and held in readiness for the whole force at an advanced supply base. In this way, a seven hours' fight definitely broke the back of Simko's resistance and liquidated a regime of terror and rapine to which the most prosperous part of the Azerbaijan province had been subjected for four years.

We stayed a few days in a village near Dilman. The Salmas plain is well watered and very fertile and comprised some sixty large and prosperous villages, which had been partly inhabited by Azeri Shia Moslems and partly by Christian Assyrians, a semitic race whose language is akin to Arabic. A great number of them had been massacred by Simko's Kurds in 1918, the few who escaped fleeing to Tabriz or Russia. I saw a field covered with bones and skulls on the Shakar Yazi plain. These belonged to a group of some 2000 Assyrians fleeing to the north who had been overtaken and massacred by the pitiless Kurds. Many of the villages were abandoned and all were half-ruined by the Shakkaks of Simko.

From Salmas our cavalry column marched towards the Somai-Baradost plain, surrounded by mountains, to the west of Urmia and after a few skirmishes with isolated groups of Begzadeh Kurds turned towards the east. Traversing the rich Urmia plain, containing more than 300 villages, we entered the town which had been four years under Simko's occupation. The entire population, reduced to 4000 or 5000 persons (it had numbered 25,000 before the war), came to greet us. They were all in rags, haggard and destitute, because they had not been allowed to leave their villages to attend to their fields and as a result the water-channels were mostly filled with sand and silt and the land uncultivated. The cavalry bivouacked in the fields close to the town, some officers being billeted in Urmia, but I and my officers preferred to be in tents with the squadron.

Urmia brought luck to my cousin Yusuf. The owner of the house in which he was lodged was a rich man who owned several large villages in the region and had one very pretty daughter. He told my cousin that he had made a vow, that if the Government's Army liberated Urmia from Simko's intolerable yoke he would give his daughter in marriage to the first unmarried officer who should enter his house. Yusuf Khan was the happy man.

From Urmia we went back to Salmas, passing through the Abdoi Shakkaks' region, whose chief, Omar Aqa Simko's uncle, submitted to the Government. From Dilman one column moved to Kohne Shahr and from there to Chahrik, which had been abandoned by Simko. Approaching this place from the east we noticed in the midst of a level plain a large modern house built in stone, with many outbuildings such as stables, kitchens, etc. Behind the house a square fortress dominated the countryside. Only when quite close did we discover that the fortress stood on a rock in the middle of a deep canyon through which a river flowed and that access to it could only be obtained by means of a narrow winding path with steps cut into the rock. This eagle's nest was built by Simko's father and the modern house by Simko himself and filled with furniture brought from well-to-do houses in Urmia. There was even a piano and an elaborate telephone system communicating with Kohne Shahr, Dilman and other places. Simko used to throw his prisoners from the wall of the fort to the bottom of the canyon, where they were allowed to rot. Later both house and fortress were destroyed by a detachment of sappers.

At the junction of two rivers, not far from the Qalarash frontier mountains, I was instructed to go forward and establish contact with the Turkish posts, to ask them to disarm the Kurds who passed into Turkey and to move them further away from Iranian territory. I reached the frontier at 5 p.m., found a Turkish post and began my talks with the sergeant in command. He told me that he was not aware of the whereabouts of Simko's Kurds, that the posts were few and far between and that certainly it would not be possible for his few frontier guards to prevent several hundred armed Kurds from going wherever they wished.

While I was still talking with him, I heard the sound of cannon shots from the direction of the cavalry column's camp (we had a mountain-gun with the column). I quickly took leave of the Turk and hurried towards the camp. It was already dark when we reached the camping ground, but I was astonished to find it empty and that the sound of firing came from the hills above. Not wishing to expose the squadron to an ambush, I ordered Mikeladze to remain at the camp and placing outposts around the squadron and taking with me Soltanof and my trumpeter, went towards the sound of the firing. Not far from the camp site we saw a fire with several men around it. Thinking they were our soldiers, we went towards them, but hearing by their speech that they were Kurds, galloped away, a few shots whizzing past our ears.

Two miles further on, I saw a group of men and heard them speak Persian. We came nearer and found some cavalry soldiers holding their horses. I asked them what had happened. They answered that the Kurds had suddenly reappeared and attacked the cavalry column's camp, inflicting some casualties. The Colonel had brought the regiment to a safer place and occupied the hill.

I went on a little further, then dismounted and climbed the hill. I had to pass over shallow trenches from which the soldiers were firing, in order to reach the top. Colonel Kalb Ali Khan was pacing to and fro in the dark, apparently in a high state of excitement. The bullets were continually whizzing by from all directions. I came forward and saluting, reported:

'Captain Arfa-os-Soltan, commander of 3rd squadron, has the honour to report . . .'

'Go to the devil!' exclaimed the Colonel. 'Look at all these lights around us: they are the fires lighted by the Kurds who attacked us. We are surrounded on this . . . hill by these . . . Kurds and you come here with your squadron, when we are here already overcrowded!'

'Tell me then where to take my squadron!'

'I told you already, to the devil!' I saw that he was quite unreasonable.

'Will you give me this order in writing, then!'

'Go wherever you like.' I produced a map, and showed him a hill marked 1208.*

'All right, go there!'

'Captain Arfa-os-Soltan has the honour to take leave!' I executed a smart about-face and went down the hill as fast as I could, the whizzing bullets giving me a definitely uncomfortable feeling. On the way down we mounted our horses, taking care to avoid the fires lighted by the Kurds, who were warming themselves beside them as the night was bitterly cold owing to the high altitude.

I was afraid that we should not be able to find the place where we had left the squadron as it was very dark and we could not shout or signal on account of the proximity of the Kurds. I decided to go at once to hill 1208 as I had indicated to the Colonel. This hill dominated the eventual line of retreat for the column and I considered that we three with one rifle, that of the trumpeter (Selim and I having only pistols and swords), might be able to hold it and so enable the column to pass in comparative safety.

After nearly an hour's march, using the compass and the map and climbing the steep slopes of hills which all looked alike, we reached the top of the Hill 1208, dominating the countryside. It was extremely cold and we sat on the ground, with my blanket (which I always carried rolled behind my saddle) wrapped round all three of us, one of us at a time keeping awake and holding the horses, and the other two trying to sleep. Towards four in the morning, from the deep gorge beneath the mountain came the sound of a metallic clatter that I recognised as the clanking of machine-gun parts carried by pack-horses. I was glad to think that the column had managed to extricate itself from the Kurds' clutches and after the sounds ceased I woke my

* On the old Russian maps heights were marked in sazhen, each sazhen equalling 7 feet, 1208 equalling 8456 feet.

companions and leading our horses by the bridle, we started to come
down the hill again by a narrow path, bordered by a deep ravine
on one side and the abrupt rise of a mountain on the other.

Looking back, I saw Kurdish horsemen galloping along the
crest of a hill to the mountain peak that we had just left. We
tried to reach a bend in the path which would protect us from
their bullets, but it was too narrow and steep for us to move fast.
I was walking in front, the trumpeter in the middle, and Selim
in the rear, and we were coming down pulling at the horses'
bridles without looking behind us, when suddenly, crack! crack!
whizz! the rain of bullets began. No use to stop and reply, we
were fine targets, without cover on that narrow path. I remembered the *Tir aux Pigeons* stand at Monte Carlo, beneath the
Casino, and thought that at least the pigeons had wings to fly
away with, whilst we had only our slow legs and were bound to
even slower horses.

Just then, a more ominous sound than that of the bullets made
me look round; I saw the trumpeter's horse on its knees and the
soldier trying vainly to make him rise. This was disaster. If the
horse was wounded and could not rise and move, we would be
forced to throw him over the precipice in order to allow Selim
and his horse to pass. I slipped from under my horse's belly to
help the trumpeter, and whipping my horse from behind,
encouraged it to go down the path without stopping and waiting
for us. Luckily the horse was not wounded and had only slipped
on the smooth stones of the path, and by our common efforts we
managed to lift him on to his feet so that we could go on.

During all this time the Kurds were shooting at us, and every
second we were expecting to be hit and to roll into the deep
ravine below. Luck was with us and we reached the blessed bend
safe and sound and from there the bed of the Zolu Chai, whose
tree-bordered banks were in pleasant contrast to the barren hills.
We followed this until it brought us to the cavalry column's
new camp at Temir Ova by about 2 p.m. I was delighted to find
my squadron there. Mikeladze reported that the heights around
the place where the squadron had been left the night before having
been occupied by the Kurds, they had been obliged to retire two
miles up a ravine, which accounted for our not having seen them.
He had left an outpost of three men at the former place to direct
me, but when I had come down from the hill, in order to avoid

the fire of the Kurds, I had made a detour and in the darkness had mistaken one ravine for another.

After our column's retreat from Qalarash as a result of Simko's counter-offensive in that region, Kalb Ali Khan reported the situation to headquarters and General Zahedi arrived with the Ahmadi infantry regiment and a mountain battery. The offensive was resumed, our regiment again in the first echelon. Our scouts were met by fire from a range of hills to the south of Tamir Ova. Kalb Ali Khan ordered two squadrons (including mine) to attack at once. We galloped in mounted formation up the hill shouting and waving our swords and the Kurds abandoned the heights and fled towards the mount Sari Tash which dominated the whole region. Apparently Simko's forces did not number more than a thousand men, the others having dwindled away during the retreat, as happens usually with tribal forces who disperse after a battle, whether it is successful or not.

The Kurdish positions on the heights suffered artillery bombardment, under cover of which the battalions progressed up the slopes. Our cavalry column was executing a turning movement in order to cut the line of retreat of the Kurds. Simko did not resist for long, and abandoning Sari Tash retreated with his men along the ridge, finally crossing into Turkey. This time the Turkish authorities took charge of them, ordering Simko to take his men to a safe distance from the Iranian frontier, where they were ultimately disarmed.

The Teheran regiments returned to the capital after having disarmed the remnant of Amir Arshad's private army which had passed under his brother Sardar Ashair into Karajadagh, as well as the Karasonni and other former allies of Simko's in western Azerbaijan.

Back in Tabriz I asked for six months' leave to go to my father's at Monte Carlo, as I was troubled by a recurrence of malaria, which I had contracted during my Mazanderan campaign, and a weakness of the lungs, and I decided to take Rustem with me. Whilst I was busy with my preparations something happened which saddened us and aroused our indignation. A notice had appeared on the walls of the Soviet Consulate, announcing an amnesty to all Caucasian refugees and inviting them to return to Russia. After some hesitation, a few Armenians decided to go back. Our friend Begzurabof, former commander of the disbanded Armenian volunteer battalion, being amongst them. We tried to dissuade him and one night at a restaurant with our friend the Soviet Consulate's secretary, we asked him if the amnesty covered Begzurabof. He said that it did and next day the same assurance was given by the Consul, together with the necessary passes. Begzurabof departed with a dozen companions and crossed the frontier at Jolfa. We were appalled to hear that he had been arrested and shot on reaching the Russian side of the bridge.

Two weeks after that, another notice appeared again on the walls of the Consulate, urging the refugees to return, but this time there were no buyers. Not being a refugee, I asked for a visa to pass through Jolfa, Tiflis and Batum on my way to Istanbul, but after consulting Moscow, the Consulate regretfully declined to give me one, without stating any reason. I was at a loss what to do to reach Monte Carlo when one day at a party I met the representative of the new Turkish Nationalist Government, which had been established in Ankara by Mostafa Kemal Pasha in opposition to the Allied-controlled Sultan's Government's Embassy in Teheran. He procured for me the necessary facilities to travel through Turkey as far as Trabzon, where I could board a boat for Istanbul. As the region was very insecure on account of the Kurdish robber bands infesting it, he was having great difficulty in sending his diplomatic bag to Ankara and he said that he would be very grateful if I would take it and deliver it at Inebolu on my way and that I would be allowed to wear my uniform and to be accompanied by an armed escort from my regiment. I accepted eagerly and bought four horses, one for me, two for my soldiers and one to carry my luggage. This comprised a trunk, a small carpet, a folding-table and chair and a bedding-roll.

On the 22nd November, after taking leave of my aunt and cousins and of my officers, who accompanied me as far as the Aji Chai bridge outside the town, I left Tabriz with my little caravan, consisting, besides myself, of Rustem, now promoted sergeant, Ibrahim the other soldier and a hired man who led the pack-horse. We travelled as people did before motor-cars, steam engines and even wheel carriages were used, in the tracks of the Seljuks and other Turkomans who had invaded Asia Minor from the east after having crossed Iran.

Journey through Turkey

The first stop on my journey was Shabister, a large and prosperous village, the centre of the district of Gunei Mahal. The village is surrounded by extensive walled orchards and vineyards and is renowned for its delicious Askeri grapes, devoid of pips, which are dried and exported as sultanas. We then went to Sharafkhaneh railhead on the Urmia lake, which had been the starting point of Lahoty's recent rebellion and had been the principal supply centre of the Russian IXth Army Corps during the 1914–1918 war. It had been abandoned by the Russians after the revolution with its very important stores of war material. The greater part of this was taken by the Iranian Army though some of it was appropriated by Kurds, the local population and merchants from Tabriz who sold caravan loads of it in the bazaar for several years. During their occupation of Azerbaijan from 1911 to 1918, as well as the railway from Tabriz to Jolfa, the Russians had built four ports on the shore of the lake at Sharafkhaneh, Golmankhaneh (which served Urmia), Danalu (which served Maragheh) and Hayderabad in the south. They had also built, with parts transported by the railway, three little steamboats which used to ply between these ports. All this had been handed over to Iran by the 1921 treaty.

I reached Khoi on the sixth day after leaving Tabriz. Everything was calm, last year's tension had disappeared and people were going about their business in the Salmas district in complete security.

At my next stop I had a disagreeable surprise, being awakened with the news that the pack-horse was dead, its carcass all swollen. According to my soldiers it had been bitten by a snake. I tried to buy a horse but none was available, so the luggage had to be divided into two loads, each carried by a donkey. These donkeys had to be hired from village to village and this increased my expenses and slowed down my march so much that it took me three days to reach Maku.

When approached from the east, Maku looks attractive, with multicoloured houses at the foot of a high and steep mountain: it is only on coming nearer that one realises the extraordinary formation of the mountain, the upper part of it literally overhanging the old town which is in a defile, making it easy to defend. Since the seventeenth century Maku has been a part of the Iranian Empire, but previously was several times under Ottoman occupation. The Khanate is inhabited by Jelali and Milanlu Kurdish tribes and by Orusanlu, and Airomlu Shia Turki-speaking Azeri. The Khans of Maku were originally from the Jelali Kurdish tribe, but at the beginning of the last century the Bayat Maku family replaced them. The origin of this family is romantic. Bayat was an officer of Nader Shah, from the province of Arak, and when the Shah was assassinated near Quchan in 1747 his widow clad in his cloak and taking some of his jewels fled with Bayat. They rode to the west, as far as Maku, where they married, finally ousting the Kurdish Khan.

During the 1914–18 war Eqbal-os-Saltaneh, who was trying to be on good terms both with Russia and Turkey, aroused Russia's suspicions. He was invited by the Russian commander in that sector to come to his camp for conversations, but once there was arrested and sent to Tiflis, where he was freed subject to police surveillance. After the revolution, in 1917 he was allowed to return to Maku. The Russians had built a narrow-gauge railway line from Shahtakhti on the Aras river, between Erivan and Nakhchevan, towards Kara Köse, passing through Maku, in order to secure their communications with the forces operating in the Eleskirt and Van regions. After the revolution, the inhabitants of Maku had removed the rails and used them in the construction of their houses as beams to support the roofs. The newer houses have a Russian look about them due to the proximity of Russia and the constant intercourse between Maku and the Caucasus. This has now completely stopped, the Russian frontier being closed since the reoccupation of the Caucasian Republics by the Soviet Army.

I halted at a caravanserai and sent Rustem to the Governor, to ask him to tell me of a suitable lodging for the night. The Governor came himself with many apologies, reproaching me for not having let him know beforehand of my arrival and took me to his home, a pleasant house with an iron roof painted green in

Russian style. I was having tea in his drawing-room, furnished with plush armchairs in the Russian fashion, when a telephone call came from Baghchejik, the Khan's palace, situated about six miles from Maku on the road to the Turkish frontier. The Governor (a relative of the Khan's and appointed by him) was ordered to invite me to Baghchejik to be the Khan's guest as he had known my father when he was Iranian Consul-General in Tiflis. I was very glad to have the opportunity of meeting the Khan or Sardar about whom I had heard so much and who was one of the most characteristic representatives of the old order in Iran.

A carriage came to fetch me, and accompanied by the Governor I drove to Baghchejik, a large house standing in a big park full of fine trees. We drove into the garden and halted in front of steps leading to a terrace. A tall gaunt old man of about seventy-five in sardari frock-coat and black astrakhan cap came to the door to meet me and took me in his arms. 'His Excellency the Sardar,' said the Governor.

The Sardar took me by the hand and led me into an enormous drawing-room furnished in the Russian version of the mid-Victorian period. After some conversation, chiefly about his friendly relations with my father at Tiflis in the nineties, he conducted me to another big room. The only furniture consisted of a beautiful carpet and velvet curtains and on the floor a luxurious sleeping place had been prepared. Inviting me to rest, the Sardar took his leave. Immediately Rustem came into the room: seeing it empty of chairs and tables he ordered the Sardar's servants to bring my folding armchair and table to make me comfortable. Rustem was an ideal servant and very much aware of his dignity and importance as cavalry sergeant, and everywhere he went ordered people about with great authority.

The next day, the Sardar took me to a wing of his palace which he had transformed into a museum. There were some interesting things, for instance arms and armour including steel helmets found on the Chaldiran battlefield not far from Maku, when a decisive battle between Shah Esma'el Safavi and Sultan Selim the Grim of Turkey, had been fought in 1514. He also showed me a collection of books written by my father.

The Sardar used to work half the night with his secretary, administering the affairs of his Khanate and corresponding with

Teheran as if he were an independent ruler.

We lunched at a gorgeously appointed table, all the dishes being spread upon it before we took our seats. Amongst the guests was a burly man of about fifty, the Khan of the neighbouring Khanate of Avajik, vassal to the Khan of Maku, who had come to pay homage to his suzerain. That night he came into my room, sat on the carpet by my bed and whispered that the Sardar was a treacherous man, that he was intriguing with the Russians and the Turks, that he had been in alliance with Simko, and that the Central Government ought not to have confidence in him. I listened to all this, having heard it before, and answered him with generalities.

After two days I took leave of my host, who kindly lent me a camel with a camel driver to carry my luggage up to Trabzon, from where I was to send it back with my orderly Ibrahim.

After leaving Baghchejik I crossed a plain covered with black petrified lava blocks ejected by the now extinct Ararat volcanoes, passed through the village of Bazargan and arrived at the frontier post. The Turkish sergeant in charge of the military frontier was quite bewildered at seeing an Iranian officer with two Iranian soldiers, who wished to penetrate into Turkish territory. All this region had been subject to the Ankara Government since 1920 so he had to obey the instructions given by that Government's representative in Tabriz, and he let us pass.

Even before reaching Maku the two Ararat peaks had been continuously in sight, that of the lesser Ararat (13,000 ft.) to the east and the greater Ararat (16,300 ft.) to the west, but actually at Maku they were hidden by the mountains dominating it from the north. Bayazit was a little town on a hill, with an old fortress situated in a wide valley lying between the Ararat (Büyük Agri Dagh) and the Tendürek Dagi group (10,300 feet), which was treeless and desolate. The town had numbered 15,000 inhabitants before the war, but not more than 3000 were living there when I passed. The whole region of Eastern Anatolia, known to Western geographers as Armenia, had been desolated during the 1914–18 war by the tide of the belligerent armies, Russian, Turkish and at the end of the war Armenian. When the Russian armies invaded the region in 1915, the Armenians living there and numbering more than one million souls thought that the Ottoman Empire would collapse at once, and all the

Mozaffar-ed-Din Shah at his coronation, 1896

The author with his father and tutor,
Mirza Mohammad Saed, in 1901

The author in 1900

Prince Mirza Reza Khan Arfa-ed-Dovleh, the author's father, 1902

Mohammad Ali Shah Qajar at his coronation in 1907

١٥٢١
1912
Istanbul

The author as a cadet, Istanbul, 1912

The author's future wife, Hilda, on the
Russian Front, 1916

Soltan Ahmad Shah Qajar, sitting, with his brother
Crown Prince Mohammad Hassan Mirza

The author as a lieutenant in Switzerland, 1915

The author at Saumur Cavalry School, 1924

Turks and Kurds be driven out of Armenia which would be subjected to Russia. In order to precipitate this issue, groups of Armenians armed with rifles smuggled before the war from Russia started attacking the Turks from the rear, notably at Van. Many acts of sabotage were committed behind the front whereupon the Ottoman Government headed by Talaat Pasha decided to remove all the Armenians, including women, children and old people, from Eastern Anatolia to the southern villages of Halep (Aleppo), Sham (Damascus) and Mosul.

The Armenians were taken from their homes, where they had to leave everything they possessed, concentrated in camps on the roads, formed into columns and taken on foot for hundreds of miles under the escort of gendarmes who were relayed at each stage, without any sort of arrangements having been made for their food, shelter or medical care. The population was hostile, especially the Kurds, who maltreated them in every way and often refused to sell them food, or asked such prohibitive prices for it that the destitute Armenians had to march without food until they dropped dead.

This forcible ejection of more than one million people resulted in ninety per cent of them dying on the march. They had not been systematically massacred, like the Jews in Germany during the Second World War, but were destroyed as a result of exposure and hunger, like the 2,000,000 Germans (out of 11,000,000) who died on the roads of Germany in the autumn and winter of 1945–6, when they were displaced from east and west Prussia, Pomerania, Silesia and the Sudetenland to West Germany, although in their case the population was friendly and the distance much less.

When the Russian Army progressed towards the interior of Anatolia it was preceded by a certain number of irregular volunteer Armenian battalions, burning with the desire for revenge. They began to massacre the Moslem population, this massacre becoming general after the revolution and the departure of the Russian officers and soldiers, when the Armenians were left alone on the Turkish front. The number of Moslems killed was not far short of 600,000, but this was not known abroad; people in Europe and the U.S.A. being chiefly interested in the Christian Armenians, whose plight has been publicised by the American and other missionaries in Turkey. These massacres

and deportations accounted for the emptiness of the region I
was traversing.

I was told long afterwards that a section of the Jelali Kurdish
tribe, part of which lived in Iran, had escaped massacre by taking
refuge on the upper reaches of the Büyük Agri Dag (greater
Ararat) with their families and flocks. Being well armed they
had been able to resist until the end of the war all attempts of
the Russians and Armenians to subdue them, thanks to the
extremely difficult terrain, although for more than three years
Agri was upwards of 100 miles behind the front.

I continued my march towards Diyadin. I could not cover
long distances between stages because the camel was slower than
our horses, so I used to ride ahead with Rustem and then wait
at the end of the stage for the camel and camelman who marched
on foot, escorted by Ibrahim on horseback.

On the second day after leaving Bayazit it began to snow and
became bitingly cold. I had reached a place covered with little
mounds with big holes in the ground, which proved to be an
underground village, and taking shelter inside one of these
holes, I discovered that it opened into spacious caves where
people and cattle took refuge and were well protected against
the rigours of the Anatolian plateau's winter. It was warm and
I was sitting on a felt rug in my stockinged feet by a brazier,
sipping hot tea, when I heard shots fired from not far away. I
realised that something was happening to my camel and its
escort. Hurriedly putting on a pair of slippers I always carried
in my saddle-bags, and seizing my pistol I ran out followed by
Rustem with his rifle. Outside, the sound of the shots was loud.
I ran about in the snow, firing my pistol in the air and shouting
commands in Turkish in order that the brigands—as surely they
were—should believe that they were in the presence of a unit of
Turkish soldiers or gendarmes. Rustem also fired a few rounds
and the firing from the opposite side stopped. Some two or three
hundred yards away we saw a dark form on the white snow,
with people behind it. It was the camel which had been made to
kneel by the camelman who was holding the horse of his escort
so that he could shoot at the brigands from behind the camel.
We brought them safely to the village, and they told me that
three armed Kurds on foot had tried to take possession of the
camel, but that when Ibrahim threatened them with his rifle,

they had disappeared in the darkness, then started firing on my men from behind some boulders. They had vanished into the night as soon as they heard us shooting. After this we appreciated our evening meal.

Next day, near Diyadin, I passed through a village where I could imagine myself in Iran. The inhabitants were wearing sardaris as in Azerbaijan, with black sheepskin caps and talked Azeri, although since leaving Bazergan I had only seen Kurdish villages and Kurdish dresses and heard only Kurdish speech. When I asked them from what part of Iran they had come and settled here, they told me that they were from the former Khanate of Erivan, that they had emigrated after the Russo-Persian war of 1826–8, and being Shia, they had not mingled with the Sunni Kurds, and so had retained their customs, speech and clothes, the village being entirely inhabited by them.

In Diyadin the local Governor persuaded me to allow a gendarme to accompany us, for the country was insecure, as I had had occasion to see for myself. At the next stage I had to pass the night in a very dirty little village, where the Kurdish *muhtar* (headman) put at my disposal a little hut consisting of two rooms, the back room having neither window nor door to the outside and entered only through the first room. I occupied the inner room while my three men and the gendarme settled in the outer one, our beasts being tied outside. When I was preparing to go to bed, the gendarme came to my room with Rustem and told me that as he understood Kurdish, he had overheard the *muhtar* saying to another villager that they intended to cut our throats after we had gone to sleep and rob us. I told the gendarme that we were not chickens to have our throats cut by such low ruffians, and that my men and I would keep watch and dispatch the first would-be murderer who would dare to enter our rooms. Nothing happened in the night, but the next morning when we were about to load the camel we discovered that it had disappeared, although it had been properly tied up like the horses, which were still there. I knew that the rascally *muhtar* was responsible for the theft.

I emerged from the hut, told the gendarme to summon the *muhtar* and asked him sternly what had happened to my camel. 'How could I know?' he said. 'You will have to know,' I said— and telling Ibrahim and the camelman to throw him to the ground and to hold fast his feet, head and arms, I ordered Rustem to flog him with his Cossack whip. The gendarme was standing by, looking very uneasy. After the third stroke, the man began to cry. After the fifth, we heard the camel's bells ringing from behind the village huts and a relative of the *muhtar* appeared leading the camel. 'I found it outside the village,' he said. He did not explain how the camel had untied itself. I paid the *muhtar* for the food, fodder and lodging, and we moved towards Kara Kilisa (now Agri). After Eleskirt the weather became still colder and the snow deeper, and the plateau with its high snow-covered mountains was extremely bleak.

At one stage, halting for the night in an underground habitation, I was ushered into a cage in the middle of the room, inside which the whole family, men, women and children, were sleeping on the ground and Rustem had my camp-bed put up for me in the midst of them. In the rest of the cave, around the cage were the animals, cows, sheep, goats and poultry. It was certainly unusual to see people in a cage and animals walking freely around it!

Between Kokse and Velibaba we passed suddenly from the Kurdish to the Turkish region and the villages and their inhabitants changed completely. People and houses were much cleaner and gone were the Kurdish costumes, men and women alike wearing the wide Turkish *shalvar* or trouser narrow at the ankle, the men being for the most part bearded and wearing on their heads the fez with the *sarik* or narrow turban, instead of the fringed head-dress of the Kurds. People were calm, silent and dignified.

I passed the night at the village *muhtar*'s house. After I had had my dinner, the *muhtar* asked my permission to bring a few notables of the village to visit me. I was glad to see them. They came one by one, saluted and sat on the ground around the room. After a few minutes' silence, the *muhtar* told me that these *aqas* (gentlemen) wanted to ask me a few questions. Then one of them said: 'We have heard that the victorious Turkish Army has entered Istanbul. What has happened to our Sultan?'

'He abdicated,' I said, 'and left Istanbul on a British warship.'

A deep silence followed, the villagers pondering over what I had said. 'Who will be the Sultan, then?'

'There will be no sultan, only a Khalif, and he is the Sultan's cousin, Abdul Mejid Effendi.'

'But how is it possible for the country to be without a sultan?'

'There will be a Republic.'

'What is that!' I tried to explain it to them, but they did not or did not want to understand and kept on saying: 'But without a Sultan, there could not be a State!'

I think that this was the opinion of the majority of the Turkish peasants. In the Kurdish regions, nobody had bothered about such questions because they were more interested in their own affairs than in those of the Empire, but the Turks considered the Empire, the Sultan, the Khalif, as belonging to them and were concerned about their fate.

I traversed the Aras river at Köprüköy, then passed through Hassan Qal'e, the stronghold of Uzan Hassan (1467–77) of the Ak Koyunlu (White Sheep) Turkoman dynasty which ruled in Azerbaijan and Eastern Anatolia from 1378 to 1502. Uzun Hassan had married the daughter of the last Byzantine Emperor of Trebizond, Despina, their daughter becoming the mother of Shah Esma'el, the first Shah of the Sefevid dynasty who reigned from 1502 to 1524, and re-established a united Empire in Iran, with his capital in Tabriz. I was approaching Erzurum, and looking at the snow-covered hills on both sides of the road, the long high straight ridge of the Kargapazari barring the horizon and dominating the plain to my right, the superimposed peaks of the Sakaltutan and Palandöken with the winding pass of the Deveboyunu on my left, I remembered these names had been in the history of the 1829, 1856, 1877 and 1914–18 wars. The Turks had defended every inch of the ground and the Russians conquered fort after fort after bloody fighting. The town was surrounded by fortifications, outside which hundreds of old cannon were lying on the ground. I had to walk a good half an hour round the moat before finding a gate through which I could enter the town, and as soon as I succeeded in doing so I went straight to the address of an Iranian merchant, which had been given to me in Tabriz.

Erzurum, covered with a deep layer of snow, charmed me. There were no wheeled vehicles to be seen, all traffic being by sledges which glided noiselessly over the snow, the horses' bells tinkling merrily as they trotted swiftly through the streets.

There were very few trees to be seen, and the country is mountainous to the east and flat to the west. The population is entirely of Turkish stock, sturdy, virile and warlike.

The second day after my arrival, a captain came from the army headquarters, asking me to call on the General in command of the Eastern Turkish Army, General Kazem Karabekir Paşa. The General asked me about the new organisation of the Iranian Army, about Reza Khan, about our operations against Simko, and about relations with the Soviets and the position of the British. I answered his questions as well as I could, and asked him in my turn about the relations of the Eastern Army Command with the Soviets.

'Excellent,' he said. 'They know what we mean, and we know what they mean!'

I stayed about ten days in Erzurum and the Soviet Consul asked me to lunch, with my Iranian host and several notabilities including two or three Turkish senior officers. At the end of the meal he proposed a toast to the friendship between Soviet Russia, Turkey and Iran, 'struggling hand in hand against the Imperialism of the Great Powers'!

While in Erzurum I was told a story which illustrates that in spite of outward friendship and collaboration, the Turks were very careful to prevent any kind of subversive activities or Communist propaganda in their country.

The year before, the Soviet Government asked the Turkish authorities to allow a mission of goodwill of seven persons, some of whom were Turks and some Russians, to come to Kars, Erzurum and other Turkish towns and hold meetings emphasising the friendship between the two nations. The Soviets were at that time helping the Turks in their war effort against the Greeks, and the Turkish Government authorised the arrival of the mission. The leader of the party was a former Turkish prisoner of war who had become a Communist and stayed in Russia. They arrived at Kars by train and at a meeting arranged by the Turkish authorities, made fiery Communistic speeches, expressing the hope that after a short time Turkey would also become Communist, and join the Soviets in her struggle for World Revolution.

The Governor of Kars telegraphed this to Erzurum, and when the 'goodwill party' arrived at Erzurum by the narrow gauge railway it was met at the station by a hostile crowd who attacked the train with sticks and stones. The railway authorities told the Communists that they would certainly be killed if they tried to come out of the train, and so the train was taken to Ilica, a small station beyond Erzurum, which was at that time the terminus of the narrow gauge line built during the war by the Russian Army. From there they were conveyed under an escort of gendarmes to Trabzon, and there entrusted to the president of the syndicate of the boatmen, a tough Laze who put them on a little sailing boat in order to take them to Batum. The boat returned after an hour and it was announced that the party had been taken to its destination. The distance from Trabzon to Batum by sea is 120 miles! This was the last goodwill mission to be sent from Russia to Turkey.

After leaving Erzurum I marched towards Kop Dagi, a mountain noted for its terrible snow-storms which sometimes prevented the passage of caravans and travellers for weeks. When I arrived at a small village I was told at its foot that there was a snow-storm on the summit and that the road was impassable on account of drifts. I had to stay for three days in this village, until finally the storm subsided and a caravan going to Trabzon opened the snowed-up track with the big padded feet of the camels. It was so cold that my boots stuck to the stirrups and in spite of my warm woollen gloves, I frequently had to let go of the reins to warm my hands and we moved in a cloud of steam coming from our horses' nostrils. To the north of the pass, the weather was much milder. We reached the little town of Bayburt without further difficulty and I had to pass the night in a hotel room already occupied by five other people. Most of the hotels in provincial towns in Turkey still rent beds rather than rooms.

I crossed the main range of the Pontus (Anadolu Daglari) at the Hadrak Pass, from which a magnificent view opens on to the wooded slopes of the mountains descending towards the sea to the north and on the barren mountains covered with snow to the south. It is not unlike the passes in the Alborz mountains in Iran, where there is the same contrast, even sharper, because the Alborz are higher than the Pontus and allow less of the northern moisture to pass to the Iranian tableland, which is more arid than the Anatolian plateau. The temperature had become still milder, the snow had disappeared and conifers had given place to deciduous trees, bare at this season.

After Machka, a town built in a clearing in the forest, the road wound along a swift-flowing river, amidst magnificent forest trees, steep hills and rushing torrents and then—the sea— Thalassa, Thalassa! At this exact spot 2400 years ago this same spectacle of the blue sea, so heartening for Mediterranean men, had gladdened the eyes of Xenophon's Greeks. They thought of the Aegean. I was transported by a vision of the blue shores of the Côte d'Azur to which I was bound and by the thought of seeing my family.

In Trabzon I dismissed the camel, giving a good tip to the camelman with a letter of thanks to the kind Sardar. I did not know that the Sardar would, like many others, fall victim to the inevitable trend of history, and be swept away with vestiges of an anachronistic feudalism. I sold my three horses as well as my surplus luggage and sent back my second orderly, Ibrahim.

In Trabzon, much more than in Erzurum, one felt the impact of the events in Western Anatolia, and the elation that had followed the sweeping victory of the Nationalist army in September, which had in one day given to the Turks the mastery of what remained of the Ottoman Empire and was to constitute modern Turkey. The Sultan, who during the foreign occupation of Istanbul had tried to save his throne and dynasty by sacrificing the interests of his own nation to those of the victorious foreign powers, had to escape in a British ship, thus putting an end to the 620-year-old Ottoman monarchy. The Allies had reluctantly to accept the result of the ordeal by battle in Asia Minor, and to evacuate their posts from the Black Sea ports, even before their departure from Istanbul and the Straits which followed the Treaty of Lausanne.

Three days after my arrival, I saw the *Gül Jemal*, the finest steamship of the Turkish marine, anchoring in the roads of Trabzon for the first time since the Armistice, for until then it had been in the possession of the Allies.

I went to see the Governor who had known my father in Istanbul and he arranged passages for me and for Rustem on the return journey of *Gül Jemal* to Istanbul. I was given a first-class ticket for myself and a second-class one for Rustem, being an officer of the army of a friendly Moslem country. I learned then that Reza Khan had sent his personal A.D.C., Colonel Kopal, to Ankara with a Qoran and a sword with a golden scabbard studded with precious stones as a gift to Mustafa Kemal Pasha to congratulate him on his brilliant victory. Although Mustafa Kemal had little use for the Qoran, the gesture was much appreciated and received wide publicity in the Turkish newspapers.

The passengers had to be taken by rowing-boats to the ship as there was no quay, and Rustem never having been in a boat of any sort was so terrified of the sea that he implored me to have him tied to the bottom of the boat. However, after we boarded the *Gül Jemal* he became quite accustomed to the ship and behaved as if he had passed all his life at sea. I delivered the diplomatic bag in Inebolu to the Nationalist Government's representative. Having telegraphed my arrival to my uncle, he came to the boat and took me together with Rustem to his house at Pangalti.

Istanbul was still under Allied military occupation, but the attitude of the occupation forces towards the Moslem population and the Turkish military and civil authorities had changed very much. After the Turkish victory against the Greek Army, which had been authorised to land at Izmir (Smyrna) by the Supreme Allied Council at the instance of the Greek Prime Minister Venizelos in May 1919 and had afterwards invaded Western Anatolia, repulsing the Turks to not very far from Ankara, the Allies had not been able to prevent the Turkish Army from crossing the Dardanelles into eastern Thrace. Now Istanbul was between two Nationalist-occupied territories, its administration being gradually transferred to the Nationalist Government.

Peace negotiations had started at Lausanne, on the basis of the new situation resulting from the resurgence of the Turkish Army. The decision to evacuate Istanbul had already been taken and would be put into effect as soon as the new peace treaty should be signed; the Treaty of Sèvres, completely dismembering the Ottoman Empire, having been considered null and void by all parties.

One of the new features of life in Istanbul was the presence of many White Russian refugees. They began to arrive in Turkey in 1918, but the bulk of them came in 1920 when the Red Army invaded the Crimea and General Baron Wrangel's White Army, with many wives and children, numbering 160,000, embarked in the ships which were in readiness in Sevastopol. After they arrived in the Bosphorus, the Allied authorities not having decided what to do with them, they were left for some days on their boats packed like sardines, several women giving birth and a few people dying before they were finally allowed to disembark in Istanbul. Many of them went from there to Bulgaria and Yugoslavia, only very few finally remained in Istanbul. At the time I arrived (Christmas 1922) many Russian cafés and restaurants had been opened by refugees, and were attracting many customers among the Allied officers.

One day I went with my uncle Ali Akbar Khan to visit the Iranian Ambassador, Mofakham-ed-Dovleh. The Ambassador was a distinguished gentleman of the old school, and apparently still very much attached to the Qajar dynasty. He asked me if I would like to see Mohammad Ali Shah, who had come to Istanbul from Russia on account of the revolution. It was decided that Mofakham-ed-Dovleh would arrange an audience for me and the next day we all three drove to the residence of the ex-Shah, at Bebek, where the Ottoman Government had put at his disposal the former palace of an Egyptian prince. We were received by the minister of the ex-Shah's Court, Shahab-ed-Dovleh, who sat with us for a few minutes, then went out and re-entering the room, bowed deeply, announcing: 'His Imperial Majesty the Shahinshah'!

We rose quickly, I saluted, being in uniform, while the Ambassador and my uncle made deep bows according to Court protocol. A short, moderately fat man with a small black moustache, in a frock-coat and a Persian cap, came swiftly into the room and held out his hand to be kissed. I shook it standing at attention. The Shah sat down and motioned us to be seated. He had a kingly presence and an authoritative manner and spoke in a pleasant voice. The Ambassador introduced me as Arfa-os-Soltan, the son of Prince Arfa-ed-Dovleh, captain in the Iranian Army. The Shah immediately asked me about Iran, Azerbaijan, the operations against Simko, the Lahoty rising and Sardar Sepah, but never mentioned his sons Ahmad Shah and the Crown Prince Mohammad Hassan Mirza. I answered all his questions as best I could, and seeing him so much interested, I remembered Ahmad Shah in 1920, and how bored and apathetic he had been when I was telling him about the campaign in Mazanderan.

The Shah's questions were all to the point, and I had the impression that he was well informed about what was happening in Iran. After nearly an hour, he rose and dismissed us and Shahab-ed-Dovleh accompanied us to the door. Mohammad Ali Shah went later to Europe where he died in 1925.

I had a civilian suit and overcoat made for me, but Rustem continued proudly to wear his cavalry sergeant's uniform, and on the 31st December we took the Simplon-Orient Express to Milan, bound for Monte Carlo, and at the frontier station of Ventimiglia I fell into the arms of my father and my brother Ibrahim who had come to greet me, the latter in a flamboyant Iranian Army infantry officer's uniform. We took the train to Monaco, where I arrived after an absence of three years and two months.

My Marriage and the Diaghilef Russian Ballet

I arrived in Monaco in the middle of the Monte Carlo season. Life had returned to the pre-war standard but everything was much more expensive and there were many changes. The public was not the same. The grand dukes and German princelings had been replaced by North and South Americans. Since the war dancing and cocktail drinking had become general, jazz orchestras had replaced the tsiganes and fox-trots the waltz tunes. Dancing was no more a drawing-room entertainment, but a daily exercise in public places. The luxury was the same, but the furs and jewels of the wives and mistresses of war profiteers overshadowed those of the former aristocrats and music hall artists. These were the roaring twenties, when people who had escaped the horrors and privations of the war threw themselves without restraint into the enjoyment of the pleasures of life.

I was very happy to see my brother Ibrahim, who was now twenty-one years old and having finished Saint-Cyr and become a sergeant-major, had just been promoted sub-lieutenant of the Iranian Army. His uniform had been ordered in France, according to the descriptions which I had sent him from Tabriz and which had apparently not been quite understood either by the tailor or the hatter, so it looked more like the uniform of Lieutenant Welia from *The Merry Widow* than anything else. Having one eye weaker than the other he wore a monocle and being tall and blond was very striking in appearance. He was socially very shy, but did not show it, being highly cultured and an excellent conversationalist. He addressed me formally as Captain, saluting me in a stiff military way, clicking his heels, and the military atmosphere was further enhanced by Sergeant Rustem. My brother had friends among the French officers of the Nice Garrison and had arranged that three horses should be at our disposal whenever we wished, so he and I followed by Rustem used to ride out in our Iranian uniforms, attracting considerable attention by our exotic appearance, particularly on the Promenade des Anglais.

Some days after my arrival I met at dinner at Danishgah a very slim and attractive young woman gracefully using a folding lorgnette, whose name I did not catch at once but who was, I was told, a ballerina of the Diaghilef Russian Ballet which had lately arrived at Monte Carlo and was rehearsing for the ballet season which was to follow the operas. I fell at once under the spell of her delicate charm and I noticed that everybody else at the table was also attracted by her. We were talking French, but when I learned that she danced in the Russian Ballet I talked to her in Russian, and as she answered me so fluently in that language I thought she was a Russian. From that day, this slim ethereal creature haunted my thoughts. During the weeks which followed I met her several times, and I learned that she was really English in spite of her perfect French and Russian and that her name was Hilda Bewicke. One evening my father invited her to dinner with her mother, a delightful woman to whom I lost my heart on the spot. Afterwards we all went to the Opera.

Two or three days later Hilda invited me to dinner at her flat in Beausoleil where she was living with her mother, who was a widow. It was a perfect evening. I told her about my journey across Turkey and about life in Iran and she told me of her adventures on the Russian Front where she had served as a V.A.D. and interpreter in the hospital organised by Lady Sybil Grey and Lady Muriel Paget which had been sent to Russia from England in 1915. Of course she also talked much of the ballet and of Pavlova with whom she had been before joining Diaghilef.

The ballet season had begun then. The Russian ballets enchanted me beyond words, the music, the décor, the choreography and the dancing being all so different from what I had been accustomed to see in the Ballets of Monte Carlo. I saw *La Belle au Bois Dormant*, *Prince Igor*, *Petrouchka*, *L'Après-Midi d'un Faune*, the *Spectre de la Rose*, *Les Femmes de Bonne Humeur* and others, Hilda being soloist. She was particularly charming as one of the two Porcelain Princesses in *La Belle au Bois Dormant*. I became acquainted through Hilda with most of the members of the Ballet, particularly with Liuba Chernisheva and her husband Grigorief, who was the regisseur. They were great friends of Hilda's and I liked them both for their Russian warmth and frankness. I was by now head over heels in love with her and had decided to ask her to marry me which I did over a *tête-à-tête* dinner and she said that she would. We returned in silence to Beausoleil after which I wandered for two hours in the empty streets gazing at the stars and the dark sea, my thoughts in a tumult and longing to tell my parents what had happened.

The next day was one of triumph! My father, my step-mother, my brother and my sister Fatimeh (who was then seventeen) congratulated me warmly and my mother, to whom I had telegraphed the news, sent me a cable. Meanwhile, Hilda had told Grigorief of her engagement and he had informed Diaghilef, who was far from pleased at the idea of losing one of his outstanding artists and summoned her to the Hôtel de Paris to discuss the situation. I occupied a table in the hall of the hotel in order to observe them. Hilda did not see me, but Diaghilef did and looked annoyed. He was a man of overpowering personality and very handsome, in manner a typical Russian aristocrat. He talked to her for nearly an hour with great persuasiveness as I could judge by his gestures from where I sat, anxiously awaiting the result of the interview. Finally they left together and when I saw her later that day she told me that in spite of all the arguments he had used she had told him that her decision was irrevocable, but that he had persuaded her to finish the season at Monte Carlo and to go with the Company to Lyons and to Montreux. I decided to go with her to Lyons and that from there we would go to Berne where we could be married at the Iranian Legation and then go to Montreux and Paris together.

Meanwhile the ballet performances continued and I now saw them more often from the wings than from the front of the house. At the end of May the Company left for Lyons where they were to give one performance and I travelled with them. From Lyons we went to Berne where we were married on 1st June. We then rejoined the Company at Montreux, and left after a few days for Paris where we took rooms in a little hotel close to the Opera. I had never been to the Paris Opera House and was to see it for the first time from an unexpected angle. We used to enter by the *Entrée des Artistes* and would often lose ourselves in the innumerable passages and staircases of that huge building. I knew most of the members of the Company: Nemchinova, Miassin, Idzikowski, Woijzekowski, Chernisheva, Sokolova, Khokhlova (afterwards Madame Picasso) and many others. I was thrilled to meet Stravinski and to hear him play the piano himself as I did once at a rehearsal and to watch Ansermet conducting. I had a tremendous admiration for Diaghilef whose creative genius, vast artistic culture, organising ability and gift for handling people were without parallel and were all exercised with the easy nonchalance of a grand seigneur. Grigorief was the ideal regisseur and administrative manager, completely devoted to the Great Man, and organising the material side of things including the transport of the Company and their accommodation in a most efficient way, with a minimum of knowledge of foreign languages.

After leaving Paris we went to London, where we were to stay with Hilda's aunt at Vale House in Chelsea. Hilda's uncle and aunt treated me at once as a nephew so that I felt at home immediately and became very fond of them. Their butler Hunt had been with them for thirty years and Charlotte, his wife who was the house parlour maid for twenty-five, whilst Mrs. Young the cook was looked upon as a newcomer, having only been there for ten years. In this house I took a great liking to English family life as it was then, a mixture of ease and formality: altogether the three months I passed there with Hilda were among the happiest in my life. I came to know many of Hilda's friends, among them Vera and Harold Bowen, Marie Rambert whom we called Mim (now Dame Marie Rambert), Teddy and Florrie Grenfell (now Lady St. Just), Muriel Gore and many members of her large family. But my leave of absence, already prolonged by six months, would soon be over and as I wished to spend a month with my mother in Geneva before returning to Iran, it was time to go. However, by great luck, just before the day of our departure I received an order from Teheran to join a Military Mission which was coming to Paris with some sixty officers who were to be attached to various French military schools to perfect their studies there. I had been attached to Saumur to follow the senior course. This was grand news and we flew to Paris so that I might present myself at the Hôtel d'Iéna, the headquarters of the Mission, whose chief was General Jahanbani. I was to accompany him on manœuvres, and having received permission to take

Hilda with us we left for Montélimar, where we were all billeted in an enormous old house with suites of rooms filled with old furniture which had belonged to Diane de Poitiers, the mistress of Henri II. The climate and geographical frontier between the Midi and the rest of France passes between Orange and Valence which lent great interest to these manœuvres. Several high-ranking Generals arrived from Paris for the final critique, amongst them Maréchal Pétain, and after the official commentary was over, General Jahanbani, noticing that Maréchal Pétain and Général Guillaumat were talking together, told me to try and hear what they were saying, as the opinions of two such high authorities would be of great interest. Accordingly I approached to hear Pétain say, 'Oh, so it was you who pinched that little brunette from me in Oran', which strategical information I imparted to my General to his great amusement.

After the manœuvres we were able to spend three weeks in Geneva before returning to Paris. We visited many military factories in the neighbourhood of Paris and at Creuzot (in the Seine-et-Loire) as we were to buy tanks, armoured cars, planes and caterpillars, and after completing these purchases we went to London where we ordered four Vickers-Armstrong armoured cars and were invited by the British Navy to visit the naval installations in Portsmouth including a torpedo launching school.

We were met at the station by a guard of honour mounted by a naval unit, and a captain who took us to the Admiral's headquarters. Vice-Admiral Freemantle received us and we were shown the school, and afterwards went on board a battleship where Vice-Admiral Goodenough entertained us for luncheon after showing us the ship. During the lunch, one of the officers of the ship who was sitting next to me told me that his wife had a friend who had married an Iranian. I asked him what her name was. 'Hilda Bewicke,' said he.

At the end of October, Rustem arrived from Monaco to be with us at Saumur where I was to take the senior course at the Cavalry School. Before leaving Paris I took him to the top of the Eiffel Tower and showed him the panorama of Paris with all its palaces, churches and monuments at our feet. I asked him what he thought of it. 'Not bad,' said this peasant from Avaj, determined not to be impressed.

In Saumur we rented a seventeenth-century house in a large

garden which included a big Canadian pine tree. Hilda was with child, and her mother came from England to stay with us, and after the birth of our daughter, whom we called Leila, both my mother and my father visited us there. Saumur is in a traditionally royalist region and our cook Marie was a staunch believer in the old regime and used to read *L'Action Française* every day from cover to cover. She was seventy years old and nearly six feet tall, and for some unknown reason always wore a hat, even in the house. There were of course many accidents with horses at Saumur and for this reason the town boasted two 'Boucheries Chevalines' where the meat was considerably cheaper than elsewhere, and it was Marie's ambition to feed Rustem and my French orderly on this meat without their realising it. 'For,' she would say, 'how can the masters make both ends meet if the Hall makes a God of its stomach?' One day, I remember, she burnt her hand rather badly but refused to take any notice of it, saying that it was nothing compared with what awaited her in Purgatory. She was enchanted by my father's title of Prince and after his visit our little daughter was always spoken of by her as '*Mademoiselle la Princesse*'.

My French orderly, who was a very simple peasant from Central France, was completely enslaved by Rustem to whom he accorded the title of *Maréchal des logis* and whose boots he cleaned. Rustem used to bring my horses to and from the school, and as he was an excellent horseman he enjoyed considerable prestige with the soldiers. Life at the school was hard and I shall never forget the cold at 6.30 in the morning. The instructors formed a group known as the *Cadre Noir* on account of their black uniforms, and all were superb horsemen.

Towards the end of the course at Saumur we moved into camp at Coëtquidan in Brittany where the Military Academy of St.-Cyr was to be transferred after the Second World War, its original home near Paris having been destroyed by American bombers during the German occupation. We were there for nearly a month, returning to Saumur on horseback in parties of five, looking after our horses ourselves and covering the 100 miles by road in about forty hours. While at Saumur I had been distressed to hear that there was a movement towards a proclamation of a Republic in Iran. I learnt afterwards that Reza Khan had become Prime Minister in October 1923 after Qavam os Saltaneh had been compromised in an attempt on the life of the Sardar, when an armed Armenian in the disguise of a woman had been caught in his apartment acting supposedly at Qavam's instigation. Ahmad Shah, who had gone to Paris in November 1923, was so annoyed at the political trend in the country and especially that his brother, Mohammad Hassan Mirza, was intriguing against him that he refused to return to Iran notwithstanding the telegrams pressing him to do so sent by Reza Khan and the Speaker of the Majles, Motamen ol Molk. It was only after much hesitation that he reached this decision having at one moment actually sent his luggage, his cars and his suite as far as Marseilles.

It was then that a strong agitation started in Iran against the absentee monarch among certain classes, and especially among the military, and the proclamation of a republic was contemplated. The clergy and the majority of the population were against the republic and demonstrated in the streets and even sought support from (of all places) the Soviet Embassy. The Soviets, wary after their Turkish experience, considered that a weak reactionary monarchy would better suit their interests than a progressive republic under strong leadership, and then showed sympathy with the monarchists. The demonstrators gathered in front of the Majles, which was in session, and as the military tried to disperse the crowd, missiles were thrown at them. The Majles showed itself opposed to the republic, and Reza Khan resigned and retired to Rudehen, a village some 30 miles to the east of Teheran. The Generals commanding the provincial divisions threatened to march on Teheran to bring him back and a group of deputies and other notabilities went to Rudehen to persuade him to resume the Premiership. He accepted and declared himself against the adoption of a republican regime, to the great satisfaction of the people and to my great relief.

Having finished my course at Saumur, we went to Paris, and finally to Geneva, where my father was representing Iran at the League of Nations, and we were able to assist at many of the meetings. My father asked me to leave Rustem with him in Monaco, as he would like to have an Iranian servant with him, and Rustem being willing to stay, I left him there.

Early in October we took leave of our relatives, who were all in Geneva, and left by train for Venice, Hilda, Leila, Nanny and

I, and after a few all too brief hours there took an Italian boat to Beyruth. It was a marvellous journey, which lasted seventeen days. A week and more than a thousand miles still separated us from Teheran by road and no road, as our way lay across the Syrian desert which had been crossed only occasionally by car. There was no road in the desert, but the sand was so firm that we were able to travel at 90 miles an hour over its vast solitude, which was broken only once by the passing of some Shammar tribesmen with their flocks of sheep and camels moving towards the south.

There is a narrow-gauge railway running between Baghdad and Khanaqin some 20 miles from the frontier and we decided to use it as we thought a rest from the road would be good both for ourselves and the car. In Khanaqin, a little town surrounded by date groves, we took to our car once more and drove on towards Iran. A high, continuous chain of mountains formed the horizon to the east. This was the Zagros beyond which lay, concealed, the Iranian plateau, though always invisible as the car sped over the plain. Suddenly behind some low hills appeared the Iraqi frontier post and beyond it an Iranian sentry on duty and the Iranian flag flying. I changed into uniform in the frontier guard's hut, and here I was an Iranian captain in my own country again.

Campaign in the Turkoman Steppe

We drove from the frontier past the little town of Kasr-e-Shirin where we saw the last date-palms before climbing the steep and winding Pa-e-Taq pass. Looking back, we could see the immensity of Iraq's plains, whilst Iran lay in front of us. We met the Iranian plateau climate and vegetation at Kerend, where the poplars, willows and chenars, adobe houses, little open shops on the corners of the streets and a much calmer and more silent population showed that we had left Arab Iraq behind and were in Iran. We had to cross three defiles, three abrupt mountain chains looking like man-made walls, which barred the plain from north to south, but fortunately reached Bissetun, which is near Kermanshah, while it was still light. Here are the famous trilingual inscriptions cut by Darius on the face of an apparently inaccessible rock and which testify to the greatness of Iran in the past and fill Iranians with hope for its renewal in the future. That night we reached Hamadan and the following night we entered Teheran through the same Qazvin Gate I had been ordered to defend three and a half years earlier. A long drive through half-empty streets brought us to our garden where we were met by our Zoroastrian gardener, Bahram, and his wife (both in traditional Zoroastrian dress) and by Fatollah, Rustem's cousin who had been left in charge of Arfaieh when I left for Azerbaijan. Almost four years had elapsed since anything had been heard of the masters and Fatollah had peopled the various pavilions in the garden with a miscellaneous collection of relatives from his village. He was clad in a long brilliant blue coat with shining brass buttons and had grown a moustache in keeping with his new social standing.

It was very hot and Hilda innocently asked for some water, but her education in how to live in Iran (as it was in those days) was to begin at once, for when the glass of water arrived it contained a number of little red wriggling worms, and when she expressed her horror and disgust at the sight Bahram calmly said that perhaps there were not enough fish in the tank! The garden, however, more than came up to her expectations, covering as it did some six acres and containing a fair number of well-grown trees and a large swimming-pool, and I must say that Hilda dealt with the situation with considerable courage. Fatollah and his suite were dismissed with thanks, a woman servant and an orderly procured and some sort of organisation set up.

I reported to the Chief of Staff, General Jahanbani, who greeted me warmly and after a few days appointed me liaison officer between the General Staff and the Military Attachés in Teheran as well as with our Attachés abroad. Among them were Lieutenant-Colonel (now Major-General retired) W. A. K. Fraser, the British Military Attaché, and Captain René Bertrand (now Général de C.A., retired), with both of whom my friendship has endured until today.

After I left Azerbaijan and during the two years I was abroad, the policy of disarming the unruly tribes and reasserting the Central Government's control over them had been pursued all over the country, with variable success.

Reza Khan's most important objective after the pacification of Azerbaijan was the establishment of Government control in Khuzestan and the Bakhtiari country, where oil was being prospected and where foreign influence was still paramount and wary of any encroachment from the north of the mountains. He knew that the A.P.O.C., and that meant the British Government which owned the majority of the shares, was giving its moral support to Sheikh Khazal of Mohammerah and to the Bakhtiari tribal chiefs, considering that it was easier to deal with them than with an independent-minded Central Government which might conceivably fall under the influence of an unfriendly Russia, and he wanted to finish once and for all with this anomalous situation.

The quickest route to Khuzestan lay through Isfahan by what was called the Lynch road, which was really a rough track not suitable for wheeled traffic, but with a bridged passage over the unfordable Karun river. The track from Soltanabad, Khorramabad and Dezful passed through the region inhabited by the wild tribes of Lorestan and it was considered too difficult to send the necessary forces to pacify these tribes.

In 1923, then, a column started from Isfahan. The Bakhtiari chiefs did not give the impression of being hostile, but nevertheless, when the column entered the rugged Bakhtiari mountain gorges, it was ambushed and lost upwards of 100 men, the remainder of the forces retreating towards Isfahan. Reza Khan was as persevering as he was unshakable in his decisions, and undiscouraged, he then undertook the pacification of Lorestan as a preliminary to the penetration of Khuzestan. He concentrated forces in Harsin on the Kermanshah-Hamadan road and in Borujerd and by a concentric movement, after forcing the mountain passes, the Government forces occupied the plain of Khorramabad and dispersing the hostile Lors, reached the Northern Khuzestan plain at Dezful.

Early in 1924, after having disarmed Sardar Moazzez, chief of the Shadlu Kurdish tribe and hereditary Governor of Bojnurd, and having established the Central Government's control in that region, a military column some 300 strong from the Mashad Division had started from Bojnurd in Western Khorasan and marched into the Turkoman Steppe. Here they were joined by some 200 Koklan mounted irregulars who were to help to pacify the unruly Yomuts, with whom the Koklans were supposed to be on bad terms. The Colonel made the mistake of dividing his force into two columns, the northern one progressing along the Atrek towards Maraveh Tappeh, while the southern with himself moved 20 miles to the south through the wooded hills of the upper reaches of the Gorgan river. The two columns were simultaneously attacked by the Yomuts, the Koklans went over to their Turkoman kin in the middle of the fight, and nearly 100 soldiers were killed while another 100 were taken prisoner. The Colonel escaped with a third of his force to tell the tale, and the prisoners were sold as slaves in the slave-market of Karim Ishan.

Reza Khan was never rash. He had decided to finish with Khuzestan and he did not divert any forces against the Turkomans, the army together with the Gendarmerie numbering then only about 40,000 men in all. He sent an officer to negotiate the buying back of the prisoners through the intermediary of those Koklan chiefs who had not been compromised in this affair. The Yomuts agreed to sell them at a good price, together with two machine-guns which had fallen into their hands, but kept the rifles and the horses.

In pursuance of his plans for Khuzestan in the beginning of the autumn of 1924 Reza Khan concentrated two army groups on the borders of that province ready to advance as soon as they received orders—the northern group around Dezful under General Ahmadi and the southern in the Behbehan region under General Zahedi. To begin with, General Zahedi's force attacked and defeated a Bakhtiari force led by Amir Mojahed, who had allied himself with Sheikh Khazal after the latter had denounced Reza Khan's Government in a proclamation inciting the tribes to revolt in favour of the Qajar dynasty, and after Zahedi had occupied Behbehan and Cham-e-Zeydun the other Bakhtiari chiefs were cowed into submission.

My brother Ibrahim was at that time in Bushehr, where he was supervising the unloading of the military material we had bought in France and Great Britain and its transport by the Bushehr-Shiraz-Isfahan road to Teheran, most of the way by pack animals. This difficult route had been adopted because when this war material was about to be sent by boat to Basra, to be taken from there by river steamers and railway through Baghdad and Khanaqin and then through Kermanshah, Hamadan and Qazvin by road to Teheran, the Iraqi Government, then under Great Britain's mandate, had refused to allow our armament to pass, invoking the provisions of a treaty signed in 1920 in Saint Germain. According to this treaty the arms traffic and transport in the Red Sea, the Arabian Sea and the Persian Gulf was to be subject to the control of the Great Powers victorious in the World War: Great Britain, France and Italy reminding Iran that an authorisation had to be obtained for the transport of our arms. When our Government claimed that Iran was not bound by this agreement, the Foreign Office produced the signature of Prince Firuz accepting this treaty on behalf of Iran. However, the Iranian Government, acting through my father who was then at the League of Nations, rejected the validity of this signature as binding on Iran as the Majles had not ratified the treaty.

My brother had also been instructed to look into the question of the help given by the A.P.O.C. to Sheikh Khazal, and he discovered that cases with rifles and ammunition had been conveyed to the Sheikh in the Company's barges. This was reported by him to the General Staff.

After the preliminary operations in the north and south-east of Khuzestan had been concluded, Sardar Sepah came in person to the front, and ordered a general offensive. The Arab tribesmen were no match for the organised Government forces, and the tribesmen themselves were in many cases dissatisfied with the arbitrary rule of Sheikh Khazal and many of them offered their submission and returned to their villages and camping grounds. The Sheikh hoped to receive help from the British because of a document signed by Sir Percy Cox, but the British authorities explained to him the uselessness of this and he had no alternative but to surrender and ask for pardon (17th December 1924). He was sent to Teheran and rented a house there, being free to move about in Teheran and its environs, but not to go further than 20 miles from the town. Later, his estates in Khuzestan were confiscated, but given back to his heirs after the Second World War.

After the liquidation of the Khuzestan question and the establishment of complete Government control over that province, Reza Khan was shown the oil installations by the A.P.O.C. staff. He then went to Iraq to visit the holy Shia shrines of Najaf and Karbala—where Imam Ali, the fourth Khalif, cousin and son-in-law of the Prophet, and Imam Hoseyn, Imam Ali's second son, are buried. He thus dispelled the rumours spread by his enemies that he was irreligious or a Bahai. From there he returned in triumph, being met at the little village of Mehrabed a few miles from Teheran, by Ministers, deputies, notabilities and a great concourse of people of all classes. I was in charge of the military attachés (British, French, Russian and Turkish) and presented them to the Sardar, whom they complimented on his return.

The Majles then nominated him Head of all the Armed Forces of Iran, thus conferring on him a prerogative belonging to the Shah. Contrary to what some people expected, after he became Prime Minister Reza Khan did not show any less interest in the affairs of the army, all the details of the service being referred to him. Two days after his arrival at Teheran, considering that officers with a foreign military education would be more useful in the units, he ordered me to be transferred from the Staff to the Teheran Cavalry Brigade, where I received the command of the 3rd squadron of the Sangin Aslaheh cavalry regiment.

At the end of March 1925, after three years of continuous

attacks by the Yomut Turkomans on the non-Turkoman villages of the neighbourhood of Asterabad, chiefly due to the provocations and intrigues of the Mazanderan chief Emir Mokarram and of his sons (who were later caught and shot by the Government), a general offensive of all the Turkoman Yomuts and Koklans started on the borders of the entire Turkoman region, from the Caspian Sea to the neighbourhood of Bojnurd. This time it was said to be due to Soviet provocation, and that arms and ammunition were being supplied to them from across the frontier.

Sardar Moazzez, the Khan of Bojnurd, was arrested with a few of his followers and taken to Mashad and his tribe revolted and joined the Turkoman Koklans. Their combined forces repulsed a detachment of the 5th Division, comprising an infantry battalion and a cavalry squadron, inside Bojnurd and surrounded the town. This was completely isolated from the rest of the country, the telegraph line being cut by the rebels.

In the south, a party of Yomuts 2000 strong crossed the mountains and looted the villages around Bastam, near Shahrud, some of them pushing as far as Abbasabad, on the Shahrud-Sabzevar road. At the same time, Ja'far Bay Turkomans in their long boats, attacked and looted villages on the Gorgan bay, near Ashraf. Certainly, reactionary elements, probably influenced by foreign interests hostile to the establishment of a strong central government, were behind all these tribal risings, but their synchronisation which would have rendered them successful was not possible. This was on account of the distance between the different tribal regions of Iran, the dissimilitude of interests and consequent rivalry of the chiefs, the independence and indiscipline of the sub-tribes and clans, the lack of interest of the tribesmen in any kind of enterprise the direct object of which was not rapine, loot and robbery and of the fact that in all these regions a counter activity of the military elements completely obedient to the Head of the Army was, if not preventing, at least retarding the occurrence of rebellions.

Reza Khan had an unusual power of grasping the most complicated political situations and of making his moves at the appropriate time without disclosing his intentions until the last moment. He knew what he wanted, and never allowed himself to be thwarted by secondary considerations or by a reluctance to hurt the vested interests of foreign powers. He was convinced that any real progress in Iran would be impossible as long as foreign intervention continued and he therefore decided to eradicate all foreign influence in Iran. He knew that the tribes had frequently been used as the instruments of foreign pressure on the Central Government. Whenever the Government was reluctant to accept any suggestion, a little advice and encouragement from the interested powers was enough to bring about a tribal disturbance, which until the advent of Reza Khan the Government had been unable to suppress, but which would subside as soon as the Government yielded to the demands in question. For this reason—as well as for many others—he decided to suppress this lever so often used by foreign powers in the past, not only by disarming the tribes, but by suppressing little by little the tribal system, with its subservience to all-powerful chiefs, and to take them under the complete control of Teheran.

Azerbaijan had been completely rid of the troublesome elements who had held sway in that province. After the defeat of Simko—who was eventually killed when he returned to Iran—Amir Ashair Khalkhali had been caught and hanged, as well as Bahador-os-Saltaneh Afshar. The Shahsevans had also been attacked, defeated and forced to make their submission. Khuzestan too had been brought under the control of the army and it was now the turn of the Turkomans.

In the middle of May 1925 the crack Pahlavi Guards Infantry Regiment (of Shakar Yazi fame), under Colonel Puladin, was ordered to Bojnurd, and after a march of three weeks reached that town, driving the rebels towards Bedranlu, a village to the west. I had been promoted Major and put in command of the 1st group of my regiment and on the 31st May I started with 210 officers and men towards Bojnurd. I was sorry to leave my wife and small child alone in a strange country, but I had to go and as soon as I started I felt the lure of the desert with the blue mountains far away on the horizon, the scorching sun, the green poplars by the villages and the dark starlit nights in the boundless steppes.

My wife and my Colonel accompanied me as far as a little village called Tonbakui, where we passed the night, and in the morning our column moved towards fighting and adventure, towards Central Asia and the yellow-skinned, narrow-eyed descendants of the warriors of Chengiz Khan and Teimur Lang. For centuries this race had threatened the borders of Iran and many times had overrun the entire country, leaving desolation behind them—'They came, they killed, they burned, they went' —in the words of the Iranian historian, and we were now about to open yet another phase in the classic struggle between Iran and Turan immortalised a thousand years ago by Firdausi in his *Shahname*.

We remained three days in Semnan, a town on the fringe of the desert, marching from there to Damghan, also a desert city, passing a night at Ahuan, meaning 'the gazelles', a sanctuary for those animals. There is a legend that a gazelle wounded by a hunter took refuge with Imam Reza who saved its life and ordered that no one should hunt gazelles in this neighbourhood. The local population respect this order of the Imam's to this day.

Shahrud, where we stayed five days, was an important communication centre, the Teheran road continuing towards Mashad and two tracks leaving it, one to Bojnurd and the U.S.S.R. frontier, the other to Gorgan (now a good road has been built through Khosh Yaylaq to Gonbad-e-Kavus). After we left Damghan we were in a region subjected to Turkoman raids and I had to take precautions in earnest.

We passed Bastam, which two months before had been the scene of the biggest raid by the Turkomans during this century, and passing through Jajarm and Sankhas reached the little village of Tahar at the foot of the Ala Dagh, not far from our destination, which was Bojnurd. The next day we had to cross this mountain pass which was, according to our information, occupied by the hostile Shadlu tribe. I had made my preparations and sent outposts to occupy some hills commanding our next day's march, when I received an order from Bojnurd. This ordered me to return to the Jajarm-Sankhas region to watch the mountain passes leading from the north-west to the Esfarayen plain and to protect the villages of this plain against Turkoman raids. I was disappointed as I had been looking forward to taking part in the fighting which was going on in the vicinity, but recalling my outposts I went back to Jajarm. I was met on the outskirts by an elderly man accompanied by several armed horsemen. He was the Khan of Nardin, a mountainous district comprising a dozen villages, situated between the Turkoman steppe and Jajarm, who had come with a hundred horsemen of his Teimuri (Turki) tribe to put himself at my disposal for operations against the Turkomans. The Nardinis used to be the vassals of Sardar Moazzez, but were now with the Government. We decided that he would guard the Jajarm-Nardin pass, whilst I would go to Sankhas to guard the more eastern mountain passes from which the Turkomans raided the plain and the Teheran-Mashad road. I detached three patrols in order to observe these passes.

After I had been three days in Sankhas, I received a report from one of my patrols that a raiding party of some 200 Turkomans had crossed a pass and penetrated into the plain, and that they were following it at a distance. I marched at once with my group to the south-west, trotting and even galloping at times, but when I reached the place indicated by my patrol, the lieutenant in command reported that the Turkomans had already looted two villages, taking some thirty prisoners and escaping by the same mountain pass.

On the 6th July I was ordered to resume my march towards Bojnurd by the Cheharburjak route, climbing the steep sides of Ala Dagh and then descending into a green valley at Besh Kardash, where I camped near a pond full of enormous carp which were considered taboo and allowed to reach a great age. On the 8th we entered Bojnurd, a pleasant town in a green plain bordered by hills to the south. Colonel Mahmud Khan Puladin, the commander of the Pahlavi Infantry Regiment, was in command of the field forces. After two days the regiment attacked the village of Bedranlu in the hills west of Bojnurd, which was fiercely defended by the Shadlu Kurds, and occupied it the same evening, the Shadlu fleeing towards the valley of Samalqan, one stage to the west. I was sent to pursue them and after overtaking the Pahlavi Regiment and without halting at Bedranlu, pushed forward towards Kerriq, the first village of the Samalqan valley which after some fighting we forced the Kurds to evacuate. We then occupied the village of Ashkhane and pursued the Kurds for a few more miles to the village of Biar which dominated the valley. A few days later General Jan Mohammad Khan, commander of the 5th Division, came to the Samalqan valley and stayed for a couple of days. It was decided that this valley should be occupied jointly by the Pahlavi Infantry Regiment and by me until the awaited reinforcements should arrive from Teheran, when a forward drive would be started.

Contrary to my expectations that the whole campaign would be over in a few weeks, we remained for more than five months in that valley. I spent my time in training the squadrons, making excursions in and around the valley, surveying the region and reading the books which I had brought with me about the Turkomans and the Khorasan province. I once had an unpleasant experience. I was sitting alone in the garden in front of the house where I was billeted, having dinner attended by my orderly, Hoseyn Aqa; suddenly there was the report of a rifle shot and a bullet whizzed past my head. I upset the candle on the table and was plunged in darkness, but no second shot was fired. We never discovered the origin of the shot nor the purpose of my would-be murderer.

There were then no railways and very few roads of any sort in Iran and consequently no motor transport. All the forces had to be moved on foot from Khuzestan, a distance of more than 1000 miles, and part of them kept for a time in that region and in Lorestan to supervise the disarmament of the tribes. It was for this reason that the operations were so protracted.

In October the northern brigade was reinforced and in this way the western column with nearly 4000 men started its offensive towards the east in the direction of Gonbad-e-Kavus. The eastern column concentrated at Samalqan was also reinforced from Teheran and numbered 2000 men. A camel corps of 180 men coming from Sistan joined us later.

The pincers movement began in this way both from the east and from the west. We started from the line Biar-Ashkhaneh and after a day's march reached the westernmost villages of the Samalqan valley, peopled by Berberis as the Hazara who emigrated from Afghanistan after the eighties were called in Iran. The Hazara are a Mongol tribe, which had settled in the central part of Afghanistan in the early thirteenth century. They are Shia and speak Persian. On account of their religion, the Afghans being Sunni, they had been subjected to persecution during the reign of the Amir Abdur Rahman (1880–1901) and many of them had emigrated to Iran and India. They are very religious and hardworking and also make excellent farmers. We spent three days in Qal'e Khan and then moved towards Incheh, the first Koklan Turkoman camping place on our line of advance. It was deserted. From there we climbed the slopes of a high mountain named Goli Dagh, under torrential rain. I was shivering with cold as I had not brought any winter clothes with me, and had nothing but my military blouse and a shirt beneath it, these being soaked. Dead tired, we had to pitch our camp in the mud and it was well after midnight before we could go to bed, I in my little canvas tent bought in Geneva and which was quite waterproof.

The next day we realised that during our climb on the hill we had left the barren inner plateau and reached the green Caspian region, covered with trees and thick undergrowth. Unfortunately having caught cold and shivering with fever I had to stay in bed, my orderly Hoseyn Aqa looking after me. I was wondering how I would be able to get on without winter clothes and even a greatcoat in this cold November, when Hoseyn Aqa told me that a soldier had left a big trunk at the entrance to my tent, saying that it was for me. The trunk had been sent by Hilda with exactly everything I needed most! There were warm uniforms, shirts, woollen undergarments, a greatcoat, a waterproof coat, woollen gloves and socks and many tins with porridge, cocoa, chocolate and biscuits. It was not even locked, but nothing was missing in spite of two weeks' journey on muleback. After putting on most of the warm clothes I invited my fellow officers to share the other items and felt glad I was a married man.

After two days, General Jan Mohammad Khan, the commander of the column, arrived at the camp and summoned me to his tent. I was still very feverish, but dressed promptly and presented myself to him. The General told me that two squadrons of the Bahrami Regiment under Major Daud Khan, which had been sent towards Qarnaveh, had been stopped and surrounded on three sides by Turkomans. He ordered me to march to his rescue with my group, repulse the Turkomans, and after taking command of the whole force occupy the heights in order to protect the advance of the column towards Pish Kamar, a big Turkoman settlement at the point where the mountain slopes merge into the Turkoman steppe, which extends beyond the Soviet frontiers to the Balkhan hills east of the Caspian.*

* It may be noted that the Balkan chain in the Balkan peninsula was so named after their native Balkhans by Kipchak—Petcheneg—and other Turkomans who had invaded that peninsula, coming from Central Asia.

I ordered our tents and stores to be loaded on mules, and the horses to be saddled. After two and a half hours' march I heard firing from the west, and galloped forward to see what was happening. From a hill dominating the whole landscape I saw a circular plain bordered by hills, much lower than the one I was on. The dismounted Bahrami squadrons were occupying the slopes of the hills jutting out from the one I had reached, and the hills in front were held by Turkomans who had intercepted Daud Khan's progress towards Pish Kamar. I made contact with him, re-assembled my squadrons and executed an enveloping manœuvre in mounted order from the north, galloping on the crest of the hills and behind them in open formation.

The sight of fast-moving mounted men on their left flank and rear, with the Bahrami squadrons intensifying their fire from the front, produced the desired effect. The Turkomans mounted their swift horses and disappeared towards the west and north, leaving a few dead and taking away the wounded on their horses. We pursued them and took half a dozen prisoners.

We learned then that after a stiff resistance from the Yomut Turkomans, between Aq Qal'e and Gonbad-e-Kavus and near Qumush Tappeh, which cost us about forty cavalrymen killed in a mounted attack, the western column under Zahedi had entered Gonbad. The Koklans submitted, but the Yomuts, abandoning the foothills, dispersed in the wide plain between the Gorgan and the Atrak, taking their round tents and families with them. General Jan Mohammad Khan decided to pursue them up to the Soviet frontier, and in order to do so organised a mobile column consisting of my squadrons, four irregular groups of local Khorasani tribesmen about 100 men each—one of Zaferanlu Kurds, one of Darreh Gaz Turks, one of Hazara (Mongols) from the Afghan frontier and one of Shadlu Kurds who had passed to the Government—an infantry company, a machine-gun company and a mountain gun. I was put in command of this force of 1000 men with orders to sweep the whole plain and to force the Turkomans to surrender or to push them across the frontier.

I moved to the north, and next day arrived at Karim Ishan. This consisted of one two-storey building which was used as a Qoranic school and meeting-place of the chiefs of the different tribes, where decisions about raids were taken and booty divided and prisoners sold as slaves when the raids were successful. It was the only building in the whole steppe, the Turkomans' settlements consisting of several scores or hundreds, according to their importance, of round tents built with light reed folding frames and covered outside with black felts and inside with coloured felts or, in the case of the well-to-do, with Turkoman red and black or white and red carpets (wrongly known abroad as Bukhara). These tents were loaded on camels and a camp could disappear overnight into the boundless steppe. The tents were of different sizes but from twenty to fifty persons could shelter in one of them.

It was at Pish Kamar that we saw the first settlement of Turkomans; before that they had completely evacuated the region we were occupying. They had Mongolian features with scanty beards, shaven under the mouth and with clean-shaven skulls. They all wore knee-length red tunics with leather belts, high boots and black sheepskin caps. The women were clad in long, straight red or purple tunics with long sleeves and were never veiled. All the housework and even the work in the fields was done by women, the men, while not raiding, just sitting in front of their tents—alajiks—and drinking innumerable cups of tea.

According to history they showed great courage while fighting the Russians in Transcaspia in the seventies, but fighting with us they showed only cruelty and were not to be compared as fighting men with Simko's Kurds, the Shahsevans or the Lors. In order to frighten their enemies they used to cut off the heads of those they had killed and breaking up the bones of the skull, stuff the skins with straw, producing in this way a kind of grotesque balloon and they would mount these ghastly objects on sticks in front of their tents as war trophies.

In Karim Ishan I was joined by the Camel Corps and decided to comb the steppe with several parallel columns supported by a reserve in order to push right to the Soviet frontier, the columns then reassembling to the north of the Atrak river.

After so many nights under my tent I was glad to be able to sleep in a room and ordered my camp bed to be brought there, together with that of my adjutant. The window was open and having undressed, we went to sleep. Suddenly we were awakened by a frightful noise, bullets pouring right into our room through the window. We threw ourselves on the floor and scrambled down the steps to the opposite side of the house. The shots were fired from a little hill some 200 yards away. We brought a machine-gun on to the roof and fired two score rounds of ammunition, while a patrol was searching the hillside. The firing ceased as suddenly as it had begun. Nobody was found and nobody hit in this affray.

From Karim Ishan I sent the Camel Corps across the steppe to Chat-e-Atrak, on the frontier, where the Atrak river coming from Iran meets the Chandir flowing from Soviet Transcaspia. I moved with the rest of the column across the Gekcheh Dagh to the Qarnaveh Pass—just to the west of the scene of my first fight a few days ago. From that pass a magnificent view extended over the plain below, the Atrak valley, the camp of Maraveh-Tappeh and the frontier chain of the Sonki Dagh. I camped on the shore of the Atrak river which was fordable everywhere, at least at this season.

The infantry and machine-gun companies, the mountain gun and the Camel Corps were then taken away from me and I was left with my cavalry. I was very glad to have the opportunity of talking with the chiefs of the irregulars, inquiring about their tribes, their way of life, their genealogy, etc., all of which served me later when as Chief of Staff I completed a tribal map of the whole of Iran on the strength of which I was elected a Fellow of the Royal Geographical Society.

The chief of the Hazara was a nice young man in a sort of khaki uniform and during our evening conversations I never imagined that after a few years he would revolt against the Government and be killed while fighting. The chief of the Zaferanlu Kurds was Farajollah Khan Shoja-ed-Dovleh, a pleasant man who knew many good stories about the frontier. He came from Quchan, north-west of Mashad. The chief of the Shadlu, who used to be in the bodyguard of the rebel Sardar Moazzez, kept himself to himself and did not join us in the evenings, as also the chief of the Darreh Gaz.

The Turkomans were assembled between the Atrak and the Sonki Dagh on the slopes of this mountain, and I received the order to cross the river and clean up the southern side of the hills as far as the frontier. The morale of the soldiers was good and firing and cheering they progressed among the boulders. The

Turkomans, their backs to the Soviet frontier, had lost hope of withstanding us, as they had never thought it possible that the Government would be able to concentrate such an important force against them. We joined them on the top of the ridge and after a short hand-to-hand fight, they abandoned a few camels and fled down the northern slope into Soviet territory.

We were now on the border of Soviet Turkestan, the Sonki Dagh dominating the lower hills to the north and the boundless desert of Kara Kum which extends uninterruptedly towards Siberia. The view was magnificent but awesome. Here was Turkestan—the country from which Huns, Avars, Khazars, Kipchaks and Seljuks, Chengiz Khan's Mongols, and Tamerlane's Turkomans had invaded Europe and the Middle East, leaving behind them when they retired the Ottomans in Turkey, the Tatars in Russia, the Nogais in the Caucasus and their language in Iranian Azerbaijan, before dwindling into insignificance and finally being conquered by an invasion coming this time from the west—that of the Russians.

The crest of the ridge was narrow and rocky, but I found a flat area where our camp was pitched. Unfortunately there was no water on our side and we were obliged to take the horses a hundred yards across the frontier into Russian territory, where we found a spring. The next morning, looking down the ridge into the plain, I saw countless Turkoman tents surrounded by innumerable flocks. These were the Yomuts who had fled from Iran. Now that the campaign was over and the whole Iranian part of the Turkoman steppe in the hands of the Iranian Army, it was necessary to bring back those who had fled, to disarm them, to assure them that they would not be molested, and encourage them to start life in changed conditions under a regular administration and the protection of the law and security forces. With this in view I chose an N.C.O. who spoke their dialect and sent him with a squad of six men and a trumpeter, all mounted, with a white flag into Soviet territory to talk to the Turkoman chiefs and elders, explain to them the situation and induce them to come back.

They started towards the plain, and looking from above I saw them disappear into the distance. Now followed an anxious time. Would the Turkomans attack and destroy them or the Russians arrest them? A whole day passed and the squad did not come back. The next day, looking into the misty distance, I saw a dust cloud moving in the steppe towards the foothills. It looked thicker than if produced only by our six men and I wondered what it could be. When it came nearer, I could distinguish a group of horsemen about forty strong moving in military formation. They climbed the slopes of the mountain and halting by the spring on the Soviet side of the frontier, just below the crest of the ridge, dismounted. Our squad was there with a platoon of Red Army cavalrymen, with a Russian officer and a Turkoman civilian who was the local commissar. These two came on foot towards me and we exchanged greetings in Russian. My squad (which had not been disarmed by the Russians) rejoined their unit while the Russian soldiers were looking after their horses.

I sat down with the Soviet people, and then the commissar complained that our soldiers had crossed the frontier armed and without authorisation. I retorted that their mission was to contact the Soviet authorities, and as there was no frontier post in the vicinity they had had to go some distance to do so. He said that they had been found speaking to the Turkomans and that the Soviet Government could not authorise any political agitation on its territory. I answered that they were only explaining to the Turkomans, who had passed the frontier, that they were free to come back to Iran. He said that if we had not maltreated them, the Turkomans would not have taken refuge in Soviet territory. I then asked him why more than three million Russians had left the country, preferring to take refuge abroad and live in exile rather than go back to Russia. This made him angry and he said that they were enemies of the people, and besides had acted on provocation by the Imperialist Powers.

After that, he asked my permission to talk to my soldiers. I said that the soldiers had their duties to perform, and could not spare the time to listen to him. 'May I talk to your officers, then?' he asked. I said that I did not object to that, but my officers did not understand Russian, nor any kind of Turkish dialect. Nevertheless he began to speak in Istanboli Turkish about the necessity for all freedom-loving countries to unite against imperialism as represented by Great Britain, and to resist the dark forces of reaction. He laid stress on the already important achievements of the Soviet Union in the field of socialist planning and in securing their rights to the people. I asked him to explain more clearly what he meant by this, but he preferred to talk in generalities, probably not quite knowing himself what it all meant. He spoke for nearly an hour and then, turning to one of my officers, asked him his opinion on what he had said. The officer replied that he did not understand Turkish.

The commissar appeared somewhat confused and changed the conversation, which became more casual. I asked him to tell me about the death of Enver Pasha, who had been killed in 1922 while fighting the Red forces. After a little hesitation the commissar told me that Enver Pasha, having fled from Istanbul after the occupation of that town by the Allies, had gone to Russia, where at first he was on good terms with the Bolshevik Government, planning with them a wide-scale action against British Imperialism in Asia, but that afterwards he had gone to Bokhara and joined the revolt of the Basmachi (rebels) against the Red Army, with the idea of proclaiming a Central Asian Turki Empire, on the model of Tamerlane's, with himself as emperor. He was defeated in the field, and finally surrounded by the Reds, whom he charged with a handful of followers in an effort to escape. They were all killed, Enver Pasha's corpse being found beside that of his dead horse, clutching a small Qoran in his hand. I felt sad at learning what had been the fate of the handsome young colonel I had seen in Istanbul carried in triumph on the shoulders of the enthusiastic people in December 1912. The Russian officer, unlike the Turkoman commissar, did not make any attempt at propaganda and complained bitterly of having to serve in this wilderness where he had already been four years, so far from his home in the Voronezh province of Central Russia.

The Soviet officials stayed overnight on the summit of the mountain, and then departed, warning us not to again enter Russian territory. Notwithstanding that, one of the squadrons' cooks having volunteered to try to contact the Turkomans in order to persuade them to return, I sent him alone disguised as a Turkoman on that adventurous errand. The poor fellow was caught by the Russians and sent to Askhabad, where he was detained for two years.

On the following morning not a tent was to be seen in the steppe below Sonki Dagh, the Turkomans had all been moved away from the frontier into the interior. The operations were ended and the region was divided into districts assigned to different military commanders with their units, the district of Incheh, between Maraveh Tappeh and Samalqan falling to my group. This district was practically empty of inhabitants, the Koklans who used to dwell in it having disappeared since the beginning of the operations.

It was already very cold, and the men and horses suffered from being exposed to the frost at night, so I ordered the construction of stables for the horses and barracks for the men. We carried the necessary timber from an abandoned poplar grove some six miles away and in a fortnight I was able to shelter my men and animals against cold, snow and wind. We remained there until the end of January 1926, and while there learned about the important events that had occurred during that time in Teheran.

In November Ahmad Shah had definitely refused to return to Iran and the Majles had voted his deposition and the end of the Qajar dynasty which had ruled Iran since 1794, only five deputies dissenting from the majority of 117: Hoseyn Ala, Hassan Taqizadeh, Dr. Mohammad Mosaddeq, Modarres and Seyid Ya'qub Anvar. Reza Shah was appointed provisional Chief of State until a Constituent Assembly should decide as to the succession to the throne. The Constituent Assembly had been elected and assembled in Teheran and had unanimously designated Reza Khan Sardar Sepah as Shahinshah of Iran, under the name of Reza Shah Pahlavi, the succession to the throne being vested in his family. His elder son Mohammed Reza became Valiahd (Crown Prince), and all the Imperial princes of the Pahlavi dynasty were designated as Shahpur (instead of Shahzadehs with the Qajar) and princesses as Shahdokht, thus reviving old Sassanian titles. The ex-Shah and all the first-class Qajar princes (sons of Shahs) were handsomely treated, the latter receiving stipends of about £80 gold per month.

One evening, while sitting by the open fireplace re-reading Sir Percy Sykes' *Ten Thousand Miles in Persia* for the second time, my orderly handed me an envelope that a messenger had brought from Mashad. It contained a communication which literally translated read as follows: 'Major Hassan Khan Arfa—By order of the slaves of His Imperial Majesty the Shahinshah—may our souls be sacrificed to him—you are appointed Military Attaché in London. You are requested to join your place of service as soon as possible.'

It is impossible to imagine my state of mind on receiving this document in the wilds of the Turkoman steppes where I had spent the last ten months hundreds of miles from the nearest railway or motor road. I should see my wife and my baby girl, the Vale House and my father in Monaco and my mother in Geneva. I scarcely slept that night and the next day received a second order, to make over the Incheh district to Major Safar Ali Khan, who was coming with a battalion of the Keyani regiment to replace me. My group was to march at once to Bojnurd where I was to leave it with the rest of the regiment, and to proceed by carriage to Mashed, take leave of General Jan Mohammad Khan and from there go by car to Teheran, the Mashed-Teheran road having been lately rendered passable for wheel-transport. I announced myself at divisional headquarters and afterwards went to a public bath, where I was scrubbed, soaped and massaged by an expert bath-assistant, and then to the sanctuary to perform the normal devotions. I was deeply moved to see the crowd of pilgrims who had come from every corner of the Middle East and India kissing the railings of the silver cage built around the Imam's tomb.

It was raining and I had put on the Burberry raincoat which I had bought in London before coming to Iran, although rain-coats were little used, being considered unmilitary-looking. Meeting me in front of the Divisional Headquarters building, General Jan Mohammad Khan asked me if I had come from London. 'No, Excellency, but I am going there,' I answered with my hand at my cap. Thinking I was making fun of him he was about to become angry, but his Chief of Staff promptly said: 'It is quite true, Excellency. Major Arfa has been appointed Military Attaché in London.' The General looked at me sternly and passed on without a word.

In the neighbourhood of Nishapur my car sank so deeply in the mud that the combined efforts of the driver, my orderly Hoseyn Aqa and myself could not make it move an inch. Fortunately some twenty villagers with planks were ready at hand and managed to get the car out. Nevertheless, as it was already dark, we had to spend the night in their village. I understood that pulling cars out of mud had become for these villagers quite a good source of income, as they always received good remuneration from the grateful passengers for their work with the cars and for the lodging and refreshments provided at the village.

Between Khar and Veramin, not far from Teheran, we had to ford the Jajerud river on foot because of floods, becoming completely soaked, which was unpleasant in the February cold. Finally we reached Teheran and I was happy to be in my home again, being greeted by my wife and my brother, who had come from Bushehr, having conveyed all the war material to Teheran, and my mother-in-law who had come from London on a visit.

Military Attache in London

I had arrived in Teheran not long before Nowruz, and having been already transferred from the Cavalry Brigade to the General Staff had no regimental duties to perform, and so had time to prepare for my departure to London.

During my absence Hilda had made many friends, both Iranian and foreign. Amongst the foreigners her best friends were the Loraines, Sir Percy the British Minister and his lovely wife Louise; the Nicolsons, Harold and Vita (Victoria Sackville-West), whom I had known in Monte Carlo in 1918; Gladwyn Jebb, then a young secretary, now Lord Gladwyn after a brilliant career as Ambassador in Paris; W. K. Fraser and his wife; Captain Bertrand the French Military Attaché; and Tarbé de St. Hardouin, Secretary at the French Embassy (afterwards Ambassador in Turkey). Amongst the Iranians were Generals Sheibani, Jahanbani and a group of young intellectuals who all fulfilled in after years the promise of those days. These were Matin Daftari (afterwards Prime Minister), Nasrullah Entezam (several times Minister and Ambassador), the late Nizam Khajeh Nouri, and Ali Akbar Siassi (afterwards Minister and Dean of the University) as well as Sarah Khanum, an Iranian from the Caucasus who had lately arrived in Iran after being released from a Bolshevik prison through the intervention of the Iranian Ambassador in Moscow, and Maryse Adl, a daughter of the English composer Raymond Roze who had married an Iranian and who subsequently had a distinguished career as a singer. With all of those who are now alive we have kept our friendship.

I was sad to learn that the Khan of Maku, Eqbal-os-Saltaneh, had been arrested, the Baghchejik Palace, including the museum, looted and that the Khan had died after a few months in prison in Tabriz in circumstances that had not been elucidated.

By order of Reza Shah, all the titles, as something-os-Saltaneh, so and so-Dovleh, etc., were suppressed, and from Arfa-os-

Soltan I had become plain Arfa, having adopted the first part of my title as my surname. Also the names of the months of the Iranian Calendar were now changed, the old Persian names replacing those of the Zodiac.

With the pacification of Azerbaijan, Khuzestan, Khorasan, Gilan and Mazandaran, security had been established in the greater parts of Iran and the capital was busy with preparations for the Coronation of Reza Shah which took place on the 24th of April 1926, according to a carefully elaborated programme. There were gala dinners at the Golestan Palace and at the Foreign Ministry, and most of the Legations also entertained the Cabinet Ministers and important personages. In my capacity of Military Attaché designate I was invited to most of these entertainments.

The Coronation ceremony was preceded by a cavalcade, the Shah driving in the state-coach with a General as his standard bearer riding by the door of the coach, which was escorted by two squadrons of Guards cavalry.

I did not have the luck to be present in the throne room during the ceremony, when the Shah took the new Crown, a reproduction of the Sassanian Crown, and put it firmly on his head.

I was told that an incident preceded this act. When the Shah entered the throne room, he noticed that the French Minister, M. Bonzon (who was known as having been in favour of the Qajars), was wearing a cloak over his gold-braided uniform. 'Remove his cloak,' said the angered Shah. The protocol people asked the Minister to take off his cloak which they quickly removed to the wardrobe in spite of the protests of the monocled Minister, this action certainly not helping to change his sentiments towards the new dynasty. After a few months a dissatisfied French Legation official gave the Iranian Foreign Ministry the copy of a secret report from the Ambassador to the Quai d'Orsay, the terms of which were considered derogatory and undiplomatic. His transfer was asked for and obtained: the Quai d'Orsay were then careful to send a diplomat who would take care to be *persona grata* at the Court.

Although at that time several questions related to Irano-British interests were the subject of difficult negotiations between the two countries, Sir Percy Loraine, the British Minister, maintained the most cordial relations with the Shah and his Government, avoiding in this way any atmosphere of bitterness or hostility.

As far as I remember the subjects of the negotiations between the two countries were as follows:

1. The demand of the British Government to use Iranian territory for the operations of Imperial Airways.

The British Government wished the itinerary to follow the Persian Gulf coast, as being the shortest route to India, and to establish and control several aerodromes on this route. The Iranian Government rejecting control and upkeep of the aerodrome by the British, and insisting on the route passing through Teheran.

Finally, after a temporary authorisation to use the Persian Gulf route for six months, but not to build and control aerodromes, Imperial Airways were obliged to adopt a longer route passing over the territory of the Arab Sheikhdoms to the south of the Persian Gulf.

2. Settlement for repayment of the sums advanced by the British Government after the war, which had not been considered as loans at the time. In this matter a compromise was reached.

3. The British Government insisted that the Iranian Government give back to Sheikh Khazal his confiscated property.

This was rejected, but after the Second World War, some estates which had belonged to him were handed over to his heirs.

It was generally assumed that while the Soviet Government was apprehensive about the new regime, considering the establishment of a strong Government in Iran as contrary to its interests, the British Government was favourable to Reza Shah, a strong regime in Iran precluding any possibility of internal troubles which would help the Soviet to interfere in Iranian affairs. Besides, it was thought that once he became Shah, Reza Shah would be content to reign and would allow a free hand to his Ministers, with whom it would be easier to come to terms.

If such hopes had been entertained in some quarters, they were to be disappointed. Reza Shah had desired the supreme power not in order to indulge in imperial pomp and etiquette, but to be able to direct all the activities of the State without hindrance, his Ministers being only obedient executives who would take their orders and advice exclusively from him.

About this time a law for universal military conscription was passed by the Majles. This law rendered the Army more efficient, as well as less expensive, as the young conscripted soldiers were much better disciplined than the former volunteers. These were great grumblers often addicted to opium smoking, drinking and gambling and had been accustomed to behave in an outrageous way towards the civilian population. Reza Shah ordered all the sons of grandees and chiefs of tribes to serve as privates in the units, together with the sons of their servants and peasants, setting thus a good example of democracy.

A few days after the Coronation and the taking of the oath at the Majles, a military review took place on the Meidan-e-Mashk, in the centre of the town, with the participation of all the units of the Teheran garrison, numbering then above 12,000 men. During the parade, my regiment received a standard from the hands of His Majesty, and was renamed the 1st Pahlavi Guards Cavalry Regiment, for services rendered during the Turkoman Campaign. I had been proposed for the Order of Sepah by General Jan Mohammad Khan, but an event caused all this General's proposals to be rejected by the Shah.

The commander of one of the Camel Corps squadrons which had been part of my column for a few days, was a Mazandarani lieutenant named Lahak Khan Bavand of the clan to which Reza Shah also belonged. As has been mentioned earlier, one of the Mazandaran chiefs and his sons who had provoked the Yomut Turkomans' aggressive attitude by their intrigues had been shot by the Government and this had provoked the indignation and hostility of the members of that family, one of them being Lahak. This highly emotional man did not conceal his feelings and his imprudent words having reached the ears of General Khozai, who then commanded the 5th Mashad Division, he summoned Lahak and advised him to be more discreet. Lahak promised the General to abstain from any rash action, and in order to keep him out of mischief he was transferred to the Sistan Brigade and incorporated in the Camel Corps.

Unfortunately, after General Khozai had been replaced by General Jan Mohammad Khan, and the military operations against the Turkomans had started, the Camel Corps had been brought from Sistan to the Turkoman Steppe, and after the end of the campaign was assigned to occupy the district of Maraveh Tappeh. It has not been elucidated if Lahak Khan had been incited to revolt by Soviet agents, but as local revolts started more or less at the same period in all the regions close to Soviet territory, Azerbaijan, Gilan, the Turkoman Steppe and Khorasan, and at a time when the Soviet Government was particularly opposed to the new regime in Iran, it is permissible to doubt whether these risings were spontaneous and unconnected.

Being homesick the Baluch soldiers of the Camel Corps (who were volunteers, as were all the soldiers of the Iranian Army at that date) rebelled at the instigation of Lahak Khan, and arresting those officers who did not join them or failed to escape, marched from Maraveh Tappeh to Incheh, where I had been two months before. The battalion quartered there joined the insurgents, a few officers succeeded in getting away but others were arrested and sent to Bojnurd, where the garrison also rebelled. At the same time, the population of the Maneh plain, to the north-west of Bojnurd, revolted against the Government, killed an official of the Finance Ministry and proclaimed a Socialist Soviet Republic. Lahak arrived at Bojnurd, where he was joined by the Maneh people who were Shadlu Kurds, ordered the officers who had been arrested to be shot, and marched by way of Shirvan towards Quchan and Mashad.

The Shah ordered Jan Mohammad Khan to advance towards Quchan with the remaining forces of the 5th Division, but it was reported that these forces were not to be trusted and he was afraid that they would join the rebels. An important column was then sent from Teheran to Sabzevar with orders to advance from there directly to Quchan, avoiding Mashad, and attack the rebels in that region. But before those forces could establish contact with the rebels, the Zafaranlu tribe, siding with the Central Government, attacked the rebel force of Lahak numbering 700 soldiers beside a few hundred armed civilians. Without officers, badly led by Lahak who lacked experience, military ability and the necessary authority, this force could not withstand the Zafaranlu tribesmen's attack. The civilians dispersed, and the soldiers with Lahak himself fled to the frontier town of Bajgiran. After looting it they crossed into U.S.S.R. It was the end of the rebellion, but not of General Jan Mohammad Khan's and Lahak's ordeals.

It had been reported to the Shah that the disaffection of the men of the 5th Division was mainly due to the maladministration and corruption which reigned in that unit for which the

General was held responsible. In consequence, taking the former Chief of Staff, General Jahanbani—who had been replaced on the Staff by General Sheibani—with him, the Shah went to Mashad, ordered Jan Mohammad Khan to be arrested and summoned a court martial, which condemned the General to degradation and a term of imprisonment. The degradation was carried out in front of the Division assembled on the parade ground of Mashad and he was then sent under escort to Teheran. After a period spent in prison he was released and spent the rest of his life looking after what remained of his properties, part of which I believe had been confiscated by the Government.

Jan Mohammad Khan was a tall, handsome, proud and haughty man, clever but cruel and unscrupulous, and his fall was met in the Army and especially in his division with a feeling of relief and satisfaction. General Amanollah Jahanbani was appointed in his place, and being a calm, kind and intelligent man, always considerate and courteous to his collaborators and subordinates, offered a perfect contrast to his predecessor.

What happened to Lahak was told me many years later by his brother Shervin Bavand who had also been several years in U.S.S.R. As has happened more often than not with the foreign revolutionaries who after discomfiture in their own country have taken refuge in the socialist paradise (see El Campesino), after a few months he realised that independence of judgement, revolutionary enthusiasm, originality of thought and an inclination for free discussion were welcome only when used in capitalist countries with the object of undermining and destroying their structure. Inside U.S.S.R. quite different characteristics were considered desirable. He asked to be allowed to leave Russia to go to Europe or America. But if one can enter paradise at will, one cannot come out of it as easily. His request was refused, and as he insisted, the guardian angels became suspicious and he was imprisoned. During long years he was sent hither and thither, from one prison to another, from one camp to a farther one, until finally he was released. His first act then was to send to His Present Majesty Mohammed Reza Shah a petition begging for pardon and asking to be allowed to return to Iran. He managed to smuggle this petition to the Iranian Consulate in Baku, which had not been closed at that time. The Soviet authorities learned of this and he was again arrested and removed to a distance. A

few months ago I learnt that finally he had been allowed by the
Soviet authorities to return to Iran.

Before leaving for London I was summoned to the Palace to
be presented to Reza Shah by the Chief of Staff, still General
Jahanbani. I was so overcome by the imposing presence of the
Shah that when he asked me something in a very low voice,
having not heard what he had said, I muttered an indistinct
reply. Addressing himself to Jahanbani, he then said with an air
of doubt, 'Is he intelligent?' 'Oh yes, Your Majesty,' answered
the General, afraid that the Shah would reproach him for having
chosen a half-wit for this post. The Shah looked at me in a
dubious way, while I tried, I am afraid without great success,
to look clever and intelligent.

Having completed my arrangements we started for London.
Besides Hilda, her mother, Leila, her nurse and myself, Vita
Nicolson also travelled with us, and I acted as courier, my know-
ledge of Russian proving most useful. We arrived at Bandar
Pahlavi and after a night in the hotel took the boat to Baku.
Being in possession of diplomatic passports we had no difficulties,
everybody was very polite, and in Baku we boarded the Moscow
Express composed of sleeping cars of the 'Compagnie Inter-
nationale des Wagons-lits' which happened to be on Russian
territory when the revolution started and which the Soviet
Government had taken over in spite of protests from the
Company.

It was already very hot and stuffy in the carriages so we tried
to open the windows, but the guard told us to shut them because
thieves might use hooked sticks with which they could remove
things, and he would then be held responsible. Although we said
that we preferred losing things to being suffocated, the guard
was adamant and we spent a very uncomfortable night. Fortunately as we journeyed north the temperature became more
bearable. At the stations we were importuned by dozens of
haggard, dirty, starving boys and girls in rags, begging for alms.
We were astonished to see the same children at subsequent
stations. When asked about them, the guard told us that they
were homeless children, called *bezprizorniye* (deprived of care),
and that they were travelling with the train, concealed between
the carriages, begging on the trains being their mode of life.
When I wondered why the Government did not do something

about them, he said that the Government had many other worries.

After three days in the train we arrived at Moscow, Vita Nicolson being met and taken to the British Embassy, while we were taken by *droshkis* (horse carriages) to the Hotel Metropole, where we were given a spacious room with solid old-fashioned furniture. This hotel was a relic of the past, breathing the respectability of bygone days. The uniformed porters, the head waiters in tails who had been there since pre-revolutionary days, reminded one of Old Russia rather than of present-day Europe. The food was good and the prices far from exorbitant. The hotel was exclusively occupied by foreigners, chiefly German businessmen.

The Russians were busy wooing the Chinese, promising them support in their struggle against Imperialism, which term at that time signified the British.

The first night we went to the Bolshoi Theatre, to see the ballet *Krasniy Mak* (the Red Poppy). It was a propaganda show. The action took place in a Chinese port; a nasty drunken British merchantman's captain was seen ill-treating Chinese coolies, when two handsome and kind young Soviet naval officers, disgusted by the brutal colonialist ways of the Englishman, rescued the coolies, and punished the imperialist as he deserved. Ballerinas in Chinese clothes afterwards danced for their entertainment and the Soviet and Chinese (Kuomintang) flags were displayed at the end as an apotheosis, to the great dismay of several grotesque Englishmen with red whiskers and long teeth. Another evening we went to see Tschaikovski's *Pikovaya Dama*, which was beautifully presented. The house was full and the poorly dressed audience, all obviously workers, was listening with the concentration and appreciation of connoisseurs.

We went to the Iranian Embassy to pay our respects to the Ambassador and his Russian wife. He was a charming and culti-vated man famed for his good looks and had made himself popular both before and after the revolution. His son Abdul Hoseyn, who was one of the Secretaries, had inherited his father's good looks and was in later years to inherit also his Embassy. At the same time that I had been posted to London, General Shaqaqi, who was the son of an old friend of my father's, had been appointed Military Attaché in Moscow. He had been at Saint

Cyr and was a first-class horseman and a good soldier but had a temper which was to be the cause of trouble for us both in the future. We had been friends with him and his wife, who is a distinguished painter in Teheran, and their presence in Moscow helped us pass a week there very pleasantly before entraining for Warsaw, Vienna and Monaco.

At that time the Russian frontier was at a little station called Niegoreloye where passports were very carefully examined, after which the train was invaded by Russian Frontier Guards who filled the corridors in all the carriages and the train very slowly advanced towards the Polish frontier station of Stolbtzi. Just inside U.S.S.R. territory a wooden arch had been erected on which was written in Russian on the side facing those about to enter Poland 'Proletarians of the World Unite', and on the side facing those about to enter Russia 'Welcome to the workers of the West', and as the train passed under the arch, one by one, rifles in hand, the Soviet soldiers sprang out of each carriage whilst the Polish soldiers also with rifles at the ready climbed into them from the other side. Since then many people have had occasion to observe the drabness of the iron curtain countries but in those days, before the Second World War had destroyed so much of the beauty and charm of the Free World, the contrast between the two was indescribable and Warsaw, with its be-flowered station and the train which took us there with its elegantly served meals, seemed like fairyland. Arrived in London, after a short visit to my father and a few days in Paris, we were received at the Vale House with the same warmth and kindness as ever and I lost no time in presenting myself to Nader Arasteh who was the Iranian Chargé d'Affaires. I also presented myself to the Chief of the Military Intelligence Department who gave me directions for the coming month which was to be a very pleasant one—I was given honorary membership of the Guards and the United Service Clubs and I also became a member of the Royal Automobile Club.

We were presented to the King and Queen at a Court held at Buckingham Palace. Everything was perfectly organised and I shall never forget the enchanting sight of the lovely young débutantes, betrained and befeathered, awaiting the moment of their presentation. I was tremendously impressed when the King and Queen entered preceded by two chamberlains walking

backwards and took their places on their thrones with the Prince
of Wales the future Edward VIII standing behind the King, and
the Duke of York the future George VI standing behind the Queen.
Apart from the débutantes about a dozen diplomats were presented, Their Majesties acknowledging our bows and curtsies
with a gracious inclination of the head. After the ceremony was
over, we passed into a vast apartment where refreshments were
served. The women were gorgeous in Court dress with ostrich
feathers on their heads and all the men who were not in uniform
wore knee breeches and silk stockings with the exception of the
United States Ambassador. He it was said had absolutely declined
to part with his long trousers, saying that he was a political man
and that if people in the United States heard that he had worn
Court dress his career would be ruined. A solution was found by
the Ambassador producing a medical certificate stating that on
account of a peculiar disease it would be dangerous for him to
wear tight breeches. The Soviet Ambassador, however, was very
correct with his black breeches and silk stockings in contrast
to the first Soviet envoy, Krassin, who, I was told, had displeased King George so much by his ignoring of protocol that
he was heard to murmur, 'Take them away, they murdered my
cousins'. Sir Austen Chamberlain in white breeches and stockings
and with his monocle looked exactly as if he had stepped out of the
famous picture of the Congress of Vienna in 1815 (although as
far as I know monocles were not worn then).

Soon after arriving in London I had the luck to meet many
interesting people whose conversation and reminiscences helped
much to increase my knowledge of the contemporary history of
Iran and of the Middle East in general. One of these was Ja'far
Pasha al Askari the Iraqi statesman who was then King Feisal's
representative at the Court of St. James and who was killed a
few years later in Iraq. Another was Mr. Norman, whom I met
at the house of a mutual friend, who had been His Majesty's
Minister in Teheran at the time of the *coup d'état* of the 20th
February.

We lunched at our Legation with Sir Percy and Lady Cox
and he talked about the 1919 Anglo-Persian Treaty, regretting
that it had not been ratified and applied in time, but hoping that
with the advent of Reza Shah's strong rule Iran would be able
to put her affairs in order. I was impressed by his strong

personality and keen intelligence, which were enhanced by a striking physical appearance. He was a man of the old school, more an Empire builder than a diplomat, and his failure in Iran was not his fault but due to circumstances, whilst his success in Iraq must be attributed in great part to his own skill.

Hilda had an aunt—Mrs. Stuart Menzies—who had written a number of books of memoirs which had had a great success a few years earlier and at her house I met Lord Headley, a handsome old man who had been converted to Islam when he was young. He invited us to his house where he received us in Arab dress with the *kefie* on his head and showed us many books and other treasures from Arabia. He told us that at the age of twenty he had studied many different religions and having come to the conclusion that Islam was the most rational as well as the most inspiring, he had been converted to that faith, performing the pilgrimage to Mecca.

One delightful week-end we spent with Vita and Harold Nicolson in the lovely old farm-house on the Knole estate in which they lived before they went to Sissinghurst Castle. Among the many interesting people we met was a Dr. Young, who had been associated with the Anglo-Iranian Oil Company since its early days and been a witness of the extraordinary expansion of the oil industry in Iran from its modest beginnings. One day Vita took us to Knole to tea with her father who occupied a very few rooms, the whole of the magnificent place with its priceless treasures being kept in perfect order. It seemed impossible to believe that only a few years earlier all of its 300 rooms had been inhabited. I remember being told that twenty-seven men were employed simply to keep the roof in order!

We talked much of Harold's books, particularly of *Public Faces* which was highly dangerous reading in Teheran. Another couple with whom we were friends were Lydia Lopokhova and Maynard Keynes. She was the most spontaneous creature alive and her original use of the English language, her total lack of interest in her personal appearance and her wonderful devotion to Maynard were very endearing. Maynard would look at her with an expression at once sardonic and indulgent and was marvellous company, especially when telling revealing stories of the Paris Peace Conference in 1919.

Towards the end of this gay and happy month I received tragic news from Iran. My cousin Yusuf Khan had been barbarously murdered by his soldiers at Shahpur.

Early in June, as the result of intensive propaganda from abroad against Reza Shah's Government in all the northern provinces of Iran, an alarming agitation started in some of the Azerbaijan districts especially among the soldiers of the Rezaieh and Shahpur garrisons. In this last town the soldiers had been a particularly easy prey to this subversive propaganda on account of their deep discontent with their regimental commander, who treated them harshly. The Colonel was recalled and Yusuf Khan appointed in his place, but the harm had been done, and provoked by Communist agitators, one night the soldiers of the Shahpur infantry regiment revolted, and set out to massacre their officers. Most of the officers managed to hide themselves or to leave the town, but when the soldiers knocked at the door of their Colonel and asked to see him, the unsuspecting Yusuf Khan, thinking probably that something important had happened in the garrison necessitating his presence, dressed hurriedly and came out of the house. Here he was surrounded by excited soldiers who had already crossed the line between insubordination and rebellion. He was struck down, and when they saw him helpless and prostrate, the savage instincts of the jungle awakened in them, and they threw themselves on him like wolves, and tore him to pieces.

The next day the soldiers (all were career enlisted men) left Shahpur and marched on Khoi, which they occupied without fighting, as there were no Government forces in that town. As soon as reports of this ghastly deed reached Tabriz, two battalions were sent to Khoi. After a short fight, fifty-two rebellious soldiers were taken prisoner, court-martialled and shot, the others fleeing to the U.S.S.R. At the same time a rebellion on a much smaller scale started again in the Caspian Provinces, but was promptly put down by local forces. After a few weeks' sporadic fighting in the coastal forests by scattered bands, the leaders were caught and executed and the rank and file of the rebels surrendered or returned quietly to their villages and pastures.

I also heard of the tragic fate that had befallen Colonel Puladin. As a result of disagreements with his chiefs, Puladin had become discontented and had entered into relations with elements hostile to the new regime and Colonel Puladin being an A.D.C. to the

Shah, was entrusted with the task of assassinating him whilst he was on duty at the palace during the night. He was betrayed by a woman, arrested, court-martialled and shot, together with two accomplices.

Then the blow fell. I received a cypher telegram, and had a premonition of something unpleasant. I was right; the first words I decyphered read: 'Your post is suppressed . . .' and afterwards: 'as well as the post of military attaché at Moscow . . . for reasons of economy'.

This was bad news. My mother-in-law had just bought us a house, thinking that we would stay in London for five years. We had to take leave of all our friends, and early in September we left London for Geneva, where I saw my mother and also my father, who was there to take part in the League of Nations General Assembly. I wondered what had happened, but it was not until I returned to Teheran that I learned what had been the real reason of my recall.

Apparently at a party in Moscow, Chicherin, the then Soviet Commissar for Foreign Affairs, said something about Iran which General Shaqaqi considered as derogatory; being a hot-tempered man he had answered in brusque military terms. The Soviet Government complained and demanded his recall. Reza Shah being extremely touchy about national prestige refused, considering that the General had been right to show his displeasure, but as the Soviet Government refused to recognise him any more as military attaché it was announced in Teheran that for reasons of economy the post of military attaché both in Moscow and in London would be suppressed, and in this way I fell a victim to the misunderstandings in Moscow.

We arrived in Geneva a few months after Locarno, and Weimar Germany was again received into the bosom of the Great Powers and had become a member of the League. I was present at the historic meeting when Briand, Ramsay MacDonald and Stresemann appeared on the platform and made declarations full of hope of friendly co-operation in the future to build a free and peace-loving Europe, banish war for ever, etc. Mussolini's Italy was certainly considered rather a nuisance, but nobody seriously considered it as dangerous for the peace of the world. Soviet Russia was safely held behind the barrier of the French-supported Polish-Rumanian alliance, the Little Entente was firmly controlling Hungary and Bulgaria, and Hitler's national-socialists had not yet become threatening.

It was about this time that my father came into conflict with the interests of the Great Powers, trying to defend those of Iran and the smaller nations. Since 1923, the two chief countries of the League, Great Britain and France, not wanting to be obliged to intervene in disputes which did not directly affect their interests, had wished to change or water down the articles X and XVI of the Covenant; article X giving the right of intervention to the League in order to preserve peace, and article XVI, defining sanctions to be applied against the aggressors.

A timely reminder to the Soviets of the possibility of Iran asking for the intervention of the League in conformity with these articles may have prevented the Soviets intervening more openly in 1925 at the time of the Turkoman revolt. According to the Covenant, an article could be changed or suppressed only by the unanimous acceptance of all the members of the League, and the proposal in 1923 to modify these articles had been prevented by the single vote of Iran, represented by my father. Since then, my father, supported by several other smaller nations, especially Finland, had struggled continuously to prevent any encroachment on the essence of these two articles.

In 1926 the Locarno Treaty had to be ratified by the League, but according to this treaty the intervention of the League in disputes and the application of sanctions was to be subject to the decision of the Council of the League, which would decide each case according to its special circumstances. Iran was not among the Locarno powers, and the day this treaty was discussed it had been arranged that my father should take part in a commission concerning some maritime regulations. Nevertheless, as soon as he became aware of what was going on, he lodged a protest on behalf of Iran.

After that the Ministers of Great Britain, France and Germany in Teheran approached the Prime Minister, Mostofi-el-Memalek, asking him if it was by order of the Iranian Government that Prince Arfa had protested against the Locarno Treaty. Mostofi said that he would study the records, and telegraphed to my father for an explanation. My father answered that when he had defeated the British motion on the modification of articles X and XVI in 1923 this had been approved by the Government of that time, and that consequently he considered himself empowered to continue to oppose such modification even if they should be effected indirectly, through the Locarno Treaty. Mostofi ordered a commission comprising Taqizadeh, Hoseyn Ala and Mosaddeq to examine my father's report and communicate their findings to him. They supported my father, and Mostofi declared to the three Ministers that Prince Arfa had acted according to the instructions of the Government. A few months later Mostofi was replaced by Mokhber-os-Saltaneh, who was more amenable to foreign pressure, my father was recalled and the protest withdrawn late in 1927.

My grandmother had died and I decided to take my mother with us to Teheran, so early in October we took the train to Moscow and from there to Baku. After an uneventful journey we returned to Teheran and to Arfaieh.

Campaigns in Kordestan and Lorestan

The exterior aspect of Teheran had already begun to change. These changes were not always very happy, but one could feel a trend towards what was considered modernisation and a few important buildings began to appear. In contrast with King Amanollah of the neighbouring kingdom of Afghanistan, Reza Shah believed in changing things gradually so as not to hurt the feelings of traditionally minded people. He believed, like Atatürk, in the moral influence of discarding national in favour of European dress, considering that in this way his people would identify themselves with those of other countries and realise that as there was no fundamental difference between them and Europeans and Americans, there was no reason why they could not achieve the same advance in every kind of work as these nations had done. But he brought about this change by carefully thought-out stages.

The traditional *sardari* had already disappeared, and men were all wearing suits of European cut. The cloth or astrakhan cap had been replaced by a kind of cloth peaked cap, like a kepi, as a preliminary to its replacement by the European hat. The foreign wives of Iranians appeared now without veils, as also a few Iranian ladies. The number of schools was increasing both in Teheran and in the provinces. The camel tracks were being transformed into roads suitable for motor transport and a contract had been signed with Junkers to operate an air-service inside Iran.

The army was being expanded and little by little transformed from an interior security force into a national army whose duty was to protect the frontiers of the country against exterior aggression. All this had been possible because taxes were being collected, customs dues paid and expenses controlled. The American financial mission presided over by Millspaugh did good work and the budget was balanced without the help of a foreign loan and even without including the money of the oil royalties, which was by order of the Shah put aside in the Government's reserve.

Everybody felt, and this was quite new in Iran, that a central direction existed, all the Ministers working according to pre-conceived plans emanating from the same source—the Shah. Nobody knew what the next step would be, but he had calculated and prepared everything in his mind beforehand and planned the future of Iran both on broad lines and in detail himself. His mind was extraordinarily clear and his intelligence far above normal. To reach his goal he displayed an iron will and great patience. If faced by an obstacle, he did not try to break through unless he considered that the time had come for that, but went around it and then resumed the march towards his goal. He now set his mind to modernise the army, and as the 60-odd officers who had been sent to France in 1923 were beginning to return to Iran after having completed their studies, others were sent every year to replace them. While the work of the organisa-tion and modernisation of the army was proceeding in Teheran and at the divisional headquarters in the provinces, the work of disarming the lawless tribes and of the extension of the Central Government's control over the outlying districts was proceeding unabated.

After the end of the Turkoman campaign and the liquidation of the revolts of Lahak in Khorasan and of the Shahpur regiment in Azerbaijan, the most troubled area was the region inhabited by the Kurds, on the western frontier of Iran.

In the Kordestan province, which is situated to the south-west of Azerbaijan and is entirely inhabited by Kurds, some of them tribal and some sedentary townspeople, dissidence was endemic, but just about that time a revolt started against the Government with more than local tribal objectives.

Prince Salar-ed-Dovleh Qajar, the late Mohammad Ali Shah's brother and a pretender to the throne of Iran, who had already revolted in the same region in 1911 and was at this time in Iraq, managed to slip into Iran with a few armed followers. He had been seen at the frontier by a detachment of Iraqi police under the command of a British officer, but having no orders they did not interfere with him, merely reporting the matter to headquarters in Baghdad.

Sardar Rashid, a notorious chieftain from the Ravansar region, who had already rebelled half a dozen times in the past and been pardoned, again raised the banner of rebellion, in connivance with Salar-ed-Dovleh, many local tribes joining in the revolt for the sake of plunder. This revolt very soon extended towards the north. A cavalry squadron was attacked by the Kurds in the Ravansar district and sustained some losses. Sanandaj was surrounded from three sides, its communications with both Saqqez and Kermanshah being cut. Happily the direct road from Hamadan to Sanandaj by Qorveh had been rendered practicable for motor transport and the Naderi Guards infantry regiment (two battalions) arrived by lorries from Teheran within 48 hours followed by two squadrons of the Pahlevi Regiment and a mountain gun section, and the Kurds considered it prudent to retire. Saqqez, Baneh and Sar Dasht, which had been temporarily occupied by the rebels, were attacked from the south by these forces and from the north by a column from Tabriz, and reoccupied, the Kurds crossing the frontier into Iraq.

Sardar Rashid was also attacked from Sanandaj and from Kermanshah and fled to Iraq, together with the discomfited pretender, Salar-ed-Dovleh. The Avromi chief of Nosud, J'afar Soltan, whose haunts were close to the Iraqi frontier had remained neutral and so was not interfered with by the pursuing Government forces.

After these happenings, Reza Shah decided to finish once and for all with the periodic disturbances in Kordestan, but according to his custom, first tried to settle things peacefully by persuasion before resorting to force.

In the autumn of 1926, the Shah sent General Abdollah Amir Tahmasseb, former Minister of War, to Sanandaj to start negotiations with the different Kurdish chiefs to bring about the definite submission of the frontier tribes. Thanks to his remarkable gifts as a negotiator, Amir Tahmasseb soon acquired great influence among the tribes and succeeded in convincing many of the chiefs of the firm establishment of the Central Government's control up to the frontier and of the advantage to them of collaboration with the Government.

At the same time, negotiations were taking place with the British authorities concerning an Iraqi-Kurdish Chief, Sheikh Mahmud of Soleymaniyeh, who had previously rebelled against the Iraqi Government, and having been defeated and pursued by Anglo-Iraqi forces, had taken shelter in Iranian territory, with Mahmud Khan Kanisanani, a Kurdish Chief in the Merivan district. Sheikh Mahmud was not only an influential chief of the Soleymaniyeh district, but the head of a religious sect and so had many followers among the Iraqi Kurds and had profited by this influence to revolt several times against Iraq. As a result his properties had been confiscated and he refused to return to Iraq unless they were given back to him and his security guaranteed.

The British were anxious not to have him in the vicinity of the Iraqi frontier, where he could continually intrigue with his kith and kin from over the border. An arrangement had been concluded by which Sheikh Mahmud would be allowed to return to Iraq, where his properties would be given back to him, but he hesitated to abandon Kanisanani's hospitality, the latter declaring that if Government forces advanced towards Merivan he would defend himself.

To the south of the Merivan district in the Avroman region, there were three tribes each of which had adopted a different attitude towards the Government. Immediately to the south of Merivan, in the Dezli district, Mahmud Khan Dezli was favourable to the Government because of a dispute with Kanisanani over a village. At the same time he was very suspicious and would have rebelled at once at the slightest hint of a move to disarm him.

To the south of Dezli was the village and district of Rezav, the Rezavi being hostile to the Government without being allied to Kanisanani.

South of Rezav dwelt the warlike tribe of J'afar Soltan, which had previously taken part in the rebellion of the Javanrud tribe but which had been persuaded by General Amir Tahmasseb to support the Government, together with his Javanrudi allies, by sending a well-armed force of 1000 men under his son Mohammad Amin to co-operate with the Government forces.

On the 16th March, five days before Nowruz, I was appointed second in command of the Pahlavi Cavalry Regiment and ordered to proceed at once to Hamadan and to take over the command of the 2nd group of that regiment, comprising two squadrons with a platoon of Lewis guns, in all about 220 men.

At Hamadan, I took charge of my unit and started to put it

into shape by extensive training, as large scale-operations against the tribes which still kept aloof were about to begin.

At the beginning of 1927 our forces suffered several reverses in the Merivan and Avroman districts and the Shah came from Teheran accompanied by several officers to inspect the forces of the local division. He was not satisfied and dismissing the commander of the Kermanshah mixed regiment, replaced him by Major Haji Ali Razmara (the future Prime Minister, assassinated in 1951), who thus began his meteoric career. Returning from Kermanshah to Hamadan, he inspected the Naderi Infantry Regiment and the Pahlavi Cavalry Group, after which he said to the Commander of the Division: 'Your forces did not behave well, my hope is in these units from Teheran.' When he came in front of me, he stopped and talked to me in Azeri, which was a great mark of favour, meaning that he recognised me, knew who I was and wished to be familiar with me.

I started on horse-back at the head of my group towards Sanandaj, the chief city of Kordestan. I found myself in what I imagined a Moslem town in mediaeval times must have been like. All the inhabitants, men and women, wore the national Kurdish dress, with wide trousers narrow at the ankles, short jackets and a kind of turban on their heads. We remained two weeks in Sanandaj and I was appointed Commander of the Cavalry column and given a squadron from the 3rd Division besides my own group, and with 320 men moved due west from Sanandaj. Half-way between that town and the old fort of Merivan, which was still in the hands of Mahmud Kanisanani, I occupied the pass of Garan, in a pleasant green region covered with dwarf oaks and bushes where I remained ten days and was then recalled to Sanandaj, the Nadiri Regiment having occupied Merivan after a skirmish. The force was now to attack Rezav and the mountain of Korre Mianeh, which protects this village from the east. The infantry column was to march from Merivan to the south and attack the Korre Mianeh along its northern slopes, while I had to turn it from the south, after making a wide detour and near the village of Boridar join a Kurdish irregular detachment from Avroman, under Mohammad Amin, the son of J'afar Soltan, who was to collaborate with us, and to become part of my column.

The track I was following was extremely difficult, passing

through narrow gorges, with hairpin bends on the slopes of the mountains, skirting precipices and crossing torrents. The mountain peaks towering above our heads made it very difficult to protect the column from the front as well as from the flanks. Perched on one of the hills which dominated our track, a single man could have inflicted heavy casualties on us. I remembered reading somewhere that during the First World War, three Kurds had halted a whole Russian infantry regiment with machine-guns for several days in this region.

We marched towards Boridar, where I expected to be met by Mohammad Amin with his Avromi horsemen. Before reaching this village, we had to make a very steep descent from the crest of a ridge to a deep and narrow valley and then climb again towards the village which was built on the top of a much lower ridge on the other side. It was the longest and most abrupt descent that I have ever seen, and of course we came down on foot, leading our horses by the bridle; my knees ached for two days afterwards. Half-way down from our ridge, we were met by desultory firing from the village. I divided my detachment into three columns and entered the village from three sides under the protection of the Lewis guns, which had taken position on the first ridge. A panic reigned there, men and women rushing about and shouting 'Sur Suri, Sur Suri!'

When they saw our uniforms they became calmer, and I understood that they had mistaken us for their neighbours of the Sur Sur tribe whom they had lately attacked and plundered, and therefore were afraid of reprisals. The same evening my advanced posts reported an important tribal force encamped about three miles from there on a commanding ridge of hills. I understood it was Mohammad Amin Khan's Avromi tribesmen, but was very much astonished that they did not come towards us. I then sent an officer with a trumpeter and four men to contact them and arrange for an interview between Amin and myself, but he was told that as it was already dark they could not allow him to enter their camp, and that he must wait until daylight. This strange behaviour puzzled and disquieted me, and I ordered strong pickets to be put around our camp, which was on a little plateau above the village.

The next morning, when my liaison officer went to contact the Avromis, he found their camping ground deserted as they had departed during the night. We never saw them again, and later Ja'afar Soltan himself revolted against the Government, and after severe fighting had to take refuge in Iraq with his numerous sons. Apparently they had hoped to take us by surprise and relieve us of our arms, as they had already decided to rebel against the State.

From Boridar I advanced towards the north-west, and after having turned the Korre Mianeh, joined the infantry column, which had seen some fighting on this mountain, the Kurds evacuating it after an artillery bombardment. From there we marched towards Merivan, which is a very pleasant place, thickly wooded, chiefly by dwarf oak trees. There is a lake called Zeriva the source of the Diyala river, which flows into the Tigris below Baghdad. The infantry stayed in Merivan and I was again posted on the Garan pass,. to ensure the liaison between Merivan and Sanandaj. Mahmud Khan Kanisanani surrendered, after Sheikh Mahmud had left Iran and voluntarily returned to Iraq.

Some time after this I rode with two officers to Kanisanan. Two miles out of the village we were met by a ten-year-old boy, Mahmud Khan's son, riding a beautiful Arab stallion, and accompanied by a dozen armed retainers. He dismounted at some 20 yards from us, bowed with dignity and introduced himself, welcoming us and begging us to honour him by being his guests. He wore the Kurdish costume with grace and elegance, and had a diminutive dagger at his belt. He entertained us with a local conjurer after whose performance we left; the boy accompanied us for some distance before taking leave of us. How was it possible to call these highly polished men savages? They were simply people living in feudal times, with the rights, privileges and duties of suzerains, vassals, serfs and yeomen, such as had existed in the twelfth and thirteenth centuries in Europe. They had adopted Islam as a religion, but the democratic spirit of Islam had not reached their mountain fastnesses and centuries of evolution had passed without influencing them. They are mostly Sunni Moslems of the Shafei rite, but all kinds of sects flourish, the more important of them being the Nakhshbandi, with followers on both sides of the frontier, the Sheikh or leader of the sect residing in Iran.

I was on the Garan pass when I received a telegram in cypher from Teheran saying: 'The Bairanaband Lors around Khorrama-bad have revolted, attacked an infantry company between that town and Borujerd, and killed the captain and a hundred soldiers. Khorramabad is completely invested, all communications with the outside world are cut, including the telegraph and telephone wires, the General commanding the division is himself in the town with one and a half battalion, you must immediately march through Kermanshah on Khorramabad, break through the investing Lors and reinforce the garrison.' This sounded like a pretty tough assignment.

The Lors had been for ages as lawless as the Turkomans, but much fiercer and braver. There had been a general offensive against them in 1924, before the drive into Khuzestan, and they were supposed to have been pacified, but in reality the more stubborn elements had taken refuge in the inaccessible mountains of Lorestan. Rifles had been smuggled from across the Iraqi frontier and they had again taken the field and by a swift action, profiting by the fact that the forces of the Western Division were busy with the Kurds more to the north, had attacked and destroyed the military posts on the Borujerd-Khorramabad road and had completely surrounded this town.

I struck camp the next day at five o'clock, and took the shortest route to Kermanshah, traversing the heart of the rebellious territory, but all was calm and secure now and nowhere had I to fight my way through hostile Kurds. I spent only one night in Kermanshah and then hurried towards Harsin, where the Kurdish region finishes and Lorestan begins.

Harsin is the last big village that one sees before coming to Khorramabad, the Lors being entirely nomadic and living the year round in their black felt tents. In contrast to the Turkomans, whose *obeh* or moving village consists sometimes of over two or three hundred huts, or *alajiks*, the settlements of the Lors never exceed forty to fifty black tents, and are usually limited to about ten or fifteen. My impression on seeing the first tent dwellers after Harsin was of extreme poverty. The Lors are tall, slim, with narrow faces, hawk-like noses, piercing eyes rather closely set, and mostly dolichocephalic skulls. Their clothes are simple, usually black, and look very drab after the picturesque costumes of the Kurds and their elaborate head-dresses.

After Harsin the country was nearly deserted, because the tribes had removed their families and flocks to the mountains out of reach of the Government forces. For security reasons we had to march during the day, and in this desert plain on these August days the heat was terrible. The plain was intersected from time to time by ranges of hills, and limited to the north-east by the inner Zagros chain and to the south-west by the Kabir Kuh, an uninterrupted chain of rugged mountains forming the outer Zagros and separating the Iranian tableland from the Mesopotamian alluvial plain. The Iranian soldier is gay, sturdy, sober with a strong sense of humour, and is disciplined and patriotic. This is true for the great majority, especially those of peasant stock. Very often the soldiers sang their local songs, but they did not talk very much, the Iranians, especially from Turki-speaking Azeri provinces, being a comparatively silent people. In camp after dinner I used to walk in the dark among the men's fires where they were brewing their tea, without their noticing me. Their talk was about their village, the day's march, the prospective enemy, with some mild jokes about their comrades. They were rather chaste and I never heard dirty stories about women, or jokes in connexion with them.

On the fourteenth day of our leaving Garan, after a march of 270 miles across three provinces, Kordestan, Kermanshah and Lorestan, we reached the last stage of our journey without having met any hostile Lors when suddenly, out of the blue, appeared a single horseman in sports clothes and riding breeches, cleanshaven except for a little moustache, who saluted me in the most civil Teherani way, looking altogether quite out of place in the Lorestan wilderness. He introduced himself as a Lor landlord. He said that he was inspecting his estates when he heard that the Bairanavand Lors who were encircling the town had prepared an ambush for us in a narrow gorge called Tang-e-Robat, which was just in front of us. I was not quite sure about the man, having never met him before, but I had no special reason to mistrust him, and anyway I had to pass through that gorge to reach Khorramabad the next day and so I continued my advance under the cover of a platoon as advance guard in more or less open country.

After half an hour's march we reached a brook and I gave the order to halt, dismount and water the horses. The Tang-e-Robat was now some three miles from us, and looking carefully with my Zeiss field-glasses I thought I saw something moving on the sky-line. I realised that to advance in full view of the enemy who was on the crest whilst we were in the plain would mean long and difficult fighting.

Then I had an idea. Just on the other side of the brook there was a low chain of hills, also perpendicular to the main chain on our left and an offshoot of that chain as the Tang-e-Robat was. I ordered the forward squadron to continue its march towards the Tang, with the horses of the rear squadron following it in marching order, so that seen from a distance, the column would appear to have the same length and composition as before. Then I took the dismounted men of the rear squadron, with the four Lewis guns, on foot from behind the perpendicular ridge to the chain of hills on the left, and moved forward behind the crest where we were not visible from the heights on both sides of Tang-e-Robat where the Lors were concentrated. The mounted part of the group lingered for a while near the brook, in order to allow us time to reach the main ridge and disappear behind its crest without being seen. The attention of the Lors was concentrated on the mounted column and they presumably intended to allow the vanguard to pass and to open fire only when the main corps entered the narrow gorge dominated by the high cliffs.

Meanwhile, after a steep ascent towards the main ridge, although we were very much out of breath, we hurried towards the Tang in order to arrive there before the head of our mounted column should be engaged. We followed this main ridge as fast as we could along the crest, and having established a fire base with the Lewis guns, attacked the Lors in open order under the protection of these guns. The effect was instantaneous. Taken completely by surprise, the Lors fled to the plain after firing a few shots, and we occupied the two sides of the gorge, through which the mounted column passed in all security. After that we came down to the plain, remounted and after spending the night camping there, entered Khorramabad on the following morning with only one man slightly wounded. Our arrival in the besieged township created quite a sensation, considerably raising the morale of the besieged and lowering that of the Bairanavands. After two days an infantry battalion arrived by lorry from Teheran, and after forcing the Lors' road block on the Borujerd-Khorramabad road, entered Khorramabad from the east.

The Lors understood that the game was up, and retreated towards the Kabir Kuh, into the Posht-Kuh region situated between the Kabir Kuh chain and the Iraqi frontier, controlled by Abu Gaddareh, the Vali of Posht-Kuh, chief of the Posht-Kuhi Lors and hereditary Governor of that district, which had up to then never been occupied by the forces of the Central Government.

The Vali, who was secretly encouraging the Lors to revolt and providing them with rifles and ammunition smuggled from Iraq, proposed to the Government that he would bring this revolt to an end if he were allowed to keep his position and were entrusted with the governorship of Pish Kuh beside his own. The Government not having had time to concentrate forces in Lorestan, negotiated with the Vali to gain time, meanwhile concentrating the forces which had been released by the pacification and disarmament of the Kurds into the Pish Kuh region, preliminary to a drive towards Posht-Kuh and the definitive pacification of both sides of Lorestan. Ultimately, in 1928, Government forces penetrated into Posht-Kuh coming from the north, and occupied the whole region up to the frontier. The Vali fled to Iraq, and military garrisons were established at Elam and Mehran.

Khorramabad was then (and still is) a very remarkable little town. It is situated in a narrow valley, between the main ridge on the east and an isolated hill on the west, on which a kind of mediaeval castle, or fort, has been built. This fort called Falak-el-Aflak was reported impregnable at the time when rifles could not fire farther than 500 yards, but today it could be subjected to an effective fire from the higher hills dominating it 1000 yards away and its defence neutralised. The fort looks very formidable with its crenellated walls and towers. It was used as barracks by the garrison, which was in this way protected against a surprise attack and sniping, and still serves to store ammunition and stocks of arms.

I had been less than a week in Khorramabad, when early one morning I saw in the street, coming towards the house, a friend from Teheran, Major Gholam Ali Ansari. I was pleased and surprised to see him, and opening my window, begged him to come in.

'What have you come to do here?' I asked after the first greetings.

'To send you to Paris,' he answered.

'What is this joke?'

'It is not a joke. You have been selected to go to the Ecole de Guerre this year. You must go to Teheran without delay, and take with you fifty young officers to finish their studies at different military academies in France. Go to Paris. Here is your appointment order.' (Among the thirty foreign officers detached to the Ecole de Guerre each year, Iran's quota was one officer, the others being chiefly from eastern Europe.) It was the second time that I had received an entirely unexpected appointment to a European capital whilst campaigning in the wildest and most remote districts of Iran and I hoped that this time no untoward event would prevent my completing the assignment.

Now I had to find a car to take me to Teheran. There was only one available, the car which had brought Ansari, but the driver, showing me several bullet-holes in his car fired by Lors from the hills when they were driving from Borujerd, refused to take to the road again until it was cleared of sniping rebels. I finally persuaded him to go by paying my fare beforehand plus a good tip, and taking with me my faithful Hoseyn Aqa. Soon the road left the plain and entered a long valley following the river bed bordered by willows and bushes. My orderly, sitting in front, had his rifle ready to fire, sticking out of the open car, while I had my Browning in my hand. We passed the famous Tang-e-Zahid-e-Shir without any incident and it was already dark when we traversed the second dangerous pass at Rang Razan. After Chalan Chulan we would be out of the danger zone, but at this moment the car suddenly stopped and the driver confessed dejectedly that having forgotten to fill up on our departure the petrol tank was empty. He could find some at the big village of Razan, not very far away, and would go at once since he had an empty can. There was nothing else to be done, the car was left on the road and the driver started on foot with his empty can to find petrol. It was full moon, but the surroundings looked unfriendly and I decided that it would be better to go to the watch-tower which I had seen on the road a few minutes before our car stopped, so Hoseyn Aqa and I walked about half a mile back to it. After calling the guards, we were finally admitted by climbing a ladder which was lowered to us from above and we stayed there until the driver returned after more than two hours with a full can.

We passed through the Chalan Chulan narrow valley, and

then turning sharp to our left, came to the wide and prosperous valley of Silakhor, well cultivated and containing many villages with watch-towers, to allow the villagers to defend themselves against the raids of the predatory Lors. Borujerd, situated in this plain, is a clean and neat little town and from there we drove to Malayer. After a night in Arak we arrived at Qom, reaching Teheran in the afternoon.

I was told at the General Staff that I had to take fifty young officers and cadets, including several civilian doctors, to Paris and to deliver them to our military attaché, Colonel Riazi. After a few days we started towards Bandar Pahlavi.

On arrival there I was glad to find that the Soviet gunboat which had been at anchor in the port since Tsarist times, except during the years of turmoil and revolution, had disappeared and the Iranian flag was the only one to be seen. I was told that a few months before, Reza Shah had come to Bandar Pahlavi and looking from the roof of his little palace of Mianposhteh at the town and the port exclaimed: 'What is that?' 'Your Majesty, it is the Soviet ship.' 'Take it away!' said the Shah angrily. The Foreign Ministry then declared to the Soviet Embassy that no negotiations for the signature of Treaties of Friendship and Trade would start until the gunboat had left Iranian territorial waters, and the Soviet Government being eager to conclude these treaties, had to recall their ship.

In Moscow we were lodged in two different hotels and I took the whole party twice to the opera at the Bolshoi, and then we started towards the frontier.

On arrival in Paris I found that my course at the Staff College did not begin until November and it was then early September, so I took the Golden Arrow to London to meet my family and stayed there until the first days of November, when we returned to Paris, staying at the Hotel Lutetia, until we found an apartment and my two years' course began.

The Staff College and the Iranian Army

The Staff College, or Ecole Supérieure de Guerre, was founded in its present form in 1878, and I was now entering this venerable institution, through which so many famous French Marshals and Generals had passed, as a member of the 49th Promotion. It counted 109 officers, 80 French and 29 foreign, Major de Lattre de Tassigny, later Maréchal de France, being the head of the Promotion.

Twice a week we had very interesting lectures on international politics by Jacques Bardoux, an adviser of the Quai d'Orsay and a specialist on Anglo-Saxon politics, and on geography by the famous geopolitician André Siegfried. Jacques Bardoux was a great admirer of Great Britain and everything British. He used to say to us: 'A British diplomat is first and foremost a gentleman. Do you know what a gentleman is? It is a man who keeps his hands and conscience clean.' Another time he described a British Ambassador who in private and when off duty was the perfect type of the English 'tweedy' country gentleman, but in the exercise of his duties, was a shrewd and extremely able diplomat. 'When he came home, he put his brains in a bowl on the mantelpiece and relaxed, and when going back to his service, took them out again and put them back into his head.' Jacques Bardoux used to write once a week the editorial in the *Temps*, up to the Second World War, and died in 1960 at a great age.

In the spring we were taken to the country to work out tactical situations previously studied on the map. These excursions were delightful, taking us into the beautiful French countryside and giving us the opportunity to enjoy specialities of the French cuisine in the places renowned for them.

Once a week we were given work to do at home, usually consisting of the tactical and logistical preparation of an offensive or defensive action. I sometimes passed the whole night on these problems, while my faithful wife plied me with black coffee to keep me awake.

All our instructors were very polite and considerate, except—as is the rule the world over—the riding instructors. This species called Hippos are generally of medium height, slim, with steel-blue, cold eyes and a chronic expression of contempt. They completely ignore the existence of any susceptibilities or pride in the victims whom fate delivers to them for the exercise of their sadistic whims.

Here is an example of one of the milder remarks of our Hippo to an unfortunate senior officer: 'Of course you are fat with a protruding belly, round thighs and short arms and you are not responsible for that, but why you must sit your horse like a sack of rotten potatoes and wriggle your legs like a pulcinello I fail to understand!' I am glad to say that Saumur, and my time with the Swiss Cavalry, together with years of continuous rough riding in Iran, protected me from such sarcasm.

We had been fortunate in finding a pleasant apartment in the Avenue de Suffren opposite the Champ de Mars and only two minutes' walk from the Ecole Militaire, for which we bought the furniture principally in the Flea Market—the dining-room table, chairs and sideboard cost us, I remember, about £5. Hilda had entered the Ecole des Langues Orientales for the study of Arabic and Persian, and we were both so busy that we had very little time for any kind of social life, but we used to see Picasso and his wife who were old friends of Hilda's and General Riazi, our military attaché and his family. We asked them to dinner, I remember, on the eve of Nowruz and just at the moment (ascertainable in all Iranian calendars) when the sun passed from the sign of the Fish into that of the Ram, the folding doors between the dining- and drawing-rooms were thrown open to reveal a Haft Sin table complete with brazier and incense and all the traditional objects. Mrs. Riazi was moved to tears as she exclaimed, 'I smell Iran.' On the thirteenth day after Nowruz, according to tradition, we had to throw our growing wheat into running water which of course was the Seine. So, late in the evening we set out for the Pont de l'Alma bearing our ungainly burden. As we approached the parapet of the bridge, a policeman appeared, viewing our activities with evident suspicion—he no doubt thought we were trying to get rid of a corpse. When the green wheat emerged from the parcel he looked puzzled but relieved.

Another acquaintance was Tapa Chermoyef, who had been President of the 'Republic of the Caucasian Mountain People' for a few months during the revolution and before its occupation by the Red Army in 1920. Then many people thought that the last word had not been said in Russia and that there was still a possibility that the Bolsheviks would be defeated and for this reason Detterding, the Chairman of Royal Dutch Shell, bought from Chermoyef the shares he held in Baku and Grosni oil for £20,000!

In the space of four years Chermoyef, a former cavalry guards officer, squandered the entire sum saying when remonstrated with: 'It was just for cigarettes.'

Leila was now four years old and Picasso gave her a silver mug on which he had had engraved one of his circus scenes. A few years ago in Teheran, Sacheverell Sitwell, who was lunching with us, remarked that it was probably Picasso's only uncatalogued work!

In June I finished my first year at the Staff College and at my request was detached for a month to a battalion of Chasseurs Alpins stationed at Annecy to study mountain warfare, Iran being almost entirely a mountainous country.

The rest of the summer we passed in England and Hilda took me to visit her sister who had been a Carmelite nun since she was twenty. It is a strictly enclosed order but a sister's husband is one of the few relatives allowed to see her unveiled, although only from behind a double grill. She seemed happy and was very much interested in everything and everybody.

My second year at the Ecole de Guerre passed just like the first with the addition of visits to Belgium, Alsace Lorraine and the battlefields of Northern France.

We stayed again for some time in London and in Paris before leaving for Iran. Both my brother and my sister were there though on very different errands. Ibrahim had been entrusted by the Shah with the purchase of modern armaments for the Iranian Army, a task for which his technical ability and incorruptibility made him eminently suitable. (At Saint Cyr the two most distinguished cadets in the school were made Sergeants and Ibrahim had been honoured in this way during his two years there, which was unprecedented for a foreigner.)

Fatimeh had never been in Iran and could not speak Persian. My father had finally consented to allow her to go to Paris with her mother to attend the School of Oriental Languages. Although he had lived for fifty years in Europe, he expected his daughter to behave as a well-brought-up young lady would have done in Iran, which was very hard on Fatimeh who was exceptionally gifted in many ways. During this time my father was in Teheran where he had unfortunately been persuaded by the American missionaries to sell our garden Arfaieh to them to be used as a boarding-school for girls, with the promise that he would be prayed for every day by these grateful maidens. Although a convinced Moslem, he probably considered that prayers from other quarters would also be welcome. We were very perturbed, as not only were we very fond of this garden but we realised, which my father did not, the tremendous rise in the value of land in Teheran which was to come about in the next few years. However, before leaving for Europe he had built for Ibrahim and myself two commodious houses, which were considered at the time to be the last word in modernity.

My father had brought back with him my orderly Rustem, who having been taught by my sister whilst he was at Monte Carlo to speak, read and write French, was able to get a job as interpreter with Kampsax, the famous Swedish Engineering Firm—a big step up for an illiterate peasant.

A few months before we arrived in Teheran, relations between Great Britain and Iran had deteriorated owing to what the British considered to be 'a lack of co-operative spirit' on the part of Reza Shah.

Contrary to expectations Reza Shah was becoming more and more independent-minded with the reinforcement of his Government as a result of the liquidation of every kind of opposition. Having become the Shahinshah he was the highest power in the State, so that action against him was no longer possible. All internal opposition had been stopped by alternately playing the politicians and former grandees one against the other and confronting them with a police and army blindly obedient to their Supreme Chief, thus giving them only the choice between submission or exile. All the tribes and hereditary governors who used to counteract the Central Government's moves by creating at inopportune moments local disturbances had been subjected by force, disarmed and rendered impotent, at least in the north and west of the country. The budget was balanced, and needing no new loans the Shah could not be influenced financially. He had concluded a new treaty of friendship and of trade with Soviet Russia, and had reached an agreement concerning the Caspian Sea fisheries on a 50-50 basis both as to administration and to profits. The Ministry of Justice had been completely re-organised, modern civil and penal codes adopted and the capitulations suppressed. The Government had acquired the right to fix the customs taxes as it wished, a tobacco monopoly had been established and the construction of a railway from the Caspian to the Gulf undertaken. This was contrary to the British wish that the line should pass from Teheran to the Iraqi frontier. A National Bank had been founded which was soon to undertake the issue of bank-notes, and a few gunboats were ordered from Italy which would challenge the complete domination of Great Britain in the Persian Gulf, where none of the countries having a seaboard had flown their flags before. It was anticipated that the Shah would soon ask the A.P.O.C. to change its statutes and substantially increase the royalties paid to the Iranian Government, and that the stipends paid until then to Sheikh Khazal and to the Bakhtiari chiefs, which were counted in the 16 per cent royalties paid to the Government, would be paid to Teheran. Only the Central Government was now responsible for law and order in the region of the airfields.

All this had undermined the influence of Great Britain in Iran and it was obvious that time was likely to accelerate the process. This was understood not only by the British but also by the southern tribes who believed in the past that the British were their natural protectors against any encroachment by the Central Government on what they considered their rights.

In 1929 the extensive region to the south and south-west of Isfahan, where the important tribes of the Bakhtiari, Qashqai, Khamseh, Boveir Ahmadi, Mamasseni and others dwelt, had not yet been brought under control by the Central Government, except for the bigger towns, and these tribes were all armed and provided with ammunition by gun-running from Masqat and the Arab Sheikhdoms of the Trucial Coast. Their chiefs understood that their turn to be disarmed and subjected was coming, and for the first time they united and started a general revolt against the Government, thinking that they had the moral support of the Paramount Power in the Gulf—Great Britain. They were supported in this opinion by the attitude of individual Englishmen, especially among junior A.P.O.C. employees, who did not conceal their disapproval of the reassertion of the Central Government's control and of its disarmament policy in the south of Iran. Although the Bakhtiari were traditionally hostile to the Qashqai, this time they joined them and in a few weeks the whole southern part of Iran was ablaze, Shiraz being practically cut off from Isfahan which was threatened from the west by the Bakhtiari.

Of course the British Government was ready to mediate between the Shah's Government and the tribes, but the acceptance of such mediation would have been tantamount to the recognition of Great Britain's influence in the south of Iran and would have confirmed the tribal chiefs in their belief that Great Britain was their protector, and that the Central Government accepted this fact.

The Shah understood the situation and decided to take action compatible with the position he wanted Iran to occupy in the world: that of a completely independent country resolved on protecting its interests and at the same time maintaining its prestige and national dignity. He ordered General Sheibani, the former Chief of Staff, whom he knew to be a brave and able man, to proceed at once to Fars and to take command of all the forces situated in that province. At the same time, General Shahbakhti, who was also fearless and devoted to the Shah, was sent to Isfahan, to lead the forces in that region, and to drive the Bakhtiari to the west where they could be attacked in their strongholds.

All this had happened while we were still in Paris, so that I was expecting to be sent to Shiraz as soon as I arrived in Teheran. We travelled again through Moscow and Baku, where we noticed a further deterioration in the food situation.

In Teheran, we settled in our new house, Arfaieh A (Arfaieh B being Ibrahim's house), but in spite of my asking to be sent to General Sheibani's forces operating around Shiraz, I had to resume my duties as second in command of the Pahlavi Guards Cavalry Regiment, and after a few days was detached to the

Military Academy, as lecturer on general tactics and Director of tactical training. I used to deliver four lectures on tactics during four hours, and after lunch rode out into the country to supervise the field exercises of the cadets.

On the 21st March 1930 I was promoted lieutenant-colonel, and shortly after that with the financial help of my mother-in-law we bought our first car, a small Peugeot limousine which I drove myself.

As my wife and myself are fluent in Russian we were often in Russian-speaking society, the leaders of which were General Yazdanpanah, Assad Bahador (former Minister in Russia and later Minister of the Court) and his Polish wife, and Abdul Hoseyn Teimurtash, Minister of the Court, and his Armenian wife. Teimurtash was a brilliant, active and highly intelligent man, a former cadet of the Imperial Russian Nikolayevski Cavalry School. He was extremely good-looking and a terrible heart-breaker, and was considered the most powerful man in Iran after the Shah, to whom he appeared completely devoted. We were often at their parties, which were always gay and characterised by the polished lightness and sophistication of aristocratic circles in Russia before the revolution.

One day in May 1930 I was summoned to the General Staff. The Chief of Staff, General Mohammed Nakhchevan, who had replaced General Sheibani, told me that His Majesty had been pleased to appoint me Commander of the Pahlavi Guards Cavalry Regiment. I was elated. This was exactly what I had longed for, an independent appointment in which I could work according to my own ideas! I went straight to Jamshidiyeh some five miles away where the adjutant Captain Modabber was waiting for me. I was being shown the regiment's quarters, when the special trumpet signal announcing the arrival of the Shah sounded, and I rushed to the entrance just as His Majesty alighted from his car, and reported myself and the regiment to him. The Shah listened to my report, then a tour through the barracks began. He stopped in front of the windows of one of the armouries and said angrily: 'These sons of burned fathers can't even keep their windows clean!' And with his cane he broke all the window panes, while I calculated rapidly the price of the Imperial anger which I would have to pay out of my 135 tomans' monthly pay (£20).

After having walked in silence through the barracks, Reza Shah returned to his car. Then I gathered up my courage and said: 'I have a petition to present for Your Majesty's consideration.' With one foot on the car's step, the Shah looked at me inquiringly: 'Speak!'

'I give Your Majesty my word to train this regiment according to Your Majesty's wishes, but I beg that Your Majesty will not visit the regiment again for three months. I also respectfully report to Your Majesty that I took command of this regiment only one hour ago.'

The Shah looked at me with his golden eyes as if appraising me, for what seemed to me a very long time, then entered his car, and was gone.

Now began for me a period of strenuous work absorbing all my thoughts and all my time. I gave myself one whole month to go thoroughly into the situation of all the branches of the regiment's activities, and to prepare a rational plan of instruction for the recruits as well as for the older soldiers, translating this into time-tables, progression charts, etc., tightening the discipline and putting the units into shape. At the end of the first month I began to work according to the plan of training I had prepared. I did not forget that I had only two months left before having to show the result of my work to the Shah. Every day I had to pass at least two hours in the different departments of the General Staff and the War Ministry, to try to get the officers, N.C.O.s, soldiers, horses, equipment, etc., necessary to bring the regiment up to establishment. My insistence and complete disregard of the rules of the game of polite procrastination, although rendering me obnoxious to the gentlemen sitting behind the desks, allowed me to reduce the shortcomings of my regiment to an appreciable extent. I asked for the transfer of Major Mikeladze and Captain Selim Lohras (formerly Soltanof) from Tabriz, and got them by order of the Shah.

At the end of August, exactly three months since his first visit, the Shah came and made a tour of the regiment, while I gave him extensive explanations about the training, etc. He did not say a word, but I understood that he was satisfied.

In November my mother-in-law arrived in Teheran in fulfilment of a promise she had made to spend Christmas with us but towards the end of December she fell ill and on the 13th

January she died. This was a great grief to us all. The Christian cemetery in Teheran is in a beautiful garden shaded by big trees and it is there that she is buried.

My work was at that time very arduous, because apart from the ordinary training we had to prepare ourselves for the great military parade held yearly on the 3rd Esfand (21st February), the anniversary of the *coup d'état* of 1921. Reza Shah attached special importance to this parade, which was intended to show the nation—as well as foreigners—the might of the Iranian State and the increasing effectiveness of the Army. The Teheran garrison then consisted of two full divisions, an artillery brigade and four cavalry regiments, with sappers, miners and signallers, and all these units were preparing themselves feverishly for the review.

I had decided to organise a cavalry display consisting of a *jigitovka* (Caucasian Cossacks' trick riding), a musical ride, a competition of swordsmanship and some firing from the horse at the gallop at targets, tent pegging and ring lifting. I had also prepared a mock fight comprising reconnoitring, establishing contact, dismounting, advancing under fire, remounting on horses brought up at a gallop and a cavalry charge, all to be performed in ten minutes. I had also written a little sketch about how a conscript was taken to his regiment, sent to fight some dissident tribes, wounded, decorated by his colonel, and finally greeted in his village by his parents and fiancée, finishing with an apotheosis while the cavalry band played the National Anthem. This play was to be performed by soldiers with the co-operation of three girl artists at the barracks after the review and march-past, in the regimental canteen hall, in front of all the soldiers.

When the day came, all the phases of my private tattoo had been rehearsed many times, and in spite of some opposition I managed to introduce it into the general programme of the review. Some 20,000 men had been assembled on three sides of the race-course of Jelaliyeh to the west of the town, and from 1 p.m. the crowds assembled on the western side of the parade ground. At half-past one we mounted our horses. Dozens of times I rode along the squadrons, on the flanks and the rear, to see that everything was in order.

At 2 p.m. the Shah arrived and mounted his big white horse. The commander of the parade, General Shaqaqi, commanded:

'Garrison! Attention! present . . . arms!' and lifting his sword in front of his face, galloped full tilt towards the Shah, stopping his horse abruptly a few yards from him, and lowering his sword he reported the troops ready for the review while the first band struck up the National Anthem. After taking the report, the Shah, followed by four aides-de-camp and Shaqaqi, went to the front of the first regiment, where colours were lowered while the soldiers shouted continuous hurrahs while the Shah was passing in front of their line. Then it was the turn of the second regiment, and so on until all the forces had been reviewed.

When the review was ended, the Shah trotted towards his special tribune, allowing Shaqaqi to order the stand at ease. The General again galloped to the middle of the parade ground and lifting his sword high above his head: 'Garrison! Arms . . . down!' A single sound was heard as eighteen thousand rifle butts touched the ground and two thousand swords were thrown into their scabbards. After that an infantry battalion performed rhythmical rifle drill in a really unsurpassed manner. I have seen such performances in several armies, but never such precision and variety of movements executed during six minutes without any words or even signs of command.

Then came our turn. In order not to make the Shah wait, everything was made ready on the ground during the infantry's performance, and the whole display started, lasting twenty-five minutes, without any hitch. I was standing by the Shah's platform throughout. Then the units marched past the Shah. When it was finished, I galloped to Jamshidiyeh, and assisted at the performance of my play, and thanked the soldiers for their excellent performance at the cavalry display and march-past.

When I came back, Hilda rushed to tell me the news. General Shaqaqi, Inspector-General of Cavalry, who had acted as commander of the parade, had just called by order of the Shah, announcing that His Majesty, highly satisfied by my regiment's performance and its visible progress in training and appearance, had been pleased to appoint me his honorary aide-de-camp.

After that I designed a special badge for the regiment, to be worn by the officers, which was accepted by the Shah. I also fixed the 24th April (day of Reza Shah's coronation) as the regiment's feast, and on that day organised a cavalry display with a surprise number. Five of my officers, who had passed through the Saumur

Cavalry School, had trained their horses to perform Spanish riding school figures, which had up to then never been seen in Iran. I invited the Crown Prince, who was twelve years old, and several Cabinet Ministers and Generals with their wives to the performance.

The next day, after the morning exercises, I was working in my office when my adjutant, Modabber, announced that an officer had brought a horse from the Imperial stables and wanted to see me. I received the lieutenant and thinking that the horse had been sent to me to be trained, told him to put it in the 2nd squadron's stables. The lieutenant smiled, 'But His Majesty is sending this horse for you as a gift,' he said. I could not believe my ears. The Shah was very chary of making gifts to anyone. They told me that the horse had been bought at the Saumur Cavalry School by Colonel Riazi especially for His Majesty, and sent by railway through Russia to Tabriz, and then by lorry to Teheran, and that it had cost some 20,000 tomans. It was a magnificent bay animal and besides being beautifully trained by Saumur's *cadre noir*, had a smooth trot and a gentle temper.

This Imperial mark of favour provoked among the other colonels and even generals some jealousy and hostility towards me, especially as the Shah ordered a circular to be sent to the regimental commanders of all arms to visit my regiment and to follow my example for the training and administration of their units.

One day a general told me that the horse which had been given to me by the Shah was not a very good animal according to Iranian taste, and that he had a very beautiful Arab stallion which he was ready to exchange for my horse. I understood at once what was his purpose and answered him that this horse was the most precious of my possessions as it had been given to me by my beloved Sovereign, and the General departed disappointed at having failed in his little plot.

The Shah's kindness to me emboldened me to say to him one day when he came to an open-air exercise, that it was the custom in monarchical armies to honour some Guards regiments by appointing members of the reigning family as Colonels-in-Chief, and that it would be the utmost honour for the Pahlavi Regiment, which already bore His Majesty's name, to have H.H. the Crown

Prince as its Colonel-in-Chief. The Shah smiled, but as usual did not answer. Next day I had a telephone call from the Chief of Staff authorising me, by order of His Majesty, to present an official demand for the appointment of the Crown Prince.

After it had been accorded I prepared a silver-embroidered saddle-cloth, specially designed shoulder-strap badges with the word Crown Prince in gold, the regimental badge to be worn on the breast, a pair of silver spurs and a silver-topped stick, all on a silver tray. After having asked for an audience I went to the palace at the head of a regimental deputation comprising, besides myself, a senior officer, a junior officer, an N.C.O. and a trooper, and presented these insignia to the Crown Prince. After that I invited the Crown Prince several times to assist at the regiment's manœuvres and field exercises which he always attended on horseback.

Reza Shah decided to send his son to study in Europe. Up to that time the Crown Prince, as well as his full brother Prince Ali Reza, had attended the military primary school, in a special class with the sons of army generals and colonels. It was decided to send the two princes with their tutor Nafici and two other boys (Teimurtash's third son and a boy named Fardust, who is now a brigadier-general and still close to the Shah) to Switzerland for five years, during which time he was not to return to Teheran.

Being the Commander of the Crown Prince's regiment, I asked permission to accompany him to Bandar Pahlavi, with a guard from his regiment. Reza Shah and all the members of the Imperial family as well as a few Ministers and generals were of the party. The Imperial family remained one night in Bandar Pahlavi, and the next day a Soviet training ship with naval cadets, specially sent to take the Crown Prince to Baku, entered the port. A battalion of the Rasht Brigade and my regiment's squad were on the quay, waiting for the Prince to arrive. He drove with his travelling companions, and insisted on having his car taken on board the ship. The Soviet naval cadets were aligned on the ship's deck and when the Prince came near the ship the Iranian units, and then the Soviet cadets, stood at attention and presented arms. The Crown Prince boarded the ship, which at once left for Baku while the soldiers cheered from the shore.

I went from there to the Shah's palace. He was in the garden, the persons of his suite standing respectfully in a circle around him. He was pacing up and down and looked much affected. 'It is very hard for me to part with my beloved son,' he said, 'but one must think of the country. Iran needs educated and enlightened rulers, we, the old and ignorant must go.'

I was extremely moved by these words. How much greater Reza Shah appeared to me then than the notorious Shah Abbas, who wanted glory for himself alone, murdering one and blinding two of his sons because he feared them as a possible danger to himself and because he did not wish to have worthy successors to share with him the esteem of the nation and so diminish his glory in the eyes of history.

My brother was still buying weapons for the army, and Reza Shah held him in high esteem. Our army had now a uniform infantry armament, and Ibrahim was ordering mountain guns from Bofors, in Sweden. He used to come to Teheran to ask for fresh instructions, staying with us, as his own house was let.

One day while he was in Teheran, Reza Shah summoned him and said that he was not satisfied with the training and discipline of the Military Academy. As Ibrahim had been an instructor there and knew it well, the Shah ordered him to pay a visit to the School, and after inspecting it unobtrusively to report to him how things were. The Academy was commanded by a colonel, but at the same time was under the direct supervision of the Chief of Staff. After visiting the School, Ibrahim reported to the Shah that the discipline was slack, the training inadequate and the officer corps unsuitable for the task of forming cadets into officers. The Shah asked Ibrahim what to do. 'Appoint my brother Hassan, who, as I have heard, has earned the satisfaction of Your Majesty with his work in the cavalry. He is tough and a strict disciplinarian, and that is what the Academy needs above everything else.'

The Shah accepted, but said that I must continue to look after the cavalry also, because I had given it a beneficial shake-up, and it would revert to the former sad condition if I were to leave it. So I was appointed Commandant of the Military Academy, at the same time keeping command of the Pahlavi Regiment, and an organisation called 'Cavalry Commission' whose duty was to supervise the training of the cavalry units was formed under my leadership, so I had three full-time jobs on my hands. Later the Shah cancelled the Chief of Staff's direct supervision of the Military Academy.

In 1932 I was promoted Colonel, and on the day of the Nowruz Salam, while passing in front of the senior officers assembled in the Golestan Palace for the usual New Year ceremonies, the Shah halted in front of me, saying: 'You answered those sons of burned fathers very well.'

I was taken aback until I remembered that a few weeks before I had read a rather nasty article against Iran and especially against the Shah in the *Near East and India*, from 'a correspondent' whose identity I guessed. I had sent a very sharp reply to the paper, which had been published, and no doubt this had been reported to the Shah who had been pleased with it. It was a great mark of favour, His Majesty not being very generous with such marks of appreciation, as was shown during another Salam, when after having heard the congratulatory speech of the War Minister, which apparently he did not find to his taste, he said to the trembling General, alluding to his predecessor who had died lately: 'How sad that he, who was so good has gone, and you who are so bad are still here.'

One day the Shah came to my regiment on inspection, and said to me pleasantly: 'Now, what have you to show me today?' I had just completed the arrangement of a new veterinary infirmary, and was taking the Shah there when, to my horror, I noticed in the middle of the cleanly swept expanse of the courtyard a black object which I suspected to be something quite out of place there. The Shah was making straight for this . . . object. I was plunged in deep anguish, when glancing to my right, I saw my adjutant, Captain Modabber, following us some thirty yards behind. I was talking to the Shah, my hand lifted at my cap, and could not turn my head or make a signal without the Shah noticing it. Although I was half a step to the left and to the rear of the Shah, the sun was behind us so he would have noticed the movements of my shadow. All the same, I managed to turn my head imperceptibly to the right and catch the eye of the adjutant, indicating the black spot in front of us. Being quick-witted Modabber ran straight towards it and stood on it with both feet, saluting when the Shah came near. 'What is this man doing here?' he asked. 'Sir, he is the adjutant, and is here in order to execute any orders Your Majesty might be pleased to give.'

The Shah examined the captain, who was nearly as tall as himself, beginning at his head. As he gradually lowered his eyes, my dread increased, but luckily the Shah did not look below the adjutant's waist, and I quickly spoke of the infirmary. Of course, when he came back, both the adjutant and the obnoxious object had disappeared.

Reza Shah was very outspoken, and the higher the rank of the people who were in his presence the more they feared him. One day he went to visit the Hamleh Regiment at Mehrabad (where the Teheran civil airport is today), but when Mikeladze, who had been appointed commander of this regiment on my recommendation, came to report to him, the Shah interrupted him and said: 'Mount your horse, gallop to town, go to the Ministry of Roads and say to the Minister: "You . . . etc., how dare you leave this road in such disrepair? I give you until tomorrow to have it repaired!" '

Mikeladze galloped to town, entered the Minister's office, then, standing at attention, delivered word for word the Imperial message.

'Tell His Majesty that the road will be immediately repaired,' said the trembling Minister. On his way back to Mehrabad, Mikeladze was overtaken by several lorries full of labourers with picks and shovels, who at once began to work on the road, which was repaired in a little more than an hour!

Another time while driving in his car, the Shah was stopped by a soldier, who complained of the bad quality of the food in his regiment. The Shah drove to the regiment, went straight to the kitchen, tasted the food and immediately dismissed both the colonel commander of the regiment and the general commanding the division, who not even daring to take his divisional car, returned to his house on foot.

During the summer I had to be at the Military Academy's Summer Camp at Aqdassieh, ten miles from town, and so entrusted the regiment to Major Lohras, who was then second in command. I began looking for a place where I could live with my family during the two summer months, when one day the owner of a small estate called Larak, which was contiguous to Aqdassieh, proposed that we should occupy his garden, sleeping under tents, whilst he continued to occupy his house. He was a very hospitable man, but in this case his offer was not entirely disinterested as he hoped by having the Commandant of the Academy as his guest to be protected from the cadets, whose raids on his fruit trees and interference with his water supply had plagued him in the past. We visited the garden, which was enclosed by mud walls in the middle of an eighty-acre estate, and contained some centenarian plane trees, and accepted the offer with alacrity. We were thinking of buying a country place near Teheran, my wife had sold the house in London and at the end of the two months the proprietor offered to sell his property to us as he wanted to go to Monte Carlo to try out a wonderful system at roulette. The property pleased us, and in May 1933 Hilda bought the place. Our long-cherished desire to own a country house was fulfilled and we found ourselves the happy owners of a small country estate, quite near to town, which we could reach by car in twenty minutes.

We bought a flock of eighty sheep and two oxen which were on the place, and a little later a cow with her calf. Unfortunately, having sent the cow to graze in a mountain valley some three miles away, a leopard devoured the calf and wounded the cow so that we had to kill her. We then bought three good milch cows, and these were the nucleus of the herd which we have still in Larak, and the beginning of our dairy farm.

It was at about this time that King Faisal I of Iraq came to visit Reza Shah, accompanied by Nuri Said, then Prime Minister. He brought three fine Arab stallions as a gift to the Shah, who took him to visit the Military Academy, where I had to give the necessary explanations to the Royal party. It was during this visit that Nuri Said concluded an agreement with our Foreign Ministry concerning the navigation rights on the Shatt-el-Arab, according to which, although the frontier would continue to be on the low-water line of the Iranian shore, a space of five kilometres on both sides of the ports of Abadan and Khorramshahr, and up to the middle of the river, would be considered as Iranian Territorial Waters. Before that, ships moored on the Abadan quay had been considered to be in Iraqi waters, and this anomalous situation created many difficulties. After the 1958 Iraqi revolution these questions again arose and have not yet been satisfactorily settled.

Early in 1932, two Turkish delegations came to Teheran. One

of them under Jelal Bayar, the head of the Turkish Ish Bankasi (afterwards President of the Republic and now in prison), was to negotiate a trade and financial agreement with Iran. The other was headed by Tewfiq Rushtu bey (later known as Ruştu Aras), the Turkish Foreign Minister, who had come to propose the exchange of an area on the top and eastern slopes of the lesser Ararat with an area of the same surface on the west of Rezaieh. He also hoped to settle a land dispute in the Qotur region, where the Turks had never recognised the frontier line as it was settled by the 1913–14 Turco-Iranian Frontier Commission in which Russian and British members had participated, saying that this line had been enforced by foreign pressure and had occupied a fairly wide slice of their territory. The Turkish Minister was assisted by a General Staff colonel, and I had been appointed on the recommendation of Teimurtash, as military assistant to our Foreign Minister, Mohammad Ali Forughi (who had before that been Ambassador in Ankara, and was afterwards several times Prime Minister).

Forughi was a very gentle and cultured man, and one day, while dining with Atatürk in Ankara, the latter insisted on stressing the strategic necessity for Turkey to have the flank of its defensive position on the Aghri mountains chain facing Russia protected by the lesser Ararat, the eastern slopes of which belonged to Iran, in order to complete its system of defence, and Forughi had said that this question could be discussed in Teheran. Atatürk had seized upon this and had prepared a proposal for an exchange of territory, which had to be put to us by the dynamic and purposeful Tewfiq Rushtu.

During the negotiations, which had been agreed to in principle but were now concerned with the details of the new frontier line, the Turkish colonel and myself failed to agree on the fate of a hill to the west of Qotur. I claimed the necessity of its becoming Iranian as it overlooked the Qotur valley, while the Turk insisted on it remaining in Turkish territory. The two Ministers remained silent, smiling at our uncompromising ardour.

Finally, Tewfiq Rushtu said that they had complete confidence in His Majesty the Shahinshah, and that they were therefore ready to accept him as arbitrator. 'Let Colonel Arfa go to the palace, explain the case to His Majesty, and his decision will be accepted by us.'

I took the maps and plans and drove to the palace, and while I was putting the maps on the table, the Shah entered and asked me what it was about. Showing the hill on the map, I was explaining in detail the strategical advantages of having that hill in our possession, when I realised that the Shah was not looking at the map but at me, with a somewhat quizzical expression in his yellow eagle's eyes. Embarrassed, I became silent.

'Is there not another hill, higher than this one, in the vicinity?' he said.

'Yes, Your Majesty.'

'Well, then why not ask for that also?'

Then, after a pause, he said, in a serious and inspired manner: 'You do not understand me. It is not this or that hill which is important: it is the settlement, once and for all, of our frontier disputes with Turkey. The disagreements between our two countries in the past, which have always been to the profit of our enemies, must cease, and a sincere friendship based on our mutual interests be established between Iran and Turkey. If we are allied and united, I do not fear anybody.' After these words he left the room.

I put my maps together and went back to the Foreign Ministry, where the commission was waiting for the Shah's answer. When I entered, they asked me eagerly what the Shah had said. 'His Majesty said that being friends and brothers there are no strategic considerations between us, and we can share the hill.'

So it was decided, and the slope facing Qotur was included in Iranian territory while the western slope remained Turkish. The Turks evacuated the territory which was to become Iranian and the barren slopes of the Ararat were given to them in exchange for a region of similar area, containing six Kurdish villages.

In 1933, events took place which deeply affected the situation in Iran, and indirectly had fateful consequences for my family. When the oil concession had been given by Mozaffar-ed-Din Shah to William Knox d'Arcy, oil was still far from being of the immense importance it is now, because steamers were still burning coal, motor-cars were only just beginning to be used and aviation was still in its infancy. Although the presence of oil deposits had been discovered by the French mission of de Morgan, it was not at all certain that it would be found in Iran in quantities which would warrant its exploitation. The conditions of the concession were entirely to the advantage of the concessionaire, the Iranian Government's share being only 16 per cent, and all the calculations of the profits were left to the concessionaire. It is not within the scope of this book to enter into the details of this question, which has been fully treated by many informed authors. A majority of the shares of the A.P.O.C., formed in 1909 with the participation of the Burma Oil Co., had been purchased by the British Government in 1914. During the First World War the needs of the British Navy, which had adopted oil fuel, were provided by Iranian oil, no accounts being given for that period to the Iranian Government, and the final settlement for all oil extracted until 1920 being fixed at a sum of £1,000,000 as the Iranian Government's share.

In 1931, the share of the Government was some £1,300,000, but the next year it fell to £306,000, and the Government refused to accept it. Negotiations which started several times proving fruitless, the Shah decided to cancel the concession and negotiate for a new concession on more favourable conditions. (November 1932.)

The situation became strained, British warships appeared in the Persian Gulf, and the Iranian forces in Khuzistan were reinforced.

The British Government complained to the League of Nations, Mr. Benesh was appointed arbitrator, and finally the two parties were invited to open direct negotiations in Geneva. Davar, the Minister of Finance, and Hoseyn Ala, were sent as the representatives of Iran.

One morning I was working in my office at the Military Academy when a letter from the Foreign Minister marked 'Urgent—Confidential' was brought to me. It was signed by the late Soheili (afterwards Prime Minister and Ambassador in London), the Secretary General, on the part of the Minister, Forughi, and the contents were as follows:

> 'His Excellency the Foreign Minister asks you to be kind enough to write your opinion on the Anglo-Iranian oil dispute, as he understands that you are well informed on this question. He will be much obliged if you would let the Foreign Minister have your reply before tomorrow morning, when a courier will be dispatched to Geneva to our representatives, to whom it might be useful.'

I set to work, and before night I had prepared a paper containing our case from the technical, financial and moral points of view.

I typed it in French and in English, and sent it to the Foreign Ministry at 7 o'clock next morning. The Ministry thanked me for this afterwards, and these notes were useful to me at the time when the oil concession question came again to the fore in 1950.

In addition to the armaments he was buying, my brother Ibrahim was now ordered to buy planes for the Iranian Air Force, and also anti-aircraft batteries. The selling of arms is not only a commercial business proposition but entails political and strategical commitments, because if arms are bought by a country not possessing an established war industry of some importance on its territory, from a foreign country, it presupposes that this country is considered by the buyer as not likely to become hostile or likely to join hostile powers in the eventuality of a war, as the supply of ammunition and spare parts as well as the replacement or completion of the acquired war material would then be impossible.

Millions were now passing through his hands and the very special nature of the purchases he was making might very well have enabled him to enrich himself without actual dishonesty, but content with the international prestige his unusual integrity gained for him he allowed the State to profit from any discount offered to him by the firms concerned. He was also subjected to solicitations and pressures from several governments both directly and through highly placed personalities in Teheran and in Embassies abroad but he was absolutely incorruptible. All impartial persons who dealt with him recognised his inflexible rectitude and the moral courage and extraordinary capacity he exercised in the accomplishment of the important mission entrusted to him by his Sovereign. Because of this there was considerable resentment against him.

As our father had passed nearly sixty years of his long life abroad and had twice married foreigners, he was without the family connexions which were and indeed still are of capital importance in Iran. We were almost like strangers in our own country so that except for myself, who held a not very influential position in the army, Ibrahim had no one to counter the hostile intrigues that were being woven against him on all sides.

Eager to secure the best armament at the lowest price, he was obliged to travel continuously all over Europe and America ordering some things in one place and some in another. This process took time, and an accusation of procrastination was brought against him, which gained some credit with the Shah, who was impatient to see his army in possession of a modern, unified armament.

In 1931, the Shah ordered yearly autumn manœuvres to be held in the neighbourhood of the capital, with the participation of all the garrison units. I was appointed a member of the manœuvres committee, and took part in them either as Chief of Staff of one of the opposing forces, or commander of a cavalry division formed for the manœuvres with three or four cavalry regiments and accessory units.

In October 1932, after the manœuvres had taken place and the Shah had conveyed his appreciation to the committee and the executants, I took one month's leave to make a trip to the south of the country, which was then still quite unknown to me.

The beauties of Isfahan have been so often described by travellers that one fears to be disappointed at the reality but it surpassed my expectations. It is interesting to note that it is an early and excellent example of town planning. Shiraz, the city of poets, lovers, wine and roses, is still famous for its gardens and the charming hospitality of the Shirazis. Persepolis (Takht-e-Jamshid in Persian) is only sixty miles away. Its ruins are amongst the most impressive in the world, especially to an Iranian caring for national prestige. We were lucky enough to see them by moonlight in all their eerie splendour.

The road to Bushehr was then extremely narrow and the lorries using it had to back three or four times to pass each of the innumerable hairpin bends by which one reached sea level from the high Iranian plateau. It is a sad little town, having lost all importance as a port, but is still redolent of the romance of the Persian Gulf. We saw there the newly bought ships of the infant Iranian Navy, two gunboats and four sloops, which were waiting in the roads to be inspected by the Shah that day, before going to the newly built port of Bandar Shahpur. Bushehr is joined to the rest of the world by a very narrow causeway several miles long, built to enable traffic to cross the salt marshes, and we travelled over it at breakneck speed—held up once by a party of camels for an agonising ten minutes—for fear of meeting with the Imperial car, which would have necessitated our throwing our beloved Peugeot off the causeway into the marshes.

From there we followed what was then a mere track along the coast towards Ahvaz, at that time a dirty little town of some 6000 inhabitants, and Mohammerah (now Khorramshahr) with its winding narrow lanes and canals. We stopped for a night at Ganaveh, where a young employee of the A.P.O.C. (the Anglo-Persian Oil Company) offered us hospitality. He was an excellent example of the young Englishman of those days on service in a strange country, having organised his little house with comfort and even elegance and filling his spare time in that lonely post by helping the local inhabitants for whom he had organised a dispensary.

On my return I received a telephone call from the Military Academy, saying that two days before His Majesty had come to the Academy, and being dissatisfied with the way the commands were given, had become very angry and dismissed the commander of the battalion and a couple of other officers. This was bad news. A few days afterwards, I was relieved of the command of the Pahlavi Cavalry Regiment, in order to concentrate on the training of the Military Academy, and after a moving farewell ceremony, entrusted the regiment to Major Selim Lohras.

At the end of December 1932, we learned with stupefaction that Abdul Hoseyn Teimurtash, the brilliant and up to then apparently trusted Minister of the Court, had been dismissed from his post and was under house arrest. It was said that Teimurtash was gambling at the Iran Club, losing sometimes sums up to ten thousand tomans (£1500 gold) in one night, and that the Shah had ordered an inquiry.

As we used to take flowers to Tatyana Teimurtash every Christmas Eve, we considered it would be ungracious to refrain from doing so because her husband was in disgrace. We drove to the Teimurtashs' home, which was heavily guarded by police and gendarmes who would allow nobody inside the house but took the flowers to be presented to Tatyana. No doubt the bouquet was searched for a written message before being handed to her, if indeed it even reached her. But although the police

recognised us, as I was in uniform, I did not get into trouble for
my gesture.

Two newspapers praised the Shah for having dismissed
Teimurtash, and he ordered the police to give the editors brooms
and make them sweep the Sepah Square, because, he said,
'Yesterday they were praising and flattering him, and today they
are abusing him, without knowing why he had been dismissed,
and that shows baseness.'

The Commission of Enquiry presided over by the Chairman
of the Bank Control Committee, gave an unfavourable report,
and Teimurtash was transferred to prison.

It was further rumoured that while on a mission in the
U.S.S.R. he had lost a suit-case containing very important secret
documents, which had probably fallen into the hands of the
Soviet authorities, and that he was suspected of sympathy, if
not of understanding, with them. Other sources found a connexion between the cancellation of the A.P.O.C.'s oil concession
and Teimurtash's disgrace.

A short time after, Teimurtash died in prison of a heart
attack, taking his secrets with him to the grave.

About this time Karakhan, the Assistant Soviet Foreign Secretary, came to Teheran, bringing presents to the Shah from
Stalin. Among these presents were a light tank and a beautiful
chestnut Don Stallion which was given to the Shah in the course
of a ceremony at the Military Academy. On this occasion I took
Karakhan (who was later liquidated by Stalin during one of his
great purges) to visit the School's museum, directing him
straight towards a red flag with Persian inscriptions. He asked
what it was, and I answered in a casual manner that it was the
flag of the short-lived Gilan Socialist Soviet Republic, taken by
our forces when they reoccupied that province, having defeated
the Communists. Karakhan, being an Armenian besides a
diplomat, merely said: 'How interesting.'

In April 1933, after long negotiations, an agreement had been
reached by which the A.P.O.C. was granted a new concession to
cover a period of sixty years by which the area conceded was
reduced to 100,000 square miles and the Government's royalties
raised to 20 per cent amongst other minor advantages. The new
conditions were considered favourable, but the prolongation of
the duration of the concession was privately criticised, no one

daring publicly to offer any opinion. Some said as a counterpart, a new Treaty of Commerce was signed at the same time with the U.S.S.R.

In the autumn of that year, the intrigues against my brother had begun to bear fruit, and he was ordered to put his accounts in order preliminary to his recall to Teheran. Little by little, a political character was given to the accusations against him, and this did not fail to react on me. On the pretext that I was too severe for the examinations and that several warrant officers who were to be commissioned had received insufficient marks and failed, and that my severity prevented the army from acquiring the commissioned officers it wanted, I was relieved of the command of the Military Academy and transferred to the Army Inspectorate, a new body whose chief was General Jahanbani. I was succeeded at the Academy by my old friend and chief, General Yazdanpanah, former commander of the 1st Teheran Division.

All sorts of wild rumours were being spread against my brother: it was said that he had disappeared, that he had been arrested and extradited, and several people meeting me in the street looked quite astonished, saying they had heard that I was also arrested. All these rumours were false but my brother was recalled to Teheran, and after a time appointed to command the anti-aircraft group of two batteries.

Atatürk and the Shah. Baluchistan

The Central Government having reasserted its control along all the coast of the Persian Gulf and the Arabian Sea, customs and Gendarmerie posts had been established in the ports and smuggling and gun-running, which most of the shore dwellers took part in, had been seriously hampered. It appeared that the newly appointed Government servants, whose one desire was to return to the north on account of the trying climate of the sea-shore, lacked the necessary tact and understanding to deal with the local population, which was then subjected to military con-scription, the payment of taxes and other signs of administrative reform without as yet having reaped the benefits from these.

Many of the people had been employed in the profitable industry of shipbuilding in Bandar-Lengeh and other places. Most of the famous dhows plying in the Persian Gulf had been built there from timber imported from India, and Lengeh had become towards the end of the nineteenth century an important trade centre of the Gulf, the dhows distributing merchandise imported from abroad to the neighbouring ports and especially to the Trucial coast of Oman. Since the British India Steamship Co. had adopted Sharjah as a port of call this port had assumed the role of distributing centre formerly held by Lengeh, and the construction of dhows had also ceased, throwing many people out of work. All these combined causes resulted in mass emigra-tion of the coastal population, composed of a mixture of Baluchis (chiefly to the east of Bandar 'Abbas), Lors, Arabs and Negroes. These Negroes were the descendants of black slaves imported from Zanzibar when in the nineteenth century that island and Masqat-Oman were under the same sultan, who had also rented for some thirty years the entire Iranian coast from Khamir to Gwatar. Most of these emigrants went to the Arab coast and to what was then British Baluchistan.

In order to find out and report on the exact position so that the necessary measures to improve the economic situation of the coastal inhabitants could be taken by the Government, General Afkhami, Chief of the Intelligence Department of the General Staff, together with myself, was appointed and we started on the 29th January 1934. I had with me my orderly, Sergeant Barat Ali, a seasoned soldier who had taken part in much tribal fighting. I was delighted to have this opportunity of seeing these regions, which were unknown to me although I had read a great deal about them.

As we passed the Hazrat Abdul Azim Gate of the town it began to snow and we advanced with great difficulty, the visibility being very poor. All that night and the next day snow fell in such quantity that the road to Qom and also to Teheran was impassable and all telegraph and telephone wires out of action. It was the coldest winter with the heaviest snowfall experienced in Iran for thirty years, all the roads in Northern and Central Iran being snow-bound for weeks and communications completely disrupted.

The next day an engineer from the Ministry of Roads arrived with several lorry loads of workmen and the local peasants were also mobilised. After three days of strenuous work in which we all joined, we finally arrived at Qom. From there the road was open, and on the 3rd February we reached Isfahan. Part of the road was still covered with snow and we saw dead camels half buried in drifts before reaching Yazd. This town is famous for its silk and its sweetmeats, and for the wind-towers on the house-tops, designed to catch the breeze and convey it to the rooms below during the summer heat. Yazd is on the fringe of the central desert of Iran and water is brought from the foot of the high mountains situated to the south by extensive underground water-channels. For this reason the well and channel diggers of Yazd are known as the best in Iran.

From Yazd it took us one day to reach Kerman, and driving from Kerman to Sa'idabad in the Sirjan district of the Fars province we found ourselves in spring weather, as it is much lower than the inner part of Iran, and from there to Bandar 'Abbas the temperature became warmer and warmer until having passed a narrow defile between very steep rocky hills of a light blue colour, called Tang-e-Zagh, we reached the sea at Bandar 'Abbas, known before 1622 as Gombrun. Bandar 'Abbas has no quay, the ships anchoring in the roads. The town was small and there were a few solidly built buildings on the waterfront, the most important being the custom-house, which had been built at the beginning of the eighteenth century by the Dutch. Most of the inhabitants were living in reed huts, about one-third of them being Negroes who had been imported by the Masqatis. Water was scarce, supplied by tanks in which rainwater was collected, and by a source at some distance from the town, but Yazdi channel diggers were busy digging a water-channel from the Kuh-i-Genu, a high mountain situated about 18 miles from Bandar 'Abbas.

Dr. Lincoln, the British Vice-Consul, arrived two days after us. He resided part of the time in Kerman. He was rather sore at having to remove a mast erected outside the garden of the Vice-Consulate on which the Union Jack used to be flown every day. This he had to do on account of an order from Teheran stipulating that flag-posts of the Legations and Consulates could be erected only on the walls or roofs of buildings, and not planted in the ground, it being considered that this implies possession of the land on which the flag-post is erected. I told him that it was very easy to remove the flag-post and have the flag flown on Sundays from the roof of the Consulate. He said that the flag-post and flag were visible from far off and that ships were accustomed to this landmark. I replied that would be all right as we would tell the port-commander to erect a flag-post near there from which the Iranian flag would be flown. He did not answer, but seemed unconvinced.

It was about the same time that Iran asked the British Government to dissociate the Persian Gulf Residency from the Consulate of Bushehr, and to remove the Residency to a place outside Iranian territory, and also to evacuate the British naval installations from Hanjam island, which used to be a British naval station in the Persian Gulf. Both were removed to Bahrein.

Since 1820, the British had established a coaling station at Bassidu, on the most western point of the island of Qeshm, and although this station was not used any more as British warships were nowadays burning oil, it was kept as a cemetery for British people and every day a lonely guard hoisted a Union Jack there. One day an Iranian gunboat approached the place, disembarked a party, and replaced the Union Jack by the Iranian colours.

British authorities felt shocked, but as no legal ground existed for their presence at Bassidu, they had to acknowledge the accomplished fact.

On the occasion of the 3rd Esfand (20th February) anniversary of the *coup d'état* there were festivities in the town, and I was astonished to see groups of Negroes executing dances with African rhythms. There was an invitation to Government House and all the notabilities were there. We were quite surprised to see them all leaving at eight o'clock, and asked the Governor for the reason for this early exodus. He smiled and said that as the diet of the population consisted chiefly of fish, shrimps and dates, this food known to be endowed with particular properties, they were all in a hurry to return to their wives. 'Then we will not detain you,' we said, departing to our lodgings. Colonel Bahador (the Governor) did not try to persuade us to stay.

We remained two days in Bandar 'Abbas, during which time we visited the islands of Hormoz and Qeshm, situated in the Strait of Hormoz. Hormoz, which used to be a very prosperous trading centre in the Middle Ages, had been captured by the famous Portuguese sailor d'Albuquerque in 1507 and retaken by Shah Abbas with the aid of the British East India Trading Company's fleet in 1622. After that the town had been transported to the mainland, and Bandar 'Abbas founded on the opposite shore, but the fort built by the Portuguese had remained nearly intact until 1916 when, unfortunately, General Sykes who had been sent to Iran during the First World War to organise the South Persian Rifles and had tried to start recruiting in Bandar 'Abbas, destroyed part of the walls of the fort in order to carry its stones to the mainland to be used for the construction of barracks for his future recruits. After a while he moved to Kerman, and the project of building barracks was abandoned, the stones still lying unused near Bandar 'Abbas in 1934. We saw several old cannon bearing the Spanish coat of arms, as Portugal had been temporarily united with Spain.

There is ochre in Hormoz, which is exported abroad in fairly important quantities. Qeshm was practically abandoned by its inhabitants, only three families of fishermen remaining in the little town bearing that name on the eastern side of the island.

On the 22nd February we embarked on the British India ship *Barpeta* whose captain was very friendly. That night, my orderly Barat Ali told me that an Iranian subject coming from Sharjah, after fleeing from conscription in Iran, was on the boat going to Karachi. When we arrived at Jask, I told the captain that he must disembark the Iranian. The captain refused to do so, saying that the ship was British. I replied that we were in Iranian territorial waters. He then decided to leave Jask at once. Profiting by his absence for a few minutes I occupied the captain's bridge with Barat Ali, his rifle at the ready, and prevented the ship from leaving. In the meantime, a motor-boat with the port health officer and a policeman arrived and I handed over the recalcitrant recruit to them. The captain was very much annoyed and telegraphed the whole story to his Company, but they answered that the proper thing had been done as the man should have been handed over to the Iranian police. The captain was relieved and thanked me warmly for having prevented him from acting in an incorrect manner which would have been the cause of trouble all round, as General Afkhami would certainly have reported the matter to Teheran.

After anchoring at Masqat, which has a double bay and a good harbour dominated by a Portuguese fort, with the Sultan's palace on the water-front, we went to Chahbahar on the Gulf of Oman, and entering the wide bay were taken ashore in a small Baluchi rowing-boat, the *Barpeta* continuing towards Karachi. Chahbahar is a small town, with tropical vegetation. It was here that I saw banians and mango trees for the first time. After three days in Chahbahar, a little motor-launch took us to Gwatar, the easternmost port on the Iranian coast, on the bay of the same name facing Jiwani, on the Indian (now Pakistani) side. As we sailed along we saw many flying fish, dolphins and twice I saw coming out of the sea a big round head looking very much like that of a seal. As there are no seals in this region, I think these must have been dugongs, sea mammals supposed to explain the origin of mermaids. We disembarked at Gwatar after a whole day sailing in the launch having followed, though in the opposite direction, almost exactly the route of Nearchos on his famous retreat from India. He had embarked in the neighbourhood of Gwatar and disembarked at the head of the Persian Gulf near Jask. This little township was quite deserted, except for a Gendarmerie post, a customs official, and a few lean starved dogs whose masters had abandoned them,

The author's wife in the *Sleeping Beauty* ballet, 1923

The author when a cavalry captain, 1923

Reza Shah Pahlavi

The Crown Prince Mohammad Reza, Colonel-in-Chief of the Pahlavi Guards Cavalry Regiment in 1951. The author is behind the Prince to the right

The meeting of two great rulers, Ankara, 1934. *From the left:* Ismet Inönü, Atatürk, Kazem Özalp, President of the Turkish National Assembly, and Reza Shah

Prime Minister Hakimi with the author

The author when Chief of Staff, 1944.

Mohammad Saed, the author's former tutor,
when Prime Minister in 1950

Queen Elizabeth being greeted at Ankara airport by the author, 1960

The author signing the Bilateral Agreement between Iran
and the U.S.A., 1959

together with their homes, to go to Jiwani or to Masqat.

On our way back we encountered a terrible storm and had to lie at anchor for the whole night near some rocks protruding from the sea, as the engine was out of order and the mechanic could not repair it in such rough weather.

Next day the storm subsided and we found ourselves not far from a little coastal village perched on a cliff with boats hauled up on the beach below, one of which came and took us to Pasa Bandar, a miserable-looking fishing village. We climbed up the cliff and saw a primitive process of salting fish. The bellies of the fish were filled with greyish salt after their entrails had been removed and thrown on the ground where millions of flies were regaling themselves on them. The stench was indescribable. As a farmer I grieved over the waste of fertiliser. We went the next day to Chahbahar where we embarked in the *Barpeta* on her return journey from Karachi, very pleased to see our friend the captain again.

We returned to Teheran by the same route, and arrived there the day after Nowruz. I was pleased to see Ibrahim at Arfaieh, but when he told me the circumstances of his recall and the ordeal through which he was passing, I was very concerned. A few days later, I learned of the death of my uncle Ali Akbar Khan at Ramsar on the Caspian Sea. He had married a girl of fifteen, the daughter of Aziz-os-Soltan, who had become a kind of Mascot of Nasr-ed-Din Shah's. Once, while hunting in the country, Nasr-ed-Din Shah had been overtaken by a storm, and had sheltered in a peasant's cottage. Hearing a child crying in the next room, the Shah went there to see what had happened and at that moment the roof of the room he had just left fell in as a result of the heavy rain. The Shah would almost certainly have been killed by the falling beams and he considered that the child had saved his life by its cries and so he took him and his parents to his Court where he became such a favourite that he afterwards married him to his grand-daughter, the daughter of Kamran Mirza Nayeb-os-Saltaneh, and it was their daughter that my uncle had married. He had three children by her and then still-born twins who caused her death before she was twenty. My uncle was so affected that he died of a heart attack six months later.

In the spring of 1934 Reza Shah decided to accept an invitation by Atatürk to visit Turkey. He hoped to further his policy of a *rapprochement* with Turkey in order to counterbalance the opposing pressures of Great Britain and Russia. My chief, General Jahanbani, had proposed that I should be included in the suite and to my great joy the Shah accepted this proposal. The suite comprised Kazemi the Foreign Minister, three Court dignitaries, Generals Jahanbani, Afkhami and Kopal, myself, three captains and a lieutenant to act as orderly officers.

According to protocol the Shah was met at the entrance to each province by the Governor in morning coat and top hat and by the military and Gendarmerie commanders, the suite wearing lounge suits. Apropos of these regulations I heard that on one occasion a provincial governor anxious to comply with the rules, greeted his Sovereign in morning coat, joined the suite for the next stage and proceeded to change into a lounge suit in his car. Unfortunately something on the road caused the Imperial displeasure and the cars were stopped. The governor, whose car was immediately following that of the Shah, was sent for. The poor man emerged in shirt and underpants, whereupon he was immediately relieved of his post, but was reinstated after explanations. The second night was passed in Tabriz and the third in Maku where we were entertained in the palace of the late Sardar by his son, who was doing his military service as a soldier in an infantry regiment stationed in Maku and had obtained leave of absence for the occasion. On the 10th of June we arrived at the Turkish frontier by the road I had followed on horseback twelve years earlier.

The Shah alighted, and after taking the salute of an Iranian battalion which presented arms while the Iranian and Turkish anthems were played, passed the frontier line on foot under a triumphal arch, the same ceremony being repeated on the Turkish side. General Ali Sait Pasha, Commander of the III Army of Eastern Anatolia, reported to the Shah, and presented the other members of the reception party. At Surbehan, we left the direct Erzerum road and proceeded towards Igdir by the pass of Mount Aghri. At our feet lay the wide valley of the Aras, its southern part belonging to Turkey, while the northern was in Soviet territory. Looking through field-glasses I could see the dark mass of the gardens surrounding Erivan, the cradle of my family, which was now the capital of Soviet Armenia with no Moslems left, as all had been massacred or expelled. Behind Erivan appeared the imposing mass of the Alagoz mountain.

Our next stop was at the little town of Igdir, chief centre of the Surmali district which had belonged to Iran before 1828 when it was annexed by Russia together with the Khanate of Erivan of which it was a part, its population being still Azeri and Shia.

The provinces of Kars and Ardahan had been ceded to Turkey by the Treaty of Brest-Litovsk and this was confirmed in 1921 by the Treaty of Kars. We passed the night in this little town where the population greeted the Shah with enthusiasm, for they were still attached to Iran. Next day we followed the Aras river, here some 50 yards wide, on the northern side of which the Soviet frontier posts were clearly visible. Kars looks quite Russian, but is now entirely inhabited by Moslems: the orthodox churches erected there during the forty years of Russian occupation had been turned into clubs and Government offices.

As we travelled over the green country between Kars and Sarikamish with its wooded hills in the distance, Ali Sait Pasha described to the Shah, who listened with great interest, the battles which had been fought there both during the 1914 war and during earlier wars in 1829, 1854 and 1876–7. Normally, after Sarikamish the country is again barren like Iran, but this year on account of the heavy snowfall of the last winter, the whole region from Teheran to Trabzon was green and covered with wild flowers of all colours.

Erzurum, our next stop, had undergone some changes since I was there in 1922 and outside the old town, surrounded by a moat, a new town had begun to emerge. From Erzurum we reached Machka, where the Shah was met by a welcoming party consisting of Tewfiq Rushtu Bey, the Foreign Minister, Fahreddin Pasha Altai, the Commander of the 1st Army, and the Admiral Commander-in-Chief of the Turkish Navy. The party accompanied us to Trabzon, where the Shah and his suite were taken by motor-launch to the imposing battle-cruiser *Yavuz* of 23,000 tons, which had recently been modernised. The roads of Trabzon were full of every kind of craft, from rowing-boats to steamers. All these boats were lavishly beflagged and filled with people. Beside the *Yavuz*, two destroyers were anchored, and while His Majesty's launch was passing close to them and then nearing the *Yavuz* the crews, ranged on the decks, greeted it by three *Yashas* (long live).

The Imperial ensign was hoisted on the *Yavuz* as soon as the Shah appeared on deck, while the naval band played the Iranian national anthem, and the ship's guns fired a 21 guns' salute. The officers of the ship were presented to His Majesty, and he was given details of the ship's armament and equipment, to all of which he listened with great attention. I set to work to prepare a kind of *Who's Who* of Turkish personalities for the Shah, who wanted to study this at night. Fortunately I had assembled the material for this in Teheran, and was able to produce it after a couple of hours' work.

The next morning the Shah landed at Samsun where he was saluted by the guns of the cruiser *Mejidiye,* and while all the ships in the harbour, as well as the railway engines and the factories, greeted him with sirens and whistles, he boarded the train for Ankara.

On the 16th June the train entered Ankara station and we leaned out of the windows and saw the Ghazi in his evening dress and top hat, the civilian high authorities on one side and the generals on the other. The Shah, looking grave but benevolent, came down on to the platform, followed by us. The Ghazi, looking at the Shah with his piercing blue eyes approached smiling and they shook hands, gazing into each other's eyes as if weighing each other up. Their scrutiny was the beginning of an historic friendship between the two greatest men of our epoch. This policy of Reza Shah's begun in 1922 had now reached its fufilment. The Iranian Reformer had come to visit his Turkish counterpart to learn and to try to gain an ally. Afterwards, he would be able to see to what extent he had succeeded. The two rulers now facing each other were as different physically as they were mentally, but they were alike in their ideals and in their extraordinary strength of character and the authority which emanated from them. Ghazi Mustafa Kemal Pasha, President of the Turkish Republic, was a man of middle stature, fair, with regular features and with a cast in one of his blue eyes which produced an extraordinary impression, as if he was looking in every direction at the same time. He had a commanding personality, an authoritative voice and great charm.

After the presentation of their suites, the two Chiefs of State passed through the station and emerged on the square on the other side of it, where they were greeted by an enthusiastic crowd. We entered the cars and drove towards the Halk Evi, a kind of political club of the Republican People's Party, the leader of which was the Ghazi, which had been prepared as a residence for Reza Shah. The members of the suite were lodged at the Hotel Ankara Palace, a modern hotel built and administered by the Government. The Shah was left in his apartment, the Ghazi taking leave of him and going to his country home of Chankaya. At eight o'clock we came to fetch the Shah at the Halk Evi, and drove to Chankaya, where the Ghazi was giving a gala dinner for him. All the high civilian and military dignitaries were present, but although no ladies were invited a choir of young girls from the Ankara conservatoire played and sang selections from European operas.

After this performance many Turkish high dignitaries were presented by the Ghazi to the Shah, including a short man with a round face, round eyes and round spectacles, whom I recognised as having seen in Teheran in 1932. 'You see this man,' said the Ghazi, 'I gave him a sack of silver, and he made me a bank.' The man was Jelal Bayar, then Governor of the Ish Bankasi and afterwards Prime Minister and President of the Republic, later imprisoned at Kayseri. The Shah shook hands with him and talked about his visit to Iran and the work he had done there. The dinner was served very late, and the Shah, who rose every day at 5 a.m. and was accustomed to go to bed not later than 10 p.m., left Chankaya before the end of the meal, ordering us to remain. The Ghazi accompanied His Majesty to the Halk Evi, while we remained at table, and when he returned, kept us up to the small hours of the morning. During the evening, the Ghazi asked General Kopal, whose Turkish was perfect: 'Are you ready to die for your Shah?'

The General rose to his feet, snapped to attention, and barked in a military manner: 'We are ready to die for him, Pasham!'

'Good,' said the Ghazi. 'My Generals here are all ready to die for me!'

Looking from the terrace of Halk Evi one could see the new town and part of the old Ankara. The old town, built on twin hills, on the higher of which is an old fortress which has existed since time immemorial and had been reconstructed successively by Romans, Byzantines and Turks. Ankara, called Ancyra, was the capital of Galatia, so called because of the Gauls who had settled there and to whom St. Paul's Epistle to the Galatians was addressed. Ancyra had belonged to Iran in Achaemenian times and again under the Imperial Seljuks (1037–1157) and the Ilkhans who were ruling in Tabriz in the thirteenth and fourteenth centuries, as an old inscription on one of the gates of the town attests. The Ottoman troops occupied it shortly afterwards, but in 1402 Amir Teimur (Tamerlane) defeated Sultan Yildirim Bayazid in the Ankara plain, and for a few months it was occupied by the Turkomans. It must be noted that the Ottomans themselves were of Turkoman stock.

Until 1920 Ankara, although the oldest city in Turkey, had only some 45,000 inhabitants, but it was a railhead and the nearest place of importance to the front line when Turks and Greeks were fighting for the mastery of Anatolia. If the Greeks had been successful in occupying it the whole Turkish defence would have been shattered, an important centre of communications would have been lost, and the morale of the defenders severely affected. After the first Inönu battle in 1921, Ismet Pasha, commander of the northern wing of the Turkish Army, although forced to retire, inflicted such severe casualties on the Greeks that they lost much of their offensive power, and so were defeated later at the battle of Sakaria. It was from Ankara that the counter-offensive had been started, and for this reason it became the symbol of the New Turkey, uncompromisingly patriotic and resolutely progressive.

A military review was organised in honour of the Shah, the 8th Division and accessory units marching past after having been inspected by the Shah and the Ghazi driving in an open car in front of the assembled troops. I was surprised and pleased to see Sir Percy and Lady Loraine waving to me from the diplomatic tribune and I went to see them afterwards at their Embassy.

Before the review, the Shah, the Ghazi and several persons of the suite including myself, lunched at the house of Ismet Pasha, the Prime Minister, hero of the two Inönu battles, at the second of which he had completely defeated the Greek Army opposed to him. His charming wife received us, and after lunch one of his sons, a little boy of ten, recited a poem in Turkish in honour of the Shah, who thanked him graciously. Learning that I was a cavalry officer, Ismet Pasha took me to see his horses, of which he was very fond. He told me then that as a little boy he used to stand at the corner of the street near the gate of the Iranian Embassy in order to admire the four beautiful black Russian horses that drew my father's carriage.

One evening while the Shah and the Ghazi were dining *tête à tête*, the Secretary General of the Foreign Ministry, Numan bey Menemenjioghlu, took us to his house to hear some Turkish music, which was at that time forbidden by the Ghazi, in his desire to suppress everything that had a link with the East. Later, however, he authorised it again, because the Turks were so attached to their music that even he could not prevent them from playing it.

That same evening, after dinner, the Shah, the Ghazi, Ismet Pasha, Jelal Bayar and Sir Percy Loraine were playing poker. At a certain moment the Ghazi rose from the table and looking at the Shah's cards, advised him what to play. The Shah followed his advice and won, Sir Percy losing to him. The Ghazi then said to the Shah: 'You see, when we are united, we win!' Many years afterwards, when I was Ambassador to Turkey, I reminded Jelal Bayar of this incident which he also remembered.

On the 19th June, the Shah attended a meeting of Parliament. When he entered, the deputies rose from their seats cheering him and the Speaker, Kiazim Pasha, announced that it was proposed to honour the occasion by passing a law similar to the one which had been passed some years earlier in Iran, introducing the compulsory adoption of a surname. The Assembly passed the law by acclamation, and thus Ghazi Mustafa Kemal became Kemal Atatürk (Father of the Turks) and Ismet Pasha, Ismet Inönu, after his victorious battles. Next day the Shah visited the newly built imposing building of the General Staff. He was met by Marshal Fevzi Chakmak, the Chief of Staff, Atatürk being also present. After having visited in detail the different sections, the Shah took Fewzi Pasha, who was as tall and solid as himself, in his arms, saying: 'I wish you to be the Chief of Staff of both our armies.'

Next day we left Ankara by train, travelling by night. Reza Shah retired at ten o'clock, and we were left with Atatürk, who as usual drank and played cards, or talked a good part of the night. He was in great form, telling of his adventures in 1912 during the war in Libya, when he tried to pass through Egypt disguised as an Arab, arousing British suspicions by his fair complexion and blue eyes, but finally in spite of difficulties reaching Libya where he fought for a time against the Italians. He was continually making fun of two of his old companions who played up to him, but I learned afterwards that in the first years after the establishment of the Republic, when People's Courts were organised by Atatürk to fight against reaction, these two presided over these Courts in a very tough way.

Our civilians and even generals were unable to stand up to him in his drinking, and dropped from the contest one after the other until I was the only one left. That pleased him, and lifting his glass he said to me: 'I see you are a real cavalry officer. I appoint you to command the 6th Cavalry Regiment.' I heard afterwards that when drinking he used to give extraordinary orders, the Ministers or generals who were near him taking note of them and saying in an earnest manner: 'On our head!' (meaning: I obey), but not executing these unless they were confirmed later in the day, and I had occasion to observe this habit a second time that same evening.

When our train entered the Ushak station, the platform was full of people waiting to greet Atatürk and Reza Shah, although it was midnight. Atatürk opened the window, and scores of people tried to seize his hand, the Ghazi looking quite pleased by this mark of his popularity. Then suddenly, his face became flushed with anger and snatching back his hand, he shouted in a terrible voice: 'How dare this so and so damned fellow try to touch my hand, he is, like all his kin, the enemy of the people, take him and destroy him.' Looking out of the window, I saw a *molla* who had had the misfortune to have tried to shake Atatürk's hand, throwing his white turban in the air, and then plunging into the crowd he disappeared with a dexterity engendered by fear. People rushed towards the turban, but the man was gone. Atatürk continued to shout: 'Tomorrow this town must be razed to the ground. Let the Governor come.' The Governor, in morning coat with his top hat in hand, was ushered into the carriage, pale and trembling. 'Dismiss him at once!' 'I obey, Pasham, on my head!' promptly said Ismet Inönu, writing something in his notebook. Of course the next day nothing happened, but Atatürk had not forgotten the incident as he ordered that from that day *mollas* should be forbidden to wear their clerical clothes outside the mosques, this measure being applied to representatives of other religions also.

Two days were spent in Izmir where the Shah, as was expected, ordered flowers to be put on the grave of Atatürk's mother, after which we went to Chanakkale where Atatürk showed him over the battlefields of the Dardanelles, where he had himself commanded that historic defence. From there we embarked in a Turkish boat for Istanbul where an apartment had been prepared for the Shah in the enormous Palace of Dolma Baghche, which has its own quay stretching for several hundred metres along the Bosphorus. The immense size of its innumerable apartments and the collection of handsome if not always beautiful objects was impressive, particularly the seven-ton chandelier suspended from the ceiling of what is reputed to be the largest room in the world!

The Palace was built by Sultan Abdul Majid (1839–61) but his son, Sultan Abdul Hamid (1876–1909), who lived in perpetual fear of assassination and considered it to be too vulnerable on account of its frontage to the sea, had retired to the neighbouring Palace of Yildiz which is built in the midst of a vast park surrounded by high walls, but his brother Mohammad V returned to it in 1909. The apartment which had been modernised for the use of Reza Shah was used afterwards by Atatürk whenever he came to Istanbul and it was in the room that had been the Shah's bedroom that he died. During his visit the Shah assisted at some heavy artillery practice to the west of Istanbul and unfortunately I had to translate and explain to the Shah the commands given in Turkish by the commanding officer, so that I could not put my fingers in my ears and open my mouth as others did and the result was two cracked ear-drums, which accident has seriously impaired my hearing ever since.

Once, I remember, whilst Atatürk was conversing with the Shah during some manœuvres on the Asiatic side of the Bosphorus, he mentioned that several Turkish military terms such as horde, in Turkish *ordu*, had been adopted in foreign languages. He was very pleased when I remarked that the word 'Hurrah' used in all countries and in Russia when attacking, was a corruption of the Turkish *Vurha* meaning strike! This had been the war cry of Subutai's invading Mongols at the beginning of the thirteenth century, and also the word *uhlan*, used in several armies to designate a certain type of cavalry dressed in

Polish-type uniforms, came from the Turkish word *oghlan*—which means a lad, and was the name of the Tatar mercenaries serving in the Middle Ages with the Polish armies.

On the twenty-sixth day after our arrival in Turkey, the Shah took leave of Atatürk and embarked with his suite on a Turkish boat headed for Trabzon, accompanied by Ali Sait Pasha, who travelled with us as far as Maku. All the members of the suite received a present of a gold watch with the Ghazi's signature engraved on the back, in memory of the visit.

On the whole, the Turkish visit must be counted a success, although perhaps Reza Shah had had hopes of obtaining more positive results from it. In any case, a great and durable friendship was established between the two Chiefs of State born of their great admiration for each other. One day when the Shah was not present Atatürk said to me in an inspired manner, 'I admire your Sovereign so much that if I had not been President of Turkey I would go to Iran to serve him as you do.' And when the escorting Turkish party left us at Maku, the Shah turned to us saying, 'We have been privileged to see a very great man.'

Before this visit our relations with Turkey had not always been happy. Apart from continual frontier difficulties during the Khalifate, the Turks had had a grudge against us for not recognising their Sultan as Khalif of all Moslems, but since then the relations between the two countries have always been excellent, which shows the wisdom of the Shah's and Atatürk's policy. Undoubtedly the Shah profited much more from observing the progress accomplished in Turkey than he would have done by visiting a more advanced country, which would have been different in every way from his own, and on his return he set to work immediately to apply what he had learnt there. From the political point of view he felt himself much less isolated than before, and with a freer hand in his dealings with other nations.

It may be supposed that when Reza Shah embraced Marshal Fevzi Chakmak, saying to him that he would like to have him as Chief of Staff of the two armies, his idea had been that Turkey might conclude some kind of military alliance with Iran, but this had not materialised. Atatürk at that time had very good relations with the U.S.S.R., and clearly did not wish to be involved in the east. After a couple of years, having cooled towards Soviet Russia on account of that country's opposition to the regaining by Turkey of her right to fortify the straits, Turkey was more open to suggestions of an alliance, but other factors intervened to make her desist from such a project, and up to the conclusion of the Baghdad Pact (afterwards CENTO), the relations of the two countries remained only those of sincere friendship.

In the course of 1934, our relations with Afghanistan deteriorated on account of continuous raids by Afghan bands into Iranian territory, and certain claims of the Afghans on a border region where the frontier had not been clearly defined. At the same time, the Baluch tribes of the Sarhad district of Iranian Baluchistan having heard that the Central Government intended to issue identification cards and to enforce compulsory conscription, had become restless, in particular the Esma'elzai tribe of Jom'e Khan, located to the west of Zahedan. This tribe was receiving some help and encouragement from beyond the Indian frontier, where Jom'e Khan had many relatives and sympathisers. According to reports in Teheran, the British frontier authorities had been rather slack in preventing the comings and goings of the rebels and their friends across the frontier and some fantastic stories about an impending Irano-Afghan war were being circulated among the credulous Baluchis. Secret reports had also reached the General Staff at Teheran concerning mismanagement, corruption and atrocities towards the local inhabitants on the part of General Alborz, the commander of the Baluchistan Brigade, which were certainly contributory to the revolt of the Baluchis in that district.

Baluchistan had been one of the last regions of Iran to be pacified and brought under the control of the Central Government. As its name indicates, it is inhabited by Baluchis, who are a people made up of a mixture of several races who met in the desert lands on the confines of ancient Iran. This mixture was the result of invasions and migrations of Dravidians from the east (the language of the Brahuis in the eastern part of Baluchistan near Kelat is related to Dravidian dialects), Arians and Mongolo-Turcs from the north and Semites from the west. The proportion of Semitic and Arian influence is stronger in Western, (i.e. Iranian), Baluchistan, and that of the Dravidian, Pathan and Indo-Arian in the Eastern, which used to be the British and is now the Pakistani part of it. There are about 400,000 Baluchis in Iran, 800,000 in Pakistani Baluchistan and perhaps about 100,000 in Afghanistan. They are all Sunni Moslems, simple, very brave, and backward, for which last the different governments under whose control they lived must bear the blame. They had been practically independent until 1923, when Reza Shah had sent the newly organised Sistan Brigade to occupy the town and old fort of Khash, in the district of Sarhad.

In 1924, at the western end of Iranian Baluchistan, forces coming from Kerman occupied Bam. This city and district, although administratively part of the Kerman province, is partly inhabited by Baluchis, and in 1928 the Shah had ordered General Jahanbani, then Commander of the Mashad Division, to move into Baluchistan and to put an end to the factual independence of Sardar Dost Mohammad Khan in Bampur and Sarawan. Using the method which had contributed to his success during his campaign of 1922 in Azerbaijan against Simko, Jahanbani had taken his time organising a forward supply base, which was necessary on account of the desert nature of the region, before he advanced methodically towards Sarawan and then to Fahraj (now Iranshahr) and Bampur. Dost Mohammad Khan surrendered and was sent to Teheran, where he was kept under police supervision but allowed to go hunting in the neighbourhood of the town accompanied by a police officer. One day while duck shooting near Veramin, he asked the officer to retrieve a bird he had shot, and when the latter took a few steps towards the fallen bird, killed him cold-bloodedly with his pistol and escaped into the desert, using camels which had been prepared beforehand by his retainers. He was pursued by the Gendarmerie and finally caught, brought to Teheran, tried and executed. Further operations were conducted in Baluchistan, by which the remaining dissident tribes were subjected, with the exception of the Esma'elzais and Yarahmadzais, who after a period of outward submission again revolted against the Government. The Chief of the Yarahmadzai, Jiand, a ninety-year-old man, had been arrested and died in Mashad, but his son-in-law Shahsavar took the tribe into the wilderness near the British frontier, refusing all contact with the Government, while Jom'e Khan revolted in Shuru, west of Zahedan (formerly Dozdab), keeping the road from the north to that place under the constant menace of raids.

In order to take command of the operations against Jom'e

Khan, which were dragging on without any positive result, ascertain the accusations against General Alborz, and clarify the attitude of the British authorities, the Shah ordered General Jahanbani to go to Baluchistan, and Jahanbani selected me as his Chief of Staff. He took with him also a Baluch chief called Sardar Idu Khan Riqi, who is one of the more colourful characters in General Dyer's *The Raiders of the Sarhad*, and who had apparently been more or less under surveillance in Teheran although he professed complete loyalty to the Government. We started on the 20th December 1934, and on the evening of the 22nd arrived at Mashad, the road had been considerably improved since 1926 in the days of my Turkoman campaign. From there we left for Zahedan.

We passed the night at Gonabad and visited the tomb of Soltan Ali Shah, one of the first Sheikhs of the Sufi Dervishes, the present Sheikh residing in that town. On our arrival in Birjand we were the guests of Amir Showkat-el-Molk, a very courteous, distinguished old gentleman, who had been the hereditary Governor of Qainat and Sistan and Warden of the marches on the Afghanistan frontier. Contrary to most of such Frontier Lords, as soon as Reza Shah had organised the Mashad Division in 1922 he had written to the Shah, asking him to send an officer to take charge of all the arms and ammunition he had in his possession and declaring his loyalty to the Government. The Shah had a great regard for him, and for a time he had held the office of Minister of Posts and Telegraphs.

Here too we met Assadi, a former manager of Showkat-el-Molk, who was hanged the next year for having instigated the Mashad people to revolt in protest at the adoption of the European hat, which the fanatical minded considered incompatible with Islam, while the ringleader, a *molla* called Sheikh Bahlul, managed to escape to Afghanistan. On that occasion people in Mashad poured into the Imam Reza Shrine as a protest, but the Shah ordered General Matbui to drive them out by military force. This act allowed the Shah to order the unveiling of the women all over Iran, without any open expression of discontent on the part of the population. This order remained in force until the occupation of Iran by foreigners, when veiling or unveiling became optional and nearly all women of the lower classes and a great number of those of the middle classes reverted to the veil, without using the *picheh* or face cover as before. All ladies of the upper classes and many of those of the middle class are now unveiled, and the veil is fast disappearing among young girls who have been to school.

To the south of Birjand the road lies for many miles in a flat desert plain with mountains visible to the east and sometimes to the west. We reached Hormak, close to Kuh-e-Malek-Siah, the point where the three frontiers of Iran, Afghanistan and British Baluchistan meet, and one day's journey brought us to Zahedan. Here we learned that two days before Jom'e Khan had attacked a military convoy killing twenty-two soldiers, and had also massacred the garrison of a post comprising eleven men, taking their arms.

The next day we flew in a Junkers First World War plane to Shuru, the former dwelling-place of Jom'e Khan, which was now occupied by the operational detachment of the Baluchistan Brigade. There we met General Alborz, who made a very un-favourable impression on me. He was a large man with cold eyes and a hard expression, with a haughty manner which did not please General Jahanbani, who was his senior and being very courteous himself appreciated politeness and good manners in others. After reconnoitring by air the place where the convoy had been attacked, and where we could see the three abandoned lorries, we returned to Zahedan which remained our head-quarters until the 12th March, although we visited the country extensively by car, by air, on camel-back and even on donkeys. I was ordered to fly over the Pir Shuran Mountains to the west of Shuru, where Jom'e Khan had taken refuge with his tribe, and dropped a few ten-kilo bombs at hazard which did not cause any harm, as I could not see anyone. In the meantime, the Kerman column was approaching from the west, and the Esma'elzai understood that we meant business. It was here that Idu, one of his four wives being the sister of Jom'e, became useful. He contacted Jom'e Khan who finally agreed to be disarmed on condition that there should be an amnesty and the flocks which had been taken from him given back.

During the negotiations with Jom'e Khan we went to Korin, a place to the south of Shuru and nearer to Jom'e's camp. There we stayed eight days under tents, the cold was so intense that one morning the temperature inside the tent was – 11° Centigrade, and we were day and night wrapped in our *pustins* (sheepskin coats).

After the submission of the Esma'elzais, the important tribe of the Yarahmadzais with its allied Gomshadzai tribe, showed a desire to come to terms. We had then flown to Khash, in the middle of the Sarhad district and its former administrative centre, now displaced by Zahedan. There is an old fortress in Khash, which was used during the war by General Dyer of Amritsar fame as the headquarters of his Brigade. From Khash we went by car to Gusht, a village at the foot of the range of hills which separates the inner plain of the Sarhad from the steppeland bordering the British ´frontier, inhabited by the Gomshadzai tribe. I found extreme poverty in all these villages, the tribesmen living in black felt tents, the peasants in the villages in reed-built huts, but all in the most primitive manner, their diet consisting exclusively of maize and dates of a poor quality.

General Jahanbani asked the headman of this village to find somebody who could be sent to the Gomshadzais behind the hills to take a letter to their chief, asking him to come to Gusht to settle the question of their disarmament and submission to the Government. The headman, himself a half-naked barefoot individual, chose the most miserable-looking wretch in the village and after giving him both a letter and verbal instructions, we sent him on his errand, going ourselves on camel-back to the Sarawan district and leaving the cars at Gusht.

When we returned to Gusht, the emissary whom we had sent to the Gomshadzais declared that he never could have imagined that such wild savage people existed! 'I would never have consented to go there if I had known what they were like,' he said.

After having settled the first part of his mission, General Jahanbani started the second part of it, which was to inquire into the conduct of General Alborz. It appeared that this man had every possible vice without any redeeming quality. He mismanaged the administration of his unit and misappropriated important sums of money, and treated the Baluchis with extreme cruelty. We visited a cave where a score of prisoners were kept chained by their ankles to a beam, where they lay amongst their excrement, food being thrown to them in the darkness. Of course, Jahanbani ordered them to be released at once. All this was conclusive, a detailed report was sent to Teheran, and the

Shah ordered General Alborz to be sent to Teheran to be prosecuted to the great relief of the population and his officers and
soldiers.

Now began our third task which was wholly political and
consisted in the clarification of the British attitude. As a result
of reports received from Baluchistan, the Iranian Government
had complained to the British Government about the incessant
violations of Iranian territory by Baluchis from British Baluchistan, and the lack of co-operation of the British frontier authorities in preventing these bands and in tracing and punishing them.
The British Government decided to send a commission, comprising the British Consul-General at Mashad, Lieutenant-
Colonel Daly, the Deputy Commissioner of British Baluchistan,
Mr. (later Sir) Clarmont Skrine, and the British military attaché
in Teheran, Major Pybus.

Colonel Daly gave the impression of being critical of nearly
everything that had been done in Iran since our *risorgimento*,
although he refrained from saying so directly. Major Pybus did
not forget that he was military attaché to the British Legation
accredited to the Imperial Iranian Government, but he complained about the ostracism to which all foreigners were subjected, as Iranian officials, both military and civilian, were
tacitly forbidden to have any intercourse with them as it is still
today in the U.S.S.R. 'We do not ask you to marry our sisters,'
said he, alluding no doubt to me, 'but still we would like to meet
you and talk to you outside service occasions.' As for Clarmont
Skrine, a shrewd and able negotiator, he was (and still is, although
retired), a perfect diplomat, well informed, keen, clever and
always courteous. Many years afterwards he was kind enough
to sponsor me as a Fellow of the Royal Geographical Society,
and I never fail to see him whenever I am in London.

At first, General Jahanbani and myself were the Iranian members of the mixed commission, which met alternately at our
house and at the British Vice-Consulate, but after a few meetings,
Jahanbani went to Khash, and I was left alone to deal with the
three British. Our complaints were under two heads—the
inability of the British Indian frontier authorities to prevent
Baluchis from their side of the frontier from coming to the aid
of rebels on our side or of raiding themselves, and the refusal
of the same authorities to co-operate with the Iranian gendarmes

in following up the raiders when they took refuge in British territory.

After several meetings it was decided that the British members of the Commission would telegraph to Teheran for further instructions, and a meeting was fixed for the next day at 8 a.m., but at seven o'clock, they all arrived at my house saying that they were very sorry, but they had been recalled and were obliged to leave immediately.

Following the departure of my British friends I took a plane to Khash, where General Jahanbani then was. The landscape from the air was dominated by the huge mass of Kuh Taftan, a nearly extinct volcano, partly covered with snow, above the conic top of which a yellowish cloud was visible as the sulphuric vapour poured from the crater. The pilot, a young lieutenant, asked me if I would like to fly over the top to see what the crater looked like, and being interested I said that I would. Our plane was again a First World War Junkers with two seats, one beside the other, open to the air and protected only by a wind-screen. The pilot flew the plane directly towards the mountain, and after a few minutes I had the impression that we had come dangerously close to it without having noticeably gained in height. I looked at the pilot and saw that he was ghastly pale.

'What is the matter?' I asked.

'Colonel, I forgot that the Junkers plane cannot fly higher than 4000 metres, and this mountain is just higher than that. We are too near to be able to turn, so I'm afraid it is all up with us.'

There was nothing to be done, so I contented myself with reciting the *Fateha* (the first verse of the Qoran) in expectation of a sudden end. And then, when we were perhaps not more than a hundred yards from the side of the Taftan, the plane was lifted as if by magic, passed over the top at not more than fifty yards from the crater, and then dropped again, continuing its course at the previous altitude. It appears that there was a current of warm air exhaled from the crater, and it was this current which had saved us. I had time to see a small depression on the flat top full of yellow-grey liquid with bubbles on its surface, as if it were boiling, and the vapour we had seen from afar was exhaled by this liquid.

From Khash we went by car to Iranshahr, by a terrible track in the sand in which we sank several times. This place, formerly called Fahraj, is built in the midst of date tree groves, and possesses a very large mud fort where a whole brigade could live in comfort. It was comparatively new and had been lately repaired by the army. After a day there, we rode on donkeys to Bampur, 18 miles to the west, where the little township was dominated by a large rectangular fort erected on a hill. This fort was old and in a neglected condition. I was lucky to see it on this occasion as a few years later it suddenly collapsed for no apparent reason, and today there is only a heap of earth where it used to stand, an object of awe to the neighbourhood.

We returned to Iranshahr on camels, which are much more comfortable to ride than donkeys, especially as I had a very good riding camel. These riding camels, called *Jammaz*, are of a quite different race from the ordinary burden-carrying one- or two-humped camels. They are much more delicately built and travel for miles with a regular elongated gait, between the amble and the trot. From Iranshahr we returned to Khash where I completed the tribal map of Baluchistan, which I was drawing according to information gathered from my conversation with the chiefs of tribes in every locality I had visited. I had also prepared genealogical tables of the principal tribal families and a short history of Iranian Baluchistan.

While at Zahedan we had visited Zabol, in the Sistan district, on the Afghan border. This region is enclosed between the Hamun-e-Helmand, an extensive lake on the west, the Afghan frontier and the bend of the Helmand river on the east and north, and the Nur Ab river-bed to the south. Being irrigated by the Helmand river coming from Afghanistan, it is very fertile in contrast to the semi-desert country which encircles it, but is entirely dependent for water on the Helmand. There are two primitive dams there which are repaired every year by the local inhabitants, where the water is divided, being taken by the Afghans for the irrigation of their part of Sistan called Chakansur, and also flowing into Iran and ultimately reaching the Hamun, which is partly in Iran and partly in Afghanistan.

In the north, close to Afghanistan, there is an island on which is a Sassanian fortress, called Kuh-e-Khojah. When the snowfall is heavy in the Hazara district of Central Afghanistan, where the Helmand has its source, the water occasionally overflows from the Hamun-e-Helmand through a natural channel called Nur Ab again to the east, and recrossing the Afghan frontier reaches a vast depression called Goud-e-Zerreh. The population of Iranian Sistan was then approximately 150,000, half of them being Persian-speaking and the other half composed of several Baluch tribes who migrated there from Baluchistan proper, the most important of them being the Narui, related to the tribes of the same name in central and southern, or coastal Baluchistan.

The climate in winter is very mild but is exceedingly hot in summer, whilst on account of the marshes, millions of mosquitoes would render life insupportable were it not for a strong wind which blows continuously for 120 days and so serves to disperse them. Zabol is a small town, with a few gardens with date trees, and we spent the night there. The next day, there being no road, we went on horseback up to the shore of the Hamun. It is very difficult to understand where the shore ends and the marsh begins as an extensive forest of reeds, which continues for many miles, covers both the shore and the lake, making it impossible to find one's way without the help of local fishermen and hunters. They sail about in extraordinary rafts made of interlaced reeds but having the shape of small flat-bottomed boats, in which a maximum of three persons can sit, one of them pushing the raft, which is called a *Tutin*, with a pole, as the Hamun is shallow everywhere.

We returned to Zahedan by the same route and from there to Mashad, where Hilda joined me and we stayed one week. We made an expedition to Fariman, some 60 miles from Mashad, to see a dam constructed under the Sassanian dynasty which had recently been repaired by order of the Shah and was once more irrigating the surrounding districts. Having passed Nowruz at Mashad we returned to Teheran, visiting the tomb of Omar Khayam at Nishapur on the way. There is a charming contemporary account of a conversation held with the poet one day in the bazaar, when he expressed the hope that he might be buried in some place where spring blossoms might fall on his grave, and when we saw his tomb in the garden of a mosque at Nishapur it was covered with fallen cherry blossom just as he had wished it should be.

Hilda and Leila had gone to London for two months and I not only felt lonely but had a presentiment of impending disaster. It was not long in coming. The next day I was informed that

Ibrahim had been arrested. I went at once to the Army Chief Prosecutor to ask him the reason for this and to obtain permission to see my brother. The Prosecutor was polite but non-committal and promised me to ask for the authorisation of the General Staff—this meaning the Shah. After two days I was allowed to see Ibrahim but in the presence of the Prosecutor, and I learned only that his arrest was in connexion with his purchase of arms.

That evening I wrote telling my father of what had happened, and early in September he arrived in Teheran hoping to be able to do something to help his son. But no kind of intervention was possible with Reza Shah and I learned later that Ibrahim's enemies were determined to bring about his fall and that an Air Force officer, who had been sent to England to buy planes after my brother's recall, had reported that Ibrahim had purposely delayed the purchase in order that during the period of tension between Great Britain and Iran, which followed the cancellation of the A.I.O.C. Concession, the Iranian Army should be at a disadvantage and that he had acted in the matter on instructions from the British Government. This was the accusation on which he was to be tried.

I forget for what reason the final session of his trial was held at night and of course *in camera*. Ibrahim's former subordinate and great friend, Captain Deihimi, and I awaited the verdict outside the court-room, and at eleven o'clock the Counsel for the defence emerged announcing to us that he had been condemned to three years' hard labour. We returned home to break the news to my father. I immediately set to work on a report recalling Ibrahim's whole career and family background and the impossibility that there could be any truth in such an accusation which could only be the work of enemies moved by envy. By five o'clock the report was ready and at seven-thirty I took it to General Zarghami, the Chief of Staff, begging that he would give it to the Shah during his eight o'clock audience before the Minister of War should take the verdict to be signed by the Shah at nine o'clock. Meanwhile, Hilda drove to the Central Telegraph Office and sent a telegram to her Carmelite sister, 'Pray that a great injustice may not be done.' This telegram, we heard afterwards, was delivered to her sister, who was Prioress, shortly after two o'clock in the morning, and waking all the nuns she gathered them to the chapel to pray as Hilda had asked them to do.

Zarghami, who was a kind and honourable man, took my report and allowed me to accompany him to the palace. Half an hour later Zarghami emerged saying that he had given my report to the Shah, who had read it attentively without saying a word and had not returned it to him, which he considered to be a good omen. The War Minister then entered and presented the verdict for the Shah's signature. His reply was to efface the sentence with a red pencil and the next day Ibrahim was released from prison.

Nevertheless Ibrahim had to leave the army and he worked for a time for the Scandinavian engineering firm of Kampsax. After a few months, a difficulty having arisen between the Government and an American firm which was selling armoured cars to Iran, Ibrahim proposed to settle the affair in a manner favourable to the Government if he were allowed to go to America. The Shah agreed, and thanks to the fact that the director of the firm in question held Ibrahim in great personal esteem, he succeeded in his mission, and on his return was re-integrated into the army and became Director of Studies at the Military Academy.

On the 19th February 1937 the Trans-Iranian railway, which had been begun in 1927, reached Teheran from the north, connecting the capital with the Caspian Sea, the through connexion from the Caspian to the Persian Gulf being ultimately effected after two more years. It was the last public function at which my father took part. Just as he was preparing to return to Monaco he caught cold at the funeral of an old friend, and contracting pneumonia, died on the 19th March 1937, at the age of at least ninety-three or ninety-four years, nobody knowing exactly when he was born.

About a year before this my sister Fatimeh had married Gabriel Bonneau, a young French diplomat whom she had met when they were both studying Persian at the Ecole des Langues Orientales in Paris. The day before my father died a letter arrived from Kabul, where Gabriel was Chargé d'Affaires at the French Legation, announcing the birth of his first grandson, and I was able to read this to him.

It was a sad end for this loyal and devoted servant of his country and his Sovereign to see his son, so brilliant and outstanding by every standard, languish in prison for months on false and preposterous accusations and though finally pardoned, not rehabilitated during his father's lifetime. The bitterness of this has remained with me to the present day, far surpassing any resentment over personal grievances I have felt as a result of later vicissitudes.

In August 1935 I was appointed Inspector of Cavalry and attached to the newly organised Staff College, and I became lecturer on Military History and Geography and cavalry tactics both at the Staff College and at the Military Academy, where one of my students was the Crown Prince, who had returned to Iran in 1936 and had entered the Military Academy. Apart from the routine work, two or three times a year I had to take the officers of the Staff College on a frontier reconnaissance journey in order to study the strategico-geographical features of the terrain.

At this time we were leading a nomadic life, spending six months of the year at Larak and six months in our town house of Arfaieh, but we always spent Fridays and holidays at Larak, where we had to supervise the farm work. I shared with Hilda a love of animals, and a keen interest in them, and we always managed to have some wild creatures as pets at Larak. The mongooses, brought from Khuzestan, followed each other for years, but unfortunately as we had also many dogs—sometimes more than twenty—they usually came to a sticky end after a few months or years. However, we kept one of them for seven years in complete freedom, taking it with us to town in winter. Besides occasional gazelles, we had a badger which was quite tame and on good terms with the mongoose, and with a bear Hilda had bought in town as a cub and who grew to enormous dimensions. The badger had an unpleasant habit of rushing at people's legs and biting them in play but as I always wore high boots I did not mind the badger's caresses, and was amused at the shrieks and cries of his victims. After three months the badger disappeared from the garden, returning to the wild.

The bear, whose particular friend was a small Pomeranian, was most amusing to watch when in summer she would lie in the water on her back pouring water over herself from a can, and in winter when she would throw snowballs in the air and catch them with her nose. She also used to climb into the elms in the avenue, and drop from there beside some terrified passerby, who perhaps did not know that we kept wild animals freely roaming on the estate. When fully grown she became difficult to manage, and we had to attach her at night to a big mulberry tree. In the end she died as a result of a snake-bite.

One day while in town we found a jackal cub on the cellar stair, nobody ever knew how it came to be there. We kept it for a few days in our bedroom, but it roamed about all night, preventing us from sleeping, so we took it to Larak and freed it in the garden, where at that time we had not yet acquired our pack of dogs. It was never seen during the day, but came at night into our bedrooms and used to lick our toes, a tickly experience, its tongue being rather rough. It also disappeared after a few months, like the badger.

And then we had a wolf. This animal was brought to us by our shepherd who found it in the mountains, abandoned by its mother. It was just a few days old and hardly bigger than one's hand, and my wife raised it on cow's milk. She said that she had never realised what the French expression *une faim de loup* really meant until that animal by the sheer force of its hunger made her get up and go to the cowshed to get milk from the cow in the middle of the night! He grew up amongst all our dogs and had a particular—but platonic—affection for a white spaniel bitch, but when all the rest of the canine population rushed barking to greet us whenever we arrived, the poor wolf could only howl. He was altogether a superb creature with a splendid coat and beautiful topaz eyes, but although he slept in the drawing-room and never attempted to leave Larak except for brief excursions up the mountains he was not civilised, his expression being totally different from that of any dog, and we were to have terrible proof of this. When autumn came we went to town and I ordered our gardener to buy bread for the wolf, but apparently he gave it occasional carcasses of dead sheep and goats, thus accustoming the wolf to eat meat, which it had never done until then. As a result of this changed diet, one day entering the gardener's room and seeing his one-and-a-half-year-old son sleeping under a blanket, the wolf seized the child by its head and was dragging it outside when the boy's eight-year-old sister came in. Although terrified by what she saw, she had the courage to seize the wolf by the tail and a tug-of-war began between the girl and the wolf. Luckily the mother appeared at that moment, chased the wolf away and rushed the child to Arfaieh, where my wife took it at once to the doctor. The little boy had been nearly scalped, and it was more than a year, six months of which were passed in hospital, before the child recovered. Of course, after that we had to have the wolf shot but we were very sad about it, because we felt sure that if it had continued to be fed with bread it would not have attacked the poor child.

In spite of the troubles with our rather strange pets, we had an extremely pleasant life in Larak. My wife soon became an expert on cow-keeping and dairy-farming, and every detail of the life of the farm interested us intensely.

As a result of Afghan encroachments and claims on Iranian territory, the Shah proposed to the Afghans to refer the frontier question to the arbitration of Atatürk. The Afghans had a great sympathy for the Turks, who are Sunni Moslems like themselves, and since 1919 there had been a Turkish military mission with the Afghan Army (at the time of writing, there are still two Turkish officers acting as instructors at the Kabul Military Academy, although the instructors in the army units are now all Soviet Russians), and accepted this proposal. Atatürk delegated General Fahreddin Altai, Inspector of the first Turkish Army, to act as arbitrator and preside over the mixed Irano-Afghan Commission which was to settle definitely the stretch of frontier left undemarcated between the northern stretch, settled in 1891 by an Irano-British Commission, General MacLean representing the Afghans, and the southern part settled in 1872–3 by another Irano-British Commission, the British chief of which was General Sir Frederick Goldsmid.

In 1937, on the proposal of Reza Shah, Turkish, Afghan and Iraqi delegates gathered in Teheran, and after a few days signed the Pact of Saadabad, which was a kind of pact of friendship, but did not contain any clauses of mutual defence, as unfortunately many people in Iran and in Iraq were wrongly allowed to believe. Many years after that, Rushtu Aras, who was at that time the Turkish Foreign Minister and represented his Government at Saadabad (the summer palace of the Shah near Teheran), told me that before their gathering at Teheran the Iraqi Government had been encouraged by the British Government, and that the Soviet Government had let the Turks know that they had nothing against such a Pact, and this may be taken as a proof that it was far from being a defensive alliance.

At the beginning of November 1938 Atatürk died, and I was ordered to go to Turkey with Generals Mohammad Nakhchevan and Kopal, to represent the Iranian Government at his funeral, an infantry company being also sent to take part in the last march past. We travelled by car to the frontier, and then took the narrow-gauge line train to Kerkuk. Having travelled without stopping some 600 miles we were tired, and having undressed, went to sleep, each in a separate compartment, the train being due at Kerkuk at seven the next morning. When I awoke we had arrived at Kerkuk, and to my horror I saw a guard of honour with a band and the regimental colours, two or three officers with drawn swords and two civilians in morning coats drawn up on the platform to greet us. There was no corridor between our compartments and it was only after much battering on the wall that I managed to establish communication with my neighbour and he with his, until at last, unwashed and unshaven, we descended to the platform. After inspecting the guard of honour, the Governor and the Brigadier took us to a Rest House where after a wash and a shave and a copious breakfast, we were able to forget the morning's adventures.

From there we went by car through Arbil, and arrived at Mosul, and after lunching with the Governor and the Commander of the Division in a fine garden on the bank of the swift-flowing Tigris we proceeded to Tel Kotchek, where in the middle of the desert we saw an incongruous sight—a train, waiting for passengers, with no station or building of any kind in sight. Since then the line has been extended to Mosul and finally to Baghdad, and now the Russians are helping Iraq to push it to Basra.

In Ankara we were again lodged at the Ankara Palace, our welcoming party of three being led by the Chief of the Operations Department of the Turkish General Staff, Colonel Assim bey, who gave me much extremely interesting information about recent political developments in the Middle East.

Atatürk had died in Istanbul, at the Dolma Baghche Palace, and his body was transported by train to Ankara, his chosen capital, symbol, like himself, of the New Turkey, where he was to be buried. It is interesting to note that throughout the night after he died in Istanbul relays of *mollas* read the Qoran and recited special prayers beside the body of this atheist. Atatürk had refrained from giving instructions that this should not be done. The carriage carrying his coffin was covered by an enormous Turkish flag, and military planes flew over the train in continuous relays the whole way from Istanbul to Ankara. At the stations and along the line thousands of people were gathered to salute the remains of their war- and peace-time leader, their Ata, trusted chief and father. All the foreign delegations, comprising civilian and military dignitaries from many countries, were present at the railway station on the train's arrival. The body then lay in state in a closed coffin covered with the Turkish flag in front of the National Assembly, opposite our hotel, and the whole night thousands of loudly weeping people passed in front of the coffin which was guarded by four officers with drawn swords.

The next day at ten o'clock, the military detachments sent by the different countries, comprising besides the Iranian infantry company, British Marines, German and Russian naval cadets, a French detachment and a crack Bulgarian infantry company, marched past the catafalque. The chiefs of the delegations included Count Ciano and von Neurath, but I cannot remember who the others were. At 11 a.m. the funeral procession began, the coffin being carried on a gun-carriage drawn by six horses, the mourners following on foot, among them one woman, Atatürk's sister, who bore a strong resemblance to him. After nearly two hours the cortège reached the Ethnographical Museum, where Atatürk was to remain until a mausoleum should be constructed (which was ultimately done in a very splendid manner). During the progress of the procession, people and even soldiers presenting arms wept, and one had the impression of seeing the genuine grief of a whole nation.

I met Sir Percy and Louise Loraine again, he worked hard to improve relations between Turkey and Great Britain. Before he came to Turkey, as a consequence of Lloyd George's policy of helping the Greeks against the Turks, the Mosul question and the unsympathetic attitude of the British Press towards Nationalist Turkey, relations were frankly bad. The first step towards their improvement was the private visit of Edward VIII to Atatürk, made possible by the lessening of tension between the two countries, when it was realised in England that the Turkish Nationalist Government was there to stay. Then came the

Montreux Conference of 1936, when Great Britain supported the Turkish desire to suppress the neutral zone of 5 kilometres on both sides of the straits and to have the right to fortify them against Soviet Russia, who wanted the freedom of passage and demilitarisation of the straits to continue. The reason for this reversal of British policy was the deterioration of British relations with Mussolini's Italy, which was now feared by Turkey and distrusted by England and France.

After the Montreux Conference, the relations between Turkey and U.S.S.R. ceased to be as close as they had been up to then, and it was said that Atatürk's new orientation towards France and England did not accord with the views of Ismet Pasha and Rushtu Aras, and that it was for this reason that shortly after the signing of the Şaadabad Pact Atatürk appointed Jelal Bayar in place of Ismet Inönu, and that the hatred of these two men for each other dates from that time. I remember having once asked Rushtu Aras for the reason of the complete subservience of Turkey to Soviet policy. He answered me that as the Western Powers were on bad terms with Turkey, she had to look for friends and support elsewhere.

The reason also was that Russia at that time had not enough military and political strength to be a menace to Turkey, and that since 1936 the Western Powers were seeking the alliance of Turkey, France having even abandoned the Sanjak of Alexandretta (today Hatay) to Turkey in order to suppress any kind of friction between the two countries and to gain the political, and eventually the military, support of Turkey in case of a crisis in the Middle East.

On the 2nd December 1938 we took the train at Haider Pasha, detrained at Riyaq and reached Damascus by car. On the way there we visited the site of the Khan Maislun battle between Feisal's Arab Army and the French forces commanded by General Gouraud, and the tomb of General Azmi, the Commander of the Arabs, who afterwards retreated to Damascus, Feisal fleeing from Syria, and later becoming King of Iraq (1920) to the great annoyance of the French. From Damascus, we travelled by Nairn service bus to Baghdad and at Rutbeh, in the middle of the desert where we stopped in the night I tasted for the first time a cup of Arab coffee, a few drops of very strong and bitter liquid in a tiny cup without a handle.

Although I had been Inspector-General of Cavalry and Armoured Forces since 1936 which was a major-general's job, I had remained for seven years a colonel, due to Ibrahim's unmerited losing of the Shah's favour, and had ceased to expect any promotion, but the day before Nowruz I was summoned to the General Staff, and entering the waiting-room found my brother there. We were ushered together to the Chief of Staff's office, and General Zarghami delivered to us the following Imperial message.

'You are promoted to the rank of General and (my brother) Lieutenant-Colonel, but you must serve your country and not be influenced by foreigners.' The allusion was transparent, and I found it insulting. I felt the blood rush to my face, and said to Zarghami: 'My brother and I have served our Sovereign and Country loyally up to this day and without consulting him I can say that we are neither of us ready to accept these promotions, and we ask to be relieved of service in the Army!'

General Zarghami allowed a half-smile of sympathy to appear for an instant on his bearded face and said calmly: 'You realise that I could not possibly say that to His Majesty; accept the promotion, and time will dispel these ideas, as everybody knows that you are two faithful and patriotic officers.'

Sometime after Nowruz, the Crown Prince who had been betrothed to Princess Fowzieh, the beautiful sister of King Faruq of Egypt, departed to Cairo, where the marriage ceremonies were to take place and from where he was going to bring his bride. Many Royal personages and high foreign dignitaries had been invited for the ceremonies which were to take place in Teheran, including the Earl of Athlone, the Duke of Spoleto, General Weygand and General Fahreddin Altai, other governments being represented by their Ambassadors and Ministers. Several foreign military units had been sent from their countries to take part in the military parade which was to be held on the Jelaliyeh racecourse.

At 3 p.m. on the 16th of April, the Ministers, high dignitaries in morning coats, the generals in full-dress uniforms with their ladies dressed up and by order wearing hats, rather an adventure for most of them, were at the railway station awaiting the Crown Prince and his bride. The Imperial Family arrived and then the Shah. At 4 p.m. we heard the train's whistle, and it slowly entered the lavishly beflagged station. The Princess's mother, Queen Nazli, and her three sisters together with the Princess and the Crown Prince alighted from the Imperial train, and were greeted by the Shah and the Imperial Family. The Queen and her four daughters were all extremely beautiful, the mother looking like their elder sister. They were warmly acclaimed by the population assembled on the square in front of the station and in the streets as they drove to the Crown Prince's palace, the Queen and her younger daughters being taken to the Sahibgranieh Palace in Shimran.

I was instructed to accompany Prince Ali Reza, the Shan's second son, to meet the Earl of Athlone on his arrival at the airport, and to be attached to him during his stay in Teheran, other generals being attached to the other exalted guests. The British detachment arrived by train from Bandar Shahpur, and caused great interest when they marched with their band and pipers from the station to the Military Academy, where lodgings had been prepared for them. The Turks and the French had also sent detachments, but the Russians had sent only a military delegation.

A week of festivities followed during which there was an exhibition of gifts sent by Royalties and Chiefs of State, prominent among these being a sports plane given by the Praesidium of the U.S.S.R. As in 1914 at the coronation of Ahmad Shah, all the foreign envoys seemed on the best of terms, especially the genial special representative of Germany, Graf von der Schulenburg, formerly Minister in Iran, who had come from Moscow where he was at that time Ambassador and who knew everybody. Yet in a few months' time they would be at each other's throats, and after two years our then Soviet and British friends would bombard and invade us, while this same von der Schulenburg would be hanged on a butcher's hook for his participation in the plot against Hitler in July 1944.

At the end of the ceremonies the foreign guests departed, and life in Teheran returned to normal.

Since the last war, public opinion in Iran was for the most part sympathetic to Germany, admiring the rehabilitation of that country since the coming of Hitler to power, but his invasion of Czechoslovakia met with general disapproval, and his non-aggression treaty with Russia in August 1939 had aroused dismay, accentuated by the unprovoked and brutal attack on Poland on the 1st September 1939.

The drive of the Russian Army into Poland and the Baltic States, and the Finnish War, created a feeling of deep indignation against the U.S.S.R. and of fear lest Iran should be the next victim.

The attitude of the U.S.S.R. towards both Iran and Turkey stiffened during this period of the war, especially after the Baltic States had been occupied and Bessarabia wrested from Rumania with the tacit approval of Germany. And it was clear that the Soviets had decided to profit by the war in which the capitalistic countries were engaged, and by their temporary accord with Germany to re-establish their influence in all the regions which had been subjected to it before the First World War. Concerned about this state of affairs, the Iranian and Turkish Governments sent their special envoys to Moscow, Sarajoghlu from Turkey, and Hamid Sayah from Iran. They stayed about three weeks in Moscow, but were not even received by Stalin, and returned to their countries without having achieved anything, the Soviet Foreign Minister not being ready to give them any non-aggression guarantee.

In the spring of 1941 everybody was expecting a Soviet drive into Iran with German approval, as the German radio was every day fiercely attacking the Shah and the Iranian Government as being reactionary and under British influence. During those days Britain regained some popularity, and then came the 22nd June 1941. The German aggression against the U.S.S.R. raised the hope that the impending Soviet menace against Iran would subside, and the announcement of German victories in Russia was greeted with unconcealed enthusiasm by all sections of the population. The United Kingdom having automatically become Soviet Russia's ally, shared that country's unpopularity, though of course to a lesser degree. The Iranians realised that a Soviet victory would mean that the northern part of Iran would be annexed to Russia, as it would have been if Russia had been victorious after the First World War.

The newspapers appeared with big headlines announcing the German victories, and a loudspeaker giving the news on the Sepah Square brought a crowd of listeners who cheered and applauded the announcement of each Russian town fallen into German hands.

As a result of a *démarche* by the Soviet and British Ambassadors, the loudspeaker was removed and the newspapers ordered to publish the Pars News Agency's news without any headlines.

Meanwhile some preparations for defence had been started in Iran. If properly led and employed according to the possibilities of the terrain for rear action and defence the Iranian Army would certainly have been a hard nut to crack. Unfortunately, the dispositions adopted precluded any possibility of any real defensive action.

In the spring of 1941, the Shah ordered the Supreme War Council to prepare a strategical plan for the defence of the territory in case of an invasion from the north, and this body appointed a commission to prepare the plan. As General Razmara (the future Prime Minister) and myself had different views on this matter, we were each of us charged to prepare a plan. The one which I prepared consisted in concentrating the majority of the forces in the mountainous region of Lorestan and Bakhtiari, where the necessary war material and food stores would be prepared in advance, and where the Shah and the Government could retire while light mobile forces could execute rear-combat action in depth, destroying the roads, railways and bridges to delay the advance of the enemy.

Razmara's plan was to occupy the frontier line and to defend the territory along the whole frontier. Of course his plan was adopted, nobody daring to present my plan to the Shah, nor daring to say that it would be impossible to defend a frontier of 1500 miles with five or six divisions disposed in a thin line against the Soviet Army.

I think that the Shah did not really believe that the army could successfully defend itself against the Russians and the British along its frontiers, but that on the other hand he did not consider it would be able to withstand protracted fighting even in the mountainous region of south-western Iran, where attacking forces would encounter great difficulties. But he wanted to keep up the nation's morale by pretending to believe in the Iranian Army's ability and preparedness to prevent any invaders from penetrating the country. This attitude was reinforced after Britain had become Russia's partner and ally as a result of the German invasion of the U.S.S.R. on the 22nd June.

In my opinion the situation on the Russian and African fronts would not have allowed the Allies at that time to engage the important forces in Iran which would have been necessary to overcome a decided defence, and they would have probably agreed to negotiate with the Iranian Government.

Although the Shah feared Russia and was suspicious of the British, he was far from being pro-German, as he was represented at the time by Allied propaganda, being daily attacked and abused by the German radio whose chief Persian speaker was then Shah Bahram Shahrokh. The German radio accused the Shah of being subservient to the Allies and advocated the overthrow of the Monarchy and the institution of a republic on the model of the German Third Reich.

In May there happened what was described in the British Press as Rashid Ali's 'revolt' in Iraq. This definition is misleading, Iraq being at that time an independent country and Rashid Ali the legally appointed Prime Minister, but like most Iraqis he was a nationalist, with strong anti-British feelings and on this account was sympathetic to the Germans. Certain of his measures made the British believe that in the event of a German advance into Egypt, Iraq was capable of joining the Germans, thus creating a dangerous situation at the rear of the British Army in the Middle East, and it is quite possible that Rashid Ali's group secretly entertained such ideas. In any case the British High Command decided to bring from India an infantry brigade, in addition to the one which was already in Iraq, in accordance with the military provision of the Anglo-Iraqi Treaty. As this same treaty subordinated the increase of the British forces beyond this brigade to consultation with the Government of Iraq, Rashid Ali protested, considering this act as a violation of the Anglo-Iraqi Treaty and Iraq's sovereign rights, and the Iraqi Army received the order to resist a British advance. The Regent, Abdulillah, Feisal the I's nephew* and uncle of the infant Feisal II, left

---

* Abdulillah, son of King Ali, was the nephew of King Feisal I. His sister Aliya married King Feisal I's son King Ghazi; their son King Feisal II was then the nephew of Abdulillah.

```
                    Sharif Hoseyn
                         |
        ┌──────────┬─────┴─────┬──────────┐
        |          :           |          :
       Ali         :        Feisal I      :
        |          :           |
   ┌────┴────┐                 |
Abdulillah  Aliya ═══════════ Ghazi
                   |
                Feisal II
```

Baghdad and joined the British. The Iraqi Army surrounded the British R.A.F. base at Habbaniya, but the stout defence of the British and the appearance of a motorised column from Transjordan put an end to Rashid Ali's resistance. After thirty-five days he fled to Iran, with the Mufti of Jerusalem, Haj Amin El Hoseyni, and a few other nationalist leaders. From there he proceeded to Germany, the Mufti of Jerusalem going to Turkey, whilst others remained in Iran and were arrested by the British after their occupation of this country, remaining interned until the end of the war.

I was then journeying about the western and north-western frontiers of Iran and on the Iraqi frontier was told by Kurds, who had come from Rawandiz in Iraq, that people there were disillusioned because Iran and Turkey, although co-members with Iraq in the Saadabad Pact, had not come to Iraq's aid. In the same way when afterwards the Allies invaded Iran, I heard many people complaining that Turkey did not come to her aid. In both cases people misunderstood the provisions of the Pact, which in effect did not contain any clause of military co-operation in the case of one of the members being attacked.

When I arrived at the Russian frontier at Jolfa I went to the bridge, half of which was in Iranian and the other half in Soviet territory. On the Iranian side a soldier was standing in front of his sentry-box, but on the Soviet side, the Russian sentry was inside his box, looking out of the lucarne. As soon as I set my foot on the bridge, the Soviet sentry shouted nervously without coming out of his box: 'Stop, or I fire.' 'But I am still on the Iranian side of the bridge,' said I. 'Stop, or I fire,' repeated the sentry in a shrill and panicky voice. I stopped and looked at the opposite bank of the river, where I saw a group of soldiers armed with tommy-guns looking at me with hostile curiosity from behind barbed-wired fences, which had not been there last year.

I learned in Tabriz that two Soviet spies had been caught during the last month, and sent to Teheran for inquiries.

On our way back, in Zanjan, Teheran radio announced that British forces had invaded Syria from Iraq, and that the Vichy French forces had been overcome. I understood at once that our turn was coming.

After the German aggression against U.S.S.R. had taken place, for some fifteen days the Soviet attitude towards Iran had become more conciliatory, but after the first week of July, when the intensity of German pressure and the magnitude of the Russian losses, especially in heavy war material, rendered speedy help from the Western Allies an imperative necessity, both the U.S.S.R. and Britain adopted towards Iran an openly threatening attitude. As German submarines were destroying approximately one-half of all ships transporting war material to Murmansk, and Turkey, having speedily fortified the straits after the Montreux Conference, did not show any disposition to allow such transport through the Dardanelles and the Bosphorus, the only alternative route was through Iran.

Seeking to justify their coming intervention, the press and radio of both countries accused the Iranian Government some-times of allowing the Germans to organise bases for aggression against the U.S.S.R. on Iranian territory and sometimes of being unable to control the several thousand [sic] Germans who were in Iran nominally as technicians or tourists, but, according to them, in reality to create centres of espionage, terrorism and sabotage directed at Soviet Russia.

No doubt these stories were believed by the majority of British people, and in any case they served to prepare public opinion both at home and abroad for the impending invasion of Iran, but the truth which emerged after the arrest and expulsion of all the Germans resident in the country was that their total number including women and children did not exceed 600. These people were all under careful surveillance by the Iranian Secret Police, and as nowhere in the world was discipline in the army and order in the administration stricter than in the Iran of Reza Shah, and the principal preoccupation of the Govern-ment was the maintenance of Iran's neutrality in the world conflict in all manifestations of the national life, it would have been impossible for them to indulge in the activities attributed to them by the Allies.

On the 19th July 1941 the British and the Russians separately made representations, asking for the expulsion of all the Germans from Iran, as they were endangering the security of Soviet territory. The Shah's Government considering this request an infringement of Iran's Sovereign rights and neutrality, refused to consider it. On the 16th August the Allies reiterated their demand in more threatening terms, and the Shah agreed to send away all the Germans except those whose presence in the technical services of some Government factories was considered absolutely indispensable.

While important Soviet and British concentrations were taking place on the northern and western frontiers of Iran, no troop movements were allowed by the Shah, all the Iranian units remaining in their garrisons. A small force from Kermanshah was nevertheless moved to Pa-e-Taq near the Iraqi frontier and occupied a defensive position there. But this defence, although organised in depth, had no mobility, as the distance between the different positions was too great, and after being outflanked, the forward forces lacking means of transport, were not able to retreat towards the rear position. Some 30,000 reservists were recalled to the colours, but were not amalgamated with active service units and could not be used.

The situation in Europe was extremely critical for the Allies. France, considered after the First World War the strongest European Power, had been defeated in the first few weeks and knocked out of the arena. Britain was restricted in her island, Italy had joined Germany, and the U.S.S.R. was sustaining defeat after defeat, the German armies rolling swiftly towards the East, which meant towards the Caucasus and the Iranian frontier. Being cautious and thinking about possible future developments, the Shah might have been ready to accord a right of way to the Allies for supplying Russia through Iran after a show of resistance under duress. Apparently the Allies did not see it this way, and that was the reason why they invaded Iran without an ultimatum, in order not to allow the Iranian Government to discuss terms or possibly yield to it.

I had always thought that it was the Soviet who insisted on invading Iran, but in 1959, during a conversation, Rushtu Aras, the former Turkish Foreign Minister, who was Turkish Ambassador in London in 1941, told me that the Russians would have been content with the Iranian Government's consent to allow war material to pass through Iran, and its assurance to protect the lines of communications, but that the British, fearing a repercussion of a possible defeat in Egypt, did not like to have a nearly 200,000 strong Iranian Army at their rear. They insisted on the occupation of the country and control over the Iranian Government.

In the first week of August a friend who came from Baghdad told us that the British were hastily preparing additional accommodation in the hospitals. This information disquieted me even more than the rumours about tanks and armoured car manœuvres on the frontier, and I considered it my duty to report it to the Chief of Staff. On hearing this he smiled and said that in order to frighten a child people talked of bogeys, and that in the present case, there were persons instructed to show the bogeys to us. Taking the hint, I said coldly that I had considered it my duty to give to the Staff any information that came to my knowledge, and that it was for the General Staff to draw its conclusions.

In Iran, as in certain other eastern countries, all the British were considered to be a blend of Lord Curzon and T. E. Lawrence (as people thought them to have been), and having an English wife it was thought impossible for me not to be in contact with the Intelligence Service and subservient to British interests. This belief on the part of certain important and influential persons and others less important afterwards led to many *quid pro quos* and sometimes allowed me to obtain valuable information.

Unfortunately, the events proved that the bogey was no fancy and no make-believe, as on the 25th August 1941, at 4.45 a.m., the British and Russian forces attacked Iran simultaneously from the north, west and south-west.

Reza Shah and Iran

Much has been written about Reza Shah's personality and work by sympathisers, critics, opponents and people who have tried to be, and sometimes succeeded in being, impartial. Most of them saw him once or twice, or at most a dozen times, and many did not see him at all or had no occasion to speak with him. I saw him certainly more than one hundred times, and had the honour of speaking with him on many occasions between 1921 and 1941, but I am no psychologist and find it hard to explain what I really think and feel about him.

Our relationship was professional. I was an executive far removed from the level of command, but nevertheless on account of his direct interest in every detail of all branches of national activity, and particularly of the army, I was frequently in direct contact with him. My life, my work, my happiness or distress depended directly on him. He was my hero. I had a boundless admiration for him and for his work and completely shared his ideals.

Being a simple soldier, my impressions of him were also simple. They can be given in one word. He was *great*. What was great in him? His single-minded devotion to one object—the regeneration of Iran. He was not a nationalist in the sense which is given nowadays to that word and which is a product of nineteenth-century Europe, his patriotism stemming rather from that of the Achaemenian and Sassanian Kings perfectly expressed by our great national poet Ferdowsi in the tenth century: 'If there be no Iran let me not be.' His determination, the power of his will, the magnetic authority which emanated from him subdued his most resolute opponents: the magnitude of his conceptions together with his care for the least details, his love of order and discipline and his dislike of waste and negligence—all were at the service of this one great objective. He was not content for Iran to be a second-class independent country. He wanted it to

attain to greatness, as in the times of the great Persian mon-
archies, not by annexing foreign lands, but by developing the
resources and uplifting the morale of the nation, and for this
reason any subservience to foreign countries was abhorrent to
him. He never wanted to take foreign loans, and on the contrary
he accelerated the repayment to Great Britain of the 1911 loan.
He had no personal charm, and did not seek popularity. He considered it his mission to work for the Iranian nation not by
courting her, but by administering to her the medicines he considered useful for her health even if they were bitter, without
taking the trouble to enclose them in sugar-covered capsules.
He knew what Iran needed, and had no intention of consulting
anybody on the subject because his objectives were clear to him:
independence from foreign influence either political, economic
or cultural, expansion of Persian culture, economic self-sufficiency, extension of education, democratisation of all institutions,
modernisation of the administration, emancipation of women,
the application of social justice, and the moral regeneration of
the nation.

Unlike many, he did not say: 'We must have social justice in
order to prevent the spread of communism', but 'We do not care
what regimes other countries have, we want social justice
because it is good!'

He never promised anything in his rare speeches. He merely
said that this, this and that *must* be done. He was a benevolent
autocrat, but at the same time he was very careful not to touch
the country's Constitution. There was a Majles, there were
deputies, but they passed all the laws presented by the Government and their proposals were always accepted by the Cabinet,
as these proposals coincided with the desires of the Shah, who
received them once a fortnight at the palace and talked to them
about what should be done. What he said was always concise and
to the point.

The Shah spoke little, in a low voice. While speaking, he
looked at his interlocutors with calm, steady eyes, which seemed
to belong to a superhuman being, looking from the depths of
centuries past into the centuries to come. He looked superhuman,
but he was a mortal and a human being and so had his shortcomings. Although perseverence and patience were two of his
great qualities, sometimes he became impatient, especially for

small causes, and allowed his temper to get the better of him. Of a very strong build and great physical vigour, he only very rarely indulged in the show of it during his twenty years of power. He was suspicious of all until their loyalty was proved by their behaviour. He was averse to the spilling of blood, but did not hesitate when he considered it necessary in the interest of the country.

At the beginning of his rise to power he deployed great political talent against the elements who were opposing him either on personal grounds, because they did not want a soldier of fortune to become their leader, or because they felt that his tendency was to democratise the country and suppress their privileges, not by attempting to win them over, but by dividing and so weakening them. Later, when he was firmly in the saddle of power, he simply ignored them, because they were cowed, as he thought, for ever. He despised most people who approached him, because he knew, or thought that he knew, their selfish nature, their hollow vanity, their natural arrogance subdued by fear and their supineness when confronted by force. At the same time, he was a dedicated man devoid of egotism, and ready to sacrifice everything including himself for the greatness of Iran. He was proud, but not vain, and he wanted himself and all Iranians to be worthy of pride. He genuinely disliked praise and I was once rebuked for having used laudatory epithets for him in my *Cavalry Journal*.

His morals were irreproachable. Although he had two wives, he was not much interested in women. He drank one small glass of brandy after dinner, but the legend about his smoking opium is absolutely false, and at least after his assumption of power he never touched this or any other drug and tried to eradicate the use of it in Iran. In many descriptions of Reza Shah I have seen the term brutal applied to him. If his personal appearance suggested brutality because he was tall and strong and had a severe countenance, I never noticed any act of brutality on his part after he became War Minister and later Shah. I heard that he had been blunt and rough when he was a sergeant, but a good sergeant must be that, especially with the uncouth rascals who were the Cossack troopers of his time. He was physically and morally fearless, but at the same time politically cautious and knowing how to bide his time, methodical and secretive. The background of Reza Shah must be taken into consideration in order to appreciate his extraordinary capacity to detach himself from the atmosphere of his surroundings and to grasp the significance of what he was told of the conditions prevalent in the modern world. He understood the exact value of any contemplated change, and adopted it without hesitation if he considered it useful for the progress of the country.

He has been accused of rapacity because of the many estates and villages which he acquired, but there was a reason for this which, as was usual with him, he did not disclose even to his closest subordinates—I do not say collaborators because really no one could be so described. He wanted to regenerate village life and to organise the agricultural work of the country according to better methods, and to see that the peasants strove to improve the quality and increase the quantity of their products in order to raise their standard of living. He could only do this by a close and direct supervision which would not have been possible had these estates not belonged to him. This is clearly indicated by the hundreds of attractive cottages for peasants he ordered to be built on his estates, which were abandoned and destroyed after his abdication by the ignorant peasants who are now seeking to restore them. Without any doubt his idea was to introduce ultimately agrarian reform, and the villages, which had been under his direct administration, were destined to become the models for the others, and this explains why in the later years of his reign he began to acquire estates in all the provinces.

If we consider the highly individualistic, unruly and sceptical character of the Iranian people, their lack of respect for and confidence in their rulers and the habit of the upper class to rely on foreigners for advice, it is astounding that Reza Shah succeeded in rising from the ranks to the highest office of the State and in imposing his will on a nation, the majority of whose influential men were if not only hostile at least unsympathetic. It can only be explained by the extraordinary irradiation of authority and moral strength that emanated from him, and the awe inspired by his imposing physical personality together with the skill he deployed in his use of these attributes, first to come to power and then to hold it.

The officers of the Cossack Division, where he served, were mostly composed of men who, like Reza Shah, had been promoted from the ranks. When he made them swear to collaborate with him before marching on Teheran they knew that any other commander would, if such an operation were a success, put them aside and replace them by younger officers of more education; whereas Reza Shah promoted them and gave them key posts in the newly organised army. In this way, their feeling of loyalty to their chief was supported by a sense of personal interest. Unfortunately, some of the younger officers with more education considered that the higher posts ought to be given to them and disliked having to serve under rough and uneducated commanders whose origin was humble and who lacked the refinement of the upper classes. They became discontented, and this led to revolts such as that of Major Lahoty in Tabriz in February 1922, or to plots like that of Colonel Puladin in 1926. On account of this the Shah became highly suspicious of the educated officers, and although utilising them for instructional jobs, kept the older uneducated officers in the key places. In this way he kept the army completely loyal and blindly obedient, but lost some officers who might have rendered useful service.

Personally, having for years suffered from the humiliation of seeing my country in a state of such weakness that she was obliged to bear with continual interference in all branches of her political, administrative, social, economic and even spiritual activities, I felt at once an unbounded gratitude to the man who put an end to this shameful situation and restored national prestige in Iran and before the world.

The Shah received no help from the non-political-minded masses of the people, in whose interest his reforms were directed, but although the secret which he kept about the projected reforms, which were all to the advantage of the working classes, did not allow them to realise the extent of the Shah's solicitude for them, little by little people understood that he was working for them, especially in the country. Security from brigands and tribal warfare, the curbing of the central and provincial authorities' exactions, the buildings of roads and railways, the expansion of education, the reform of the administration of justice, the improvement of health and hygiene: all this, even though not advertised in advance by State propaganda, created a feeling of confidence in the public at large.

The disarmament and the bringing under the control of the

Central Government of the warlike tribes deprived the discontented elements of the means to create trouble and assured the supremacy of the State.

If war had not come with the consequent occupation of Iran for more than four years and the abdication of Reza Shah, his rule would have continued until its natural conclusion, and the Crown Prince would have succeeded his father in a normal way, the country continuing to advance steadily in the way of modernisation and progress. But fate had decided otherwise. The work of Reza Shah in Iran has been described in many books and articles. I will try to give a résumé of it under four headings according to the importance Reza Shah himself gave to each although he carried them on simultaneously, as the attainment of each of them depended on the others.

1. *Freeing Iran from foreign political and economic domination.*—Since the Turkmenchai Treaty of 1828, Iran had been subjected to a capitulatory regime, extended by the most-favoured nation clause to all other European countries.

The port installations of Bandar Pahlavi had been conceded to Russia, including the lighthouses, the quays, the customs depot buildings, etc., and it was the sole Iranian port in the Caspian. A Russian warship was permanently anchored there.

The island of Ashurada on the south-eastern coast of the Caspian Sea had been since 1841 under Russian occupation.

Soviet forces occupied part of Gilan and Mazanderan.

A military force called the South Persian Rifles (S.P.R.), organised during the 1914–18 war by the British, was in charge of security duties in the southern provinces of Iran, especially Fars and Kerman, under British military authorities. There were British military units in Bushehr, Hengam island and in Iranian Baluchistan, and since 1911 British post-offices functioned in some places.

At Bushehr, Jask, Bandar Abbas and Khorramshahr, the police and sanitary inspections were effected by the British. The British Consul-General in Bushehr was at the same time British Resident in the Gulf, which was understood by the local population to mean that the British had the same rights on the Iranian as on the Arab shore of the Persian Gulf, which was not legally the case. British vessels entering Iranian ports did not hoist the Iranian flag as is the international custom, which was interpreted by the local inhabitants as signifying that Great Britain was the protecting power of all the lands adjoining the Persian Gulf.

The local chieftains on the shore of the Persian Gulf received subsidies from the British in order not to interfere with their installations, as no Iranian police or gendarmerie existed there.

The finances and monetary policy of the country were practically directed by the British, as the Imperial Bank of Persia, a British concern, had the concession right to issue bank-notes and was in charge of all the financial operations of the Government.

Foreign telegraph connexions were in the hands of the British Telegraph Department and the British Indo-European Telegraph Co., which controlled in this way all the Government's communications.

The A.P.O.C. was a state within the state and considered itself completely independent in Khuzestan, having only some kind of co-operation with the Sheikh of Mohammerah whom they treated practically as an independent ruler.

The Iranian Government was not free to fix the customs duties, and could not take more than 5 per cent *ad valorem* on imported products, foreign importers generally managing not to pay more than 2 or 3 per cent.

This was the situation that faced Reza Shah in 1921. He liquidated all these servitudes according to the following time-table:

In 1921 Soviet forces evacuated Iranian territory.

That same year, the S.P.R. were disbanded, being replaced in south Iran by units of the Iranian National Army and Gendarmerie.

By 1923 all British military units had left Iran, and the British post-offices closed.

In 1927 the port of Bandar Pahlavi with all its installations reverted to Iran and the Russian warship departed, the Ashurada island being also occupied by the Iranian frontier guards.

In 1928 the capitulations were abrogated, and Iran declared its right to fix the custom duties. The different foreign powers concluded bilateral treaties regulating their trade relations with Iran.

By 1930 the British port and health authorities in Iranian

ports were replaced by Iranians. The Gulf Resident was transferred to Bahrain, all foreign (including British) ships had to submit to Iranian regulations and to hoist the Iranian flag. The British naval base from Henqam was also transferred to Bahrain, and the island occupied by Iranian gendarmerie.

The subsidies to the chieftains in Iranian territory were stopped.

In 1930, the Imperial Bank of Persia's concession having lapsed, the Government founded the National Bank of Iran, which began the issue of Iranian bank-notes.

In 1931 the concessions to the Eastern Telegraph Department and Indo-European Telegraph Company, which had also terminated, were not renewed, and the Iranian State Telegraph took over all their material and started to operate the international lines.

In 1933 the A.P.O.C. (which had later become the A.I.O.C.) concession was cancelled and replaced by a more favourable concession, which substantially increased the royalties of the Iranian Government.

Already in 1924 the Sheikh of Mohammerah had been arrested and brought to Teheran, and the province of Khuzestan brought under Government control.

All this had been attained through constant pressure, as the British had tried to bring the Iranian Government to renew the Bank and Telegraph concessions, and the negotiations to replace the capitulations treaty were hard and protracted, and those for the reassertion of the exterior signs of Iranian sovereignty in the Persian Gulf not as smooth as people afterwards imagined them to have been.

2. *Internal security and the establishment of a strong Central Government.*—Reza Shah amalgamated the different armed organisations into an army, with a proper territorial and tactical organisation, a High Command (himself), a General Staff, services, a Military Academy and later a Staff College, an Air Force, a small Navy, universal military conscription, a unified armament and military factories for munitions. The army's medical and veterinary services received the Shah's special attention, studs were organised in several regions of Iran, and a Gendarmerie was charged with order on the roads and rural security, the army's duty being restricted to the protection of the country's frontiers.

As stated before, the lawless and turbulent tribes had been disarmed, and brought to order; many of them settled on the land, only a few men being allowed to take the flocks to the summer pastures under the protection and surveillance of gendarmes. A few tribal chiefs were brought to Teheran, where they were allowed to live in their houses under police supervision, that is they could not go farther than 20 miles from the town without special authorisation. Others had their estates exchanged with estates in other provinces, far from their tribes, in order to prevent them from intriguing with their former tribesmen.

The police organisation was extended, all police in the provincial towns controlled from the Central Police Organisation in Teheran, the secret and political police being very efficient and order was strictly kept all over the country.

If security had not been established, none of the other reforms could have been implemented.

3. *Administrative reforms and economic progress.*—These consisted in—The reorganisation of the general administration of the country, the creation of a civil service with a table of ranks and regulations for the conditions of service, promotion, etc.— The organisation of the Judicial system—The promulgation of laws—The building of roads and railways—The reorganisation of the country's finances on the basis of a budget—The making of provisions for external trade—The creation of a national industry—The modernisation of agricultural methods and the extension of cultivation.

As mentioned in the first part of this book, the economy of Iran was a mixture of the economies practised in Europe from the Dark Ages, until the end of the nineteenth century. For instance, agricultural methods were more primitive than in the Middle Ages. Industry was non-existent. Wheeled transport by carts was used only on the Teheran–Rasht–Enzeli, Tabriz–Jolfa and Qazvin–Hamadan roads, otherwise pack animals were the only method of transport. Building materials consisted chiefly of unburnt bricks (*adobe*) and mud mixed with straw, roofed over with beams on which were laid branches supporting mud roofs, stones being used only in some mountainous regions and domed roofs chiefly in the south and south-centre of the country.

Administration as understood in Europe and America was non-existent before the Constitution in 1907, and since then had remained embryonic. The laws were the religious laws of the Sharieh, which, admirable in essence as they are, do not correspond to all the necessities and complications of life today and were administered by the clergy only, whose interpretation of the law varied according to the knowledge or inclination of the judges, especially in cases of lawsuits.

Reza Shah understood that all this was wrong, and knew that it was different and, as he thought, better abroad. After becoming Prime Minister, he grouped around him a number of young and active men who had been educated abroad and who displayed initiative and willingness to work with him, such as Abdul Hoseyn Teimurtash, Firuz, Ali Akbar Davar, Mudir-ol-Molk Jam, Dadgar and a few others, and ordered them to prepare for him blue-prints of the necessary administrative reforms. With his extraordinary intelligence he at once understood what was presented to him, discerned what was at the time possible, and what had to be postponed, and ordered their application, himself controlling all the details and correcting the mistakes and the errors of judgement of his subordinates. He never allowed their influence to become paramount, and subjected the application of their projects to the general lines which he had himself drawn up for the progress of the country.

An American financial mission under Dr. A. C. Millspaugh helped to solve financial problems, but when Millspaugh tried to direct the work according to his own, and not the Shah's ideas, he had to quit, his contract not being renewed. The National Bank was organised by Germans, but when their work failed to come up to his expectations they were replaced by Iranians, an Iranian officer becoming the Governor of the Bank, which he administered for years very ably, becoming afterwards Minister of Finance.

Following the example of Atatürk, the Shah ordered Davar, who had been a lawyer educated in France, and some others to prepare a penal code and a civil code largely inspired by the French codes, and these having been passed by the Majles, the Ministry of Justice was closed for three months during which a new Ministry on modern lines was organised, the new personnel becoming entirely lay.

In order to give work to the clerical personnel who had lost their jobs through his reorganisation, he created notarial offices in which all deeds, marriages, births, deaths, etc., had to be registered, and had the jobless *mollas* appointed notaries, but in each such office a Government official had also to be present, and all deeds had to have his approval. A General Registration Administration was created, as well as a Cadastral Administration, with offices in all the provinces and districts, and all properties and estates had to be registered, delimited and evaluated, so as to limit disputes.

The Shah was careful to preserve the Sharieh law in questions of marriage, births, inheritance, wills, etc., because he did not want to upset the religious feelings of the great majority of the people, but in order to work towards the emancipation of women he ordered some laws to be supplemented. In this way it has become possible to put in the marriage contract such stipulations as the obligation of the husband not to take another wife—the right of the wife to divorce with the same facility as the man— the right for the wife to choose in what place to live.

Being a soldier, the Shah was well aware of the importance of communications, and he grasped very quickly their importance from the economic point of view. In a few years 17,000 miles of roads were built or transformed from pack animal tracks to motor roads, 1700 miles of the Trans-Iranian railway completed, with branches towards Tabriz and Mashad begun, all this being financed by a tax on sugar, thus avoiding the necessity of taking a foreign loan which the Shah considered highly undesirable as furthering foreign political influence in the country. This development of communications ended the danger of local famines, when one region suffered from a bad harvest while in another grain was rotting because of the lack of means of transport.

In order to expand and modernise agriculture, the Shah founded an agricultural college at Karaj, 30 miles from Teheran, and agricultural research and experimental stations in the provinces, where better seeds were given to the peasants and more modern methods taught to them. But the real experiments and teaching of new methods took place on the estates of the Shah, where these were applied with considerable success, although provoking some discontent among the peasants, who had for centuries been accustomed to work only sufficiently to keep themselves and their families alive, never working in winter, and not understanding the possibility of raising their standard of living. In order to have grain in an emergency and to keep it in better condition the Shah had ordered a large silo to be built in Teheran, with seven others in the provinces. As will be seen later, the Teheran silo was very useful in keeping the town from starvation during the war.

The Shah believed in self-sufficiency for the country, and strove to create as many factories as possible. Many of these worked at first at a loss, but the Shah considered that with time they would improve their methods and the quality of their products and become profitable. Besides, he thought that it was good for the morale of the nation to see that Iran could also have industries, and manufacture industrial products.

It was for the same reason that the Shah began to build imposing public buildings, like the Police Headquarters, the Ministry of Foreign Affairs, the War Ministry, the Teheran Railway Station, the National Bank, the Ministry of Justice, the University, the Officers' Club, etc., and began the huge Ministry of Finance. He considered that it contributed to raise the prestige of the State and to impress on the people that Iran was again a great and powerful nation, as it had been in the past.

4. *Social reforms and cultural progress.*—The Shah was a democrat, though not in the sense that the people ought to be at once allowed to govern themselves, but that they must be rendered able to do so in future, and that democratisation must come by stages, according to the capacity of people to absorb and digest it. He rightly thought that the best way to democratise a nation was to educate it, because educated people will not submit blindly to the exploitation of reactionary landlords or unscrupulous political adventurers, and would also better resist foreign interference. Though he had himself received a very scanty education, he appreciated its value and from the beginning laid particular stress on it. He was especially interested in the establishment of primary schools for boys and girls, because he considered that the greatest possible number of people must know how to read and write, and that higher education must come after that.

I remember being told that when the Shah decided to create a university with several faculties, a French architect, who was brought to prepare the plan of the buildings of the different faculties, was rather disappointed when the Shah told him that for the present only the faculties of medicine and law would be built, the others being constructed later. 'First, we must teach the peasants and the workers how to read and write, and then we can look after higher education.' All the same, he did not neglect secondary and higher education, and was in fact the founder of it in Iran. He ordered official text-books to be prepared and all education unified. In 1921 there was only one teachers' college in Iran, and it was very rudimentary. In 1941 there were 36 elementary teachers' colleges and one secondary training college, providing the schools with qualified teachers. The number of primary schools rose from 440 with 44,025 pupils in 1922–1923 to 2424 with 253,837 in 1941, and that of secondary schools from 47 with 9399 pupils (they were very rudimentary, and except one, the rest of them had a lower standard than the primary schools at the end of Reza Shah's reign) to 301 with 24,112, and the only high school, with 91 students, became a university with 8 faculties, with 2500 students. Besides this, Reza Shah instituted adult education with a two years' course, the teaching taking place in the evenings, and more than 150,000 persons were enrolled in about 2000 classes.

There were besides these many technical and professional schools. Teaching the recruits to read and write was an obligation of all the unit commanders, who were refused promotion if their soldiers were not able to read, write and apply the four rules of arithmetic at the end of their two years' service. This was very strictly observed, as all units of the army were inspected twice a year by special commissions.

The Shah gave very great importance to physical education for boys and girls, and boy scouts and girl guides were organised on the international model, with the proper uniforms. An imposing sports stadium was constructed and several others planned, and sports competitions became obligatory in the army and all the schools. Races took place twice a year in Teheran, once a year in the Turkoman steppe and once or twice a year in different provincial towns.

All schoolboys had to wear uniform of grey cloth with peaked caps, and the girls grey overalls, and all were taught to be clean and tidy. A professional school for girls had been established after the Shah had seen the Ismet Pasha's Girls' School in Ankara, where domestic arts were taught to girl students from poorer classes. Foreign Missionary schools and proselytism were first discouraged and later prohibited, in the case of schools not prepared to submit to the Education Ministry's programme. This prescribed the Persian language as medium of teaching, allowing foreign languages to be taught only as a second language, and ordering Islamic religious teaching for the Moslem children. A few foreign schools, which had accepted the Government's regulations, have been allowed to continue their work.

The old Qoranic schools where *mollas* used to teach children to read and write, elementary arithmetic and the Qoran, continued to exist, as in many villages (of which there are 45,000 in Iran) no other schools existed and still do not exist. They are run with money from pious donations, and are not included in the above-mentioned statistics, but thanks to them the number of illiterates in Iran is much lower than is imagined, and does not surpass 60 per cent—which is still enormous.

Reza Shah did not try to suppress religion, but succeeded in preventing the *mollas* from interfering or opposing reforms. In order to raise their standard the Shah ordered them all to pass examinations, and only those who had been able to pass them were authorised to wear the Moslem religious costume, with the long robe and white or (for the descendants of the Prophet) black turban. They were attached to mosques and religious institutions. Each regiment had a Ghazi-Askar or military chaplain whose rank was lieutenant or captain, and who used to come on Fridays and religious holidays and preach to the soldiers. They also took part in military ceremonies and supervised the swearing-in of cadets and recruits.

Every year Reza Shah used to send 100 young students, some of them with Government scholarships, to foreign universities and technical schools, and today most of the higher administrative posts are occupied by these people.

Reza Shah wished to raise the standard of public health, and it was for this reason that the first faculty of the Teheran University to be founded was that of medicine. He ordered dissection to be included in the medical courses, as before that it had been (wrongly) considered incompatible with Islam, and therefore forbidden. A Pasteur Institute was established on the model of that of Paris with a French director, vaccines were prepared and vaccination against smallpox became compulsory, that against other diseases being performed during epidemics. There were only half a dozen Government hospitals in the entire country, two of them with about 60 beds being in Teheran. In 1940 there were more than 150 hospitals and a 500-bed hospital was being erected near Teheran.

All this seems very little today, but it had all been created from nothing by means of the scanty Government budget, without any outside help, without external or internal loans, by a ridiculously small number of specialists and technicians, inspired and directed by a man who, before being faced with the task of ruling a State in the twentieth-century world, had never imagined the existence of the manifold complicated political and technical problems of a country's administration today.

The younger generation and some foreigners take what was accomplished by Reza Shah for granted, failing to realise the spiritual, political and material conditions which prevailed in Iran in 1920, when this predestined genius of a man undertook the gigantic work of changing a mediaeval, feudalistic, anachronistic country into a modern State, having, it is true, many shortcomings, but still modern, and capable of improvement.

Those of the older generation, if not prejudiced, or basically hostile, cannot fail to appreciate and admire Reza Shah's tremendous achievement which has rightly earned for him the title of Reza Shah the Great.

PART III

During The Second World War in Iran—
Recession 1941–1946

Impact of War on Iran

On the 19th August 1941 Reza Shah came to the Military Academy's Summer Camp at Aqdassieh for the ceremony of the commissioning of the senior class cadets, who were to become sub-lieutenants.

The Ministers, the Generals and the representatives of the Press were present. After the distribution of the diplomas and the taking of the oath by the young sub-lieutenants, the Shah made a speech telling them that on account of the gravity of the situation the promoted officers would not get their usual one-month holiday, and must at once join their units. 'Anywhere you may be, in any circumstances, do not forget your duty towards the Army and the country,' he said at the end.

The young officers cheered him with a thunderous hurrah, and the Shah departed, leaving everybody in a state of tension, as it was known that the Russians and British had again made representations, and the declarations of Eden on the 8th of August had been menacing. On the 21st there was a Salam at the Golestan Palace on the occasion of Mabas, the anniversary of the Revelation of the Prophet. Everything looked quite normal, and nobody guessed then that this was to be Reza Shah's last Salam. The next day, which was a Friday, we had as guest at Larak the English wife of Admiral Bayandor, the Commander of the Iranian Navy, who was himself at Khorramshahr. She came with her small son, and stayed the whole day, very gay and cheerful, little knowing what was in store for her. She promised to come back together with her husband at his next visit to Teheran.

Early on the 25th Teheran radio announced briefly that Soviet and British troops had passed the frontier and penetrated into Iranian territory. 'Our forces are defending the national territory, fighting has started and is continuing on all fronts.' I drove at once to the General Staff, and asked General Zarghami to be sent to the front. He said that he would transmit my demand to His Majesty.

During the morning seven big Soviet planes flew over Teheran dropping leaflets, inviting the population to be calm and to surrender, and explaining that the Soviet forces were entering Iran because the Iranian Government had been reluctant to expel German spies and terrorists. In the afternoon I learned that Khorramshahr had been bombarded and occupied, our gunboats sunk after a stiff resistance, and that Admiral Bayandor had been killed.

A few days earlier my brother had been sent to Kermanshah and appointed Chief of Staff of the Western Forces, and I was anxious about him. That evening Zarghami announced to me that Ibrahim was all right, and that the Shah had ordered me to become Chief of Staff of Teheran's Defence Forces, under General Yazdanpanah.

On the 26th we learned of the occupation of Marand, Sofian, Bandar Pahlavi, Khoi, Maku and Shahpur by the Russians. The British had been held at Pa-e-Tak by forces of the Kermanshah Division and sustained some losses, but a battalion had been parachuted to Masjed-e-Soleyman in order to prevent sabotage of the oilfields and to protect the British personnel, who numbered some 2500 in the oilfield region. I learned that no operational instruction had been given to the army units, no destruction of railways, roads or bridges authorised, and no rear-guard actions ordered. It was clear that from the beginning the Shah did not intend to put up a real defence, and wanted only to show the Germans that Iran had been invaded by force, so that in the event of a German victory Iran could not be held responsible and treated as an enemy country.

The diplomatic representatives of the invading countries had remained in Teheran and had not been interfered with, and the Iranian representatives in London and Moscow were also not recalled, but the Allied forces continued to advance. Captain Bayandor, the brother of the Admiral, was killed at Bandar Pahlavi on the Caspian, on the same day as his brother had been killed at Khorramshahr on the Persian Gulf; and Tabriz, Rasht and Qazvin were bombarded by Soviet planes with heavy losses to the civilian population. The British warships' bombardment on the 25th had also resulted in many casualties among civilians, soldiers and sailors. I proposed to blow up the bridges, and to move the units of the important Teheran garrison by night towards the mountainous region west of Arak and to organise a defence there, but the Shah rejected this plan.

Early the next morning, when I was already working at my Chief of Staff's office at the Military Academy, I heard three successive reports of bombs bursting from the direction of Larak, and I telephoned to ask my wife what had happened. She told me that a Soviet plane flying very low, had passed over their heads whilst they were having breakfast in the garden with Leila, and had dropped a bomb some 300 yards from there which fell in a ravine, another which fell half a mile to the south in a field and a third close to the Military Academy's summer camp. At 8 a.m. it was officially announced that the army had been ordered to return to their barracks and that an agreement for an armistice had been entered into with the Allies. Nevertheless, the advance continued. According to the terms of the armistice the Russians were to occupy the northern part of Azerbaijan, Gilan, Mazanderan, Gorgan and the northern part of Khorasan, as well as Qazvin, Semnan, Damghan and Shahrud, and the British, the Khuzestan province and part of Kermanshah. The Iranian Government undertook to expel all the Germans and nationals of other enemy States, including the diplomats, and to put its lines of communications at the disposal of the Allies, to carry war material, etc., to the U.S.S.R. The Iranian Government was also to provide all kinds of facilities to the occupying forces.

Ali Mansur, the Prime Minister, had to resign, and was replaced by Mohammad Ali Foroughi, who was more acceptable to the Allies, i.e. the British, as the Russians were too busy coping with the German offensive to interfere very much in these arrangements and left negotiations with the Iranian Government to the British. In the new Cabinet, General Ahmad Nakhchevan (no connexion with Mohammad Nakhchevan, the former War Minister) became War Minister, and probably considering that in the new situation the War Minister did not need to consult the Sovereign, decided to dissolve the conscript army as a preliminary to adopting a voluntary recruited army on the model of the peace-time British Army. I do not know if he had received hints from some quarter, but the result was that thousands of soldiers abandoned their barracks and moving in long irregular columns began to go back to their villages.

On learning of this order of the newly appointed War Minister the Shah was furious, and not being satisfied with his explanations, ordered him to be put in prison. The Gendarmerie was ordered to send the disbanded recruits back and many were returned before they reached their villages, but finding that no food was available, as the month's provisions given by the commissariat had been squandered at the time of the soldiers' departure, they left the barracks again. This time they avoided marching on the roads so it was more difficult to stop them and bring them back. Nevertheless, in the end, the commissariat produced food, most of the soldiers were brought back and order was restored.

In the provinces things were worse. In Kordestan, in Azerbaijan, Khorasan and Gorgan, where Soviet forces were advancing, as soon as the order to liberate the recruits came, rifles, machine-guns and mountain guns were abandoned by soldiers returning to their villages, and officers having heard about the fate of the officers of the Polish Army whom the Soviet Army had taken prisoner, retreated to the south. They would have been ready to fight if ordered, but after the surrender of the Government and the occupation of the country by enemy forces they did not see any sense in remaining to be slaughtered like the hapless officers of the Esthonian, Lettonian, Lithuanian and Polish armies. Most of the arms abandoned by the soldiers fell into the hands of the tribes, especially in Kordestan and the Kermanshah region, and these tribes reverted at once to their lawless practices, pillaging the neighbouring villages and attacking each other.

Although according to the stipulations of the Armistice the Iranian Army was not to be interfered with, disarmed, nor taken prisoner, the Soviet forces in Gorgan arrested all the officers and took them to Askhabad where they were kept for three months, and before being freed were told to sign a paper undertaking not to act against the U.S.S.R., and to keep contact with their representatives. I am glad to say that many of them refused to sign, and the few who did, considering themselves to have done it under duress, did not regard it as binding and reported this fact to the General Staff as soon as they returned to Teheran. The country had been occupied but Reza Shah, who had to accept this fact, did not lose his hold on it and continued to wield the same authority; the army, or what was left of it, being completely loyal. Martial law had been proclaimed in the capital. This situation did not suit the Allies, who wanted to have the run of the country for themselves, and so an intense radio propaganda against the Shah began, not only from Moscow, but also from London and Delhi.

Great capital was being made out of the arrest of the War Minister, who was represented as a victim of the Shah's autocratic ways. To answer this propaganda the Shah ordered Forughi to make the deputies of the Majles sign a declaration protesting against the broadcasts from Delhi and London, saying that the Shah was not a dictator, having always respected the country's Constitution and that the Majles was loyal to the Sovereign. This proposal was met unfavourably by a group of deputies who refused to sign the declaration, stating that the radios had said nothing but the truth and that there was no democracy in Iran. Forughi transmitted this answer to the Shah who was deeply affected by this ingratitude and opportunism on the part of people who owed so much to him.

According to the stipulations of the Armistice, all the Germans living in Iran were to be expelled. They were brought to the summer residence of the German Embassy in Shimran where they camped in the extensive grounds, but several of them managed to disappear, and as the Iranian Government could not find them, the Allies seized on this pretext to order their forces to move on Teheran, the Russians from the east and the British from the west. I heard this news early on the 16th September, and thought that when the Russians entered Teheran they would at once arrest Colonel Mikeladze, who had returned from Tabriz, and have him shot as a deserter from their army. So I went at once to the Headquarters of the 1st Division, to which Mikeladze belonged, and asked to see the General, but his Chief of Staff told me that he had been summoned to the palace. I telephoned to him there, asking him to allow Mikeladze to go at once to Isfahan, supposedly on duty, and to use an army motorcycle. After some haggling he authorised this and then said: 'Do you know why we have been called to the palace? His Majesty has formally abdicated in favour of the Crown Prince, to whom we have sworn fidelity.'

I felt as if the ground on which I stood had been taken from under me. The world was foundering around us. The feeling of security given by knowing that Reza Shah was at his palace, looking after his nation, suddenly disappeared.

What had induced him to take this fateful decision? After what had happened at the Majles, the march of the British and Soviet forces on Teheran indicated that the Allies had definitely decided to get rid of him by every means possible. If he was unpopular with them, perhaps his son who was new to politics and was not compromised in the eyes of the Allies would be able to maintain himself with the support of the loyal army? The Shah was ready to sacrifice himself, but he wanted Iran to remain and his dynasty to continue to serve the country. Also, after twenty years of absolute power it was hard for him to accept the rebukes of his own deputies and the humiliations inflicted on him by the occupying Powers, who intended to dictate their wishes to him and to enforce them by the bayonets present in his capital. These were, I thought then, the reasons for his abdication.

What would happen now? Would the Allies allow Mohammad Reza Shah to reign? What would be the reactions of the people? I was sure that the army would remain loyal to the new Shah, who was already very popular with the young officers who considered him one of themselves, as he had been a good and simple comrade at the Military Academy and was a keen and able sportsman. But in a country occupied by alien military forces the army had no power to act against the wishes of those forces. If it had been able to do so it would have prevented the occupation. I knew that an article had appeared in the *Ettelaat* newspaper without a signature, blaming the British and Russians for having violated our neutrality and the integrity of our territory, and that the Allies thought this article had been inspired by the Crown Prince, which did not endear him to them.

I went to the General Staff, where I was told that Reza Shah had already departed to Isfahan alone in his Rolls-Royce, the Imperial family with the exception of the young Shah having already been sent there. As all the generals had been ordered to be present at the Majles at 11 a.m. for the ceremony of the taking of the oath to the Constitution by the new Sovereign, Mohammad Reza Shah Pahlavi, I hurried home to put on my parade uniform and went from there to the Majles, where generals in parade uniforms and Ministers and high dignitaries in morning coats were assembled, a company of Guards with their band waiting at the entrance. We were standing in the entrance hall, the officers to the right of the entrance, the civilians to the left. There was very little conversation while we waited. A few civilians tried to look casual, but the majority looked subdued and even gloomy. Then we heard from outside the National Anthem played by the band, and the greeting of the Shah answered rhythmically according to regulation by the Guards: '*Javīd-bād-Ala-Hāzrat!*' Mohammad Reza Shah entered the hall. He was in parade uniform, pale but composed. The Senior General commanded: 'Attention!' and we froze into immobility, following our new Sovereign with our eyes, while the civilians bowed deeply according to Court etiquette. The Shah did not look to right or left and went up the stairs, followed by his A.D.C.s and by us.

The Ministers had already taken their stand on the rostrum, the deputies, also in morning coats, rose and the Shah took the oath on the Qoran. It was all over in a few minutes, and the young Shah left the Majles building without speaking to anybody. I was much moved looking at the young man on whom the heavy responsibility of leading his nation through this terrible crisis had prematurely fallen, and swore to myself to serve him loyally and faithfully, as I had served his father. In the afternoon I was summoned to the palace. It was my first audience with my new Sovereign. The Shah told me that the British and Soviet forces would enter Teheran the next day, and that I was appointed as liaison officer with the British, while another officer was designated for the same duty to the Russians. We had to provide suitable quarters for them and contact their commanders.

Mohammad Reza Shah twenty years ago had exactly the same figure as he has today. He is of middle height, broad-shouldered and slim-waisted with clear intelligent eyes and clean-cut regular features—altogether a handsome man pleasant to look upon. His exceptional intelligence and great personal charm were already noticeable, and he easily won the hearts of those with whom he spoke by his pleasant manners and the interest he showed in what people said.

On leaving the palace, I drove to the British Legation to see the British Military Attaché, who was now Major-General

W. A. K. Fraser, my old friend of the twenties, Pybus having become his assistant. Notwithstanding the painful circumstances I was happy to see him and we talked of old times. General Fraser had been in command of the British forces who advanced on Baghdad against Rashid Ali, and in order not to occupy the town in the dark, which would have created a dangerous situation, there had been some delay. During this time some Arabs had looted the houses of local Jews, which produced an outcry from the powerful Jewish elements in Great Britain, and Fraser had been sent to Teheran, where he had been nearly seven years from 1919 to 1926, and where his deep knowledge of Iranian affairs was being utilised. It was decided that I would come with my car in the afternoon to fetch him and that we would drive together to Kahrizak, south of Teheran, to meet the advancing British force. I did not relish this trip, but the Shah's orders had to be obeyed.

Beside Fraser, a lieutenant-colonel came with us. While driving down the Ferdowsi Avenue, we saw in front of the German Legation buses being filled with German women and children, the men having all been declared prisoners of war, and some ninety of them delivered to the Soviet authorities, God knows to what fate, the others being interned by the British in Australia and elsewhere. These women were to be sent through the Soviet occupation zone to Turkey. While I was looking sadly at them, the British lieutenant-colonel said jokingly that it would not have been a bad thing if they had been sent through the British zone. Outraged by this vulgar joke in the face of the tragedy of these unfortunate creatures whose husbands had been taken away from them perhaps for ever, I said indignantly: 'I wonder in accordance with what law or treaty, the nationals of a country friendly to an independent and neutral State are subjected to these indignities in the name of a struggle for Freedom and Justice.' The lieutenant-colonel kept silence, but General Fraser, with great tact, began talking about the progress of Teheran since he had left in 1926.

Just before reaching Kahrizak, we saw the first jeeps and armoured cars of the Household Cavalry's mechanised brigade. We advanced to meet General Aizlewood, the British Commander, General Fraser making the introductions. Just at this moment a Soviet liaison officer coming from the column marching on the capital from the east arrived and he showed us on the map the marching disposition of the Russians and told us the time of their arrival near the town. It was decided that the British would pass the night at Rei, and the Soviet forces at Mehrabad, and that the next day they would occupy the buildings put at their disposal by our General Staff.

That evening the Russians installed a military post between Teheran and the summer resort of Tajrish, a distance of eight miles, and the Minister of Communications, Sajadi, driving with his wife, was stopped by Russian soldiers and relieved of their money and jewels, including the lady's bracelets. When the Government complained, the Embassy denied the possibility of such a happening, saying that it was probably due to robbers who had put on Soviet soldiers' uniforms! It must be said that apart from this instance and a few others, the discipline of the Russian soldiers was much better than that of the British, both English and Indians. A few days after the arrival of the British and the Russians, a fifteen-year-old English girl, a friend of Leila's, was kidnapped in broad daylight by Indian soldiers who were carrying her off in a droshky, when several Iranian officers, hearing her screams, succeeded in freeing her, putting the Indians to flight.

Immediately after the departure of Reza Shah, lawlessness, robbery and hold-ups started all over the country. My wife told me that the day after the departure of Reza Shah, as she was driving in the town, our driver turned down a one-way street and when she remonstrated, replied, 'Oh! It does not matter, now Reza Shah has gone.'

Another story was told me at this time by an Englishman about a traveller who had been held up by a brigand. After having taken all his belongings, the robber noticed a paper in the pocket of his victim, and asked him what it was. 'A telegram, announcing Reza Shah's return,' said the traveller calmly. The brigand abandoning his booty fled at once without asking for any details. '*Se non è vero è ben trovato.*'

A young officer driving in his car was killed by a British lorry driving on the left (we have the right drive in Iran). I complained to the British Commander but could get no satisfaction from him and took the matter to Fraser, who told me that General Slim, the Commander of Paiforce, was coming the next day, and that there would be a party for him at the British

Legation and I could talk to him about this affair then. The following day I was introduced to General Slim, who listened to my complaint with great attention and promised to order reparations and that care should be taken to avoid such accidents in the future. He produced an excellent impression on me, being soldierly in his manner and at the same time courteous and considerate. In 1963 I met him at a dinner at the Athenæum Club in London and we recalled this incident.

The foreign occupation had different repercussions, in the capital and in the provinces, and influenced the different classes of the population in various ways. In the army the old discipline remained, the Generals and senior officers having transferred quite naturally their allegiance from the father to the son. Among the young officers there was a feeling of indignation towards the High Command, which had not allowed them to fight the invaders, and of frustration at having worked hard at the Military Academy and in their units to no purpose, as they had not been able to put their instruction into practice when the situation for which they had been prepared arose, together with deep humiliation at seeing the invaders in the streets of the capital. They were obliged, by special order, to salute foreign officers of a superior rank, although the foreign soldiers, N.C.O.s and officers did not bother to salute the Iranians, in spite of the order they had received to do so. Foreigners walking and talking with Iranian girls, drove the Iranians to acts of disrespect towards the Allied officers and caused brawls with them in the cafés and noisy demonstrations of loyalty to the young Sovereign, who had become the symbol of Iranian independence and was supposed to share their feelings and ideals. They were unanimously pro-German and welcomed news of German and afterwards of Japanese victories with delight, thirsting for revenge. They were more anti-British than anti-Russian, because the Russians, by order, were much less conspicuous in the streets and very rarely seen in the cafés, and also never requested anybody to salute them.

The intellectuals were divided. Those who had studied in Germany after 1933 were anti-Ally and Nazi-minded, and so in sympathy with the young officers, but among those who had been there before 1933 some were inclined to Communism. Those who came from France or (very few) from England, were mostly pro-Ally, as was the aristocracy with few exceptions. The merchants and the bazaar people wanted to trade with everybody, by all possible means. The working-class peasants and small shop-keepers were naturally hostile and suspicious of all foreigners, although not showing it. A political amnesty was declared and 52 Communists, who had been imprisoned by Reza Shah, were released, and at once began political activity with the moral support of the Soviet authorities which culminated, in November 1941, in the organisation of the Iranian Communist Party, under the name of *Tudeh* (masses) in order not to frighten the public by the term Communist. They were particularly active in Azer-baijan and in other districts under Soviet occupation, but in spite of pressures and encouragement from Soviet official quarters they had even less success in the provinces than in the capital.

During Reza Shah's time a few newspapers appeared in Teheran and in some provincial towns, but as there were no parties to subsidise party-organs they were obliged to be self-supporting. After the occupation more than a hundred new newspapers appeared, some of them as organs of the many parties which had grown up chiefly in the capital, and some others representing private interests, some even subsisting chiefly by blackmailing people in important positions or by subsidies from foreign sources.

During this time we were very much concerned about the development of the new situation if the German armies suc-ceeded in crossing the Caucasus and arrived at the Iranian frontier. Doubtless the Allied armies forced to evacuate Iran would adopt the scorched-earth policy and destroy the reserves of foodstuffs in the country to prevent their falling into enemy hands. It would not be possible to evacuate 16 million people through desert regions to India or to Soviet Transcaspia, and the Iranian nation would suffer famine even worse than that which followed the First World War, when some 2 million out of a population of 12 million had died of hunger and the consequent epidemics. It was natural to assume, that in order not to incur the odium of destroying the supplies vital for the existence of the local population, the Occupying Powers would have forced the Government to order the Iranian Army to do the job of annihi-lating the means of subsistence of their own nation. To anticipate this happening I considered that the army should be vigilant and ready to oppose such genocidal measures.

We were now very much affected by the humiliation inflicted without any legal excuse on Reza Shah. After staying several weeks in Isfahan he had embarked on a British ship at Bushehr, intending to go to Canada, but afterwards he had been transferred to another ship and taken against his wish to Mauritius. This act against the former Sovereign of an independent and neutral country was deeply resented by patriotic Iranians.

Immediately after the departure of the Shah the tribal chiefs, who were under restriction, returned to their districts and to their tribal life as it had been before Reza Shah. The Qashqai tribe, which was together with the Bakhtiari one of the most powerful in Iran, was led by the four sons of its late Khan, Sohlat-ed-Dovleh, who had died in prison during Reza Shah's reign. They were: Nasser, Mohammad Hoseyn, Mansur, who was in Germany, and Khosro, the youngest but the most dynamic. They were openly pro-German, and defied both the Government and the Occupying Powers, giving shelter to several German agents until the end of the war.

In the west, a Kurdish chieftain of the Baneh region, called Hama Rashid, revolted against the Government and occupied Sardasht, Baneh and even Saqqez, on the Sanandaj–Tabriz road. He was opposed by my brother Ibrahim, who after several months of fierce fighting with varying success, finally defeated him, but only after General Amin, my class comrade at Kuleli and Harbiyeh, had been killed. My brother, promoted Colonel, was then appointed Commander of the Kordestan Division.

In the Turkoman steppe, the Turkomans reverted to their old way of life, and most of the Government employees departed, but there was no concentrated revolt against the Government. Farther east, the Bicheranlu section of the Zafaranlu tribe revolted, as well as Solat and Montaser of Hazara. Their revolts were dealt with by local Government forces and liquidated, Solat being killed.

Iran under Occupation

On the 30th of September General Yazdanpanah, when I called to congratulate him, told me that he intended to appoint me as head of the 2nd Bureau (Military Intelligence), and asked me what I thought of it. I begged him to allow me to remain at the Inspectorate. He was far from pleased. After a few weeks he renewed his offer and I again answered that I would obey an order, but if it was at my discretion I preferred to stay where I was. After a few days I was superseded by General Mohammad Hoseyn Firuz, who had been forced to leave the army in 1928 during the Southern Tribes revolt and had returned to the army after Reza Shah's abdication, and I was attached to the General Staff, which meant that I had no regular job, but was on full pay. General Yazdanpanah told me that he had wanted to have a General Staff brilliantly organised, and for this reason would have liked to appoint me Chief of the Military Intelligence Department, and His Majesty had accepted this, but as I had refused they had given the Cavalry General Inspectorate to General Firuz, while the Military Intelligence was still at my disposal if I would care to take it. I felt very hurt and said that I was always ready to obey orders, but when asked my opinion considered myself free to give it.

At this time, I became the guardian of the two daughters of Dr. Naqi Khan Qaragozlu, a great friend of ours, who had died some years before. Their mother, Katherine, is an American woman, who is one of our greatest friends. A little eccentric and very highly strung, she found it very difficult to get on with their former guardian, who, being an ex-*molla* of the old school, considered that girls should be brought up in the old ways with no sport, no going out and very little education, and although the girls were considerable heiresses would allow no money to be spent on the things Katherine considered necessities for her daughters. She asked to have me appointed in his place and was, I

think, satisfied with me, as my ideas about women were exactly
contrary to those of my predecessor. The two girls, Mary and
Turan, were about the same age as Leila and all three were
excellent horsewomen.

On the 7th of December, after the attack on Pearl Harbour,
Japan entered the war against the British and the Americans,
but not against the Russians, and Japan became popular in Iran
on account of some speedy victories.

The Allies proposed a Tripartite Treaty to Iran, regularising
her relations with the occupying powers, but a section of public
opinion was against this. Patriotic organisations were formed to
oppose it, in which some cadets from the Military Academy
participated: demonstrations were held in the streets, and the
Prime Minister Forughi was physically attacked in Parliament.
Nevertheless, the treaty was signed and several of its opponents
arrested.

In the middle of February 1942 I received the order to inspect
the western divisions, from Kordestan to Khuzestan, reporting
on their situation and on what had happened there since the
invasion of Iran. Taking four officers with me, I started at once
for Sanandaj via Hamadan and Kermanshah, where I stayed for
three days inspecting the division. I had hoped to see my brother
in Sanandaj as he was then Commander of the Kordestan Division, but he was fighting the Kurds on the Saqiz road, that town
having been in their hands since the murder of General Amin.
Sanandaj having been included in the British zone was occupied
by a token British force. I received a call from two British
officers, who told me that in spite of the fact that my brother was
continually opposing them in everything they had the greatest
esteem for him.

I started with two of my officers by car towards Divandarreh,
on the Saqiz road. We could not go farther than Baqerabad,
half-way to that place on account of a heavy snowfall, so we
lunched there and finding horses, proceeded along the snow-
covered road. After 15 miles darkness prevented us from advancing further, and we passed the night in a small Kurdish village
which was half-buried in snow. I enjoyed this ride in the bracing
winter air among sparkling snow-covered hills, which reminded
me of my journey on the Anatolian Plateau just twenty years
before. That day we covered 35 miles. Our next stage was over

an interminable plateau, covered by three to four feet of snow and swept by an icy wind blowing right into our faces. Luckily a military column had passed that way after the last snowfall and we were able to follow in their tracks. On reaching Miranshah at 4.30 p.m., we went straight to the camp outside the village, and at last I found Ibrahim who was in his tent, working to prepare a raid on the enemy-held village of Sunnateh, on the far side of the Qezel Owzan's upper reaches, the enemy in question being the Kurdish rebel chief Hama Rashid.

Next day at 4 a.m. the whole detachment of about 1200 men started in pitch darkness through the snow towards Sunnateh. We passed through the village of Junian at daybreak, where a loyal Kurdish force of the Tilekuhi tribe, whose chief Ali Khan had been murdered, together with General Amin by Hama Rashid and who were thirsting for revenge, joined us. The rebels were taken by surprise. The mountain-gun shelled the height which dominated the village, the infantry attacked, covered by machine-gun fire, and we galloped with the cavalry squadron up the slope and reached it when the last Kurds were fleeing down the opposite slope and then up a ridge towards a crest situated three miles away. Ibrahim ordered the gun to fire just beyond the crest, and calling a young cavalry captain of athletic build, he introduced him to me as 'Captain Ali Zolqadr', and ordered him to take a platoon and pursue the Kurds up to the crest of the ridge. The captain saluted, and mounting his horse galloped off alone, forgetting in his eagerness to join the fight to fetch his platoon. We saw him gallop past the fleeing Kurds without interfering with them or being interfered with by the panic-stricken rebels, and disappear behind the crest, going directly under the shells of our guns. Ibrahim ordered the guns to cease firing, and a platoon was sent after Zolqadr, but before it reached the crest we saw him through our field-glasses returning with a score of armed Kurds, whom he had taken prisoner single-handed, and was driving towards the camp.

This extraordinary 'Douglas Fairbanks' of a man, of whose conquests among the European ladies of Teheran I had heard many scandalous details, was a Caucasian, the son of a millionaire horse-breeder, who had emigrated during the Russian revolution to France, and afterwards to Iran. He had enlisted in the French Foreign Legion, and for five years had victimised his co-religionists in Morocco, after which he had come to Iran where he enlisted as a specialist mechanic of armoured cars. Afterwards he was commissioned sub-lieutenant, as the Moslem immigrants from Russian Azerbaijan, which had belonged to Iran until 1828, were still considered as Iranian subjects, and had finally been promoted captain. He had lost a front tooth in some accident, but when I suggested his replacing it he confided to me that he hoped by not doing so to reduce the attentions lavished upon him by the fair sex. Naturally he was a great drinker, and sometimes after emptying his glass he would chew it up and swallow it! After my brother's death he left Iran and enlisted again in the French Foreign Legion, serving in Indo-China and Algeria, and after the completion of his second five-year term, married a young White-Russian *émigrée* and settled down in Teheran, where he is now running a restaurant and where he personally supervises the making of excellent *kababs*.

We returned to Junian, and in the afternoon started on our journey, which was comparatively easy going as this time the wind blew on our backs, and thanks to our special caps with ear-flaps we had no frost-bitten ears. After two days more riding we arrived at Baqerabad where we found our car waiting for us. Altogether in seven days we rode 180 miles on snow-covered tracks before reaching Sanandaj again. From there I continued my inspection, crossing the Lor country now quite peaceful and finishing my tour at Ahvaz. This town had also improved very much since 1936, when I had last seen it. There were many wide asphalted avenues and squares planted with palm trees, and it had lost its Arab character, through the immigration of many Isfahanis. I inspected there the military units, and noticed the buildings destroyed by the British air-bombing, and on the 12th March I returned by train to Teheran. During this time Foroughi had resigned and been replaced by Soheili, who was *persona grata* with both the British and the Russians, as he was more amenable to further concessions to the occupying powers.

My reports about the military situation of Western Iran were presented to the Shah, and after two days I was received in audience and had the honour to lunch with His Majesty. The conversation was about the shortcomings of the army and of what should be done to remedy them, the Shah laying particular stress on the necessity for improving the financial situation of the officers.

After a few days General Yazdanpanah called me to the General Staff and asked me if I was now willing to accept the Military Intelligence Department. I replied that I would be happy to accept it if he could reappoint me at the same time to the Cavalry Inspectorate. He promised to present this proposal for the approval of His Majesty, and on the 31st March I received the dual appointment. The Army Studs and Remount Department had also been attached to the Cavalry Inspectorate.

I prepared my weekly report on the political and military situation, with details of the different political parties which had sprung up like mushrooms in Iran during the last six months, and General Yazdanpanah presented it to the Shah. Apparently the Shah was interested, as he ordered that in the future I should myself bring my reports every Tuesday. After two months, I asked General Yazdanpanah to relieve me of the Military Intelligence duties as my assistant was now perfectly able to direct this department, but notwithstanding this, the Shah ordered me to continue to bring him every Tuesday reports on the war and the internal political situation of which I was well informed, thanks to various contacts I had made in the last months.

It was about this time that some 120,000 Poles of the army General Anders had raised in U.S.S.R., about 70,000 of them being soldiers and the rest civilians with many women and even children, who were supposed to be attached to this army in some capacity, arrived in Iran through Bandar Pahlavi, and were located in a camp to the east of Teheran. These Poles had been taken prisoner by the Soviet forces of 1939, and had since been in different P.O.W. camps. Their appearance aroused great compassion in the population as they were in a pitiful condition, suffering from undernourishment and disease. Many of them told tales of utter horror.

According to an agreement between the Soviet High Command and the Allies, all the Polish war prisoners were to be released to form a Polish Army, which would join with the Allies in their war against Germany. It was first intended that they should fight on the Russian front, but Stalin not wishing to have these non-Communist elements free in U.S.S.R. territory, agreed to send them through Iran to the Middle East, where they would be reorganised and engaged on one of the fronts which it was intended to establish in Western or Southern Europe. General Anders, released from prison, had been charged with the organisation of this army. He was very popular with his army, who owed their release from Soviet camps and prisons to his patient and tireless endeavours.

My mother was very ill at that time, and needed somebody to look after her constantly. I went to the Polish camp to inquire whether there was anyone there who could act as nurse for her, and a suitable young woman was found. Pani Zosia Krychowska was the wife of an officer who had been taken prisoner by the Germans whilst she had been taken to a labour camp by the Russians, and she proved kind and capable, remaining with us till the last of the Poles left for South Africa. My mother had been ill for months, and had become very weak. The doctors could do nothing for her, and she died on the 19th June. We laid her to rest in the Orthodox Cemetery, as she was born in that faith, and in spite of her English father had always felt herself Russian at heart.

An outward change was seen in the Soviet Army. New uniforms were introduced, with golden shoulder straps exactly like those of the Imperial Russian Army, and parade uniforms in dark green cloth were adopted for high-ranking officers. Up to this time the National Anthem of the U.S.S.R. had been the 'Internationale', but they now adopted a special new Anthem.

In spite of the presence of the invading forces, the life of the army had to continue, and the studs and remount services having been attached to the Cavalry Inspectorate there was new and interesting work for me. The horses spent the summer months grazing in the Lar valley, which lies in the middle of the Alborz range at an altitude of 7500 feet. The valley is 25 miles long and from 3 to 4 miles wide and is perfectly flat but surrounded by lofty ridges of the Alborz mountains with 18,000 ft. Mount Damavand, the highest mountain in Iran, on its eastern side. The Lar river, which is full of trout, flows down the middle of the valley and after skirting Damavand joins a torrent coming from the south by a waterfall before turning north towards the Caspian Sea. Thanks to the altitude and its considerable rainfall it is carpeted by long grass and innumerable wild flowers and remains green throughout the summer. To this delectable spot I took Leila and the two Qaragozlu girls, all four of us covering the 40 miles which separate the valley from Larak on horseback in one day through wild gorges and magnificent mountain scenery crossing a 10,000 ft. pass.

There are no trees in the valley on account of the bitter winter winds and no habitations, and the studs' personnel, at the head of which was Colonel Manuchehr Makui, a former veterinary surgeon of my Pahlavi Regiment, were living in tents. It was hot in the day but quite cool in the shade, and so cold at night that we slept under two blankets. The Colonel had his family with him, and was most hospitable. We rode the whole day, changing horses several times, galloping freely on the flat turf of the valley. We made several excursions in lateral valleys, and I rode nearly half the way to the summit of Mount Damavand, passing the night under a light tent three yards from a block of ice.

According to Iranian mythology Iran was once inhabited by hairy giants (*Divs*), whose leader was snow white and covered with spots like a leopard. These *Divs* made great trouble in the country until Teimures, a legendary king of the Keyan dynasty (whose descendants the Sistan people claim to be), decided to get rid of them, and finally succeeded in exiling them behind the Alborz mountains, where they are still supposed to be. In a valley lateral to the Lar there is a mound from under which strange sounds are heard, which are said to be produced by a mill grinding grain for the use of the *Divs*. Of course we were anxious to visit this place, and as we came near to it we heard uncanny sounds. The Colonel's wife and family preferred to remain at a distance, but we continued our investigation and discovered a hole on the top of the mound with a wreath of dead birds and insects at its mouth, from which a strong sulphurous smell emanated, and sounds like those produced by a giant boiler coming from within, but to our disappointment the *Divs* did not manifest themselves in any other way.

Two weeks later we returned to Larak carrying two baskets full of trout, which we had bought from an old fisherman, who remembered having taken trout to Nasr-ed-Din Shah (killed in 1896), who used to come sometimes to hunt in the valley.

After this happy interlude it was hard to be back in the troubled atmosphere of Teheran. Those people, who had been traditionally privileged before Reza Shah had come to power and for whom the reforms of the last twenty years had been anathema, were afraid that at the end of the war and after Iran had been evacuated by foreign forces the young Shah with the support of the army would revert to his father's methods and continue the democratisation of the country. They were agitating against the regime in the Majles and in the press, and this was not without its influence on the British, to whom these people were continually suggesting that the Shah was opposed to them. For many of the British members at the Legation, the Shah represented the regime of his father, and until the middle of 1943 the relations between the Palace and the occupying authorities were not always happy. In July, Soheili resigned and was replaced by Qavam, who was openly hostile to the Pahlavi dynasty, as he had been imprisoned in 1923 and afterwards expelled from the country by Reza Shah, having been implicated in a plot against him when he was War Minister.

The Russians at this time pressed on Qavam a demand to deliver to them 100,000 7·92 rifles made in Iran, 3000 light machine-guns model Brno, also of Iranian make, and 1000 heavy Maxim machine-guns, which were in the arsenal. These arms were delivered to them in their cases in Teheran. We did not understand then the reason for this request, as these arms were not in use in the Soviet Army; on the other hand we had still enough arms left in our units and arsenals for our own army which had by then been reduced to 100,000 men plus 15,000 gendarmes. The reason became apparent after two years, when we discovered that the Soviet-organised army of the puppet-state of Iranian Azerbaijan was armed with these rifles in an attempt to make the world believe that this armament had been taken from Iranian units, and not provided by the U.S.S.R.

The situation of my wards' estates in Hamadan being confused, as they were not in touch with their farmers and bailiffs, I took a few days' leave and went to Hamadan with them by the direct route through Noberan, in order, again, to avoid Soviet-occupied Qazvin. We had a pleasant journey, as my young companions were witty and gay, but as we were following a track which had, I think, never been used by a car before, we had to open the road in some places using the pick and shovel I had taken the precaution to bring, and sometimes even to summon the help of the local villagers. Arrived in Hamadan, we were met by villagers from the Qaragozlu estates with horses, and we rode the remaining 13 miles by a track which led through picturesque hills and villages surrounded by gardens with green trees, nearly all of which belonged to some member of the numerous Qaragozlu family.

The Qaragozlu are an important tribe of Turki-Mongolian origin, which had been brought from Turkestan by Chengiz Khan at the beginning of the thirteenth century, and first settled in Syria. After nearly 200 years, Amir Teimur (Tamerlane) brought them back from Syria and settled them in the region between Qazvin and Hamadan, together with other Turki tribes, such as the Inanlu and Baghdadi Shahsevans and the Shamlu. From then on, the family of the chiefs had ruled their tribes as vassals to the successive dynasties which succeeded each other in Iran. Now the tribes are all settled in villages and the chiefs have lost their standing as rulers, having been superseded in this role even before Reza Shah by the Governor of Hamadan representing Teheran. The former regent of Iran, the late Nasr-ol-Molk Qaragozlu, belonged to this family, his daughter being the wife of Hoseyn Ala, the present Minister of the Court, and his brother Amir Tuman, was the paternal grandfather of my young wards.

A three-hour ride brought us to Varkaneh, our destination. The village is on a hill and close to it on another hill was a big garden with pine trees, in which Dr. Naqi Khan and his wife had built a charming house in a rustic style using the stones of the country. From here we visited the five other villages belonging to the girls before returning to Teheran.

At this time the Military Academy was in camp at Aqdassieh, a garden immediately adjacent to Larak, and my great friend General Shahab was Commandant. One day I sent my chauffeur over with a note asking Shahab to dinner. Whilst I was waiting for the answer I heard the sound of a shot and a few minutes later my man arrived telling me that whilst presiding over a commission under a tent in the garden, a cadet, who had been expelled from the Academy for misconduct, had fired at him, killing him almost instantaneously. I arrived at the camp too late to say goodbye to this man who, scrupulously honest, brave, cultivated and patriotic, had been sacrificed to his uncompromising sense of military rectitude.

I was then appointed deputy Chief of Staff, keeping the Cavalry Inspectorate. Meanwhile, the economic situation was daily becoming worse. The Government was obliged by the Allies to provide foodstuffs for the occupation forces, and as it had not the financial means to do so it was compelled to print bank-notes. These surplus bank-notes not having the necessary gold backing, the value of our money fell rapidly, prices soared and the people being unable to supply their needs became discontented. A reliable divisional commander was needed in Teheran, and I proposed to General Yazdanpanah to transfer Ibrahim to the command of the 2nd Teheran Division. The Shah agreed, and one evening I was astonished to see an ambulance stop in front of Arfaieh, four people coming out of it. These were Ibrahim and his three aides, Mokhber, Zargham and Saberi. Ibrahim was so fond of these three that he brought them with him in the only vehicle to be found at Sanandaj, the ambulance, relying on me to arrange for their transfer afterwards. This was, of course, done.

On the 8th December people assembled in front of the Majles clamouring for cheaper bread. The police were overpowered and the Majles occupied. Ibrahim was ordered to restore order with the 2nd Division and with great difficulty managed to reoccupy the Majles at midnight.

The next day, people assembled again in greater numbers, and looted some shops on the Shahabad street. Ibrahim received the order to fire on the crowd, but refused, saying that he was prepared to resign his command but not to fire on the people, as he thought that they could be dispersed with patience and persuasion. Qavam telephoned to General Yazdanpanah, ordering him to disperse the crowd which was shouting slogans against him, by firing on them, as the fire-engines sent against them had been put out of action and taken by the crowd and the police were helpless. General Yazdanpanah replied that the military authorities did not consider it wise to fire on the crowd in the circumstances, and that an officer would be sent to explain the situation to the Prime Minister. Qavam accepted grudgingly the postponement of the order until after seeing the officer, who was to be me.

I went to the office of the Prime Minister, and told Qavam that firing on the crowd would result in terrible bloodshed, and that the people were only asking for bread. He told me that they were shouting slogans against the Allies and the Government (meaning himself). I said that the commander on the spot, who was aware of the situation, was opposed to the firing.

'I order you to disperse the crowd by firing if necessary.'

'Very good, sir,' said I. 'Then kindly give the order in writing.'

'Is a verbal order not sufficient?'

'No, sir. According to army regulations, operational orders must be given in writing.'

'Very well,' said he, taking up a pen, but after a few seconds of hesitation he told me to go, saying that he would send it later. He never sent it, and firing was averted.

On my way back to the General Staff, I passed through the Parliament Square, which was filled with a crowd of several thousand people. Of course I had to leave the car in a side street, and walked on foot to the middle of the Square, people opening their ranks to allow me to pass. Then I addressed the crowd, saying that the army was of the nation, and the nation should consider the army as the guardian of its rights, and that it would do everything possible to lighten their burden, that His Majesty the Shahinshah would never allow them to be harmed and was day and night thinking about his people. After me, Ibrahim emerged from the Majles and also addressed the crowd, after which violence subsided, the people dispersed, and a deputation of young men came to the Staff to thank the army for its peaceful intervention.

On the African front the British Army had just defeated the Germans at El Alamein. The British Air Attaché in Teheran, Wing-Commander Greenwood, was instructed to invite an Iranian Military Mission to fly to Libya to study the El Alamein battlefield. Our Government designated my brother and three senior air force officers, and on 18th January 1943 they left on a British military plane, accompanied by Greenwood and the head of the British Council in Teheran. There was a terrible wind, and our air force commander advised them to wait until it should subside, but Greenwood said that it would be all right, as the pilots were experienced.

Half an hour after their departure, their plane sent a radio message that the weather was too bad and they were returning, but they never came back. For one week the surrounding country was searched in vain, but finally on my return from a flight over the salt marsh to the east of Qom, I received a report from the Gendarmerie that the wreckage of the plane with the ten passengers and crew had been discovered in the snow not far from Noberan. It was a terrible shock for everyone and an incalculable loss for Iran. My brother's extraordinary intelligence, remarkable ability in everything he undertook, his deep knowledge of the technicalities of his profession, his wide culture, high moral qualities together with his social gifts, made him an altogether exceptional being, esteemed and admired even by those who were for some reason opposed to him. He had seemed destined to render the highest services to his country and to his Sovereign. He had been extremely popular in the army, and his funeral was attended by hundreds of officers, whose grief was deep and genuine. We buried him in the family tomb which we had together erected over our father's grave. By order of the Shah he has been posthumously promoted Major-General, and in 1962, nearly twenty years after his death, the Military Academy's promotion had been named: 'Promotion of Major-General Ibrahim Arfa'.

In February Qavam had to resign and Soheili came once more to power. He was not compromised with the anti-people stand of his predecessor, and had much better relations with the Palace. As in the year before, the anniversary of the *coup d'état* of the 21st February 1921, which had been the principal national holiday after Nowruz and on which day a military parade was always held, passed unnoticed, as it had marked the beginning of Reza Shah's rule. Nevertheless, I organised a reunion at my home to commemorate it in which many loyal officers of all ranks participated, patriotic speeches being made and the Shahinshah toasted.

One of the Germans who had managed to go underground when the others had been arrested and delivered to the Allies, was a man called Meyer. He was not a professional secret agent, as had been assumed at the time by the Allies and the Iranian authorities, but he managed to communicate with the German Government and had received from them instructions and a radio transmitter-receiver. He went to Isfahan and it was said that he had entered into communication with General Zahedi, the Commander of the Isfahan Division, but had afterwards returned to Teheran. I was then approached by two of my friends, who wanted to arrange a meeting with Meyer, but I refused and advised them to have nothing to do with secret agents of foreign powers. After a short time, Meyer was apprehended in Teheran by the Allies and all his papers and code seized, and the names of those Iranian officers whom he had mentioned in his documents were disclosed.

On the 19th June General Yazdanpanah announced to me that he was tired and unwell, and as he had taken two months' leave I would be acting Chief of Staff during his absence. I did not realise then that he was not to return to the General Staff.

About this time General Zahedi was arrested in Isfahan by the British in dramatic circumstances which have been related in detail in Brigadier Fitzroy Maclean's book *Eastern Approaches*.

At the beginning of July a military column of 900 men commanded by Colonel Shaqaqi, which was operating in the mountainous region of Semirom to the south of Isfahan, where the summer pasture grounds of the Bakhtiari, the Qashqai and the Boveir Ahmadi meet, had been surprised by a superior force of several thousand armed tribesmen commanded by Khosro Qashqai and Abdullah Zarghampur. The column was completely defeated, the unfortunate Shaqaqi being killed besides many of his officers and men. It has been afterwards revealed that this defeat was due to the fact that Shaqaqi did not expect this sudden offensive action on the part of tribes which had appeared to be peacefully grazing their flocks in the vicinity. I had to break this news to the Shah, which was a great blow for the army's prestige, both in the eyes of the Iranians and of foreigners.

A fortnight after this, as disquieting news was received about the tribal situation in Kordestan, the Shah told me that a good divisional commander was needed for the Sanandaj Division, and asked who I considered would be suitable for this job. I answered that General Razmara having commanded a brigade in the western part of Iran was well acquainted with the Kurds, and being clever and brave, would be a good commander there. The Shah said that he intended to appoint Razmara Chief of Staff, as General Yazdanpanah would receive another appointment, and I would replace General Razmara as Commander of the Teheran Training Centre. I thanked the Shah, and after handing over the Staff to General Razmara, took over the Training Centre.

A couple of weeks after this I learned that a list containing more than forty names of officers, besides many civilians, for arrest had been communicated to Iranian authorities. They included my close friends Colonels N. Batmanglij and Ariana, and many others, and among the civilians, Matin Daftari, former Prime Minister, and Sajadi, former Minister, in all close to one hundred persons who were presumed to have been involved in fifth column activities. The names of most of these people were mentioned in Meyer's papers which had fallen into the hands of the Allies. They were transferred to Arak. General Razmara had protested against these arrests, and after only forty-five days at the Staff he was replaced by my great friend General Riazi, and appointed Chief of the Shah's Military Bureau, a newly created post.

The late Nosrat-ed-Dovleh Firuz's son Mozaffar Firuz, who was bitterly hostile to the Shah and the Pahlavi dynasty, went to Palestine and to Egypt, where he made active propaganda against the Shah. While in Palestine he met Seyid Zia-ed-Din Tabatabai, who had been expelled by Reza Shah in 1921 after three months of Premiership. He had settled there on a farm. On his return Firuz announced that Seyid Zia-ed-Din would come after a short time and take the power into his hands, implying that this would be the end of the Shah. Meanwhile rumours were spread that a Qajar prince, named Hamid Mirza, the son of the late Qajar Crown Prince Mohammad Hassan Mirza, was a candidate for the throne. At the same time Mozaffar gave it to be understood that if a Qajar had to be chosen Shah, no one was more suitable than himself. Mozaffar Firuz had a striking physical appearance and a flamboyant and adventurous character. He was extremely clever, with an implacable determination and immeasurable ambition. He was very friendly with General Razmara, with whom he had close family ties, but was ready to sacrifice him, if necessary, to his ambitious plans. I have no doubt that Razmara understood this very well, and had the same attitude towards Mozaffar.

In September, Seyid Zia arrived in Teheran, and with the aid of Mozaffar, who became the editor of his newspaper *R'ad Emruz* (so named after Seyid Zia's pre-First World War newspaper *R'ad*), organised a party called *Eradeh-ye-Melli*— the will of the People—which at once began anti-Soviet activity, supported by rich merchants and landowners who had a grudge against the Pahlavi regime, and at the same time were afraid of the Russians.

On 13th November Majles finished its term, and the election campaign began in the country. In two constituencies the Soviet military intervened directly in the polling, and Dr. Keshavarz was elected deputy of Bandar Pahlavi in this manner. In certain others, Soheili ordered the local authorities to support Tudeh candidates to please the Russians, who were complaining that the British had a much stronger influence in Iran than they had, and the British themselves advised the Iranian Government to be more accommodating with the Russians.

It must be noted that the British were extremely correct, and even tried to be friendly with the Russians, while the Russians were suspicious, often insulting and nearly always hostile towards the British, and later towards the Americans. They condescended to allow the Western Allies to help them, at the same time complaining that their aid was insignificant. They considered their collaboration with them as something abnormal, not to say shameful, and merely temporary. While the final objective of the Western Allies was to defeat Germany, this was only an intermediate objective for the Soviet, whose final one was the communisation of the world. I heard then many high-ranking British people, passing through Teheran, say that the West must meet the Communists half-way, but the Soviet did not intend to come even one step forward, expecting the others to come the whole way towards them. This attitude was well reflected at the Teheran Conference, which lasted from the 28th November to the 1st December.

One week in advance of this conference special security forces with a host of secret and semi-secret agents flooded Teheran, to ensure the safety of Stalin. By pretending that there was a plot to kill one of the Chiefs of State, the Russians managed to arrange that all the meetings should be held inside the Soviet Embassy, and Roosevelt was lodged inside their Embassy's compound to save him the trouble of coming and going from the U.S.A. Embassy. Only twice did Stalin quit this compound: once to pay a call on the Shah—Churchill also went to see him—and once to dine at the British Legation, which had been promoted to the rank of Embassy on the occasion. It was on that day that the joint declaration about the safeguarding of the independence of Iran and the securing of its political and economic wellbeing after the war had been made. A corridor of tent-walls had been erected on this occasion across the road between the British and Soviet Embassies.

It was at this conference that the fate of Poland was sealed, the U.S.S.R. allowing an independent though diminished Finland to subsist, but including Poland in its sphere of influence. This with the approval of the Western Allies, who had started the war ostensibly not to allow Hitler to occupy the Danzig corridor but were now abandoning the whole of Poland to the tender mercies of its hereditary enemy—Russia.

While visiting the Shah, Stalin had promised him to give to the Iranian Army, as a gift, a regiment of tanks and a wing of war-planes. This sounded very well, but afterwards the Russians demanded that the tank regiment be located at Qazvin under Soviet instructors, who would be allowed to choose themselves the cadres for this unit, and that the air force wing at Mashad should operate under the same conditions. It was clear that the moment the Soviet judged it convenient, these 'Iranian' units would march on Teheran and back a *putsch* designed to bring to power a Tudeh Government, as had been done in the Baltic States, afterwards declaring that it had been a genuine revolution by the Iranian people! Of course, we had to decline Stalin's kind offer.

Although the fate of Iran was not discussed at the conference, it was understood that after the war the country would be evacuated without any restrictions being put on its freedom and independence. I was informed by a usually trustworthy source that in the entourage of Stalin the formation of independent entities in Iranian Azerbaijan, Gilan, Mazanderan and Gorgan had been envisaged, which would after a time secede from Iran and join the Soviet Republics of Soviet Azerbaijan and Turkmenistan; and in the same way, with the co-operation of the Tudeh, the coming to power in Teheran of a progressive Government would also be encouraged, this Government to be in close alliance with the Soviet Union. The subsequent events proved this information to have been well founded. On the 2nd December the Heads of States departed.

About this time the U.S. Persian Gulf Command was organised. Although being a military organisation, composed of armed service men under a U.S. General and comprised at one time nearly 20,000 men, this command did not include fighting units, and was in theory part of the British occupying forces, as the U.S. had not participated in the Tripartite Treaty with Iran.

An agreement was come to between the Iranian and U.S.A. Governments for the engagement of a U.S. military mission headed by General Ridley for advice on the working of the administrative section of the army, and another with Colonel Schwartzkopf for the reorganisation of the Gendarmerie. Already since November 1942, Dr. Millspaugh had again been engaged by the Government for the supervision of the financial administration of the country. Our policy then was to bring as many Americans as possible to Iran, to be witnesses of the Soviet political encroachments and by their presence act as a deterrent for the more open violations of our independence and interference in our internal affairs. Of course this policy was not agreeable to the Soviet, and met with violent outbursts on the part of the Tudeh Party.

In October I had been appointed Commander of the 1st Guards Teheran Division, which was the most important unit of the Iranian Army, with 14,000 men and 400 officers. I very quickly put this unit into shape, as it had been before the occupation, and started intensive training. As I continued to be Inspector-General of Cavalry and in this capacity had under my control the Teheran Cavalry Brigade of two regiments and an armoured car group, I happened to be in command of the major part of the Teheran Garrison. Both the Tudeh and the Eradeh-ye-Melli, knowing my complete devotion to the Shah, professed to be afraid that I would engineer a *coup d'état* in his favour, close the Majles, imprison the Tudeh people, and restore the situation to what it had been before the occupation. Of course, there was not a word of truth in this, but as the Chief of Staff General Riazi was my great friend, our opponents considered that he was supporting me in these plans.

At the end of December 1943, President Beneš arrived in Teheran on his way to Moscow, where he intended to sign a treaty of friendship and co-operation with the Soviet Government. The Shah had invited him to stay three days in Teheran, and I was appointed his aide-de-camp for the duration of his

visit. I had met him in 1926 in Geneva at the League of Nations,
but he had aged very much and moved with a peculiar gait,
keeping one shoulder higher than the other. He was lodged at
the Empress Mother's palace and lunched with the Shah, but
dined with the Czech Minister and me. One day I asked him:
'Do you not think, Mr. President, that by becoming too close
with Soviet Russia, with which country you will probably have a
common frontier after the war, you risk installing Communism
in your country?' Beneš smiled and answered: 'My dear General,
I know my people very well. It is I and my friend the late
Masaryk who *made* Czechoslovakia. They will *never* become
Communist.' I remembered this conversation five years later when
Czechoslovakia became one of U.S.S.R.'s Communist satellites.

I took him to visit the museums, and noticing that every time
we were driving by Reza Shah's statues, I corrected my position
and saluted militarily (as I still do now), he said that I was right
to honour the man who had done so much for Iran, as he understood that everything he saw had been done by him. 'But,' he
said, 'Reza Shah's most important contribution to Iran has been
his son, your Shah. When I met him first on my arrival, it was
intended that our interview should last for a quarter of an hour.
It lasted more than one hour, because I could not tear myself
from the interesting conversation with this remarkable young
man. I do not say that as a compliment, but I have never met a
head of state so well informed, with such brilliant intelligence as
your Sovereign. You can be proud of him.'

In February 1944 Soheili resigned and was replaced by
Mohammad Saed, who had been Foreign Minister in the
preceding Cabinet.

That year I had the pleasure of finding again an old friend of
the Paris Ecole de Guerre days. This was Lieutenant-Colonel
Milovan Gligorievic, who had come to Teheran as a military
attaché to the Yugoslav Legation. He was as always good company and a sincere and faithful friend. After several months in
Teheran he left for Egypt, where he had to pass through an
ordeal at the time of the Suez crisis in 1956, having been
arrested by the Egyptians as a British spy but finally released as
a result of his frank and fearless attitude during his trial.

In order to show the Teheran people that in spite of the
occupation, the Imperial Iranian Army presented still an

appreciable strength, I decided to arrange a military parade of the 1st Division and Cavalry Brigade in the Bagh-e-Shah Cantonment, and to invite His Majesty and the Ministers. As the units were rehearsing the different parts of the programme, which necessitated the daily coming and going of the cavalry regiments from their cantonments to Bagh-e-Shah, hostile elements represented this as the preparation of a *coup d'état*, pretending that with the Shah's approval I intended to arrest the leading personalities during the parade and proclaim a military government. Seyid Zia-ed-Din's friends and particularly Mozaffar Firuz took this matter to the Majles, and the Government was requested to take immediate steps to deal with my supposed *coup*. As a result of this agitation I was dismissed from the command of the Division, and after a couple of days the Cavalry Inspectorate and Direction was dissolved, and I was put at the disposal of the War Ministry. General Razmara became Chief of Staff for the second time, General Riazi replacing him as Chief of the Shah's Military Bureau.

We were living at Larak, and having nothing to do in town, I stayed there, amusing myself with looking after the irrigation of the fields and the grazing of the cattle.

In July I rode to Lar with my daughter, and spent a week with Colonel Makui riding and climbing the hills. It was while we were there that the news of Reza Shah's death in Johannesburg was announced by Teheran radio. Leila and I were so much affected that we left the camp and wandered for two hours in the valley, talking of the tragedy of this end in exile of the man who had regenerated Iran and fallen a victim to the circumstances arising from the war.

After my return from Lar I was appointed Military Governor of roads, railways and ports, all the installations on them up to 1 km. being in my jurisdiction. My duty was to supervise the transport of the war material sent by the Americans and the British to the U.S.S.R., and to prevent the stealing of arms, ammunition and supplies which had lately reached quite important proportions in spite of the British, American and Soviet forces, who were supposed to look after this, but in reality contented themselves with securing the lines of communication against sabotage.

We were on very friendly terms with the British Embassy

people, the civilians as well as the military, especially the Ambassador, Sir Reader Bullard, Alan Trott, General Fraser, Colonel Pybus, Colonel Gastrell and Anne Lambton, and I took great pains to try to explain to them the true situation, and especially the moral and spiritual attitude of the army, which was completely devoted to the Shah and the Monarchy, and the patriotism of the common people.

Anne Lambton has written an excellent grammar of the Persian language which she knows thoroughly but she also knows many Iranian dialects including Raiji, the dialect of the region surrounding Kashan. One day when she was visiting us I called up one of our men from that part of the world to talk with her. They conversed together for some time without our understanding a word and the following day this man said: 'The lady who was here yesterday must have been a relative of our Khan's because she knew all about us.' Certainly a handsome tribute to her mastery of the dialect.

First among our Iranian friends was Amine Pakravan who, having carried off a French literary prize for her novel (written in French) *Le Prince sans histoire*, is internationally known. Her father was a friend of my father's and now her grandchildren are friends with mine.

Amongst a host of others the Suratgar couple stands out. She, an Englishwoman, is lecturer at the Teheran University and her husband, who has a vast knowledge of English literature as well as of his own, is Rector of the University of Shiraz.

One day I had a telephone call from Colonel Kazem Sayah, who was much attached to Seyid Zia, that the Seyid wanted to come and see me. I fixed a rendezvous and they came together, and I had a very friendly talk with them, Seyid Zia showing himself quite ready to co-operate with the Shah and the regime. Seyid Zia was also very friendly with the Prime Minister Saed, who was traditionally loyal to the Monarchy and devoted to the Shah.

With the war drawing towards its end, the Soviet Government was showing an increasing interest in Iran, and began to be more politically active than they had been during the crisis years of the German advance, when the British were the chief actors on Iran's political scene. This interest manifested itself also in the cultural field.

One day a friend of ours, Fatimeh Sayah, who had passed

most of her life in Russia where she had been a professor at
Moscow University and who was now a professor at Teheran
University, asked if she might bring to Larak Knipper, a well-
known Moscow conductor who was interested in collecting
Iranian musical folk themes. He was the brother of Olga
Knipper, the famous actress from the Moscow art theatre, who
had married Anton Chekhov. To our great surprise he and his
wife arrived in a car from the Soviet Embassy which they dismissed, remaining for several hours alone with us. They were
delightful people and we were glad to be able to help them by
getting many of our work-people to sing their popular melodies
into the recorder he had brought with him. The astonishment of
some of these people at hearing their own voices was worth seeing!

The Soviet Government had wished to have Knipper appointed Director of the Teheran Conservatoire but the Iranian
Government had not accepted, and he had to leave.

A more serious interest for Russia was the oil question, and
the Soviet Government relying on its powers of persuasion—or
pressure—sent the Assistant Foreign Secretary, Kaftaradze, to
negotiate for a concession on the basis of 51 shares for the
U.S.S.R. and 49 for Iran, covering the territory of the Northern
Provinces. Saed having refused, the Soviet authorities became
extremely angry, and provoked the Tudeh Party to start violent
demonstrations in Teheran as well as in all the Russian-occupied
territory. In Teheran the Tudeh people were openly escorted by
armed Soviet soldiers, and in several parts of the town clashes
with the police occurred. As a result, General Razmara ordered
the Military Governor to close the Tudeh Party's headquarters
and to remove their signboard. This act infuriated both the Tudeh
and the Russians against Razmara, who up to then had managed
to keep good relations with them. In Azerbaijan the Soviet
authorities made the population sign petitions and telegrams,
demanding that the Government accord the oil concession to the
Russians, and force the resignation of Saed.

In Tabriz, a violent demonstration took place in the streets,
and the commander of the newly reorganised army detachment
(two infantry battalions), General Khosrovani, having dispersed
the Tudeh demonstrators, was expelled by the Soviet Commander and was replaced by Colonel Derakhshani, a much more
yielding officer.

In the course of my duties I had to collaborate closely with the Soviet General Kargin, a very pleasant and courteous man, who gave me interesting information about life in the Soviet Army. Being very strict in my work, I gained the confidence of the Soviet military authorities, and was authorised to go on a tour of inspection of the roads and Bandar Pahlavi port in the Soviet-occupied zone. I was the first General allowed to do so after the occupation, and travelled with an A.D.C. in my Government car to Qazvin, Rasht, Bandar Pahlavi, Astara, Ardabil, Tabriz and Zanjan. Everywhere I saw the Soviet soldiers well dressed and disciplined, saluting smartly like the men of the old Imperial Army. Amongst them were many girls dressed and armed exactly like the men except that they wore skirts instead of breeches. I was told of an actual incident which showed that any looting or misbehaving by Soviet soldiers was sternly suppressed by their superiors, who forced on them an iron discipline. A merchant coming from Teheran was stopped at the Qazvin Gate by a Soviet sentry, who allowed him to pass after payment of a few *tomans*. The merchant went to the Soviet forces' Qazvin headquarters and complained to the Commander. The latter asked him to return in an hour. When the merchant did so, the Commander paraded the men just relieved from sentry duty in front of him, asking him to designate the man. When the merchant pointed towards a soldier, without saying a word the officer drew his pistol and shot the man dead.

Having returned from this trip, I started the next day with my wife by train towards the south. We went through Ahwaz to Khorramshahr, where I inspected the newly built quays at which four big steamers were moored, and we established contact with the British authorities.

On the 9th November Saed had resigned, probably under Soviet pressure, and Bayat had become Prime Minister. About this time, the moderate deputies of the Ettehad-e-Melli group, backed by Seyid Zia's followers, demanded the dismissal of Razmara, and the War Minister, Ibrahim Zand, as well as General Yazdanpanah proposed to the Shah to appoint me Chief of Staff.

On the 21st December 1944 Zand took me to the palace, and I was told by the Shah that he had decided to appoint me Chief of Staff of the Army.

My Work as Chief of Staff

According to our organisation established in conformity with the fundamental laws of the Constitution, the Shah was the Commander-in-Chief of the Army, not only nominally but effectively, and the Chief of Staff was directly responsible to the Sovereign whose Chief of Staff he was in exactly the same way as the Chief of Staff of a division or of an Army Corps is responsible to his divisional or corps commander. This system is still maintained today. I followed strictly this regulation, reporting to the Shah every detail of the service, and executing to the letter His Majesty's instructions.

We had to fight not on the frontier, but inside the country and even in the capital, against foreign-inspired subversion, chiefly represented by the Tudeh Party, but also by the Southern Tribes, principally the Qashqai, whose aim was now not only to return to their tribal way of life but to become autonomous and even independent in a wider field of action, and if necessary with foreign support. This was the situation as I understood it:

Stalin had decided to extend Soviet domination on Iranian Azerbaijan, Gilan, Mazanderan, Gorgan and the northern part of Khorasan, and political and economic influence on the rest of Iran. The Western Allies (U.K. and U.S.A.), although not ready to recognise such pretensions, were not sure of being able to prevent Russia from fulfilling its first aim, but had decided to resist Stalin's endeavour to reach its second objective.

According to the terms of the Tripartite Treaty, the U.S.S.R. and U.K. had solemnly undertaken to respect Iran's independence and territorial integrity, and even the U.S.S.R. found it difficult openly to violate these terms. But on the other hand its behaviour in Iran made it difficult to believe that the Soviet Army would be ready simply to evacuate the regions it had occupied and it was clear that the Soviets were preparing an action which would give them a pretext to do so, whilst giving a semblance of legality to the continuation of the occupation beyond the period of six months after the end of the war, as fixed in the treaty. For this, it was not enough for them to occupy large tracts of Iranian territory; they had to have in Teheran an Iranian Government which would be to such an extent subservient to them, that it would itself officially ask them to remain. This situation would be legalised later through a referendum which would have the same result as those of June 1941 in Esthonia, Latvia and Lithuania. For this they had to bring the Tudeh Communist Party to power by means of a revolution in Teheran, and according to the information received from different agencies they had seriously begun to prepare for such an event since the beginning of 1945.

When handing over the Staff to me, General Razmara gave me a list of some one hundred officers suspected of being sympathetic to Communism. There were half a dozen colonels, the others being of lower rank. About sixty of them were already known to me for their extremist opinions or Russian sympathies: the others were unknown to me, none of them, however, occupying important posts.

The War Minister, Ibrahim Zand, had had a Russian education. His Russian was perfect, and he was considered by the Russians as friendly towards them. In reality he was a highly patriotic man with unshakable moral principles, loyal to the Shah and to his country, which fact the Soviets were soon to realise. I was in the same position, as Russian was my mother tongue, and I had always shown myself friendly to them socially, and had collaborated efficiently with General Kargin to stop robbery of the supplies destined for the U.S.S.R. The day I was appointed Chief of Staff, the Soviet Ambassador Maximof congratulated Zand on his choice, saying: 'You have found a good Chief of Staff.'

Something happened, however, in Azerbaijan which brought about tension in my relations with them, which was destined to grow during the whole time of my tenure as Chief of Staff.

As lawlessness was growing in Azerbaijan, the Russians authorised the Iranian Government to send forces there from Teheran and to organise a division with two battalions in Tabriz, two in Rezaiyeh and two in Ardabil, without any artillery, cavalry or other troops. Gendarmerie units were also re-established in their former posts on the roads, but civil servants who did not show themselves 'co-operative' were sent to Teheran.

At the end of winter, disturbances began in the Mahabad region, where the Kurds, encouraged by the circumstances, expelled the gendarmes. I ordered the Kordestan Division to send a detachment comprising one infantry battalion, one cavalry squadron and one artillery section (2 mountain guns), from Saqqez to re-establish order. The Russians protested, saying that they were ready to allow one battalion from Tabriz, but no units from outside their occupation zone, because it would 'disturb the balance of forces in Azerbaijan'.

I said that the Soviet Army which had destroyed the might of the German Wehrmacht had no reason to fear a squadron coming from Saqqez, but they remained obdurate. I then ordered the detachment, which had assembled at Saqqez, to march on Mahabad through Bokan, but at Bokan they were stopped by Soviet forces and had to return to Saqqez, Mahabad remaining in Kurdish hands. I understood that their intention was that we should send a battalion of raw soldiers from Tabriz, numbering 500 men without guns and without cavalry protection, to be slaughtered by the Kurds in the mountain defiles of Mahabad, where Malekzade and later Halu Qorban had met their fate, and then announce that the Iranian Army had not been able to cope with the Kurds, which would prove that the Kurds deserved independence!

Some time before I became Chief of Staff, Doctor Mohammad Mosaddeq, former Governor of Fars, Finance Minister and President of the Majles, who was then a deputy in the newly elected Majles, having made insulting remarks about the deputies, calling the Majles 'a nest of thieves', had temporarily left it. In December 1944 several hundred students who were his supporters went to his house and took him in a triumphal procession to the Majles. This led to a demonstration. In order to prevent disorder, I occupied the Majles with an infantry company and closed the doors, preventing the crowd from entering. Arriving on the spot, I ordered the military units not to act against the crowd which was gathered in front of the Majles, and in this way prevented bloodshed, the crowd dispersing by itself after a couple of hours. During this time I stayed inside the Majles and had talks with the newly elected deputies of the 14th Legislature.

Most of them were well disposed, but all the time felt themselves under the threat of a renewal of strong Government, which was the reason they had asked for my dismissal from the command of the 1st Division in April, and Razmara's dismissal from the Staff in November. I tried to inspire them with confidence, and think that for the time being I succeeded in doing so.

The Soviet authorities having refused to allow the detachment from Saqqez to restore order in Mahabad, were insisting now that a battalion from Tabriz should be sent there. As I had refused to do this for the reasons mentioned before, the Soviet Military Attaché told me that the Soviet Commander of the occupational forces, General Sovietnikof, would be arriving from Qazvin when there would be a reception at the Soviet Embassy which would provide an opportunity to talk with him on this subject. At the reception, the Soviet Military Attaché conducted me to the bar where there were innumerable bottles of vodka and General Sovietnikof, a tall strongly built man in the new green parade uniform with a quantity of medals on his chest, was standing. The Colonel introduced me, saying: 'This is General Arfa, the Chief of Staff, known here as the father of the Iranian Cavalry, which he reorganised.'

The General greeted me warmly, patted my shoulder and pouring out a tumbler of vodka, handed it to me, saying: 'Now, General, you must drink this to our glorious Soviet Army.' Seeing that he had poured out a very small glass for himself, I protested, saying that I would only drink my glass if he would pour a glass of the same size for himself, and although he said that he had already drunk much and did not feel well, I poured him a tumbler like mine and looking him in the eyes, gulped down my vodka, afterwards turning the tumbler upside down to show that it was empty. The General hesitated, then emptied his glass, and saying, 'Bravo, General, you are a real cavalry officer', turned to go, but I retained him by his sleeve, inviting him to drink now to the Imperial Iranian Army. The General refused, saying again that he was not feeling well. Seeing that he was adamant, I said to him in a grave and severe voice:

'General, if you do not drink, something awful will happen.'

'What will happen?' said he.

'I will tell you. You know, of course, your country's history. Two hundred years ago the Imperial Russian Army having defeated King Frederic of Prussia's Army, occupied Berlin—as you are about to do now—but suddenly, the Empress Elisabeth Petrovna died and was succeeded by her nephew Peter III. This Sovereign, whose father was a German and who was born and educated in Germany, had an unbounded admiration for Frederic, and at once ordered the Russian General in command to evacuate Berlin and to conclude an armistice. After this when the Russian and Prussian officers were fraternising, it was proposed to drink to the health of their respective Sovereigns. The Russians were handed big glasses of champagne, which they drained in honour of King Frederic, but afterwards the Prussians flatly refused to do the same for Emperor Peter. The Russians insisted, but the Prussians were obdurate. Then the Russians, saying "Friedrich, *heraus*!", put two fingers down their throats— with the natural result.'

The General said with a smile, '*Kharosho!*', and taking the full tumbler I was handing to him, drank to the Imperial Iranian Army, and of course I did the same but after that he disappeared, and was not be seen for the rest of the party.

My work at the Staff comprised two fields of action, one military, and one political. In the military field I severely enforced the regulations forbidding corporal punishments, which had been promulgated during Reza Shah's time but which had been disregarded by local commanders since the foreign occupation. I ordered Soldiers' Homes to be organised in all garrisons, these being centres where recreational facilities, games, clean and cheap canteens, libraries and radios were provided and where suitable lectures were given. At the same time, I organised Associations of Officers' Wives, whose presidents and secretaries were to be elected by secret ballot and whose duties were to investigate the needs of poor soldiers' families and to give them necessary help. In order to finance these two schemes I suggested that these Associations organise tea-dances which would serve the double purpose of raising money and providing entertainment for the officers' families. These teas, for which the tickets were very cheap, became extremely popular and so fulfilled the two objects I had had in view.

Two days after I came to the Staff, the Chief of the American Military Mission, General Ridley, came to see me and expressed his concern that the budget of the army provided for only 100,000 men, although there were actually 104,000 men on active service.

When I had been in command of the Teheran Training Centre and 1st Division, I had noticed that there were too many men employed in the auxiliary services and the different offices in comparison with those in the fighting units. In the Teheran Training Centre I had sent more than 200 men from behind desks to the ranks, and in the 1st Division more than 300 men, of course provoking many protests from the influential relatives of those affected by these measures. I decided now to resort to the same system for the whole army, and with the authorisation of the Shah ordered a commission to review the organisation of the units and administrative services. After three weeks of strenuous work, it was found possible to reduce the army's strength from 104 to 100 thousand men, at the same time increasing the effectives of the fighting units by 22,000 men. Of course this measure did not endear me to those highly placed persons whose relatives were doing their military service sitting behind desks and counting the flies on the ceiling, and were now obliged to do field training in the country and drill on the parade ground to commands fiercely barked by irascible N.C.O.s and not too patient platoon commanders.

In the beginning, when the Russians were on good terms with me, as I had been appointed after General Razmara who had antagonised them by temporarily closing their club, the Tudeh were not badly disposed towards me. Through mutual friends I became acquainted with several leaders of the party, and became quite friendly with Fedakar, Iraj Eskanderi, Morteza Yazdi and Radmanesh, but I felt Kambakhsh, the most extremist of them, hostile to me from the start. Little by little, however, when they understood that I would oppose any subversion in the army and any Soviet encroachments, they became hostile and began to attack me in their newspapers, distorting facts and inventing all kinds of fantastic stories about me.

I was driving one day in my car when I saw that there had been an accident and a crowd had gathered in the street. Two cars had collided with slight damage to both, but with no victims, and the police were trying to find out who was responsible. I called the officer in charge, telling him to take care that people should not be hurt by the traffic and told my driver to take me by another road. The next day a Communist paper reported that I had myself driven into a crowd of peaceful workers, crushed several of them to death, and without stopping to see if any had remained alive, shouted mockingly from my car, 'Let these low brutes have what they deserve!'

Next day, I asked Morteza Yazdi how they could invent such an extraordinary tale. He laughed and said that of course they knew it was not true, but they considered it necessary to show me in such a light.

I became more and more convinced that in the face of these Soviet designs we had to rely chiefly on ourselves, and that the army was the only factor which could preserve the independence of the country. The Tudeh realised it also and were trying to discredit it and especially those elements they knew to be the most patriotic and loyal to the Shah. At this time General Razmara was trying to reconcile himself both with the Russians and with the Tudeh. The Russian Military Attaché Razin met him several times, and listened quite amiably to what he said in explanation of his unfriendly actions when he was Chief of Staff, but the Tudeh chiefs were less conciliatory and did not seem ready to forget the past so easily.

My relations with the Ettehad Melli group and with the several independents of the Majles were friendly, as also with the Mihan group deputies, which comprised the friends of Seyid Zia-ed-Din. With the latter group, however, I had a clash of policy. In the north, we collaborated closely against Soviet encroachments and Tudeh subversion, and they supported the army for that purpose, but in the south they were following the British policy of strengthening the tribes versus the army, which meant the Central Government.

I judged from the pattern of events that the British, supported by the Americans, were prepared to make concessions to the Russians in the north of Iran, but would not allow any encroachment in the south where the oil-producing area was situated. This they considered to be in their sphere of influence, and in order to prevent the Central Government, which might possibly be influenced by the Soviet, from extending its influence and domination there, they were fortifying and trying to unite the Southern Tribes in a sort of tribal confederation. The Erade-i-Melli Party was working in this direction and its provincial leader in Shiraz was Nasser Qashqai. The Qashqai brothers had understood this policy, and from pro-German had become for the time being pro-British, differing, however, from them in that their aim was the disruption of the country and the creation of a South Persian State or Confederation with a Qashqai at its head, whereas the British and the Americans would have been happy to save the whole of Iran. They had an alliance with Abdollah Zarghampur, Chief of the Sardsiri Sofla Boveir Ahmadi Tribe of Kuhgelu, but the Mamasseni, Sardsiri Auliya and the Bakhtiari family were divided among themselves, Morteza Qoli and his sons being with the Erade-ye-Melli, and Abul Qasem opposed to them.

Mosaddeq and his group's idea was that Iran could not be divided, and that South Iran would have to share the fate of North Iran, even if that would mean its falling under Soviet influence. The Shah's and our idea was also that Iran could not be divided, but we wanted it to be understood that if the Western Allies wished to keep the Khuzestan oil-fields and their covering regions of Bakhtiari and Fars safe from Russia and the Tudeh, they must not allow the North to be torn away. For this reason I was opposing the Erade-i-Melli in the South, and trying to create division among the tribes and even inside the tribal chiefs' families—the policy of Reza Shah—with considerable success; in this way rendering the possibility of the secession of the southern province from the Central Government very remote.

Having travelled extensively in the tribal regions of Iran before the war, it was easy for me to make or renew acquaintance with the tribal chiefs, towards whom I had always felt sympathetic even when fighting against them, because they represented a tradition of free, unrestrained outdoor life. Also they reminded me of the romantic past of the wandering hordes of Central Asia, who had crossed and recrossed the Middle East until the boundaries of modern states put a limit to their migrations. Besides, being myself an outdoor man and a soldier, it was easier for me to understand them and to be understood by them than it was for those who had not had occasion to deal directly with them, either through negotiation or through exchange of fire. Many chiefs of tribes came to see me and received either encouragement and praise, if they were loyal and law-abiding, or

H.I.M. Mohammad Reza Shah
and H.M. Empress Farah

Turkey, 1959

Front row from the left: Prime Minister of Turkey Adnan Menderes, President Jelal Bayar, the author, Mr. Zorlu, Minister of Foreign Affairs

Ministerial Council of CENTO in Ankara, 1961
From left to right: Mr. Sarper, Turkish Foreign Min., Mr. Hassan, Pak. Amb. the author, Sir B. Burrows, U.K. Amb., Mr. Manzur Qader, Pak. Foreig Min., Dean Rusk, U.S. State Sec., Lord Home, Mr. Baig, Sec.-Gen. of CENTC and Mr. Gods Nakhaï, Iranian Foreign Min.

Ismet Inönü, the Turkish Prime Minister, with the author,
Ankara, 1961

Jawaharlar Nehru with the author, 1960

During the Shah's visit to Pakistan, 1962

Front row from the left: The author, Mr. Manzur Qader, former Foreign Minister of Pakistan, The Shah, Field-Marshal Ayub Khan, President of the Republic of Pakistan

warning if I suspected them of intrigue or rebellion. In any case, I always gave the strictest orders to the military units not to oppress or annoy them and to refrain from any sort of provocation, the tribes being Iranians, and soldiers by nature, and in any emergency they should co-operate with us for the defence of Iran's independence.

One day Khosro Qashqai came to see me, to complain against the past policy of subjugation and pressure. I told him that the policy of Reza Shah was sensible and in accordance with the exigencies of a modern State, but perhaps those who had been charged with its application had made mistakes and caused undue trouble. He was a tall, handsome young man, athletically built with bold manners but not devoid of charm, and very outspoken. His brother Mohammad Hoseyn, who also came to see me, was as handsome and tall as Khosro, but much more reserved, and looked more like a man about town than a tribal chief. Afterwards I had many interviews with them, and later with their elder brother Nasser, who came to see me at Larak, and although our policies were most of the time antagonistic, our relations were always friendly.

Several Kurdish chiefs came also. The famous old Chief of the Mamish, Qarani Aqa, who had fought against us in Simko's days, but was quite friendly now, and As'ad-ed-Dovleh Debokri and the Mangur chiefs, and Habibi of Tilekuh, and many others I had known twenty years before. One day I received a visit from Mohammad Ghazi, a Kurdish *molla* and chief, and his brother Sadr Ghazi, deputy from Mahabad. Their tune was different. They talked of autonomy, and accused the local Government servants of exactions, and I understood that they were directly influenced by separatist propaganda emanating from the Soviet. I told them that in any case their future lay within the Iranian Empire, that the Kurds were a branch of the Iranian nation, our culture being the same, and we had to co-operate loyally together. I did not know, nor for that matter did they, that after less than eighteen months their fate would be sealed.

After a year and a half in Arak several of the political prisoners had been released and the others moved to an enormous new building just outside the town, which was destined by Reza Shah to be a 500-bed hospital and which was nearly completed at the time of his abdication. The contract for this building had been given to a German firm, and for this reason was known to the British as the 'German Hospital'.

I was glad to see my friends, and I think they were glad to see me. Colonel Ariana, who had preserved a magnificent morale, had even composed a hymn full of patriotic ardour during his detention.

In June 1945, Hilda and Leila went to Egypt in the suite of Empress Fowziyeh, and returned from there at the end of August. During this time the internal situation was becoming increasingly explosive. In all the regions of Iran not under Russian occupation people were holding mass demonstrations against the Tudeh, having understood the anti-national and anti-religious character of that party, and even in those regions of the Soviet-occupied zone which were not under the direct control of the occupational forces, the Soviet-supported Tudeh groups were attacked and driven away, people boycotting the pro-Soviet propaganda films shown by the Russians in the villages of the zone. This was particularly the case in the regions around Ardabil, Khalkhal, Arasbaran and Ujarud, near the Soviet frontier, where the patriotic and warlike Shahsevan tribes dwelt. As a Soviet drive against these tribes would demand the employment of important effectives, and involve them in protracted operations in a difficult mountainous region where these same Shahsevans had inflicted heavy losses on the Imperial Russian Army in 1911, the Soviet authorities requested the Iranian Government to disarm them and to restore order in these regions. This meant neutralising the loyal and patriotic elements and authorising the Soviet protégés to step up their subversive activity against the independence and integrity of the country. The Foreign Minister transmitted this request to me and I answered that I considered the Soviet request natural and that I was eager to undertake the work of disarming the civilian population of Azerbaijan at once, starting from the Mahabad Kurdish region, where the unruly elements were much the most troublesome, as they had attacked the Government offices and Gendarmerie posts and driven the officials away, but that up till now the occupation forces had prevented us from re-establishing order there as had been proved by their stopping the advance of our Saqqez detachment some time ago. After that the Russians dropped the matter.

Then I entered into conflict with the Soviet authorities on another question. Colonel Vossuq, the Mashad Division Commander, reported to me that the Soviet Commander had requested him to disperse his three battalions in posts along the roads to do the work of gendarmes, although there were already Gendarmerie units in charge of the security of the roads, which was quite normal. I ordered him to answer that he could only obey orders from the General Staff.

After a few days I received a visit from Colonel Ivanof, Assistant Soviet Military Attaché, who, after some remarks about the weather, told me that the Soviet High Command would like to have Vossuq recalled.

'Why,' I asked, showing great concern, 'if he has done anything wrong, I will not only recall him but also apply sanctions!'

'Oh no! he is quite correct,' said the Colonel, 'but you see, it happens in every army, that two divisional commanders in an Army Corps do not see eye to eye on some questions, and then one of them is changed in order to restore harmony.'

'In that case,' I replied, 'I think that as we are in our country, and you are our guests, it is up to you to change your Commander from Mashad.' Ivanof spoke of other matters and soon left.

Meanwhile, the Soviet Commander was putting pressure on the Governor-General, Ali Mansur, the former Prime Minister, who, not being informed of military matters, requested Vossuq to act according to the Russians' wishes as we were obliged to co-operate with them. Vossuq having refused, Mansur reported to the Shah, who summoned me and asked me my views. I reported to His Majesty that the insistence of the Russians over a dispersion of our Mashad forces, without anything warranting such a move, proved that they intended to make a *coup* in that town through the Tudeh Party, and for that purpose wanted to remove from Mashad forces which would have prevented such a move. The Shah accepted my views, and was also impressed by the reports Vossuq was sending to the Staff about the daily Soviet encroachments and their open encouragement of the Tudeh's subversive activities, and rejected Mansur's demand to recall Colonel Vossuq.

On the 3rd of June, Hakimi, who had replaced Bayat as Prime Minister on the 9th of May, resigned, not having sufficient support from the Majles and Sadr, a former Minister of Justice, became Premier. He was himself strongly pro-Western, but had to include in his Cabinet several Ministers with whom the Soviet authorities would sympathise.

The war with Germany having finished and Russia having her hands free, we were expecting new developments and my information led me to believe that these developments would start very soon, although I did not know exactly how or where. One of these was the dissolution of the Tudeh Party in Azerbaijan, and the formation of a new party called 'the Azerbaijan Democratic Party', with the same cadres but with emphasis on being a specially Azerbaijan organisation, which led us to expect a move towards this province's secession from Iran and ultimate union with Soviet Azerbaijan. Unfortunately, as this region was under Soviet military occupation, I could not do anything to prevent such a possibility, except by morally reinforcing the Shahsevans, as it was difficult to send them any armament.

Then, by sheer luck, we unearthed the plot which was destined to deliver the whole of Iran in a space of one night to the Tudeh Party. One day I received a report from the Commander of the Kordestan Division, saying that an officer of that Division had been found guilty of embezzlement. He had been arrested and when his house had been searched a suit-case was discovered under his bed, which, on being opened, was found to contain documents in code. The Intelligence Section of the Division had been unable to decode these documents, so the whole suit-case with the documents was sent to the General Staff.

I ordered my Chief of the Intelligence Department to decode the papers. After two days' work, he brought me decoded documents containing a complete plan for a military rising which was to take place in Teheran at a given date, with similar action in the provincial garrison, with the names of the prospective participants in this rising, for the most part coinciding with those on the list General Razmara had handed to me.

I immediately reported this matter to the Shah, who ordered me to take necessary action. I then ordered the arrest of some forty officers in Teheran, and telegraphed to the provincial divisions to arrest some thirty others and to send them under escort to Teheran. In Teheran the arrests were effected that same day without any incidents, but three officers having learned beforehand what was about to happen, disappeared and managed to escape to Azerbaijan in the Soviet occupation zone. After cross-examining the arrested officers it was learned that at a date in September, which was to be fixed by 'higher authority', the Tudeh affiliated officers had arranged to be on duty in their respective regiments by exchanging their normal duty dates with those of non-Tudeh unsuspecting officers, where during the night they were to seize the strategic points of the town, proclaim a Tudeh Government, and arrest the Ministers, army officers and high officials.

On the night of 16th August I received a telegram from Colonel Vossuq stating that eighteen officers, with half a dozen soldiers, had fled from Mashad with two jeeps and three light lorries loaded with arms, after having disabled all the divisional motor vehicles, to prevent their being pursued. As soon as he had learned what had happened, Vossuq requisitioned several cars from local garages and sent a force in pursuit of the deserters, but just outside the town this detachment was stopped by Soviet forces and turned back, although they had allowed the fleeing officers to proceed unmolested towards Quchan and Bojnurd. At this time we had no wireless in these towns, and the telegrams sent from Mashad to the military commander at Bojnurd were not transmitted, the Soviet occupying forces being in control of the telegraph. I immediately reported to the Shah, and telegraphed through Bojnurd to the captain in command of a cavalry squadron of Maraveh Tappeh to intercept the deserters. It was discovered that the officer in charge of the cypher at the divisional staff was himself a Communist and instead of communicating the order to arrest the deserting officers to the Commander of the Division, informed his friends of it and fled with them.

Next day I learned that my telegraphic order had not been transmitted to Maraveh Tappeh, with the result that when the captain had been handed an order with a faked signature of Colonel Vossuq ordering him to deliver his squadron's arms and ammunition to the lieutenant-colonel and take his disarmed squadron to Bojnurd, he obeyed, learning the truth only after his arrival there. From Maraveh Tappeh, the deserters proceeded to Gonbad-e-Kavus, and from there to Gorgan. After a meeting with the Soviet Commander, they returned to Gonbad-e-Kavus. Prompt action was needed. A glance at the map shows how near

Gonbad-e-Kavus is to Shahrud, on the main Teheran–Mashad road, and as to the south of Sharud lies the great salt marsh desert of Dasht-e-Kafir, impassable for troops, the occupation of this town, which was then the terminus of the railway, would have cut off the whole Khorasan province from Teheran and the rest of the country. A subversive movement could be started in that province and a Tudeh Government installed at Mashad.

I prepared a notice promising 10,000 *Rials* for each deserting officer, alive or dead, had it printed at the General Staff's printing press, and gave 5000 copies each to two officers, who took them by car, travelling disguised as merchants with the notices concealed in bales of cloth, by different routes, to the Turkoman Steppe, where they distributed them among the population. It was a very dangerous mission, as they would have been arrested and taken to Russia if the Soviet authorities had discovered what they were up to. Luck was with them, however, and they reached their destination, distributed the notices, and came back safely to Teheran.

Meanwhile, the deserters had returned with instructions from Gorgan to Gonbad-e-Kavus and had tried to induce the local Turkomans to revolt against the Government, and with the arms they were ready to give them for that purpose, march on Shahrud under their command, promising them all kinds of rewards (a polite word for plunder). But the Turkomans declined this offer, and as the deserters insisted, they loaded their reed-and-felt huts on their camels and disappeared during the night into the boundless steppe.

Frustrated, the rebel officers now decided to drive themselves to Shahrud, and after arming the Tudeh-minded railway workers, seize that town, thus isolating Khorasan. After having lunched with the local Soviet Commander they started to the south, but just outside Gonbad they were ambushed by local people while passing through a narrow defile, eight of the officers being killed and the others fleeing, abandoning the jeeps, lorries and arms. The soldiers managed to return, saying that they had been deceived by the deserting officers, and the remaining deserters were transported by the Russians to Azerbaijan. The Russians made difficulties over allowing us to bring back the arms, but finally we succeeded in doing it, as all endeavours to provoke the Turkomans to seize the abandoned arms before we could transport them back to Mashad failed, these tribesmen remaining loyal to the Government.

I sent a cheque for 80,000 *Rials* to be distributed among those who, by their timely action, had prevented the treacherous seizing of Shahrud which would have had incalculable results.

After these open provocations to rebellion, I considered myself obliged to publish a communiqué exposing plainly the revolutionary and subversive character of the Tudeh Party, and warning the population against being deceived by it. Of course, I was bitterly attacked in the Tudeh newspaper for this, and called a reactionary agent of Anglo-American Imperialism!

The Soviet forces were occupying several barracks of the Imperial Army in Teheran, including the Iranian Air Force Fighter Regiment's Headquarters and the aerodrome at Qal'e Morghi, outside Teheran, where they had brought a quantity of arms and ammunition. I heard from secret sources that they intended to evacuate this place without warning. Having read in the papers that they had lately done the same thing in Mukden, abandoning a great quantity of arms in the Japanese Arsenal which Mao-tse-Tung's Communists, duly warned, were able to grab, forestalling the Kuomintang forces who, although also in the vicinity, were taken by surprise, I posted men in civilian clothes around the place, and prepared a motorised detachment in the neighbouring barracks. As soon as I learned that the Red forces had left Qal'e Morghi we occupied the place where not a sentry was to be seen, although many arms were stored in empty rooms with locked doors. As soon as we moved in, the Russians reappeared, saying that they had left their material in the precincts. They were told that nothing had been touched, and that they were free to put sentries in front of the doors, or remove the material, or even reoccupy the place. They removed the material (19th October).

After Seyid Zia-ed-Din had adopted a friendly attitude towards the regime, Mozaffar Firuz became more and more aloof, and finally broke with him, his paper becoming more and more leftist, and he used to attack me violently and abuse me for my loyalist sentiments.

On the 21st October Sadr resigned, and Hakimi again assumed the premiership. On the 14th November, by order of the Government, the premises of the Central Organisation of the Tudeh

Party in Teheran were occupied by the Military Governor and their archives with many secret documents seized. A few days later the party was declared illegal and some of the leaders arrested, but those who were deputies at the Majles were not interfered with.

On the 16th November, what we had been dreading happened. I was called to the telegraph office to have a telegraphic conversation with General Darakhshani, the Commander of the Tabriz Division. He told me (by telegram exchanged on the spot) that the day before there had been risings in different parts of the province, Gendarmerie posts being attacked and occupied after stiff fighting, many gendarmes being killed by armed individuals who were not local inhabitants, but had come from elsewhere. Darakhshani told me that an attack by these elements with the help of the Soviet occupying forces was imminent and as the officers' houses were dispersed in the town, they would not be able to reach the cantonment in the morning as they would probably be prevented by the hostile mob.

Mianeh having been occupied by armed rebels, the whole province was practically cut off from the centre, and it was to be expected that the telegraph line would also be cut. The rebels were affiliated to the Azerbaijan Democratic Party, the local version of the Tudeh. I had the impression that he wanted to impress on me the impossibility of resistance, and would have liked to receive instructions embodying the inevitability of the surrender of the Tabriz garrison.

I must say here that several months before I had received confidential reports about this General, according to which he was sympathetic to the Tudeh and had secret relations with this party. In order to investigate this I had sent Captain Teimur Bakhtiar (later Chief of the Intelligence Service of Iran and a lieutenant-general), to tour in the north-western provinces. He reported to me the truth of these reports, which was confirmed later by the divisional Chief of Staff, Colonel Varahram, who had come to Teheran on leave. I had proposed to the War Council to replace Darakhshani, but unfortunately no decision had been taken up to then and he had remained at his post. I ordered him then to stay with all the officers at the cantonments, and if possible to move their families there, also to concentrate provisions for the troops in the cantonments and to survey the possible routes going from the cantonments to the south, towards the Sahand mountains, in case an evacuation forced by the Soviet Army's intervention should be necessary.

On the 20th, under the protection of Soviet forces, members of the Azerbaijan Democratic Party, consisting chiefly of people who had come from the Caucasus in the wake of the Soviet Army, held a meeting proclaiming the autonomy of Iranian Azerbaijan. One hundred and one deputies were elected, the Turki Azeri dialect was adopted as the official language instead of Persian, and it was decided to organise a national Azerbaijan Army on the Soviet pattern with Russian instructors. The process of detaching this region from Iran preliminary to annexing it to Soviet Azerbaijan, had begun.

The night before I was called to the army radio station, to talk to General Darakhshani, radio communication with Tabriz having just been established. He told me that an autonomous Azerbaijan Government had been organised in Tabriz, that he was practically surrounded by Soviet forces with tanks who threatened him with retaliation if he entered the town or tried to leave it. He had been given the choice between surrendering with arms and material to the Azerbaijan Government, the soldiers being disbanded and the officers sent to Teheran, or joining the new Government, forming the nucleus of the new Azerbaijan Army, and that the Chief of the Azerbaijan Government, Pishevari (also a man from Baku), had offered him the post of Commander-in-Chief of the new Azerbaijan Army, as he was from Tabriz. He asked me to report this proposition to the Shah, and to give him immediately a favourable reply!

I answered that I would certainly not dare to report to His Majesty that a General of the Imperial Army proposed to join an organisation in open revolt against the Central Government, and that he had either to resist by fighting, or if the attitude of Soviet forces rendered this impossible, to abandon all heavy material and to move through mountain paths to the south, and join the Imperial Iranian Army in Kordestan.

The next day he telegraphed to the Prime Minister Hakimi, that unless he surrendered before 9 p.m., the Democrats helped by Soviet forces would storm the cantonment. The Prime Minister ordered the War Minister, General Riazi, to give the necessary order. General Riazi, who was at that moment in my office, refused to give such a dishonourable order. Hakimi then called me, and I replied that I could take orders only from the Supreme Commander—who was His Majesty. When he insisted, both Riazi and I offered to resign, and finally the Prime Minister issued the order himself and sent it direct to Darakhshani. We learned afterwards that this order had been unnecessary, Darakhshani having surrendered two hours before.

On the 25th the Azerbaijan Army (a rabble of Caucasian immigrants hastily armed by the Soviet with the arms they had taken from us three years before) occupied Zanjan, where no Government troops were stationed, this town being also in the Soviet occupational zone.

The Ardabil garrison surrendered, and after two days' fighting the Rezaiyeh garrison followed suit, its Commanding Officer being arrested and condemned to death for having resisted, but afterwards exchanged with several Tudeh people who had been arrested in Teheran. Having been able to establish radio communication with the Miandoab Gendarmerie force, I ordered it to retreat towards Shahin Dezh before being cut off by the rebels, and the captain in command succeeded in disengaging his 200 men by fording the Zarin Rud river under enemy fire.

In this way, for the time being, Azerbaijan was completely separated from Iran, and became a satellite of the U.S.S.R., with a puppet government supported by an infinitesimal minority composed chiefly of foreign immigrants and enforcing its rule by terror through police-state methods under the protection of foreign occupying forces. With the collaboration of Soviet instructors, the rebels promptly organised an army on Red Army lines and prepared to invade the rest of the country. This army was reinforced by some Iranian officers who had deserted, won over to the Communist cause.

I felt that the Western Allies were ready to make concessions to the U.S.S.R., accepting the accomplished fact of Azerbaijan autonomy under some conditions. It seemed they were at that time even ready to advise the Iranian Government to come to terms with the Soviet, just as they had advised the Turks to negotiate in a conciliatory spirit with the Russians when the Soviet asked for bases in the Dardanelles and the return of the Kars and Ardahan provinces to Russia: the Turks happily decided to risk war by refusing any compromise on this subject.

One day I said to the British Ambassador, Sir Reader Bullard, that something must be done to prevent the Russians from swallowing Azerbaijan.

'We are not going to declare war on Russia for that!' he answered.

'But you have guaranteed our independence and territorial integrity!'

'That is up to London,' he replied, 'here we are just executives.'

I was on friendly terms with the American military attaché, Colonel Baker, who sympathised with our plight, and I asked him to arrange a meeting for me with the U.S. Ambassador, Mr. Wallace Murray. I explained our tragic situation to the Ambassador and the necessity to take action to prevent the secession of Azerbaijan. He showed himself without understanding of the situation, telling me that nobody wanted to take Azerbaijan, that certainly the Russians would evacuate Iran and this province in due course, and that probably these pessimistic ideas had been inculcated in me by that arch-reactionary, Seyid Zia-ed-Din! I asked him who had suggested these ideas to him, and he candidly mentioned the names of three deputies, two of whom were later associated with the Tudeh Party. After that, for nearly half an hour, he talked of the importance of the gifts the U.S. Gulf Command Office in Teheran was giving to us before leaving Iran.

I had more luck with the deputies. I arranged weekly meetings in turn in the houses of the deputies supporting me to discuss events, and to bolster up their resistance.

On the 1st January 1946 the British and American forces evacuated Iran, but the Russians remained without any official reason, thus openly violating the Tripartite Treaty according to which the Allies undertook to evacuate the country six months after the conclusion of the war with Germany or her associates, this period having elapsed after the surrender of Japan in August 1945. Not only did the Western Allies do nothing to enforce the execution of the treaty by their reluctant Soviet ally, but according to what I had been told by a British diplomat, who had been a member of the British Mission headed by Ernest Bevin at the Moscow Conference between the U.S.S.R., U.K. and U.S., they even presented to the Soviet Government proposals which would have without doubt ultimately resulted in the partition of Iran and the annexation of its greater part to the U.S.S.R.

This is what had happened in Moscow according to what was told to me by this diplomat and also told by an American member of the Conference to a Turkish diplomat at that time. It has also been briefly related in Sir Reader Bullard's *The Camels must go*. The Allied representatives proposed to Molotof to apply some provisions of the Fundamental Laws of Iran concerning the organisation of Provincial Councils, by enlarging their prerogatives in such a way that the situation which had arisen in Azerbaijan as a consequence of the events of the 16th November could be legalised, this region, although retaining its autonomy, being still considered as part of Iran. In the same way, other autonomous regions would be created in Kordestan, Gilan, Mazanderan, Gorgan, and in the south in Fars, Bakhtiari and Khuzestan. By this ingenious plan the Russians would be allowed to keep their hold in the North, where the special position they were holding from 1907 to 1917 would be restored, and similarly autonomous entities which would look for protection and advice to the West, would come into being in the southern oil-producing region. In short the 1907 division of Iran into spheres of influence would be revived, the Centre, including Teheran, being left to look after itself, this meaning that it would also fall after a time into Soviet clutches. Of course, my British informer did not describe to me the probable consequences of this plan in this crude manner, saying, on the contrary, that by this scheme we would be able 'to preserve our territorial integrity'.

It must be taken into consideration that the absorption of Poland, Czechoslovakia, Rumania, Bulgaria, Hungary and Eastern Germany had not yet been completed. The Western Allied statesmen were still considering the U.S.S.R. as a more or less normal Great Power, being loth to accept the fact that the Soviet Government is at the head of a militant doctrinal organisation, whose avowed aim was—and still is—the if possible peaceful, but otherwise forceful, adoption of their doctrine by all the countries of the world, beginning with their neighbours.

After hearing the proposal, Molotof declared that he could not talk about this matter without Stalin's authorisation, upon which Bevin and Byrnes asked to see Stalin, who seemed to be quite taken by the idea and said that he would consider this proposal.

But at a further meeting Molotof said to them that after having thought the matter over, Stalin had declared that having signed the Tripartite Treaty according to which the independence and territorial integrity of Iran had to be respected, the U.S.S.R. could not hold any conversation regarding this country without the presence of adequate Iranian delegates. When the Western Foreign Ministers asked to see Stalin again, the better to explain their views, they were told that not feeling well he had departed for a cure to Sochi.

It appears that Stalin expected to be able to swallow the whole of Iran in the near future, by putting into power at Teheran a puppet government which would claim the legal sovereignty over all the country, including the oil-rich regions of the South, and did not want to tie his hands by an agreement which would have the result of limiting his projects of expansion towards the Persian Gulf, and in this way we were saved by Stalin's greed.

After that the British and Americans tried to do, through the Iranian Government, what they had not been able to do through Stalin, and proposed to Hakimi the formation of a mixed commission, composed of Iranian, Soviet, British and American members, to inquire into the special situation of the outstanding provinces and to implement the organisation of the Provincial Councils according to the needs of each particular district. Hakimi submitted this proposal to the Majles, which referred it to a Foreign Affairs Commission, two members of which were influenced by the Soviet Embassy and two others by my friends. The proposal was rejected to the dismay of the Western Allies, who had even declared that if it were not accepted they would not support Iran's eventual complaint to the Security Council of the U.N. against the prolongation of the Soviet occupation of Iran.

For us, it was now a race with time. On the one hand, the Soviet tried by its threatening attitude to prevent our Government from lodging a complaint to the Security Council, and on the other hand, it was feverishly preparing to bring to power in Teheran a Government which would declare its acceptance of the Soviet military occupation and for all purposes become a Russian satellite.

The only serious opposing factor to this scheme then was the Shah, acting through his faithful army.

Through the General Staff's Intelligence Department, I was informed that the revolutionary elements had decided to get rid of me. I proposed to my wife that she should take our daughter abroad for a time so as not to share the danger of the day-by-day darkening situation. Hilda resolutely refused to leave me, but we decided to send Leila to America, where she would stay for a time with her aunt, Hilda's sister, and she flew first to London and then to the States.

According to the information I had, the Soviet's scheme was as follows:

1. A concentric action was to be launched against Teheran from three directions, north, south and east, by the 'Popular Army' of the Communist state of Azerbaijan plus armed Tudeh elements from Mazanderan and Samnan, which provinces had also been subjugated under the protection of the Red forces of occupation. To reinforce the morale of these elements and to weaken that of their adversaries, a Soviet detachment of armoured cars advanced to within 18 miles of Teheran on the Karaj road, whilst to the east Firukzuh and Garmsar were similarly occupied.

2. The arrival of these Communist elements in the neighbourhood of Teheran was intended to coincide with a popular revolt inside the town by the Tudeh partisans.

3. In order to help the success of this rising the Tudeh partisans in Qazvin and Firuzkuh were to prevent the transportation of supplies to the capital, thus provoking an artificial famine as had been done in February 1917 in Petrograd at the beginning of the Russian revolution. The fall of Teheran and the seizure of power by the Tudeh Party was destined to bring about the communisation of the whole country when Iran would have become a satellite of the U.S.S.R.

I reported this situation to the Shah, and His Majesty, approving the measures by which I proposed to deal with it, the following dispositions were adopted:

(a) In order to demonstrate to world opinion and to the United Nations that the separatist movement in Azerbaijan did not have the support of the people of that province as the Soviet Government wished people to believe, a small force of 1200 men was dispatched from Teheran to Azerbaijan to restore order. It was clear that such a weak force could not fulfil this task if, as the Soviets pretended, the Communist Government was supported by the four million inhabitants of Azerbaijan and Khamseh, but after the Soviet Military Attaché had tried to dissuade me from sending it the Soviet Government, preferring to take no risk, stopped this column just east of Qazvin at a distance of about 90 miles from Teheran by a concentration of infantry and tanks. This was witnessed by the British and American Assistant Military Attachés, whom I had asked their Embassies to send so that

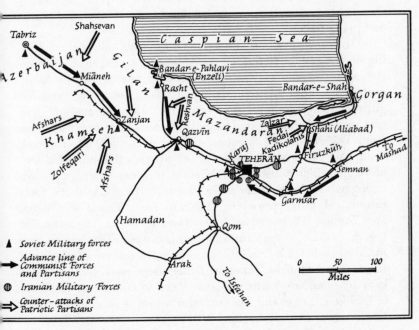

The Defence of Teheran, December 1945

they might testify to the Soviet military intervention. I ordered this force to remain where it had stopped, and they were cantoned for three weeks in the village of Sharifabad, near Qazvin.

Another column of 500 gendarmes was sent eastwards towards Firuzkuh and this column was stopped in the same manner by the occupying forces at about 50 kilometres from Teheran. Nevertheless the dispatch of these two columns was of assistance to the General Staff by obliging the Soviet authorities to define their intentions, thus justifying any subsequent measures by the

Staff and securing the support of the Government and the Majles, always inclined to see in any military action a threat to their parliamentary liberties.

(b) The garrison of Teheran being insufficient to oppose at the same time the Communist forces marching on Teheran from the outside and those preparing to rise within the town itself, some 5000 men were brought from Kermanshah, Isfahan, Kerman and Khorremabad and accommodated in tents as most of the Teheran barracks were in the hands of the Red Army occupying forces.

(c) In order to disorganise the Communist columns converging on the capital from west, north and east, and to supplement the action of the Government forces paralysed by the Soviet authorities, light arms consisting of rifles, sten guns, machineguns and ammunition, together with some officers and non-commissioned officers provided with wireless sets, were dispatched from Teheran in the direction of Hamadan via Qom and Arak. From there they went on mule-back towards the south and west of Zanjan, 200 miles from Teheran, in order to arm the loyal tribes, whose instructions were to attack the flank of the Communist column approaching Teheran from Tabriz by Mianeh and Zanjan. These tribes at the head of which were the Zolfeqari, Afshar, Moqaddam and Yamini, were organised as commandos, each led by an officer in direct liaison by wireless with the General Staff in Teheran. Other arms were sent on muleback by mountain paths to Mazanderan to be used by the tribes of Qadikola, Kojur and Alamut, who were the chief opponents of Communism in those regions.

I had previously been approached to give arms to the landowners to protect their villages against the depredations of the rebels, but I refused, saying that our aim was not to keep order in the Communist-occupied region, but to wage war against them, creating chaos in the rear of their operational forces, and ordered the officers whom I sent with the arms to use them to arm commandos for offensive warfare, and not to give them to villagers for defence against marauders.

In order to be able to direct the operations of these elements without the knowledge of Communist secret agents, whose presence was suspected within the General Staff itself, I organised a special staff composed of officers in whom I had absolute confidence and made all communications with the nationalist partisans by means of a special code without passing through the offices of the General Staff. For this purpose I installed a wireless set with operators on the roof of the Officers' Club, across the street opposite to my office at the Staff, with which I was connected by a closed-circuit telephone with a wire passing from the Club's roof directly into my office by a hole in the window.

(d) To forestall any activity on the part of the Communists in Teheran I ordered the occupation, by night and without any warning, of the strategic points in the city.

Every night, I, one of the two Deputy Chiefs of Staff, or one of the divisional commanders remained on duty at the General Staff to ensure permanent liaison with all forces throughout the twenty-four hours.

(e) The Teherani garrison composed of two divisions, one cavalry and one mechanised brigade and various elements not incorporated in the divisions, under my direct command adopted dispositions which would allow it to repulse an attack from outside and at the same time prevent any rising inside the town.

Towards the middle of January 1946 Communist action took shape. Some 5000 men under the command of a Caucasian emigrant, Gholam Yahya, armed by the Soviet authorities and in possession of artillery, began to march on Qazvin and Teheran. At one stage to the south of Zanjan they were met by the commandos armed by the General Staff. The Communists were deflected to the west, and unable to continue their march on Teheran were drawn into the snow-covered mountains where the Nationalists had the advantage of a knowledge of the country and the protection of their villages each of which became a defensive refuge. In this manner the Communists were obliged to abandon their mission.

In Mazanderan, the forest tribes of Qadikola attacked the Communists concentrated at Shahi and dispersed them after causing them considerable losses.

Finally, between Teheran and Garmsar to the south-east of the capital, a Communist group was stopped by an army detachment and prevented from proceeding.

In Teheran itself, thanks to the time gained by these manœuvres the Iranian Government, presided over by Hakimi, by order of the Shah addressed a note to the Security Council protesting against the continued presence of Soviet troops in

Iran as being contrary to the terms of the Tripartite Treaty. The Iranian case was ably expressed by Seyid Hassan Taqizadeh, then Iranian Ambassador in London and permanent delegate to the United Nations, who by his courage and an eloquence inspired by strong feelings of patriotism rendered inestimable service to the cause of his country.

Then the Tudeh began a series of attempts on my life by which means they no doubt hoped to induce me to resign even if they did not succeed in eliminating me definitely. Being aware of that, I took precautions which proved quite useful. Nevertheless, one night when I was dining at the Egyptian Embassy I had a telephone call from Larak saying that a dozen men armed with rifles had attacked the place, probably thinking I was there, and were shooting at my people, one of my soldiers having been wounded. I telephoned at once to a nearby regiment to send a mounted platoon to Larak. Returning to the table, I told the host that the call was about a service matter. After more than one hour fighting with my two soldiers and the cavalrymen, the aggressors fled, one of them being taken prisoner. This man pretended to be insane and did not answer any questions, but was tried for armed aggression.

Another time while I was in Larak, four armed individuals held up two of my workers, asking them questions about my whereabouts and if I kept arms by me in the night. During these inquiries, they were suddenly attacked by a dozen of the fierce dogs I kept in Larak, and fled without waiting for an answer!

The last such attempt at intimidation was made one night when I was sleeping at Larak. Early in the morning, a warrant officer who was in charge of the premises of the Aqdassieh Military Academy's Summer Camp which was close to Larak, came to report that in the middle of the night he had been wakened by a band of eight men armed with rifles and pistols, who had entered his house. They asked him if I had armed men in my garden (as a matter of fact I had), and when he told them that he did not know anything about my arrangements they left his house and went towards Larak. Having apparently not dared —or not wished—to climb over the wall into my garden, they returned after half an hour, ordering him to give them some bread and milk, and after having eaten, departed in the direction of the town.

One day when the Shah showed concern about my safety, I answered that the lot of a soldier was to fight, which meant to strike and be stricken, and that today our front line was not on the country's frontiers, but inside the capital. A few days after that I was honoured by receiving a signed photograph of His Majesty.

Trying to impress the necessity of resistance on the deputies of the Iran Party, I arranged for an interview with one of them, Engineer Farivar, in the house of a mutual friend. He told me that as Iran could not exist without Azerbaijan, it had to go the same way as that province. I argued with him for nearly an hour, and he said that I sounded convincing but they had a leader whom they followed and who had to be convinced also. When I asked him who this leader was, he named Dr. Mosaddeq. I then asked him to arrange a meeting between Mosaddeq and myself, and after two days, accompanied by Farivar and two friends, I was received by Mosaddeq at his house on Kakh Street. He was extremely polite, spoke about my father, whom he had known at Shiraz after his ordeal with the brigands, and then declared himself ready to listen to what I had to say.

'I would like to ask you three questions in order to understand your attitude to the political situation:

1. 'The majority of the deputies of the Majles are of the opinion that the parliamentary elections which would normally be held in two months' time ought to be postponed until one month after the evacuation of Iran by foreign (that is Soviet, as the others had already departed) forces, in order not to be influenced by their presence. I understand that you have declared that they should be held without waiting for this evacuation. Would you kindly explain to me the reason for this point of view.'

'Certainly,' he said. 'Our elections have always been influenced by the big reactionary landowners, who made their villagers vote according to their wishes. We must profit by the fact that in the Soviet-occupied zone these landowners have temporarily lost their influence and we should have democratically elected deputies at least in the northern regions.'

'But will the Soviet forces not also influence the people to vote for their candidates, as they did in 1942 in some places?' I asked.

'At least these would be progressive people, and they would counterbalance those elected in the old manner in the rest of Iran.'

2. 'In 1944, you proposed to the Majles the adoption of a law punishing with imprisonment any prime minister or minister who agreed to negotiate the granting of a concession to exploit oil in Iran before the end of the war, this of course meaning the end of the military occupation. This law was adopted. I understand that now you are in favour of granting an oil concession to the Soviet Government. How are we to understand this?'

'When I proposed this law, the Government was negotiating with an American concern called the Amiranian for a concession to prospect and exploit oil in Baluchistan. Though outwardly American, this concern was certainly under the influence of the Anglo-Iranian Oil Company, and the result would have been a strengthening of this Company's stranglehold on Iran. On the contrary, the exploitation of the oil in the northern provinces on the basis of 51 shares to the Soviet and 49 to Iran, would be profitable to our country and would provide work for our population.'

3. 'Do you think that the Tudeh Party must remain illegal or that it ought to be allowed to renew its activity?'

'I consider that the Tudeh must be as free as any other party to take part in the political life of the nation and to propagate its doctrine.'

I wanted to ask him for further explanations of his political outlook, but looking at his watch, he said that he had an engagement and he left, I having been enlightened as to his views on these questions.

One of my preoccupations was to prevent the possibility of any secessionist movement in the south, as I felt that should the Western Allies lose all hope of separating the oil-producing region of the south from a potential Soviet-protected state, they would become more eager to back our complaint to the Security Council. For this I had to fight the British-sponsored confederation of the tribes, at the head of which were the Qashqai, and also to prevent any Arab irredentist move in Khuzestan. I therefore appointed to the command of the Ahvaz Division an officer in whom I had full confidence, Colonel Afsharoghlu, my comrade from Kuleli days. I then sent my A.D.C., Captain Mokhber, to the south, to befriend those tribes who were antagonistic to the Qashqai by gifts of shot-guns, pistols, field-glasses, accompanied by adequate letters praising their loyalty to the Crown and country, with a few medals which the Shah had been pleased to bestow on them. Mokhber had an extremely pleasant personality and being a shrewd and convincing negotiator was completely successful in his mission.

The precarious tribal entente which was entered into by some of the tribes of the Fars Province at an assembly of chiefs, which had taken place at Chenar Rahdar to the west of Shiraz, and at which according to our information the British Consul in Isfahan, Colonel Gault, had assisted, was shattered. This in spite of a resolution which these chiefs had written in a note to be sent to the United Nations, asking for autonomy on the grounds that they considered themselves as a minority entitled to that organisation's protection!

Meanwhile, in Khuzestan the last showdown was about to take place.

Our officers from the Azerbaijan Division which had been disbanded after Darakhshani's surrender, had arrived in Teheran. General Darakhshani was arrested, and it was decided to distribute the other officers among the different army units and administrations. In order to bolster their morale, which had been badly shaken by their vicissitudes in Azerbaijan, I invited them to the Officers' Club and made a speech about the difficulties of the situation, the hope that in the near future things would improve and the country regain its unity, and the solicitude of His Majesty the Shahinshah for all the officers who did their duty towards their country.

Afterwards I came out to take my car and go home, when an officer of the Cypher Department reported to me that an urgent telegram from Ahvaz had just arrived and been decyphered by him. Leaving the driver outside, I took the cypher officer with me in the car and he read me the telegram from Afsharoghlu: 'To the Chief of the General Staff . . . Today Sheikh Jasseb, the son of Sheikh Khaz'al, with 150 armed Arabs crossed the Iraqi frontier and occupied the Gendarmerie post of Feiliyeh, where he surprised the gendarmes taking 17 rifles from them. He intends to march on Khorramshahr and Ahvaz, and is negotiating with the British Consul and the Governor General. I am waiting for orders.'

There was no time to lose. Once he had entered Khorramshahr, with its maze of narrow winding lanes, canals and date-palm groves intersected by deep ditches full of water, his expulsion would be both difficult and lengthy, and in the meantime he would most probably receive reinforcements from across the Shatt-el-Arab. I knew that we had at that time only three infantry companies in Khuzestan: one in Khorramshahr and two in Ahvaz, one of these being raw recruits. I also knew that if I reported the matter to the War Minister he would consider it necessary to report to the Prime Minister Hakimi, who being a prudent man, hearing about negotiations with the British Consul, would consider this as an international incident and call a meeting of the Council of Ministers. As next day was a Friday and probably most of the Ministers would be out of reach for the week-end, this meeting would be postponed until Saturday, and complementary explanations requested from the Governor. All this would give to Jasseb the time to strengthen his position in Khuzestan, and as his move fell into the pattern of other developments in the south after the failure to organise the Provincial Councils, the Iranian Government would be faced with the same situation in the south as it had to contend with in the north.

For this reason I preferred not to lose time, and dictated the following telegram:

'Commander of 6th Division. Leaving the recruits in Ahvaz, you will take one company by train, which you will requisition if necessary, to Khorramshahr, join the company in this town and attack immediately the Sheikh, throwing him into the Shatt.'

I reported the matter to the Shah who completely endorsed my action.

On Sunday I had the report from Khorramshahr. Afsharoghlu had attacked Feiliyeh with two companies, taking a quantity of arms from the Sheikh who hurriedly recrossed the frontier.

After the failure of the sphere of influence policy and Teheran having successfully resisted the Tudeh, Hakimi's complaint to the Security Council was supported by the Western Allies, but at the same time they considered that the U.S.S.R. had to be mollified by a more conciliatory attitude on the part of Iran.

On the 19th January 1946, Hakimi resigned. During eight days an intense activity reigned in the Majles. Most of my friends disapproved of Qavam-os-Saltaneh, who was candidate for the premiership and considered to be conciliatory to the

Russians. He was also known to be hostile to the Shah, and all those who were opposed to the regime were working for him.

One of his most eager partisans was a *mojtahed* (member of the High Clergy), Seyid Abol Qassem Kashani. This *molla* was living in Iraq before the First World War and took an active part in the Arab revolt against the British in 1920. Having been expelled to Iran, he alienated Reza Shah by his haughty manners and remained aloof from political activity until the occupation of Iran in 1941. He then indulged in activity against the British through the Japanese Legation, which, after the departure of the German Legation had remained in Iran until Pearl Harbour. When the British wanted to arrest him he disappeared, hidden by his numerous friends, but after six months was found and arrested and detained until after the war. He then returned in triumph to Teheran and was greeted by the populace and all the personages of the capital. I went to see him with a mutual friend and was at once taken in by his frank and pleasant manners, very different from the usual pompous or artificially decorous ways of the *mollas*. He was certainly highly patriotic, scrupulously honest, devoid of fanaticism and very human, but he was bitterly hostile to the British and did not sympathise with the regime. Nearly all the Ulemas were against him, but he had great popularity among the working classes, to whom he had always been helpful. His animosity against the British made him for a time favour a *rapprochement* with the Soviet, and this was the reason for his support of Qavam.

Although not openly saying so, the British and Americans appeared to be favourable to Qavam, whom they considered able to maintain a balance between their interests and those of the U.S.S.R. This act was certainly not without influence on the Majles, and when the Shah (whose Constitutional prerogative is to designate himself the Prime Minister, with or without previous consultation with the Presidents of the Majles and the Senate) asked the Majles to give its opinion, Qavam got 51 votes out of 100; the Tudeh and Iran parties voting for Qavam.

Mozaffar Firuz, who had been campaigning for Qavam, instituted himself his political factotum, as he had been before for Seyid Zia. Seyid Zia-ed-Din's group was in the opposition, as well as many influential *mollas* who were afraid of a strengthening of the Tudeh.

Qavam gave assurances of loyalty to the Shah through several people, and even before receiving his official Farman (investiture) from the Shah asked me to visit him, which I refrained from doing until the *Farman* was promulgated (27th January 1946).

Qavam chose his Ministers chiefly among people whom he thought to be not on too good terms with the regime, Mozaffar Firuz becoming his deputy, and afterwards Minister of Labour. Mozaffar at once started feverish activity against me and I understood that my days as Chief of Staff were over, as the Tudeh had become the leading political power and the Soviet was becoming the paramount power in Teheran.

It was decided that Qavam would go to Moscow to negotiate with the Soviet Government, and it was known that the principal items of these negotiations would be Azerbaijan and the oil concession to Russia.

We feared that in Moscow Qavam would be persuaded to take back Hakimi's complaint to the Security Council about the continuation of the Soviet occupation of Iran, and in this way prevent the Council from putting the necessary pressure on the U.S.S.R. for the evacuation of the country, which ought to have taken place on the 1st of January. Our group of deputies, at the head of which Seyid Zia-ed-Din had now taken an active place, was ready to question the Government on this subject, but Mozaffar Firuz, acting on behalf of Qavam, had mobilised the militant toughs of Tudeh to surround the Majles and to prevent any deputies who were not the active supporters of Qavam from entering the building. At the same time, secret instructions had been given to the Chief of Police not to interfere with the activities of these toughs. As a result, only some thirty leftist deputies were allowed to enter the Majles, the others being attacked, beaten and bodily prevented from entering: only a few policemen were present in the square and these remained inactive.

Less than two weeks remained of the life of the 14th Legislature, after which the deputies would lose their standing, and the Government could not be interfered with until after the election of a new Legislature. Seyid Zia-ed-Din, myself and a close friend of mine, Habibollah Mohit, a deputy of Saqqez, decided to take active steps to prevent Qavam from taking back Hakimi's complaint. For three or four nights, Seyid Zia's brother, Engineer Tabatabai, came to fetch me in his car and took me to Mohit's house where Seyid Zia was waiting, and the three of us prepared a declaration which was to be signed by the majority of the deputies. This stated that on account of the Government's illegally preventing the deputies from assembling in the Majles, which was the forum of the nation, by means of the Tudeh mobs' unhindered action, the deputies had met at another place. After protesting against the illegal manner in which the duly elected representatives of the nation had been prevented from assembling freely, they solemnly declared that they continued to back the Hakimi Government's complaint against the continuation of the Soviet military forces' occupation of Iran, and were opposed to any eventual action of the present Government in withdrawing it from the Security Council's agenda. This was written in a convincing manner in Persian by Seyid Zia, who is a writer of considerable ability, and translated into English. When it was finished I privately invited some of the deputies to my house where they signed this document, afterwards giving it to Mohit, who took it to those deputies whom we knew would be ready to sign it.

After two days we had about sixty signatures on the declaration, which was more than the majority of the deputies then present in Teheran. We decided not to send it at once, but to wait until the Government showed an inclination to withdraw the complaint.

I thought that as the telegraph and post were controlled by the Government we would be prevented from sending it to the United Nations, so I went to see an Ambassador of a friendly nation who, after some hesitation, promised that if necessary he would transmit the document to its destination.

Of course, Qavam was aware of the existence of the document, but not of my arrangements for its transmission. Nevertheless, he abstained for a time from withdrawing the complaint, and Hoseyn Ala, who was then the Iranian representative at Lake Success, pressed this matter which resulted in the first serious disagreement between the Soviet and the Western statesmen at the United Nations.

Encouraged by Mozaffar Firuz, the whole leftist press was clamouring for my dismissal and the return and liberation of the Tudeh-affiliated officers whom I had arrested or transferred to the southern garrisons. In February the new War Minister, General Ahmadi, summoned me to his office, and after having praised me for the way I had defended Teheran against the Tudeh onslaught, told me that in view of the necessity for calming public opinion and conciliating the Russians, with whom negotiations were about to begin, it was necessary to replace me by a less controversial Chief of Staff. I was told that General Aq Evli, one of the officers who had been arrested and detained by the British during the war, had been appointed in my place.

After a few days, General Riazi, who had again become Chief of the Shah's Military Bureau, called on me and reported His Majesty's great satisfaction at the way in which I had accomplished my mission of defending Teheran, saying that after the situation became calmer, the Shah would express his appreciation of my services by giving me an appropriate decoration. I asked him to thank His Majesty for his kindness, and assure him that at any place and in any capacity, I would always be a faithful and loyal soldier at the service of my country and Sovereign.

My Arrest and Imprisonment

The Tudeh newspapers and their allies were not satisfied with my dismissal, pretending that I was directing the activities of the Staff from my home through the officers who were devoted to me and occupied key posts. They vociferously demanded my arrest and trial for 'treason against democracy and the people, subservience to Western Imperialism, arming the rebels and causing the mass killing of progressive elements, arresting and exiling liberal-minded young officers, associating myself with the reactionary Palace clique, storming the Tudeh premises, and instituting a reign of terror and mistrust in the Army and the Country'.

I was at first inclined to laugh at these fantastic accusations, but soon realised that they were launched by the Government itself, this then meaning Mozaffar Firuz, whose chief aim was to weaken the regime by discrediting its loyal supporters.

Meanwhile Qavam departed for Moscow, and on 5th April 1946, after his return, signed an agreement in which it was laid down that Iran would itself settle the Azerbaijan question and accept the formation of an Irano-Soviet Oil Company to exploit the oil in the northern provinces, the shares of which were fixed at 51 to the Soviet and 49 to Iran.

One evening at a dinner in a friend's house, the Tudeh leader, Dr. Morteza Yazdi, said to me that I had followed a wrong policy at the Staff as by my action the Tudeh's coming to power had been postponed for ten years. I retorted that I hoped it had been postponed *sine die*. Then he told me that as soon as Qavam returned from the U.S.S.R. I would be arrested. I said that the fate of men depended on God's will.

The next day, Seyid Zia-ed-Din telephoned to me that he had information that I would be arrested. I thanked him, saying that I had had the same information about him, and as a matter of fact he was arrested a couple of days later.

I asked for one month's leave to go to Hamadan to my Qaragozlu wards' village of Varkaneh, which was granted, but I finally decided to stay in Teheran. Nevertheless, rumours were spread by the Tudeh that I had gone to Kermanshah to stir the Kalhor tribe into revolt against the Government, as this tribe's chief, Qobadian, a deputy of the 14th Majles, was my close friend.

On the 6th I went to see the War Minister, General Ahmadi, who advised me to leave at once for the United States, telling me that all my travel and residence expenses there would be assured by the Government. I declined, saying that I was not ready to leave now, and that owing to the country's critical condition I considered it my duty to be here at the disposal of my Sovereign. He gave me forty-eight hours to decide.

At 10 p.m. on the 8th he telephoned me at Larak, asking if I had anything to say, and when I said that I had not, he asked me to be ready to meet somebody he would send to me. I understood that I was about to be arrested, ordered the entrance gate to be opened and packed a suit-case with a few necessaries. At 11 p.m. my men informed me that Larak was surrounded by Military Police and after half an hour the Chief of the Military Police arrived, telling me that he had the painful duty of asking me to accompany him to the Military Police Headquarters. I passed the rest of the night in his office where a camp-bed had been prepared, and next day was given a room on the first floor of the building, with two armed soldiers mounting guard just outside the door. I was not allowed to walk in the yard, but could take exercise for one hour in the spacious lecture-room, the windows of which were opposite to the Girls' Professional School.

The next day I was informed that I had been arrested by order of the Prime Minister, in accordance with article 5 of Martial Law, which provided that persons suspected of activity against the Government could be arrested without a regular warrant being issued and kept under arrest without trial for as long as the Military Governor should consider it necessary. This was contrary to army regulations, according to which no General could be arrested or brought to trial without the special order of the Shah, which had not been forthcoming in my case. Of course I protested in writing against the illegality of my arrest and asked to be told the reason for it.

Two days later Hilda came to see me in the presence of a

Military Police officer, but after some weeks was allowed to come alone and to stay as long as she wished. She came regularly from 8 to 10 a.m. and from 5 to 7 p.m., and brought me newspapers, books and stationery, which were not restricted. All my meals were also brought to me from my house by my personal servant, my former batman, Taqi, who is still my butler, having been twenty-six years in my service.

After ten days, Mozaffar Firuz in a press conference declared that I had been arrested for treason, sedition and association with brigands, and that I would be tried and condemned in an exemplary manner. This statement was transmitted abroad and published in British and American newspapers.

After his return from the U.S.S.R., Qavam, apparently fulfilling the promise he had given there, instructed Ala to withdraw the Iranian Government's complaint, but by order of the Shah the complaint remained on the agenda and Ala made a brilliant and very spirited speech explaining our point of view.

On the 29th, according to the secret provisions of the agreement with the U.S.S.R., the chief of the Azerbaijan puppet government, Pishevari, accompanied by a suite including several of the officer deserters, in Russian-style uniforms, arrived in Teheran to negotiate with the Central Government. Movarrekh-ed Dovleh Sepehr, a Cabinet Minister, and Mozaffar Firuz were appointed to negotiate with him about the autonomous status of Azerbaijan. From the start these two Government delegates disagreed, and finally Firuz alone continued the talks with Pishevari. Even between these two the conversations were not smooth, as Firuz's aim was to change the regime of Iran to his advantage and not the disruption of the country. It was finally decided to continue the negotiations concerning the unification of the Army of Azerbaijan with the Imperial Army in Tabriz, the Shah resolutely rejecting the reintegration of the deserters with promotion to superior ranks, which had been granted to them by the Azerbaijan rebel government.

Meanwhile, I received the official communication of the accusations for which I was to be tried:

1. To have distributed arms and ammunition to brigand bands; and
2. To have caused the death of eight officers of the army by putting a price on their heads.

During the preliminary inquiries, I had the impression that my questioners wished me to throw the responsibility for the arming of the tribes on to the Shah, which would have enabled them to start direct attacks on the Sovereign and the Monarchy. Naturally I declared that I had acted on my own responsibility and that I had the right to do so without asking anybody's authorisation. Nevertheless, both the former Prime Minister Hakimi and ex-War Minister Zand declared to the tribunal and to the press that it was with their approval that these arms had been given.

Mozaffar Firuz in a conversation with my wife said that I had only myself to blame for what had happened as he had many times warned me not to cling to a rotten rope—meaning the Pahlavi monarchy.

It was finally decided to try me for the first of these accusations, and a special court was formed, under General Fazlollah Zahedi, who had returned from British detention a few months before. Zahedi frankly admitted that Mozaffar Firuz had told him that in order to placate the Tudeh and the Russians I had to be condemned, irrespective of how the case went, as if this were not done the Government would take the case away from the military court and try me in a specially appointed People's Court, which could condemn me to a much severer penalty and would be a precedent for future cases in which army officers were involved.

During all this time the partisans armed by me were continuing to fight against the Azerbaijan 'Army', under the officers I had appointed to this task.

One day an order signed by me to the military commander of the Ardabil region, instructing him to give every assistance to a *molla* who was going from Teheran to the Shahsevan country to preach the Qoran, was produced in court (in reality, he was conveying a consignment of small arms to the Shahsevan tribes to fight against the Tudeh), and I was asked what the Chief of Staff of the Army had to do with religious preaching.

I answered that I was a Moslem, and that every Moslem was interested in promoting the teaching of the Qoran.

On the 9th May the Soviet Army evacuated Iran, but the rebel Azerbaijan Government did not show any disposition to consider itself as a part of Iran, and every day new measures were adopted which cemented the separation of Azerbaijan from the rest of the country. The crown was removed from the officers' uniforms, and towns, streets, etc., bearing names associated with the monarchy were renamed, the Persian language was superseded by Turki in the schools.

In the Kurdish-speaking western region of Azerbaijan, a Kurdish State came into being, with the 'Komuleh' Party—the Kurdish counterpart of Tudeh—in power. Their leaders were Ghazi Mohammad, Sadr Ghazi, *Molla* Mostafa Barzani who had come from Iraq and Hama Rashid, my late brother's adversary.

Then, on 1st July, General Razmara became Chief of Staff. This was how it happened, according to what Iraj Eskandari afterwards told one of my friends in Paris.

After his return from Moscow and the signing of the Agreement with the Soviet, Qavam reshuffled his Cabinet, introducing three Tudeh Ministers, Iraj Eskandari, Dr. Morteza Yazdi and Dr. Keshavarz, besides Allayar Saleh, who had joined the Tudeh Party with part of the Iran Party. Other members of this party had dissociated themselves from them to form the Vahdat-e-Melli Party.

One day, after a meeting of the Council of Ministers at the Foreign Ministry, Mozaffar Firuz asked the three Tudeh Ministers to come to his office. Once there, he took out of a drawer a Qoran, saying that he had to tell them something very secret, and before doing so wished them to swear on the Qoran that they would not repeat it to anybody. The Tudeh Ministers replied that being Communists they had no use for the Qoran, and besides, being members of the Central Committee of the party they could not conceal anything from the other members of the Committee. Therefore, Mozaffar Firuz put back the Qoran in the drawer, and said to them:

'I am now convinced that Qavam is also a reactionary and therefore no good. We must unite and bring to power a progressive Government, ridding ourselves of the Shah, Qavam, and all the old reactionary politicians.'

'How are we to do that?' they asked.

'By a military *coup d'état*.'

'How can we do that? The Army is not in our hands, we are just three Ministers, and with you we will be four!'

'By appointing General Razmara as Chief of Staff.'

'But he is also a reactionary, even worse than Arfa!'

'Not at all. He is completely in my hands and will do everything I tell him, I answer for him. For this purpose, I ask you to go to Qavam, and tell him that General Aq Evli has no authority in the Army, and though in prison, it is Arfa who still runs the Staff through his friends. The only man who can neutralise Arfa's influence is Razmara, and ask Qavam to appoint him Chief of Staff.'

The three Ministers said that they had to discuss this at the Party Central Committee, and departed. After discussion, they came to the conclusion that as Mozaffar Firuz was not to be trusted and had possibly concocted all this story together with Qavam to get rid not only of the Shah, but also of the Tudeh by a *coup* with the aid of Razmara, they would approach Qavam asking him only to replace Aq Evli without mentioning Razmara. If Qavam suggested Razmara, it would prove that he was aware of Mozaffar's plan, and this appointment ought then to be opposed. If, on the other hand, Qavam suggested somebody else, then Mozaffar could be trusted, and Razmara's nomination supported.

They went to see Qavam and complained about the inactivity and weakness of Aq Evli. Qavam said that he would choose a suitable Chief of Staff, and General Amanollah Jahanbani, who then commanded the Military Academy, was proposed. The Tudeh then believed that Mozaffar's proposition was genuine, and suggested to Qavam that Razmara be appointed.

Understanding the difficulty of the situation, Jahanbani asked to be left at the Military Academy. After much hesitation the Shah, who had not been disposed towards Razmara on account of his contacts with the Tudeh and even with one of the deserters, Captain Ruzbeh, whom he was said to have sheltered in his house, sanctioned Razmara's appointment as Chief of Staff.

The elections, which had been postponed until after the completion of the evacuation by the Russians, were now due to begin and the idea of the Soviet was to bring to power a Popular Front majority, which would be under the control of the Tudeh and their Allies, the Azerbaijan Democrats. Such a majority could only be brought about if a third so-called Progressive Party supported by the Government came into being. The idea of the creation of such a party was suggested to Mozaffar Firuz and to Qavam, each of whom saw in it his opportunity. On the 29th June, after consultations with several political leaders, Qavam announced the formation of the Democratic Party of

Iran under his leadership, Mozaffar Firúz being its chief organiser.

The Tudeh then proposed a deal—long live 'true democracy!' —the Government would arrange for the election of 50 Iran Democrats, 25 Tudeh and 25 Azerbaijan Democrats and Komuleh, and these 100 deputies would form the Popular Front, the rest of the seats (about 20) being allowed to go to independents. Qavam procrastinated, meanwhile organising his party to which flocked all those who were opposed to the Tudeh, and also the opportunists who looked for favours from the Government in power. Its success was immense, and the Tudeh realised at once that they had been deceived. Although outwardly still friendly, a bitter rivalry began in which the Tudeh very soon found that they were the losers, as Mozaffar Firuz, who was now Minister of Labour, organised Workers' Trade Unions which were affiliated to the Iran Democrats and directed against the Tudeh-sponsored Workers' Syndicate.

Qavam in the meantime was neutralising his opponents from the right as well as from other quarters. Several former deputies and even Seyid Abol Qassem Kashani were arrested, to placate the Tudeh and to free his hands in the struggle to come.

Then the Soviet made a great blunder. On the 14th of July, without any previous demands for an increase of pay or the betterment of their conditions, nearly 60,000 workers in the A.I.O.C. oil-fields and the Abadan refinery launched a strike, and on the same day, the workers of the Iraq Petroleum Company at Kerkuk and Mosul also stopped work. It was in this way obvious that these strikes were not simply engineered by the Tudeh, which had no hold on the Iraqi workers, but by the Soviet, which wished in this way to alarm the Western Powers by showing its influence in this part of the Middle East. At Abadan the strike was accompanied by mob violence with many persons killed in a most savage way.

Three British warships sailed to the Shatt-el-Arab, to protect British lives and interests (more than 2500 British technicians were working in Khuzestan), and in spite of a protest by the Iranian Government Indian troops were disembarked in Basra. Mozaffar Firuz came to Ahvaz, and made provocative declarations against the 'foreign-supported reactionaries' and the A.I.O.C.

The Western Powers realising that the situation was dangerous, and that not only the north but the whole of Iran was slipping towards U.S.S.R., adopted a more active approach to the problems in Iran. This new policy was to be conducted on behalf of the United Kingdom by Sir John Helier le Rougetel, who had replaced Sir Reader Bullard, and on behalf of the United States by George Allen, both of them being very distinguished diplomats who at once appreciated the situation, starting a definitely pro-Iranian policy instead of the conciliatory attitude towards Russian claims, which had prevailed during the war.

Developments outside Iran contributed towards this stiffening of their attitude. In the United States, President Truman dismissed the fellow-travelling Henry Wallace, and at the partial elections the Republicans won over the then much more conciliatory Democrats. The British were fighting the Greek Communists around Athens, and the halcyon days of the period immediately after the war seemed to be over.

In Teheran, to show its strength, the Tudeh organised mass meetings on the Sepah Square and other places, especially on the occasion of the visit of a mission from the World Federation of Trade Unions, which organisation was headed by Louis Saillaat. One of these meetings was to protest against the survival of the Franco regime in Spain, the other against the Kuomintang. People who had never before heard these names and were ignorant of the whereabouts of these countries, shouted slogans and lifted their fists in a fit of brotherly feelings for the Spanish and Chinese working masses. To give them more understandable matter to care about they were afterwards paraded in procession through the town, shouting 'Death to Seyid Zia, death to Arfa!' Passing in the street in front of the Military Police Headquarters, they did not realise that I was standing at the window looking at them, greatly amused by this display of revolutionary ardour.

One day I was brought a Tudeh paper with a cartoon showing me in a lavishly furnished room, reclining in a super comfortable armchair, an enormous cigar in my mouth and my jack-booted and spurred feet on a table, on which a radio was blaring instructions from London, which I was duly transmitting by telephone to my reactionary accomplices outside the 'prison'. The caption of the cartoon was 'His Master's Voice'!

Another day, a poem appeared in a Communist paper, in which all my crimes and cruelties towards the toiling masses were exposed in detail and which ended by saying that if ever a spark of commiseration towards my hapless compatriots was born in my soul, my heartless imperialistic English wife was there to extinguish it.

I occupied myself during the long hours of enforced leisure by writing about political, administrative, social and economic reforms which I considered necessary for Iran, which comprised radical agrarian reform, participation of the workers in the profits of the concern in which they were working, equal rights for women, extension of education in the villages and towns, an independent foreign policy based on close collaboration with our Moslem neighbours, and pitiless anti-corruption action.

In spite of the torrid heat—my room faced south, and the chimney of the kitchens just below was being built inside the wall beside my bed—I was always in uniform with high boots, coat and belt, as if ready to go to the parade ground. In the afternoon, my exercise hours corresponding with the hours at which my cousin, a military lady doctor, was giving lectures to the girls in the school opposite the military prison, I used to communicate with her by signs from my window. The girls, much intrigued to see me appear every day at the same hour, used to gather at their windows to look at me, smiling and waving, until my cousin came and sent them away.

At the end of July there was another rumour of the secession of Azerbaijan, and immediately in Khuzestan in some quarters close to the A.I.O.C. there was talk of attaching Khuzestan to Iraq.

On the 8th of September Mozaffar Firuz went to Isfahan, where he ordered the arrest of the Bakhtiari chiefs, Morteza Qoli and his sons. It was announced that they had been preparing a general rising of the tribes, in concert with the Qashqais and others, but that Abol Qassem Bakhtiar, their cousin, had betrayed them. The military governor of Khorramshahr, Colonel Hejazi, accused of 'reactionary activity', was also arrested and sent to Teheran. When brought into the presence of Mozaffar Firuz, who wished to interrogate him himself, the latter used offensive language, so Hejazi boxed his ears soundly, after which he was conveyed to Military Police Headquarters where he remained for some twenty days. (He is now Chief of Staff of the Army.)

General Zahedi was sent to Shiraz to forestall the rising of the tribes, but on the 20th September, all the tribes of Fars, Persian Gulf Coast and Eastern Khuzestan rose against the Government, the chief rebels being Nasser Qashqai and Abdullah Zarghampur Boveir Ahmadi.

It was said in Tudeh circles that a short time before this rising the late Alan Trott, who was then British Consul in Khuzestan, had visited the coastal region, while Colonel Gault had gone to hunt in a tribal region!

The day I read this news in the papers, I understood that the farce of my trial and detention would soon be over. It was after all the tribal confederation which I had fought the year before which saved the country and myself from the Communist danger, but there was no more talk of dividing Iran as the Soviet had shown that it was not a part but the whole of the country that they wanted, and that the south was inseparable from the north.

On the 22nd all the coast above Bushehr was occupied by the coastal tribes of Dashti, Dashtistan and Liravi. The next day Nasser Qashqai sent an ultimatum to Qavam, asking him, among other things, for the dismissal of the Tudeh Ministers, the out-lawing of the Tudeh Party, the adoption of a more nationalistic policy and the granting of autonomy to Fars. Qavam rejected these conditions, and General Razmara ordered a column to Isfahan and Shiraz to 'crush the rebels and traitors', placing it under the command of Zahedi.

The Tudeh and the Azerbaijan Democratic Government offered to arm their militants and to assume the garrison duties in Teheran and other towns in order to allow the regular forces to be sent to the south! One of the Tudeh newspapers frankly wrote that: 'In this way, we will be able to effect our revolution without any hindrance!' Razmara thanked them but did not make use of this kind and disinterested offer.

My trial was postponed as my judges were away fighting.

In spite of his rejection of Nasser's terms, Qavam sent a mission to negotiate with him, but the fighting continued and Bushehr fell. A little later Kazerun surrendered, the military forces, aware of the fact that the fighting was part of the struggle against the Tudeh, lacking in enthusiasm for a fight on what they considered the Tudeh side. General Razmara was menacing the rebels and also the lukewarm officers with trial, firing squads, etc., but not pressing too much to 'annihilate the rebels'. Zahedi was having meetings with the representatives of the tribes, but no offensive operations were started.

On the 3rd October, it was announced from Kermanshah that on the initiative of Qobadian a confederation of western tribes had been formed, issuing a declaration supporting the action of the southern tribes, and threatening to march on Kermanshah.

Qavam had to accept Nasser's conditions—without shedding too many tears about it—and reshuffled his Cabinet, reforming it without the Tudeh and Allayar Saleh. The Shah signed the *Farman* for the elections all over the country, including Azerbaijan, and the political atmosphere underwent a decisive change.

General Razmara had been brought back to the Staff by his great friend Mozaffar Firuz because by his utterances and contacts with the anti-monarchist Tudeh, he was believed to be ready to share Mozaffar's views and was, like him, hostile to the regime. Although outwardly vivacious, Razmara was a shrewd and intelligent man who seldom acted on impulse. He carefully considered the situation not only as it presented itself at the time but as it was likely to evolve, and in view of this what kind of action would be more profitable for him personally. He had no illusions about Mozaffar Firuz, whom he knew to be as egoistical as himself, and understood that he would never be able to realise his ambitions, which went far beyond being Chief of Staff, with a cold reasoning ambitious Qavam, whose aim seemed to be the presidency of a republic, or with Mozaffar Firuz, even more ambitious, who would certainly keep him always in a subordinate position. The Shah, being by his position above this struggle for power, was much more likely to bestow on him the highest office in the State—that of Prime Minister—and he had, therefore, much more to gain by showing himself loyal to the monarchy.

Still keeping outwardly friendly relations with the Tudeh, Razmara began to show himself more and more loyal to the Shah and aloof from Qavam and Mozaffar Firuz. When they understood their mistake it was too late, Razmara was firmly in the saddle and being aware of the Qavam, Mozaffar and Tudeh's machinations against the Crown, as well as of their disagreements among themselves, he was able to counter them and in this way gained the gratitude of the Shah.

The official attitude towards the 'brigands' to whom I had given arms had now completely changed. Their leaders were invited to Teheran where honours were bestowed on them and they took part in the army parade which for the first time took place on the Sepah Square, the Shah taking the salute from the balcony of the Municipal Building—while I, who had armed them and organised their defence and directed the operations which prevented the Tudeh and Azerbaijan Democrats from taking Teheran, was still in prison.

I could understand that for political reasons, in order to soothe the Soviet and placate the Tudeh, it had suited the Government to take temporary coercive measures against me, even in contradiction to the country's laws and regulations. But now that the evolution of the situation had disposed of this necessity, and the results of my struggle for my country and my Sovereign were being praised and exalted, the continuation of my detention could only be due to the hostility of the Chief of Staff who, profiting by his position and the influence he had acquired, considered it necessary for his ambitious plans to neutralise a prospective rival and opponent.

On the 28th October my wife came to see me with the news that General Darakhshani, the man who had surrendered his force to the rebels and had even wished to join them, had been released while I was still under detention. Beside herself with indignation Hilda went to the War Ministry and made such a protest that the next day I was summoned to the War Minister and released from my seven months' detention.

Entering the War Minister's office I saw there, beside the Minister Ahmadi, Generals Yazdanpanah and Razmara. Ahmadi did all the talking, praising my action against the Tudeh when I was Chief of Staff, my patriotism, devotion to the Shah, etc. He said that of course all that had happened to me was most unfortunate, but had been due to the special circumstances of that critical time, that a new court would be appointed to dispose of my case, but that meanwhile I was asked to go to my estate in Larak and undertake not to come to town before my case was settled, and that I would not be subjected there to any surveillance. During all this the other two Generals did not utter a word.

I answered that I had always acted according to what I understood to be my duty to my country and my Sovereign, and that in future I would not act otherwise. Then I rose and left them, my wife having arrived with our car to fetch me and we drove straight to Arfaieh, and the next day we moved to Larak. In spite of the distance and the lack of transport facilities, all my friends came to see me, and I was both touched and gratified that on the day the Zolfiqari brothers, Nasser, Mohammad and Mahmud, were to be decorated by the Shah, they came first to Larak to thank me, saying that the honours they were about to receive were entirely due to me.

In Larak I passed my time riding, reading, walking in the country and interesting myself in our farm. I was impatient to have my trial over and to return once more to active service, especially as new and far-reaching developments were taking place.

After having concentrated adequate forces in Qazvin, the Government announced that the Khamseh province (between Qazvin and Azerbaijan) had never been part of Azerbaijan, and would not, therefore, be assimilated to the region of the autonomous Azerbaijan, and moved its troops on Zanjan. The town was occupied without resistance, the forces of the rebel Azerbaijan Government retreating along the railway line towards Mianeh, behind the Qaflan Kuh mountain, which is the geographical and administrative southern border of the Iranian province of Azerbaijan. The population of the province greeted the Imperial Army units with enthusiasm.

About this time Tudeh-inspired disturbances occurred in Mazanderan, and a plot against Qavam's Government was discovered by the secret police. Several Tudeh leaders were arrested, others, like Kambakhsh, disappeared, and the Tudeh went again underground. Mozaffar Firuz was apparently also to some extent compromised and was appointed Ambassador to Moscow.

On the 3rd December Qavam issued a declaration, stating that in order to implement the holding of elections in all the provinces of Iran the Imperial Army had received orders to occupy all the regions where the elections would be held, including Azerbaijan. The Azerbaijan Government protested, declaring that it was a violation of the previous summer's verbal agreement between Pishevari and the Central Government, and that it would defend the region by force of arms.

I was told that at a War Council held at this time at the Palace, the Shah was for advancing without delay into Azerbaijan but that others considered that this would involve the risk of Soviet military intervention. In any case, the Shah gave the order to the army to enter Azerbaijan and to advance on Tabriz, and the army moved to the north in three columns, the principal one along the axis Zanjan–Mianeh, and two others along those of Bijar–Shahin–Dezh–Maragheh and Saqqez–Mahabad.

As soon as I learned that, I wrote to the War Minister, asking to be allowed to take part in the operation in any capacity, but I did not get any answer.

On the 8th Qavam proclaimed the Azerbaijan Government to be a rebel organisation because it was resisting the Central Government's control over elections, and declared that its leaders would be prosecuted and punished. On the 10th the main column crossed the Qezel Owzan river by fording, as the rebels had blown up the bridge, and after a short fight on the Qaflan Kuh, entered Mianeh.

The next day, the Bijar column occupied Shahin Dezh after a skirmish. On that day a group of young Tabriziss having heard of the approach of the Imperial Army, made a surprise attack on the Azerbaijan Government's headquarters and the centre of the Azerbaijan Democratic Party. Most of the rebel armed forces retreating from Mianeh towards Tabriz, being still 60 miles from that town, they met with little opposition and the whole civil population rose, joining the patriotic youths. Hearing that Tabriz had risen in their rear the rebels dispersed in the country, some 5000 were able to escape across the frontier, but several hundred were caught and massacred by the infuriated populace. The Imperial Army units received this news when still far from the provincial capital, entering the town on the 12th, when they were greeted by the Tabriz population with indescribable enthusiasm. In Eastern Azerbaijan, the Shahsevan attacked the Tudeh, killing many of them, and very soon the whole Soviet frontier was reoccupied by our army posts.

In the Mahabad region, the Shahin–Dezh column occupied Miandoab and turning towards the west, effected its junction with the Saqqez column, taking the entire Komuleh Kurdish Government in a net. Ghazi Mohammad and Sadr Ghazi were tried and hanged, but Molla Mostafa was brought to Teheran and afterwards released and sent back to Iraq.

Princess Ashraf, the Shah's twin sister, went to Zanjan and Mianeh to give relief to distressed people on the part of the Red Lion and Sun, of which she was then the Honorary President, and took Hilda with her as she had been elected a short time before Vice-President of the feminine section of this organisation. They were greeted everywhere with extraordinary demonstrations of joy expressed in Azerbaijan by the sacrifice of innumerable beasts, whose meat was distributed amongst the poor. A few weeks later the Princess made another journey, again taking Hilda with her, this time to Astara, which had been the scene of a massacre of the population by the rebels during the war. Here the people's happiness was expressed by great quantities of spring wild flowers collected in the forests.

This was the end of Azerbaijan's forced secession, which collapsed as soon as foreign protection was removed from it.

It has become the fashion, especially in foreign circles, to credit Qavam with the survival of Iran's independence, which they consider due only to his shrewdness and political ability. I will not deny him those qualities, nor say that he did not use them to the full with great benefit to Iran. But without a doubt, if Iran was saved from losing its independence it was due to the defence of Teheran in the winter of 1945, when the coming to power of a Tudeh Government would have prevented Qavam from using his diplomatic skill and the Western Allies would have found themselves faced by a situation comparable to that they were later to be confronted with in Hungary, Rumania, Czechoslovakia, Poland and Bulgaria, where neither they nor the Security Council of the United Nations had been able to intervene.

This survival was directly due to Mohammad Reza Shah's action through his loyal army, which he directed and inspired. In the same way, it was due to his fearless decision that the army had moved forward and reconquered the Azerbaijan province, whose population counts among the most patriotic and loyal in Iran.

Qavam was also helped by the evolution of the political atmosphere in the Western countries, due to the ruthless action of Stalinist Russia in the enslavement of the East European countries, and their threats against Turkey to force that country

to give to the U.S.S.R. bases in the straits and the Kars and
Ardahan provinces. And in Iran the political strike engineered by
them in the oil-fields, and the rejection of the Western Allies'
offer at the Moscow Conference, whilst the American elections
of 1946 were certainly not without their influence on events
also.

On the 2nd January 1947 I received the official notification
of the decision of the tribunal that as no offence had been committed, there could be no prosecution. I expected that after
having been unjustly dismissed from my post on the Staff,
illegally arrested and kept for seven months in detention and two
months on parole, and as all my actions had been vindicated and
officially acknowledged to have led to the happy conclusion of
the struggle for the independence of Iran, I would be rewarded
in such a manner as to compensate me for my months of detention. However, nothing happened, and nobody summoned me,
to the great indigation and sorrow of my numerous friends and
all patriotic Iranians.

At the end of January one of my friends told me that the
chiefs of the Shahsevan tribes of Azerbaijan, who had come to
Teheran to pay homage to the Shah, wanted to come to Larak
that day. My cook managed to prepare an excellent meal for
twenty-three persons, in spite of the short notice, and the chiefs
expressed their gratitude to me for having given them arms to
fight the Tudeh. My hospitality proved fatal to me, as after
leaving Larak they had the unfortunate idea of sending a
telegram to the Shah through the General Staff, asking him to
reward me for my services and give me an important appointment. General Razmara represented this as having been inspired by me, which of course was quite untrue, saying that I was
intriguing with the tribes and that my presence in Iran was
dangerous. On the 3rd February I received from the War
Ministry an order to start in three days' time to the United
States, as representative of the Iranian Army. I answered that
certainly this order would be obeyed, but that when I was
arrested the Government of Qavam, which was still in power,
had officially announced that 'I was a traitor and a criminal, and
that there was no doubt about my guilt'. As a traitor could not
worthily represent his army in a foreign country, I asked the
War Minister to give the necessary orders that the Tribunal's

verdict that no criminal action had taken place should be officially announced to the press in the same way as my supposed guilt had been.

Instead of an answer I received on the 6th March the notification that I was retired from the army. I wrote a note to the War Minister protesting against this unjust measure, but got no answer.

After twenty days a friend of mine, General Hushmand-Afshar, called on me, saying that Razmara had asked him if he was on friendly terms with me, and his answer being affirmative, had asked him to see me and to tell me that 'he [Razmara] was very sorry for what had happened, that he wished to have the honour of reintegrating me into active service, and that he would give me any appointment which I would like, without any obligation to leave Iran, and that he was ready to meet me anywhere I chose'.

I asked to think about this proposal, and the next morning answered in writing that I was retired against my desire, but now I was not ready to return because the most flagrant injustice had been done to me.

PART IV

Contemporary Iran and Mohammad Reza Shah.
Progress through Struggle and Upheavals,
1946–1963

Post-War Iran

Soon after the liquidation of the Azerbaijan separatist movement, the elections for the 15th Legislature of the Majles started. They resulted—as was to be expected—in the overwhelming victory of Qavam's Democratic Party of Iran. The Tudeh were of course completely eliminated, but there was an important minority of conservatives of the Seyid Zia group, although he had not himself taken part in the elections.

The Soviet Government was pressing for the ratification of the oil concession, which had been granted by Qavam a year earlier. This ratification was to have been made within three months but had not yet taken place as the elections had been postponed until January 1947, and there was a strong current of opinion against it. The Soviet Ambassador Sadchikof openly threatened Qavam with all kinds of unpleasantness if the concession should not be accepted, and Qavam promised him to explain to the deputies the desirability of its ratification. Soviet military forces were concentrated on our frontiers, gun-boats manœuvred in front of Bandar Pahlavi in our territorial waters and planes violated our air-space, flying up to thirty miles inside our territory.

One day Qavam summoned the leaders of the Majles groups and showed them a letter written by Mozaffar Firuz, the Ambassador in Moscow, saying that he was convinced that if the oil concession to the U.S.S.R. were not ratified the Soviet armies would re-enter Azerbaijan, as they had allowed the Iranian Government to reoccupy it only on the understanding that the oil concession accepted by Qavam would be given to them. Qavam told the deputies that they must seriously consider all sides of this matter before taking a decision.

One day a Counsellor from the British Embassy, who had come to Larak, told me that George Allen the American Ambassador was to attend a reception of the alumni of British universities and that he would make a speech. The following day I read in the newspapers that he had announced that the U.S. Government considered that as an independent and sovereign State, Iran had the right to grant or refuse concessions to anyone she chose, nobody being entitled to force her to act against her own wishes, and that the United States would fully support Iran in the defence of her rights.

This speech made a deep impression in political circles and on public opinion, and on the 22nd October when the oil concession project was presented by the Government to the Majles it was rejected by 102 votes to 2. The Soviet Government was much angered, but could not find any plausible pretext to reoccupy Azerbaijan, especially as the population of that province had shown in an unmistakable manner its attachment to the Iranian Empire to which they had belonged for 2500 years.

A fortnight after that the Chief of Police, General Saffari, called on me and told me on behalf of Qavam that he recognised having treated me badly, and would like to see me. I answered that I did not bear any grudge against them, but that if he wanted to see me I was always at Larak and he could come there. Two days later Saffari came again and said that Qavam was dissatisfied with Razmara and wanted to appoint me Chief of Staff. I said that it was the Sovereign's prerogative to nominate the Chief of Staff, and not the Prime Minister's.

During this time a crisis had developed inside the Democratic Party, part of which forming its right wing rebelled against Qavam, who also lost his Parliamentary support. Several of his ministers resigned and he wanted to reshuffle his Cabinet. On the first days of December my friends Mohit and Amir Qassem Fuladvand (who was related to Qavam) came to Larak also on behalf of the Prime Minister, telling me that he wished me to be War Minister in his new Cabinet. I reserved my answer, but on the 10th Qavam, not having been able to form a Cabinet, resigned, and after a few days the Shah appointed Hakimi to form a Ministry.

During this year the United States started to give more concrete military help to Iran, a number of army lorries and other material being provided for the army, and the Soviet Government took this pretext to send a strong protest to the Iranian Government who answered it adequately.

In June 1948 Hakimi resigned and was replaced by Hazhir, a young politician who by his activity and initiative had gained the confidence of the Shah. Hazhir wanted to introduce reforms, but met with the opposition of the privileged classes and had to resign in November, after only five months' premiership, being replaced by Mohammad Saed.

During this time Razmara proposed several times to meet and to come to an agreement with me, as my friends were agitating against him in the Majles and in the opposition press, but I avoided him because we held radically opposing views on the country's external and internal policies and I did not approve of his methods. At the same time I was also opposed to the policy of the opposition groups, both of the right and of the left, who had joined together to attack the Government and had organised an 'antidictatorial front'. They held their first meeting at the Hotel Ferdowsi, to which they invited me, but I did not attend the meeting and openly declared that I would have nothing to do with them.

Early in 1947 Leila returned from the U.S. after more than a year's absence during which she had been extremely anxious about the events in Iran and my imprisonment, and we were very happy to be all together again.

In the autumn of 1947 Princess Ashraf was invited by the Red Cross Societies of several countries, notably Sweden and the U.S., and again she took Hilda with her. My wife was very much attached to the Imperial family and I am happy to say they appreciated this, her services being constantly required for various charitable organisations started by the Shah and his sisters, and she had the honour to be nominated by special Imperial *Farman* a member of the Board of Directors of the Imperial Foundation for Social Service. She gave much time and thought to the organisation of five Infant Welfare Centres for the Foundation, and for sixteen years was largely responsible for the 'Ashraf Institute' which cares for some 250 children in the poorest part of the town.

In October 1947, together with Dr. Ahmad Human, an intelligent, honest and cultured lawyer, I organised an Association called 'the Asiatic Group', the aim of which was to foster the idea of an Organisation of Asiatic and even a few African States, more or less on the model of the Pan-American League, which would be able to resist pressures and encroachments coming from both the Western Great Powers and from the north. We came into contact with the envoys of the Asiatic nations and learned personalities, both Iranian and foreign, and edited a newspaper called *Asia Gruh*. We criticised the subservience of the Government of the time to certain foreign political influences, and owing to martial law the paper was often suspended. I gave several lectures on international politics, advocating the organisation of a group of Middle Eastern countries.

On the 4th February 1949 when the Shah was alighting from his car in front of the Law Faculty on a visit to the University, a man standing among a group of students fired point-blank five bullets from his automatic at the Sovereign. Two bullets grazed the Shah, but one entered his cheek and after piercing his upper lip came out from his mouth, happily without causing dangerous injury. The assailant was at once shot down by the officers of the suite and died instantly, and the Shah, who had kept complete control of himself, drove to the Military Hospital not far from there. After being bandaged he returned to the palace and broadcast to the nation.

This event had a tremendous repercussion among all classes, for it was realised that the disappearance of the Shah would have precipitated the country into anarchy. It provoked extraordinary demonstrations of loyalty throughout the country. It was discovered later that the terrorist was a member of the Tudeh Party, and the Police and Military Governor proceeded to arrest a number of Tudeh leaders. Other members of the opposition were put under surveillance, the 'Front against Dictatorship' was suppressed, and Qavam barely escaped arrest on the intervention of the Shah and was rushed to a plane and sent abroad.

After the granting of an oil concession to Russia had been rejected, an agitation had started for securing more profitable terms from the A.I.O.C. which resulted in a tentative agreement, increasing the royalties to be paid by the Company to the Government. I talked about the desirability of revising the terms of the concession with several British members of the A.I.O.C. staff, including Mr. Northcroft, the representative of the A.I.O.C. in Teheran, but it is very difficult to convince people in financial matters when their interests—or those of their concerns—are to be directly affected in the near future.

An important development in the economic sphere was the adoption of the first seven years' plan for the rehabilitation of the country, consisting of projects for the building of roads, railways, dams, water distribution in towns, schools, hospitals, the promotion of hygiene, modernisation and extension of agriculture, creation of new industries, etc.

Some of the provisions of the Fundamental Laws of the State, such as the creation of a Senate not having been implemented until then and other modifications being considered desirable, the Government proposed the summoning of a Constituent Assembly for which elections had to be held, the deputies of the Majles being eligible as members. During the electoral campaign which started for the Constituent Assembly, an incident occurred which was destined to have important political and economic repercussions.

The deputy of Kerman, Dr. Mozaffar Baqai, announced his candidature for the Constituent Assembly. He was then summoned by the Commander of the Kerman Division, who told him that by order of the Chief of Staff, General Razmara, he was asked to resign his candidature as a conservative was to be 'elected'. When Dr. Baqai protested, the General curtly told him that this was the order, and being afraid of possible unpleasantnesses Baqai at once flew to Teheran and took sanctuary in the Majles after which he began a violent campaign against the General Staff, Razmara and the War Ministry.

One day my friend Colonel Deihimi told me that Dr. Baqai, being opposed to some aspects of the Government's foreign policy and their handling of the oil question, would like to have my views. We had a telephone conversation and I told him of my ideas on the desirability of a revision of the A.I.O.C.'s concession, and sent him the copy of considerations on that question, which I had prepared and sent to the Foreign Ministry in 1933.

From the next day, Baqai, who is a gifted orator and has a forceful personality, began his series of attacks on the concession, asking for the first time not simply an increase of the royalties, but the total revision of the structure of the concession, implying its iranisation. After a time Baqai left the Majles, and I used to have weekly meetings with him.

I also often saw Seyid Abul Qassem Kashani, whom I liked

personally but with whose political views I was often in conflict as they were sometimes prejudiced and subjective, and I told him several times that it would be better if he left politics alone. Otherwise he was very good company and had a strong sense of humour. One day I went to see him at a hospital where he had had an operation, and found the Armenian patriarch also visiting him. After a time the patriarch, rising to go, asked Kashani's permission to bless him. Kashani acquiesced, and the Armenian, taking an enormous cross out of the folds of his robe, applied it several times to the turban of Kashani, murmuring prayers, while Kashani, keeping an imperturbably solemn look, managed a wink in my direction. After the departure of the patriarch, when I jokingly congratulated him on having been blessed so thoroughly, he said to me: 'That's nothing, you should have seen the Jewish Rabbi yesterday!'

Another day, he came on a visit to Larak accompanied by three lesser *mollas*, and I ordered my servants to remove our numerous dogs who were accustomed to come freely into the rooms and ingratiate themselves with people, as dogs are considered unclean, especially by the clergy. The holy people sat on a sofa facing the French window and Kashani began to read to me out of a book of moral precepts of Imam Ali, while I sat in front of them with my back to the windows. Suddenly I saw an expression of horror on the faces of Kashani and his beturbaned aides, and looking quickly behind me I saw my daughter, in slacks—how unwomanly —kissing a big grey bitch on the muzzle!

I thought that Kashani would rise and depart with curses and never come back to such a heathen abode, but he composed himself and looking down at his book continued to read. After refreshments he departed quite happily, and came again to Larak not long afterwards. He was far from fanatical. One day, having read in the morning paper that two reactionary deputies had protested against girls being admitted to the University, I went to Kashani and asked his view on the subject.

'The Holy Prophet said that the acquisition of knowledge was praiseworthy for all Moslems. Are not the girls also Moslems?' said he. I asked him to write this as a declaration, and to sign it, which he willingly did, and I printed it in next day's issue of *Asia Gruh*, this causing quite a sensation. Our friendship endured until the end as I saw him at his hospital in December 1961 a fortnight before he died at the age of ninety, the Shah visiting him a few days before his death.

General Zahedi was for a time appointed Chief of Police, but soon quarrelled with General Razmara, the Chief of Staff, as he did not allow any interference in the elections with the result that several nationalist politicians were elected deputies and started an active offensive for the revision of the A.I.O.C. concession. After having resigned from the Police, Zahedi was elected to the Senate and made several very strong speeches, which created a great impression.

In March 1950 Saed resigned, being succeeded by Ali Mansur, who had been Prime Minister in 1941 at the time of the invasion.

Hazhir, who had become Minister of the Court, was murdered by a reactionary during a religious ceremony. This was an unfortunate revival of the terrorism which had claimed several victims during the last years, the most noteworthy of whom was Kasravi, a distinguished historian and patriot, but to whose peculiar religious views many had taken exception. Also a journalist, Mahmud Mas'ud, who had gained the enmity of many people by his outspoken and often unfair attacks against influential personalities, which had often been influenced by other interests than those of the cause of freedom and liberty.

On the 7th May grandiose ceremonies took place for the funeral of Reza Shah, whose remains had been brought from Johannesburg first to Egypt and then to Teheran, by boat to Khorramshahr, and then by train to Teheran. Detachments of Pakistani, Turkish and Iraqi Army units with their bands took part in the march-past in front of the catafalque before the Imperial coffin placed on a gun carriage and drawn by horses was taken to its resting place in Rei, close to Hazrat Abdul Azim's shrine. The cortège passed through streets lined by troops presenting arms and followed by the Shahinshah, the Imperial family, the representatives of foreign states and the ministers, generals, etc. It was the last occasion at which I wore my General's uniform. The ceremony was very impressive, and I then remembered being told by Ernest Perron, the Shah's Swiss private secretary, that when he visited Reza Shah in Johannesburg and presented him with a handful of Iranian earth, Reza Shah had said that he wanted this earth to be put on his coffin if he died far from his country. Now his wish would be fulfilled, and he would rest in the soil of his Fatherland.

During Mansur's tenure of office the agitation against the A.I.O.C. increased very much, and the progressive deputies of the 16th Majles joined in a 'National Front' Organisation, at the head of which were Dr. Mosaddeq and Kashani, each controlling a separate and politically widely differing group temporarily allied for the struggle against the A.I.O.C. issue, the group of Mosaddeq chiefly comprising intellectuals, students and university professors, and that of Kashani bazar merchants, artisans, small shopkeepers and workers. I calculated at that time that Mosaddeq could have mustered between 1000 and 1500 people in a rally, while Kashani could easily have brought together at least 10,000 at a few hours' notice. This proportion afterwards underwent change with the addition of the former Tudeh and fellow-travellers to the Mosaddeq block.

It must be understood that all the members of this block were not blind followers of Mosaddep, and we had several meetings in Larak with Dr. Baqai and others at which it was considered that the next Prime Minister ought to be somebody at the same time in sympathy with the aims of the National Front and having the confidence of the Sovereign, the name of Ibrahim Zand, former Minister of War, being suggested.

Then, on the 18th June 1950, General Razmara was appointed Prime Minister. It was said that apart from the Imperial favour, Razmara had managed to secure the support of both the British and the Americans. In any case on the day of his appointment Christopher Gandy, the British Embassy's First Secretary, who came to lunch at Larak, praised the new Prime Minister highly. After a short time Razmara revealed himself a strong opponent of the nationalisation of the oil industry in Iran, which had become the chief item of the National Front's political programme, the others being the revision of the electoral law— the revision of the press laws—and the revision of the martial law regulations (all being revisions of negative character instead of projects of positive reforms).

Kashani, who had been arrested after the attempt on the Sovereign—although it had been proved that he had had nothing to do with it—had been exiled to Beyruth, but Mosaddeq's group was daily attacking the Government in the Majles.

At the beginning of 1951, General Razmara ordered his

Finance Minister, Gholam Hoseyn Fruhar, to read in the Majles a declaration purporting to show in great detail that the nationalisation of the oil industry was not in the interests of Iran. The technical arguments and the style of this declaration, although written in Persian, led to a belief that it had been prepared by the A.I.O.C. and translated from English. It was refuted point by point by the National Front deputies, and attacked in the progressive press, which had got completely out of hand, accusing the ministers of being traitors, sold to foreigners, etc. It was afterwards said that the Company had made more liberal propositions, but that for the purpose of bargaining the Government had not made them public.

On the morning of the 2nd March 1951 I learned that Razmara had been murdered at the Shah Mosque in the Bazar during a religious ceremony—exactly in the same manner as Hazhir. I was profoundly shocked by this news. Although hostile to me, General Razmara was a fellow-officer whom I had known for many years, and the fact that we had not been on good terms made his death affect me even more than it would have done otherwise. Although his methods were objectionable to me and I considered his immeasurable ambition dangerous for the country, I recognised that he was an extremely able man and in 1946 had rendered a great service to the Shah and the country. Many things have been said about the projects he was nurturing just before his death, but to my knowledge nothing has been proved, and he took his secret with him to the grave.

The Majles passed the law on the nationalisation of the oil industry on the 16th March, a few days after Hoseyn Ala, who had previously been Minister of the Court and Ambassador in Washington, had been appointed Prime Minister.

Hoseyn Ala, the son of Ala-os-Saltaneh, in whose Cabinet my father had been Minister of Justice in 1913–14, is one of the most outstanding statesmen of Iran. A man of lofty principles, scrupulously honest and highly cultured, he is also one of the most courteous people I have ever met. He proposed to me the post of Minister of Roads and Communications, which I accepted on certain conditions, one of them being the upholding of the oil industry's nationalisation. I was presented to the Shah together with General Zahedi, who had become Minister of the Interior.

During the few weeks this Cabinet was in power, it had to

cope with the leftists' demonstrations against the A.I.O.C., the immediate cancellation of whose concession they were clamouring for, the attacks of the Mosaddeq group who accused the Government of being hesitant and lukewarm in the implementation of the provision of this Nationalisation law, and the stubborn opposition of the British Ambassador Shepherd.

The Cabinet had also some difficulty in having its programme adopted by the Majles, this programme being considered too radical by the conservatives, and too moderate by the National Front, while the fellow-travelling Ashtianizade, who represented the Tudeh tendency, this party being excluded from political activity and from the Majles, attacked both Ala and the National Front.

Although the Tudeh was fiercely hostile to the A.I.O.C., it was not in favour of the nationalisation of the oil industry law, because this law would for ever prevent the U.S.S.R. from getting the much-coveted oil concession in the north of Iran, which had been rejected by the previous Majles. During a meeting at which all the ministers were present, Ashtianizade accused Ala of betraying the nation's interests, thereupon Abd-or-Rahman Faramarzi, the witty editor of the Keyhan daily, rose to the tribune, and amid nearly unanimous applause said that a country where Ala was a traitor might consider itself fortunate.

When Ashtianizade declared that Ala's Cabinet was composed of a majority of National Frontists, and among a few others cited my name, I heard loud exclamations from different parts of the house that I had saved Azerbaijan, Mazanderan and Kordestan, the deputies of the above-named provinces alluding to my action when I was Chief of Staff. Finally the programme was approved.

My Ministry comprised the departments of roads, ports, civil aviation, railway construction and the Iranian State Railways Organisation. My closest collaborators were Rafi, my Chief of Cabinet, a loyal and honest man, and Didevar, a relative of Seyid Abul Qassem Kashani, an able and honourable man whom I appointed as administrative under-secretary, a post which did not previously exist. I had heard that there had been defalcations in several departments and Didevar being a financial expert and also acquainted with the Roads Ministry, I asked him to examine the records and to report on any irregularities he discovered, but the short life of the Cabinet prevented me from taking action to correct them.

On the 27th April Ala summoned a ministerial meeting, and announced that between the intransigence of Dr. Mosaddeq and the categorical refusal by the British Ambassador to acknowledge the nationalisation, he did not see any possibility of continuing his work, and had presented the Cabinet's resignation to the Sovereign that morning.

The next day I drove to Seyid Abul Qassem Kashani's house. He was alone, and as we began to talk the telephone rang and he went to answer it. I heard loud exclamations, and coming back, he announced to me in an elated manner: 'God has had pity on Iran, the Majles has voted for Mosaddeq!'

I did not tell him what I was thinking, but my thoughts were far from cheerful. I knew that the real purpose of Mosaddeq in coming to power was the elimination of the Pahlavi dynasty, which he would strive to bring about by destroying the army. After a few minutes I left Kashani and drove to Larak, where I summoned my friends. We decided to support the plea for the nationalisation of the oil industry, but to oppose by every means any encroachment on the army and the prerogatives of the Crown.

We learned that the proposal of Mosaddeq for the premiership had come from a rightist deputy, who had probably presumed that as on some previous occasions Mosaddeq, when offered the responsibility of power, would shrink from it, contenting himself with criticising the Government, and by this move it would be possible afterwards to counter-attack him in the Majles. It was also said that the idea was that after a few weeks in power, seeing the impossibility of putting the Nationalisation law into force, he would himself resign and allow others to find a solution, without being able to criticise, having failed himself. Be this as it may, neither this deputy nor his friends had realised the degree of Mosaddeq's implacable determination to achieve the real aims he was pursuing.

Mosaddeq and After

From the first days of Mosaddeq's premiership, his actions followed the pattern which I had foreseen: the attack on the structure of the monarchy by every means at his disposal. This aspect of his activities was disregarded by foreign observers who concentrated on the struggle between the Iranian Government and the British Government supporting the A.I.O.C., but for us it was of paramount importance, as for those who had a true knowledge of the situation the disappearance of the monarchy would mean danger to the very existence of Iran.

As already mentioned, Tudeh and fellow-travellers were careful not to mention the rubric 'Nationalisation of the Oil Industry' in their propaganda, but replaced it first by that of 'National Struggle against the A.I.O.C.', and afterwards by that of 'Struggle against the Imperialistic Oil Companies'—meaning not only the A.I.O.C. but also any other non-Soviet companies which might eventually seek a concession in Iran. This slogan was also changed after a short time to that of 'Struggle against Imperialism', when the Americans associated themselves with the British in negotiating with Mosaddeq, these changes showing the evolution of the party line.

At the same time an organisation for World Peace, also Communist-inspired, and which gained followers among the middle and upper classes as it had been presided over by the great poet Malek-esh-Shoara Bahar until his death in April 1951, was also organising meetings and demonstrations which sometimes resulted in violence, the word 'Peace' taking then the meaning of 'Revolution' and being directed solely against the U.S. and U.K. Although the demonstrations for the nationalisation of Iran oil were for the most part encouraged by the Government itself in order to give more weight to its claims against the A.I.O.C., both the patriotic and loyalist elements and the Tudeh with their fellow-travellers participated in them as the feelings of the great majority of the Iranian people for the revision of the Concession were genuine. The Western observers of that time—and many even of this time—did not care or wish to understand this, and discarded all these manifestations as Communist-engineered and unimportant, as if the mass of the Iranian nation was not only completely devoid of patriotism, but quite satisfied with the inferior position of its nationals in the A.I.O.C. and content to receive only what the Company was willing to give them.

The story of this phase of Anglo-Iranian relations has been told in several books in great detail, and I will mention here only the principal landmarks of this dispute in their relation to the events in Iran between May 1951 and August 1953—the Mosaddeq period.

The Law on Nationalisation came into force on the 2nd May, and a commission of five members was elected to implement its provision. On the 26th the British Government took this dispute to the International Court of Justice at The Hague, the Iranian Government contesting the competence of this body to deal with what it considered a question between a Sovereign State and a company seeking a concession.

After a time the court ruled that this question was out of its competence, but advised the parties to the dispute to refrain from any move which could embitter the dispute, and to maintain the *status quo* until it should be settled by negotiations. It is to be noted that the British member of the court associated himself with this resolution, which was in effect favourable to Iran.

On the 20th June the Government decided to take in hand the exploitation of the Company, offering to the foreign (British) employees the chance to remain and work for the newly organised National Iranian Oil Company. None of them accepted, and the 2500 British employees were evacuated under the protection of the cruiser *Mauritius*, which had anchored in the Shatt-el-Arab in front of Abadan, a parachute battalion having also been flown from England to Cyprus to be ready in case of emergency. The situation had become extremely tense, patriotic feelings being stirred and military forces, including artillery, were sent from Teheran to Abadan and Khorramshahr, their arrival there provoking great enthusiasm.

Iran having but few oil specialists, the Abadan refinery was practically closed and the work in the oilfields greatly reduced.

President Truman offered to mediate, and this being accepted by Mossadeq, on the 15th July the President's Assistant, Harriman, arrived in Teheran.

The Tudeh were of course opposed to any kind of settlement, as their aim was not to reach an agreement with the A.I.O.C. under the auspices of the U.S., but on the contrary to cut all ties with the Western countries and provoke an open conflict with them, pushing in this way Iran into the arms of the U.S.S.R. In this their policy diverged from that of other political groups, among them the newly organised 'Toilers Party', whose leader was Dr. Baqai, with Khalil Maleki, Sepahbodi, and a few others, who wanted to reach a settlement favourable to Iran and welcomed the arrival of Harriman.

I had finally organised with a few friends a party called 'National Movement', our members being chiefly workers from the south of the town, our programme being loyalist to the Shah and the Monarchy, nationalist without discrimination for or against any country or bloc, with Socialist ideas. One of my friends put a newspaper at our disposal.

After having worked the whole night at the printing press I was finally able to bring ·out the first number of the *National Movement*, with articles supporting the Shah, religion and the nationalisation of the oil industry, and a leading article emphasising man's fundamental right to freedom of thought and expression.

This day coincided with the arrival of Harriman, and the Tudeh had prepared a mass demonstration against him and U.S. mediation. At about 2 p.m. the Tudeh column, comprising toughs with sticks, moved along Shahabad Street without hindrance, but when they reached Majles Square they were attacked by Dr. Baqai's 'Toilers'. The police did not intervene in time, and the Tudeh demonstration was broken up and dispersed.

The next day Mosaddeq dismissed the Chief of Police, and reproached General Zahedi, who was then Minister of Interior, with not having given orders to protect the 'peaceful demonstration of the patriotic elements' (meaning the Tudeh) against the 'brutal onslaught of the reactionary toughs'.

On the 30th August Mosaddeq rejected the joint proposal of Truman and Churchill, which failed to accept the accomplished fact of the nationalisation of the A.I.O.C. and its logical consequences.

I wrote a leading article in my *National Movement* paper, under the title 'Shah and *Prime Minister*'. In this article I stated that in Iran the Shah and the Prime Minister must always work together, and that if the Prime Minister did not work according to this principle, the result would be fatal both for the country and for himself and I cited as an example the mistakes of Qavam. I then telephoned to Mosaddeq's house asking for an interview. He answered me himself, fixing 4 p.m. that day.

I took a copy of the paper and went to see him. I was ushered into his bedroom. He was sitting up in bed, and greeted me with a profusion of compliments. We talked about the oil question, and I told him that I had brought him an article which would probably interest him and meet with his approval, and handing him the paper I took my leave. It was the last time I saw him.

In October the Security Council examined the complaint lodged by the British Government against the nationalisation of the A.I.O.C. by unilateral action of the Iranian Government. Mosaddeq had gone to New York with a delegation of which Dr. Baqai was a member and seemed to have influenced the Security Council by his speech, which abstained from taking a decision on this question.

Meanwhile, the relations between Iran and the U.K. went from bad to worse, and as a result of declarations by the British Consul in Khorramshahr, to which the Iranian Government took exception, all the British Consulates were closed down as from the 21st January 1952.

In October of that year I caught cold, developing pneumonia and afterwards pleurisy, and as a result of staying a long time in bed had an attack of phlebitis, all this keeping me in bed for nearly seven months, followed by two months of convalescence. In this way I was for nearly one year prevented from taking an active part in politics, although I was kept well informed by my friends who visited me every day.

At the beginning of February, the elections for the 17th Majles brought to a head the parting of the ways between Mosaddeq, who was leaning more and more towards the left, and Kashani, and through pressure by Mosaddeq, Maki was elected first deputy of Teheran instead of Kashani, which had resulted in a loss of prestige for this religious leader. The elections were openly interfered with by the Tudeh and pro-Mosaddeq people, and some ten Larak workers with my butler Taqi, who had gone to the nearest voting centre, were stopped by Tudeh toughs standing in front of the booths, and asked to show their voting papers. When they refused, they were prevented from voting, and when they complained to a policeman who was standing by he told them that his orders were not to intervene, and they had to come back without having been able to vote.

Mosaddeq being inclined to adopt a policy of neutralism, following Nehru's example, had first cancelled the agreement according to which a U.S. military mission was assisting the Iranian Army, but later changed his mind and the Americans remained.

It was in June 1952 that, encouraged by the Tudeh propaganda, the peasants on several big private estates began to agitate against their landlords, several of whom were expelled and two or three even killed without the Government doing much to deal with this situation.

Our position in Larak was quite different, and from the point of view of farming in Iran, original. When we bought Larak, which has an area of only 80 acres, being against the sharecropping system which prevailed in Iran, we engaged several workers who were paid a monthly wage, increasing their number after we started our dairy farm.

In order to teach our workers discipline and to have them always clean and tidy I elaborated a system which I introduced progressively and which is still applied in Larak. I provided them with complete sets of summer and winter clothes, exactly like in the army, with boots, belts, caps, great-coats, warm gloves for the winter, of a military pattern, with distinctive badges to be differentiated from soldiers. Receiving all that free, they were of course delighted. So that even when I told them that being in military uniforms, they had to accept military discipline, stand at attention, salute in a military fashion, etc., they did not mind.

We built little houses for all our workers each with a small allotment attached in which they could grow their own vegetables and made a small addition to their wages for every child up to working age for the boys, and until they married for the girls. We also provided free medicines and medical attention and engaged a teacher for the adults who were illiterate and for any of the children who for any reason were unable to attend the school in a neighbouring village. In order to encourage them to work harder they shared in the prosperity of the farm, receiving a bonus for any result above a certain norm in all branches of its activity: so much for more milk produced, so much for a better harvest, and so on. They also received a small increase of pay for every year of service with us which was forfeited if they left even for a very short time. This seniority was shown by badges worn on their arms, several of them showing today more than twenty years' service.

I provided a bugle, and one of the boys was taught to sound it at the nearest military barracks, after which all the work was done by the same bugle calls as in the army.

In his endeavour to bring down the monarchical regime, Mosaddeq was hampered by the fact that the army was loyal to the Shah, and his efforts to infiltrate it with subversive and disaffected elements had up to then proved abortive. He asked also to be given the portfolio of the War Ministry, and as this request was not immediately accepted, he resigned.

There was talk of an Allayar Saleh or a Dr. Moazzami Cabinet, both of whom belonged to the Iran Party affiliated to Mosaddeq, but finally it was decided that Qavam would again be brought to power, and he received the Imperial *Farman*, ordering him to form a Ministry. Politically Qavam had changed very much, and his brother Motaman-os-Saltaneh telephoned to me saying that he was considering proposing a portfolio to me. Qavam never succeeded in forming a Ministry. The Tudeh and all the partisans of Mosaddeq made violent demonstrations in the streets, and tried to storm the Majles. In order to avoid bloodshed the police were ordered off the streets, the job of directing the traffic being performed by militant Tudeh, some of them even wearing party badges. In this way, for two days Teheran was in the hands of the mob, the army being confined to its barracks.

On the 20th April 1953 the Chief of Police, General Afshar-Tus, disappeared. After a few days it was ascertained that he had been kidnapped by a group comprising several army officers and civilians hostile to Mosaddeq, and it was surmised that Dr. Baqai, who had also joined the opposition, had been the directing brain. His corpse was discovered in the hills some twenty miles from Teheran, the suspected people being arrested but released after the National rising of the 19th August.

Afshar-Tus was a mysterious character. I had him under my orders for a short time at the Military Academy, where he acted as an instructor. But his behaviour with the cadets was so harsh and brutal that, though a believer in strict discipline, I had to transfer him to another unit. Afterwards he was for a time administrator of Reza Shah's estates in Mazanderan, but there also was said to have treated the peasants with brutality and even cruelty. He was supposed to have been loyal to Mosaddeq, but being very ambitious, nobody knew what ideas he had been nurturing. Among other things it was said that he had been kidnapped in order to show the insecurity of Mosaddeq's regime and to deprive him of a valuable if ruthless assistant.

On the 29th June President Eisenhower wrote to Mosaddeq not to expect any financial help from the U.S. until a suitable settlement of the oil question had been reached. This was followed by demonstrations of the workers in the oilfields and the refinery in support of Mosaddeq's oil policy.

Since the Senate had been dissolved, General Zahedi, who was an outspoken opponent of Mosaddeq, had gone into hiding, and one day a friend I had in the political section of the Secret Police informed me that the next day a secret agent would be sent to Araj, a village close to Larak, to spy on me from there and report all my movements and the numbers of the cars of my visitors.

Next day I noticed an unknown man pacing on the road outside the fence surrounding Larak in company with a notorious Tudeh man from a near-by village. When I asked him what he wanted, he answered me rudely, and I understood that this was the spy.

I returned to the house and sent three Larak men to arrest the man and to take him to the near-by gendarmerie post, saying that he was disturbing the peace of the neighbourhood. This was effected, and in spite of his protests he was conveyed under escort to town and kept for a couple of days in the gendarmerie, the police wondering what had happened to their agent.

Ten days after that I saw him again, concealing himself behind a tree, half a mile from Larak. This time I sent a friend to the Chief of Police to say that if the agent, was not recalled in twenty-four hours, I would see to his disappearance for ever. The next day he was gone.

Some time after this episode, from a point which dominates the countryside, I noticed a column of cars coming from the direction of the town, and stopping not far from Larak. Having sent for my field-glasses, I could see fifty to sixty men emerge from the cars executing field exercises under the direction of an instructor standing in front of them. After half an hour they re-entered their cars and returned by the same way, but halted again in the village of Araj, where they held a meeting.

The next day one of my men told me that while in the village public bath, he had overheard two Araj villagers saying that these people were Tudeh and that they would return in force on Monday to attack Larak which was 'a den of reactionary Palace lackeys who were plotting against the people with the agents of Anglo-American Imperialism'.

I realised that this time Tudeh meant business, probably with the tacit approval of Mosaddeq. I ordered my Larak men to manœuvre on that part of the estate which was visible from Araj and telephoned to the Shimran district's military governor warning him that if, as I was told, the Tudeh hooligans came next Monday to attack Larak, I would fight them with my forty men, who would then be armed not only with sticks, but with more dangerous weapons. According to the Law, I had the right to repulse trespassers on my enclosed property, which was clearly delimited by a barbed wire fence and that in that case he would be responsible for spilled blood, as he had been duly warned.

On Monday, several lorries with armed soldiers arrived in Araj to keep order, and the Tudeh did not manifest itself, but on the next day their newspaper openly complained against the military governor's action, saying that he had prevented the 'patriotic youth from teaching a lesson to General Arfa, the brainless agent of International reaction'.

On the 10th August Mosaddeq arranged a referendum to approve his action in dissolving the Majles. In order to frighten the people into acquiescence, ignoring the secrecy of the ballot guaranteed by the Constitution, he arranged that there should be two tents in all polling stations, one for those who intended voting as he wished and one for the few bold enough to brave the threats and insults of the hefty young Communists stationed before its entrance, who made assurance doubly sure by destroying the dissentient votes, the police having been ordered not to interfere.

It was not to be thought that an administration using such

methods would hesitate to change the voting boxes or to count only favourable ones. The result was a heavy vote in favour of the dissolution of the Majles.

Being a Constitutional Sovereign, the Shah could not dumbly assist at such a tragic farce and he understood that this tragicomedy was leading the country directly to chaos and anarchy, from which it could emerge only to fall into the hands of the Tudeh. He, therefore, used his Constitutional right and dismissed Mosaddeq, appointing in his place General Fazlollah Zahedi, who was still in hiding. This order was conveyed to Mosaddeq by Colonel Nasiri, but Mosaddeq not only refused to obey the Shah's order but arrested Nasiri and also several people close to the Court. Hoseyn Ala had been before that sent to Washington as Ambassador, and replaced by Abol Qassem Amini whom Mosaddeq thought to be favourable to him, but who in reality was devoted neither to Mosaddeq, nor to the Shah, and played an independent hand.

The next day pro-Mosaddeq and Tudeh newspapers attacked the Shah without restraint, the *Bakhtar*, organ of Mosaddeq's foreign minister Fatemi, who was furious at having been temporarily arrested a short time before by army officers who had tried to engineer a *coup* but failed, even daring to indulge in the most offensive abuse which was relayed by the Teheran radio.

The Shah was at that time at Ramsar, on the Caspian Sea. In order to prevent bloodshed and a possible civil war, he decided to leave the country temporarily. His private plane being at a nearby landing-ground with his personal pilot, Major Khatem, he flew towards Baghdad with Empress Soraya and his Master of the Horse, Abol Fath Atabay.

Meanwhile, Mosaddeq had telegraphed to all Iranian Embassies abroad that the Shah was not to be met or given any assistance. As a result of this, the Iranian Ambassador in Baghdad refrained from actually meeting the Shah. The Sovereign's plane remained in Baghdad just the time to re-fuel and proceeded to Rome. In that town also, the Ambassador refrained from presenting himself to the Shah; one of the Secretaries, however, dared to come to the hotel and put himself and his resources at the Shah's disposal.

Things were moving fast in Teheran. All the Shah's pictures in the Government offices, cinemas, shops, etc., were removed by order of Mosaddeq's Government. The mention of the Shah's name in the morning and evening prayers in the military units was suppressed by order of General Riahi, the Chief of Staff appointed by Mosaddeq, whom I had put in 1945 under surveillance because of his Tudeh leanings, and in one garrison, a young lieutenant, who in spite of this order had shouted hurrah for the Shah, was arrested and thrown into prison.

The Imperial Guards Regiment, the soldiers of which are all long-term enlisted men, was disarmed and replaced at the palace gates by infantry soldiers.

Preparations were made for the formation of a Council of Regency which would prepare the way for the proclamation of the republic, and Mosaddeq's collaborators, Fatemi, Dr. Sanjabi, Hasibi and Zirekzade, had prevailed on Mosaddeq to include Khodabandeh of the Tudeh Party in this Council. Dr. Baqai was opposed to all this, but his party, the *Toilers*, had split in two, the seceders having adopted the name *Third Force Toilers Party* under Khalil Maleki. This group was more radical than the original *Toilers*, but was also opposed to the Tudeh, and Maleki broke with Mosaddeq because the latter had said that as the Tudeh Party was the strongest party of Iran he had to collaborate with it, being the Prime Minister of all the people, and not only of a faction.

On the 18th the Tudeh decided to bring down and destroy Reza Shah's statues in the town. I drove from Larak to Teheran and saw a handful of hooligans bringing down the statue of our great King in the Sepah Square, while the policemen, who were all deeply loyal to the monarchy, were powerless at this display of vandalism, having been forbidden to interfere because according to Mosaddeq 'it was the nation's will'.

After having destroyed Reza Shah's statues in the town, a party of Tudeh decided to demolish and desecrate Reza Shah's mausoleum at Hazrat Abdul Azim, in the close vicinity of that Saint's shrine. A servant of mine being on leave that day spent it at Hazrat Abdul Azim and returning late in the evening came to tell me what had happened there.

After the Tudeh people started to loot the precincts of the mausoleum prior to destroying it, the local inhabitants who are very devout, as all people living in places of pilgrimage are, regarding this action of the Tudeh as sacrilege, armed themselves with picks, axes, iron bars, bicycle chains, daggers and a few fire-arms, and attacked the miscreants in superior numbers. After a bloody battle they killed eleven of them, the others fleeing for their lives towards Teheran, while the policemen who were there calmly looked on without interfering in the struggle.

That same evening all the 400 cadets of the Military Academy's Summer Camp at Aqdassieh, with the exception of six, went on hunger strike in protest against the breaking of the Imperial statues and the omitting of His Majesty's name from the evening and morning prayers, in spite of the efforts of their officers who feared the possible repercussions which might follow these demonstrations.

Early in the morning of the 19th August my wife drove from Larak to the south of the town where Princess Ashraf's charitable institution was situated, but returned very soon, saying that in the south of the town people were demonstrating apparently against the Government, and after ten o'clock our milk distributors, who had returned from taking the farm's milk to town, told us in detail what had happened that morning. Peasants from Hazrat Abdul Azim who, as usual, had brought their vegetables and fruit to sell in the market in the south of the town, brought the news of the Tudeh's discomfiture of the evening before, stressing the fact that the police had not intervened to prevent the beating and killing of the desecrators. The market is a great meeting-place for peasants selling their produce and for workers of all kinds who gather there to await transport to their various factories.

The news from Hazrat Abdul Azim was greeted with demonstrations of approval by the workers, which were quickly followed by abuse of the Government. Some inscriptions on the walls praising Mosaddeq and attacking the Shah were obliterated, and the crowd adopted a threatening attitude. They got hold of some pictures of the Shah and of Reza Shah, and started a procession towards the north of the town shouting slogans for the Shah and against Mosaddeq as they went. As they progressed they were joined by more and more people including many off-duty army and gendarmerie N.C.O.s.

Mosaddeq, to whom these demonstrations had been reported and who had been alarmed by the proportions they had assumed, realising that the rank and file of the police was not to be trusted, ordered the General Staff to send army units against the people. Fearing that the soldiers would join the loyalist crowd, their chiefs (who were afraid of Mosaddeq) told them that the insurgent crowd were in reality Tudeh, and that the pro-Shah slogans were uttered by them only in order to deceive the soldiers. But these simple sons of the people though they were, realised that this was nonsense, and declaring that they would not shoot at the Shah's portraits, instead of barring the people's road to the Majles, reversed their rifles and joined them, first one by one, and then by entire squads and groups. The younger officers also mingled with the people, who were now progressing along all the south to north avenues towards the districts where the administrative and Government buildings are located.

At nine o'clock, the railway-station was occupied, and an enormous Iranian banner with the Shah's portrait appeared on the front of the station. At ten o'clock, Parliament Square was full of people, and improvised orators standing on the base where the statue of Reza Shah had been, addressed the delirious crowd who shouted continuously: 'Shah! Shah!' In less than an hour, tens of thousands of the Shah's pictures had been printed and distributed to motor-car owners, who stuck them on the windscreen of their cars, those who had not been able to get hold of one sticking on banknotes with the Shah's likeness instead. All the cars had their headlights full on and hooted without ceasing in sign of joy. At twelve o'clock most of the town was completely in the hands of the loyalists, the ministers having all disappeared, hidden nobody knew where.

Thinking that he could still master the situation, Mosaddeq dismissed the Chief of Police, General Modabber (my former clever adjutant of the Pahlavi Regiment), appointing one of his relatives in his place. This General drove to Police Headquarters to take charge of his office. There, he was surrounded by policemen who asked him: 'Are you for the Shah or for Mosaddeq?' 'Everybody is for the Shah,' said he. 'Then shout *Zendebad Shah*!' (Long live the Shah). The General shouted 'Zendebad Shah', and then drove back to Mosaddeq, saying that 'everything is finished. We are going, and you had better think about yourself before it is too late.' 'But where are the 80,000 people who voted for me at the referendum?' asked Mosaddeq. '*Bâd bord*' (Gone with the wind), answered the General.

Mosaddeq's house was guarded by troops under the command of a colonel who had received orders from General Riahi to resist to the end. He obeyed his orders and the attacking crowd were swept by machine-gun fire and mowed down by the tank guns, more than a hundred people losing their lives in front of the house.

The radio station was already in the hands of the people who had come by cars from the town and occupied it in spite of the presence of tanks, the soldiers joining them at once, but a pro-Mosaddeq technician had disappeared taking away with him an important part of the equipment and no communication was possible until a transmission came through from the Tabriz radio, announcing that the building of the Teheran radio was in the hands of the loyalists and that fighting was continuing in some parts of the town. This news had been transmitted from Teheran to Tabriz by telephone, and then broadcast from there.

At 2 p.m. a plane flying over the Military Academy's Summer Camp dropped a message conveying this information. At once the cadets hurried towards the town to take part in the demonstrations. I took two men from Larak and drove also to Teheran. On the way I stopped at a place where pro-Mosaddeq and anti-Shah slogans were written with chalk on the walls, and with my driver and the other men started to efface them. Seeing some twenty people looking at us, I shouted to them to come and help us; they all rushed forward and after a couple of minutes the offensive inscriptions had disappeared. Going back towards my car, I was surrounded by half a dozen young girls who insisted on kissing me— I having no objection to this loyalist demonstration. After that I had to submit to rougher kisses on the part of not too clean shaven policemen, who took me on their shoulders and lifted me on to the top of a bus, from where I made a fiery speech, shouting '*Zendebad Shah!*' until I was hoarse. After two more such improvised meetings in Shimran, I arrived at the radio station, which had meanwhile been repaired. General Zahedi had come out of his hiding-place at about half-past two and broadcast to the nation.

I was met at the radio station by young men in the uniform of the Aria Party, run by Hadi Sepehr, and they carried me on their shoulders to the studio. At this moment a colonel arrived with a paper announcing (as we understood afterwards, wrongly) the resignation of Mosaddeq. I took this paper and read it over the air. After that I drove to the town where severe fighting was still going on around Mosaddeq's house. I held meetings, addressing the crowd in half a dozen places, climbing on the roof of my car and on a public fountain in Mokhber-ed-Dovleh Square, where a monument commemorating the National Revolution has since been erected. The enthusiasm of the crowd had to be seen to be believed, people of all ages, but chiefly workers, artisans and small shopkeepers, waving and shouting without ceasing.

I then drove to Police Headquarters, from the top of the steps of which I made a speech to the crowd assembled below, and went inside to congratulate General Zahedi, exchanging warm embraces with him. It was then that the loyalists who had been arrested by Mosaddeq, including General Batmanglij, Ernest Perron and Shaban Ja'afari, were released from prison.

From there I drove in the direction from which shooting could be heard, but was stopped on my way by some officers who declared that they had been brought there with a motorised column from the armoured brigade by General Keyani, a Mosaddeq supporter, with orders to repulse the loyalists, but reaching the town both the officers and men refused to attack the crowd. The General then took flight, and having recognised me they asked me to lead them towards the fighting. I told them to follow my car, and sped towards Mosaddeq's house. When we arrived there the defending troops had surrendered, and Mosaddeq had fled in a lorry after climbing by a ladder into a neighbour's garden.

At four o'clock General Zahedi was already in charge of the situation, and cabled to the Shah in Rome that everything was settled and order reigned.

It is clear that the rising of the 19th August 1953—known in Iran as 'the 28th Mordad rising', was a genuine rising of the people in defence of their traditions and their Sovereign, the truth of which is vouched for by hundreds of reliable eyewitnesses. The only shots fired had been in defence of Mosaddeq, and not by General Zahedi's troops against the people supposedly supporting Mosaddeq, as had been circulated not only abroad but after a time also in Iran, by people who were hostile to the monarchy or who wanted to take the credit of what had happened to themselves. The decision was reached in Teheran after a few hours, but risings occurred in all provincial towns of Iran on the same day, and if the revolution had not taken place in Teheran at that date a bloody civil war might have started in the provinces.

The next day I went to congratulate Prince Gholam Reza, the Shah's brother, at the Saadabad Palace, and saw the Guardsmen, who had been disarmed by Mosaddeq, taking over their previous duties at the gates from the infantry soldiers who were returning to their barracks. After two days Mosaddeq was arrested with most of his ministers, but Fatemi was not found until several months later when he was tried and executed for high treason.

The Shah returned on the 23rd August, being met by enthusiastic crowds. I was received in audience, His Majesty showing himself particularly kind to me and talking for half an hour about the happenings of the past days.

After a fortnight an officer of the General Staff came to Larak, handing me the 1st Class of the newly created 'Order of the National Revolution', by order of the Shah. I again asked for an audience to express to my Sovereign my gratitude for his kindness. The Shah told me that he had seen me in a film. I was puzzled, but did not ask for details. It was only later that I was told that the Shah had seen a newsreel in Rome taken during the rising, in which I had appeared, and had seen me making a speech standing on the fountain steps, although I had had no idea I was being filmed at that moment!

General Zahedi established his headquarters at the Officers' Club where Mosaddeq was detained in a special apartment. The General Staff was purged, as well as the Police and the Gendarmerie. General Batmanglij was appointed Chief of Staff. After a few weeks, Colonel Teimur Bakhtiar, who had distinguished himself in Azerbaijan against the Tabriz Democrats, became Military Governor of Teheran, and after a ruthlessly conducted drive succeeded in eradicating the Tudeh which had gone underground but was unearthed and completely dislocated, all its leading members being arrested.

A few days after the Shah's return, I met Zahedi at a Salam. He took me by the arm and warmly greeting me said that he would like to see me and talk to me. I answered that I was at his disposal. A week after that he telephoned to me at Larak, saying again that he would like to see me and invited me to dine with him at the Club. I was met at the door by the new Chief of Staff, General Batmanglij, and passed some two hours alone with Zahedi, talking about what had happened. He said that he had reported to His Majesty that loyal and trustworthy officers like General Ahmadi and myself ought to be close to him, and when one of his aides came into the room with some business papers to be signed, he said to him: 'Do you know General Arfa?' 'Of course,' answered the aide, a former deputy of the 14th Majles who had been in the group which had supported me when I was Chief of Staff. 'Well, you know then that without him, we would not have been able to be here tonight,' said Zahedi, alluding to my defence of Teheran in 1945. We dined with Batmanglij and two others, and I returned to Larak.

After a time the diplomatic relations between Iran and Great Britain were resumed and negotiations started with A.I.O.C. and American Oil Companies which resulted in the granting of a new concession to an International Consortium composed of the British Petroleum Co. (the former A.I.O.C.) with 40 per cent of the shares, eight American oil companies with also 40 per cent, the Royal Dutch Shell (6 per cent British and 8 per cent Dutch) and the Compagnie Française des Pétroles (6 per cent). The A.I.O.C. was abrogated, Iran having to pay £25 million as compensation to the A.I.O.C.

The refinery and oil wells of Kermanshah were ceded to the National Iranian Oil Co., which became also the distributing organ in Iran and responsible for the administrative arrangements inside Iran. The Consortium had to pay 50 per cent of the net profits to the Iranian Government. The number of foreign employees in Iran dropped from 2500 to about 600, but afterwards rose again to nearly 1000, although the concession stipulates that the foreign technicians should be gradually replaced by Iranians. Many young students were sent to different specialised faculties in foreign countries, and a special section for oil-prospecting engineering opened at the Teheran University, the final agreement being signed on the 19th September 1954, Dr. Ali Amini, the Finance Minister (who was Prime Minister from 1961 to 1962), being the chief Iranian negotiator.

Mosaddeq was tried and finally condemned to three years' penal detention, but his tenure of power resulted in Iran's almost complete financial ruin, and it was only with American aid that the Government could run the State after Mosaddeq's collapse, nearly 700 million dollars being given to Iran under various provisions.

The elections for the Senate and for the 18th Majles in February 1954 gave rise to much discontent, as it was said that only people who had been put on special lists could be elected, these lists being given to non-official supervisors whose task was to eliminate from the ballot boxes the names of all those whose election was considered undesirable. There were loud protests on the part of persons who were thus eliminated. This discontent affected not only the intellectuals and the liberal-minded section of the population, but also many others who considered that the Government was conceding to the Consortium too many advantages, or who disliked seeing Iran fall again under Anglo-American political and economic influence, or who wanted to know in what way the enormous sums of money received or borrowed from the U.S. were being spent.

In the beginning of the spring of 1954 one or two papers mentioned my name as a possible alternative to Zahedi, and after a few weeks a great many people began coming to Larak, trying to induce me to plunge into political activity. I told them that the appointment of the Prime Minister depended on the Shah, and that General Zahedi being a strong and active Premier I did not see any reason why anybody should replace him. Nevertheless, this agitation continued until General Zahedi resigned on the 5th April 1955 and Hoseyn Ala assumed the Premiership for the second time.

One day I met Loy Henderson, who was at that time U.S. Ambassador in Teheran, at a party at Princess Shams's (the Shah's sister) Palace, and recalling his difficulties with Mosaddeq, he told me that Mosaddeq had accused him of going by night to Larak and plotting with me against him. When Henderson replied that he had certainly heard about me but had never met me, Mosaddeq refused to believe him.

I understood that secret police agents who had been ordered to watch me, having been discouraged from coming in the vicinity of Larak by my treatment of one of them, preferred to stay in town and invent stories about my supposed activity, which stories Mosaddeq believed.

In August 1954 the secret service discovered an important Tudeh organisation in the army among the younger officers, and during the next month some 600 officers whose affiliation to the Tudeh had been proved were arrested. They were tried, a few were condemned to death and executed, others being condemned to various terms of confinement, but in the following years all were amnestied by the Shah, or had their sentences reduced.

In the spring of 1955 an order to settle disputes on the subject of several ill-defined sections of the frontier between Iran and the U.S.S.R. where the Soviet frontier guards had in the past encroached on Iranian territory, a mixed commission was formed to fix the frontier-line definitely. After several months the commission concluded its work, the Russians handing back to us several tracts of territory they had occupied in the past, while we accepted the claims on several others, notably in the former estuary of the Atrek river on the south-eastern corner of the Caspian Sea. Here the water of the Atrek had become dry near its estuary because of irrigation works and evaporation, and the frontier was a subject of dispute between the two parties.

Since the signing of a defensive agreement between Turkey and Pakistan, it was clear that these two countries had in view the ulterior participation of Iran in that agreement, as two countries situated at such a great distance from one another could not contemplate military co-operation. After a time Iraq joined this pact through a similar agreement with Turkey, and with the entry of the U.K., the Baghdad Pact came into being in 1955.

The necessity of a grouping of the Middle Eastern countries had already manifested itself between the two World Wars, as a substitute for the Anglo-Russian Alliance, and a vast buffer zone between these two countries, comprising Turkey, Iran, Iraq and Afghanistan, was created by means of the Saadabad Pact. This Pact being devoid of military clauses Iran did not come to the aid of Iraq in May 1941, when this country was involved in hostilities with the British, nor did Turkey help Iran when it was overrun by the Soviet and British armies.

After the war there were two developments which showed the necessity for the formation of a regional organisation which could be used to co-ordinate the defence of the Middle Eastern region— the pressure exercised by the U.S.S.R. against Turkey, to acquire bases in the Straits and to take back the Ardahan and Kars Provinces, and the endeavour of the Soviet to annex Iranian Azerbaijan and afterwards to reduce the whole of Iran to the state of a satellite. These considerations were to the fore at the formation of the Baghdad Pact, which was actively supported from the beginning by the U.S., although for different reasons it did not officially join it. The U.S. authorities strongly advised Iran to enter the Pact, but the British showed themselves reluctant to sponsor this idea, and through their Iranian friends seemed to

advise Iran to stick to its old policy of non-alignment and neutrality. Of course the Russians were also trying to influence public
opinion in this direction, by threats of atomic bombardment,
instantaneous annihilation, etc.

During that year responsible public opinion in Iran was
divided between those who were for the Pact and those who were
against it. The former followers of Mosaddeq, the fellow-
travellers, the crypto-Communists and most of the intellectuals
on the one hand and the Anglophiles of every shade on the other,
were against it. Most of the military, an important section of the
people of Azerbaijan, part of the middle class and of the business
community were in favour of the Pact. Finally on the 11th
October, Hoseyn Ala speaking at the foreign affairs commission
of the Senate said that the Government had decided to enter the
Baghdad Pact, and this was officially announced on the 12th.

Great hopes were entertained both by the military, who
expected a swift and serious reinforcement of the army's defensive power, and by others who imagined that economic development on a large scale would be launched with Western financial
aid. After a time it was realised that these aids, which had
already been forthcoming before Iran had joined the Pact, were
not to be substantially increased or accelerated. Moreover, what
transpired from the discussions which were taking place at the
Ministerial and Military meetings of the Pact brought home to
Iranian public opinion that the policy of the Western Powers
was in many instances in conflict with that of three of the four
regional members.

Iraq was clamouring for CENTO'S support for its anti-Zionist
policy. Iran wanted more arms and economic aid, and Pakistan
desired moral and political support for its claims to Kashmir and
in face of the threat from India and Afghanistan.

The polemics on the desirability of Iran's continued participation in the Pact flared up from time to time, according to
internal or external pressures brought to bear on public opinion.
The Suez affair provoked violent cross-currents in wide circles in
Iran. The great majority of Iranians, especially among the middle
and lower classes, were pro-Egyptian on account of their Moslem
feelings, but among the upper classes the traditional Anglophiles were of course pro-British. Many others believed that somehow British policy would in the end bring down Nasser and

restore British position and prestige, and that it was folly on the part of Nasser to imagine that he could resist the U.K.

In order to placate the feelings of the Arabs, on the insistence of Iraq, no U.K. delegates took part in the Ministerial meeting which took place in Teheran.

On the 17th November a member of the extremist fanatical organisation Fedayan Islam, the counterpart of the Moslem Brotherhood which existed in the Arab countries, made an attempt on the life of the Prime Minister, Hoseyn Ala, who was slightly wounded. Although Ala, always kind-hearted, asked that the man should be pardoned, the would-be murderer was tried. When it was discovered that he had acted on the incitement of his organisation, the Chief of the Fedayan, a *molla* called Nawab Safavi, together with another member of this group who had previously killed General Razmara but had been freed during Mosaddeq's time of power, were also arrested, and all three men condemned to death and executed, thus bringing to an end the existence of this terrorist organisation.

In 1956, what appeared to constitute a very important oil deposit was found near Qom, where a purely Iranian concern, the Iran Oil Co., all the shares of which belonged to the Government, struck oil. This took fire, and had to be extinguished by an American expert flown specially from the U.S. Afterwards it was said that the oil discovered in this region was not sufficient to justify exploitation, but sceptics murmured that further research had been discouraged by foreign interests.

Only one-sixth of the country being in the zone of the former A.I.O.C. and the present Consortium concession area, the Government—Dr. Manuchehr Eqbal having by then succeeded Hoseyn Ala, who had again become Minister of the Court—at the instigation of the Shah decided to put before the Majles a law authorising the National Iranian Oil Company (N.I.O.C.) to negotiate contracts with foreign companies, on profitable terms for Iran, such contracts being subject to ratification by the Majles.

Negotiations were also started with an Italian concern, A.G.I.P., for an area of 23,000 square kilometres divided in three zones for the setting up of a joint Italo-Iranian Company in which N.I.O.C. was to have a 50 per cent share in capital, as in the profits, A.G.I.P. having to pay 50 per cent of their profits to the Iranian Government as royalties. In this way the Government would in effect receive 75 per cent of the whole profits, without infringing on the principle of 50 per cent profits which the Consortium in Iran and the Concessionnaires in Iraq, Kuwait and Saudi Arabia accorded to the oil-owning governments and which was considered sacrosanct; although the Iranian Government had the right to give concessions on any terms it liked in the territory not included in the Consortium's concession.

Nevertheless, presumably inspired by foreign interests, a campaign was started against both the concession and the Law project, some people even accusing the Government members of having taken bribes from the Italians. Imagining that having an English wife I would at once take a part in this agitation, many people came to me indignantly denouncing the Government's action. They were taken aback when I warmly approved it, explaining that it would be in the interest of the nation. I even started a series of meetings in favour of this Law in the popular parts of the town as also in Larak, several hundred people gathering every Friday to hear speeches supporting the Shah's enlightened and progressive policy.

This agitation was at its height during the journey of the Shah to Spain, but on the Sovereign's return he made a strong declaration against 'troublesome elements who were agitating against the nation's interests', the agitation subsided, and the deputies, duly and unequivocally warned, passed the Law without demur. The agreement with A.G.I.P. was signed shortly afterwards, and the contemplated joint company founded under the name of SIRIP.

Later a similar agreement was reached with the Pan-American Oil Company, and a joint company called I.P.A.C. came into being. Today both these concerns have found oil and it is expected that in the near future, the production of oil in the territory outside the Consortium zone will be stepped up.

In 1958 an agreement was signed between Iran and Turkey for the eventual construction of a pipe-line from Qom to a port in Turkey, either Mersin or Iskenderun, but sufficient oil not having been found in Qom, this project has not materialised up to now. On the other hand, extensive pipe-lines have been built in Iran, the first 952 kilometres running from Abadan to Teheran, others being constructed after 1956 between Teheran–Qazvin–

Rasht and Teheran–Shahrud, which will be extended to Tabriz in the west and Mashad in the east, and another from Azna to Isfahan and to Yazd.

In spite of the participation of Iran in the Baghdad Pact, and a strong protest by the U.S.S.R. against this move which it considered as contrary to the 1921 and 1927 Irano-Soviet treaties, the relations between Iran and its northern neighbour were fairly good. The Soviet Government had the year before ratified the frontier convention, and after twelve years the reserve of gold belonging to the Iranian Melli Bank, which had been carried to Russia during the war, was returned to Iran. In June 1956 the Shah accompanied by Empress Soraya was invited to Russia, and this visit was quite successful, His Majesty making a very favourable impression in spite of some plain talk by the Shah to the Soviet authorities when they chose to criticise Iran's entry into the Baghdad Pact.

Having completed his time in prison, Mosaddeq was released and went to his estates of Ahmadabad, between Teheran and Qazvin. At first, people were allowed to visit him freely, but as one day a bus full of anti-Mosaddeq workers from the south of Teheran started trouble and wanted to attack him, being prevented from doing so by the gendarmerie, the Government had to accord him protection. Visits to Ahmadabad were restricted, only his relatives and close friends were permitted to see him.

After the national rising of the 28th Mordad (19th August, 1953), I became very popular with the people of the poorer districts, workers, artisans, etc., with whom I had co-operated during that momentous day, and amongst whom there were many ex-soldiers and retired N.C.O.s of the 1st Division who remembered me as their friend. In addition to our weekly Friday meetings, people used also to come to Larak on religious occasions such as the Ashura days, which commemorate the martydom of Imam Hoseyn, the second son of the Khalif and Imam Ali, the Prophet's cousin, who was massacred with all his family in the desert near Karbala, in Iraq, by the Governor of that province by order of the Omayyad Khalif Yazid. Every year between two to four hundred people used to gather at Larak, where I entertained them with sherbet and tea, and took part myself in the mourning ceremonies.

During the Ashura of 1956, I heard that on the following day not only the usual group but more people from town and from four neighbouring villages intended to visit Larak during the celebrations. This would mean at least 1000 people, and I felt that as they would have come from some distance they should be offered a meal before leaving. It was five o'clock in the afternoon when I summoned the cook and told him of the impending visitation. With complete sangfroid he asked what the menu was to be and when told soup, rice and meat, fruit and tea, saluted and took his leave. A hectic night preceded this gathering, and my servants showed great initiative in executing my orders. The estate mason constructed eight enormous ovens in the gardens, animals being slain and messengers sent in every direction to borrow cooking-pots and crockery and to purchase fruit, tea, sugar, rice and so on, and somehow the first service for 500 people was ready at twelve o'clock and the second for 500 more at one. Unfortunately, the 500 who had to wait until one o'clock became hungry and attacked the 500 who were having their meal and a battle royal ensued. In the end, the two hostile parties joining together attacked the kitchen folk, who had to flee for their lives so as not to become themselves the 'martyrs' of that day! I was entertaining the leaders of the mourners including Shaban Ja'afari in the house, and as we were making patriotic speeches, we heard nothing of this row, which finally subsided with the intervention of a few gendarmes who were among the guests.

I had been so absorbed by my life in Iran that twenty-eight years had passed without my leaving the country and I felt the time had come to visit the outside world again. I had not seen my sister during all these years, and she was then in Europe, her husband being French Ambassador in Stockholm, so we decided to invite ourselves to Sweden for a week and to divide the rest of our time between Monte Carlo, Paris and London, and it was whilst we were in Sweden that a telegram from Teheran was to open a new chapter in my life by offering me the post of Ambassador in Turkey which had been held by my father fifty years before.

Ambassador to Turkey and to Pakistan

Arriving early one morning at Ankara Airport to take up my new post we were met by the entire staff of the Embassy. We drove some 22 miles passing through the town which had grown beyond recognition since I had last seen it in 1938, an imposing shop-lined boulevard having replaced the country road which used to lead past the Embassy to Chankaya, Atatürk's country house, now the residence of the President.

From the first day I found myself in a friendly atmosphere, being received by the Turks with the same warmth I felt towards them. When I presented my Letters of Credence the President, Jelal Bayar, kept me for half an hour instead of the classic ten minutes, so that I was able to remind him of the manner in which Atatürk had presented him to Reza Shah in 1934.

It is sad to remember today my visits to the ministers of whom the two most distinguished have since been tried by a popular court and hanged, whilst others are still in prison as I write.

The Prime Minister, jovial, happy-looking Adnan Menderes, was extremely courteous and easy-mannered but reputed to be tough in politics. The Foreign Minister, Fatin Rushtu Zorlu, was the son-in-law of Rushtu Aras whom I had known as Turkey's Foreign Minister since 1934, and was a man of strong personality and great diplomatic ability, who enjoyed considerable prestige with the ambassadors.

A few days after my arrival the CENTO Ministerial Meeting was held in Ankara, our Prime Minister Dr. Eqbal with our Foreign Minister Ardalan staying with us at the Embassy. The U.K. was represented by Selwyn Lloyd, the U.S. by Foster Dulles, the Iraq Delegation being headed by Nuri Said and the Pakistan Delegation by Firuz Khan Noon and Manzur Qader. The first day Eqbal, Ardalan and I lunched at the British Embassy with

Selwyn Lloyd, Sir William Hayter and Sir Michael Wright, then British Ambassador in Baghdad, our host being Sir James Bowker with whom we afterwards became particularly friendly, his witty and glamorous Lebanese wife being the *bout en train* of Ankara society. Sir James was a man of exquisite manners and great charm and was much liked by everybody.

This first winter was brightened by the visit of Dame Ninette de Valois, an old friend of my wife's, and Dame Margot Fonteyn who gave several performances at the Turkish Opera House supported by the local ballet company. The National Opera House had been founded by Atatürk, who for the furtherance of his programme of westernisation had obtained the best possible advice, inviting Dame Ninette to found the Ballet School and Carl Ebert to direct the Opera. As a result Ankara has now an Opera House which produces old and new operas (always sung in Turkish) to the great enjoyment of an ever-growing musical public.

We gave a luncheon at the Embassy in honour of these illustrious ladies, which was attended by the British Ambassador and the Minister of Education under whose auspices the visit had been arranged.

Being accredited to Greece we went in May to Athens by car driving from Ankara to Istanbul and from there through Edirne, Cavalla, Salonica and Larissa to Athens, an unforgettable drive. The Greeks were extremely friendly to us, but on account of the negotiations on the Cyprus question which had then reached a difficult phase, the relations of Greece with both Turkey and Great Britain were passing through a difficult period, and our car having a Turkish number was looked at in a not very friendly manner until the Iranian flag on it was noticed.

After having passed through the lovely regions of Cavalla, Salonica and Larissa, we halted on a high pass, near the impressive heights of Olympus, at a wayside coffee-shop. The innkeeper came and sat at our table, but as we did not speak Greek the conversation reduced itself to his trying to discover from where we came, and when he grasped it was from Iran, he became even more friendly exclaiming joyfully, 'Marathon—Darius—Soraya', and we felt that ancient wounds were healed.

The Hotel Grande Bretagne, where we stayed in Athens, had been the scene of violent fighting towards the end of the war between the British Forces and the Greek Communists, being held at one time as an island in the midst of the Communist-occupied city joined to the Piraeus only by a narrow passage through which supplies could pass. At the time we arrived there owing to the temporary unpopularity of Great Britain the hotel had changed its name, but on our second visit it had resumed it.

The presentation of Credentials was done in great pomp, the King standing on a platform in the throne-room with six Generals on his left and six high Court officials on his right. He was a tall handsome man with great dignity, but quite devoid of pomposity and very friendly. The Prime Minister, Karamanlis, was a handsome, poised, able statesman and a shrewd politician, and the Foreign Minister, Evangelos Averoff, with whom I had several interesting conversations, impressed me as an extremely able diplomat with wide and objective views on the world situation.

For reasons of economy the royal family no longer reside in the official palace but in the charming country house of Tatei some miles from the town, and it was there that my wife and I paid our respects to Queen Frederica, a great grand-daughter of Queen Victoria and a grand-daughter of Kaiser William II. She is an unusually charming and vivacious person who has devoted herself completely to the service of her country being directly active in many welfare organisations, one of which is quite special to Greece—the giving of dowries to poor girls to enable them to marry.

I had had hopes when I knew I was to go to Athens of finding one of my Demidoff relations who had been the last Tsarist Minister to Greece and had settled there after the revolution, but in this I was to be disappointed as both he and his wife, who had been the daughter of the last Viceroy of the Caucasus, had died a few years before our arrival and I was only able to visit their graves. I discovered, however, their nephew Count Sheremetief who was working as a purser on a Greek ship and who had married an enchanting lady, the daughter of the Grand Duchess Irina and Prince Yusupoff who, together with the Grand Duke Dmitri Pavlovitch, had killed Rasputin. The cousinship was certainly remote, but we accepted each other as relatives and their friendship added much to the pleasure of our Greek visit.

When we took our leave of the royal pair, King Paul graciously bestowed on me the Grand Cross of the Order of the Phoenix, which he handed to me himself.

In Turkey I tried in vain to find the old atmosphere and homely Turkish ways I had known when at Harbiye, but outwardly all this had disappeared almost as completely as the old Russian spirit from the U.S.S.R. The clean-shaven elderly men, short-skirted women and tight-trousered boys, seemed quite unrelated to the befezed bearded effendis with their ample frock-coats, the veiled hanums and the moustachioed youths with dark fezes of the time of my youth. However, as I saw more of the new generation I discovered that the Turks were still the Turks, and that Islam had still its hold on the great majority of the population and that the solid qualities of courage, perseverance and devotion to an abstract idea—whether Islam, nationalism or as among the youth of today Westernisation—animate the Turks today as yesterday. They are a tough, disciplined, idealistic people who have preserved the qualities of their Central Asian forbears, which have dwindled to nothing in their kin subjected to Russian and Chinese rule.

In Ankara society is confined almost exclusively to the Diplomatic Corps, as the Government officials do not entertain, and go seldom to parties, but in Istanbul the old Ottoman Society of princes, former pashas, industrialists and cosmopolitan businessmen still thrives, and cocktail parties and intimate dinners and teas are occasions to meet interesting people and to escape from the strictly diplomatic atmosphere of Ankara.

For the summer months we rented a *yali* or house built directly on the Bosphorus at Yenikoy, one of the few villages on the European side which has preserved something of its old-world charm. The Bosphorus is certainly the most dramatic waterway in the world, representing today as it has done for untold centuries the doorway between Asia and Europe. Very near our house Darius had crossed it on a bridge of boats and Yenikoy had in the eighth century been pillaged by the Varangian princes from Kiev and in the seventeenth by the Zaparog Cossacks who arrived in 2000 long boats which were sunk by the Sultan. Today the entry to it is heavily mined, but from the entrance to the Golden Horn it presents a gay and animated scene—steamers replace motor-buses and boats laden with vegetables, fruit, roasted corn and many other commodities peddle their goods directly to the houses on the water, whilst boat after boat filled with gay bronzed bathers and water skiers pass in a never-ending procession. Leila and her children joined us at the Yali and spent many happy hours in the water.

Konya is naturally the first place for an Iranian to visit as it is there that the great mystic poet Jelal-ed-Din Rumi, whose poetry is known and loved throughout Iran, founded the Mevlevi Order of Dervishes, known in Europe as the Dancing Dervishes, which from the thirteenth century until the day of Atatürk had their headquarters there. This religious confraternity, like all the others, has been officially suppressed and forbidden by the Turkish Republican Government, but many of them continue to exist secretly and this order and the Bektashi order have many adherents in all classes of society.

Jelal-ed Din's disciples, having lived continuously in the same place since their founder's time, have piously preserved his entire wardrobe and personal belongings which are all in perfect condition exactly as they must have been the day he died some 700 years ago. All this together with a splendid collection of manuscripts are preserved in what is called a museum, but which is actually a place of pilgrimage where scores of people, including peasants from near and far, and of course the Iranians who visit Turkey, come to pray and meditate on this great mystical poet and philosopher of the thirteenth century. There is a constant tug-of-war between the Iranians and the Turks over this Saint who though he lived all his life in Turkey wrote exclusively in Persian.

Haji Bektash, the cradle of the Bektashi sect, is not far from Kaisarieh (Cesarea of the ancients), and there again 'the museum' which has been installed there is a place of pilgrimage for the Bektashis of today. The Dervishes are people of all classes, who dress like everybody else but form a kind of freemasonry, the leaders being unknown to the rank and file. They have a very strict hierarchy, and are promoted according to rules. When we visited their extensive premises which comprise a hostelry for visiting Dervishes and other pilgrims, kitchens, store-rooms, a mosque, living quarters for residing Dervishes, etc., the custodian explained to us the customs of the order in such detail that we had no doubt that he was himself a Bektashi, perhaps holding an important situation in their hierarchy.

Not far from Haji Bektash are situated the incredible cave

monasteries of Urgup and Goreme. On account of the special nature of the soil erosion in this region fantastic tower-like formations have appeared, inside which the monks of former centuries had dug caves where they lived and worshipped, and which are inhabited today by the local peasants.

Probably no country in the world is so evocative of the past as Turkey. The Hittites, the Greeks, the Early Church, Byzantium, the Seljuks and the Ottoman Empire, are all richly represented and much has been written of all this, particularly of late years by such distinguished travellers as Freya Stark, Lord Kinross, Colonel Lockhart and Sir Harry Luke. I will not attempt to tread in their footsteps but merely record my personal conviction that the Turk of today who is ethnologically probably more Anatolian (Phrygian Cappadocian, etc.) than Central Asiatic is still essentially a Turk formed by Turkish tradition and Irano-Islamic influences, so that even the modern atheist is spiritually quite different from a Western unbeliever.

Turkey is today inhabited by two important groups, the Turks themselves with their strong national characteristics, and the Kurds, who number between 2 and 3 millions, and are of pure Iranian race. These people are being subjected to a strong process of Turkification, the Turks speaking of them as 'Mountain Turks' and pretending to believe that Kurdish is a Turkish dialect, although it has nothing in common with Turkish, being a purely Iranian tongue.

Besides the Kurds, there are some 600,000 Circassians who immigrated from the Caucasus in the last century, about 200,000 Lazes (akin to Georgians), 90,000 Greeks, 50,000 Armenians and 45,000 Jews, so that from 23 to 25 millions out of the total population of 28 millions are purely Turkish by speech, creed, thought and feeling.

In January 1958 the news of the union of Syria with Egypt created in the Middle East a new situation which was certainly not to the liking of the Western Powers nor did the Soviet seem over-enthusiastic at this development. It halted, for the time being, the process of the gradual communisation of Syria through Khalid Bektash, General Bizri and the other leaders of the small but active Syrian Communist Party. The immediate reaction was the formation of the Iraq-Jordan union, which created a peculiar situation, Iraq being a member of the Baghdad Pact, and Jordan remaining outside it. In Lebanon the revolution and civil war between the mostly Moslem neutralist section of the population which was opposing the change of the Constitution intended to make possible the re-election of the pro-Western President Camille Shamun, and the mostly Christian section which was supporting Shamun also contributed to the creating of an explosive situation in the Middle East.

At the beginning of July the Heads of State of the regional members of the Pact decided to meet in Istanbul on the invitation of President Jelal Bayar, and on the morning of the 14th July, King Faisal of Iraq with Nuri Said, the Shahinshah and Iskandar Mirza, were expected at the airport of Yesilkey, our Prime Minister Eqbal having already arrived two days before. Arriving at the airport at eight o'clock to greet King Faisal who was to be the first arrival, I saw the guard of honour ready in front of the building, but the Chief of Protocol told me in a distracted manner that according to a broadcast from Baghdad a revolution had taken place there and that the King could not come. A second message announced the murder of the royal family and the arrest of the ministers. It was then signalled to the Shah's plane not to come down in Yesilkey, but to proceed directly to Ankara, and Dr. Eqbal and I flew there at once, arriving at Chankaya fifteen minutes after the Shah.

Iskandar Mirza, who had just brought off his *coup d'état* in Pakistan, had come with General Mohammad Ayub Khan, the Commander-in-Chief, whom I had met before at the Pact's Ministerial Conference in January. We had talked much on military matters, and I admired this tall and handsome General who was the embodiment of the true military spirit.

After the CENTO meeting, there was a luncheon party on the President's yacht for the Shah and Iskandar Mirza with his Iranian wife, to which Ayub Khan, the Pakistan Ambassador and his wife, Dr. Eqbal, and my wife and I were invited. It was not a happy party as we were all conscious of the guest who should have been with us.

In August, Sir James Bowker was transferred to Vienna, and a few weeks later Sir Bernard Burrows, who had been resident in the Persian Gulf, came with his wife to replace him.

This delightful couple complemented each other in a remarkable manner—he, deeply cultured and extremely intelligent, being unusually calm even for an Englishman, whilst she was incredibly lively, gay and unconventional. They both acquired in a short time a good knowledge of colloquial Turkish, which was greatly appreciated by the Turks.

At the beginning of 1959 we went to Karachi for the Ministerial Conference of CENTO, where we found Ayub Khan already the Chief of State, Iskandar Mirza having been forced to leave the country. At this time the relations between Iran and the U.S.S.R. were passing through a delicate phase, as the Russians knew that we were negotiating a bilateral treaty with the U.S. by which this country would pledge itself to come to our help in the case of aggression, and Soviet diplomacy considering such a treaty as directed against the U.S.S.R., wanted to prevent it, and if possible persuade us to abandon the Baghdad Pact. On the other hand, the Iranian Government's wish was to suppress the articles 5 and 7 of the Irano-Soviet Treaty of 1921, according to which the Soviet had a right to send its military forces into Iranian territory if groups hostile to the U.S.S.R. were preparing to invade its territory using Iran as their springboard. Although it had been clearly specified in letters exchanged between the Iranian Foreign Ministry and the Soviet Ambassador at the time, and duly incorporated in the treaty, that this provision concerned only a possible grouping of White Russian elements for an aggression against U.S.S.R., these articles had nevertheless served as a pretext to invade Iran in 1941 in concert with the British forces, in spite of the fact that there were no White Russians nor any other foreign forces on Iranian territory.

The Soviet would have been ready to accept such a modification on condition that Iran would not sign a treaty of defence with the U.S., would abandon the Pact and would undertake not to allow any foreign military base in Iran. The latter condition could be understood in different ways, the presence of a few foreign instructors, any store of arms, or military (or even civilian) aerodromes, could be described as foreign bases for the purpose of an aggression.

The negotiations with the U.S. were dragging and meanwhile, on the insistence of the Russians, the Iranian Government had agreed that a mission from the Soviet Foreign Ministry should come to Teheran. This created quite a stir among Iran's Pact partners, especially the U.S.A. and Turkey, and even the U.K.

which had been, apparently wrongly, considered in Iran as favouring an Irano-Soviet *rapprochement*, informed Teheran of its concern. The Russians had meanwhile dropped their demand that Iran should quit the Pact, only asking for a guarantee concerning the bases, and abstention from signing the bilateral agreement. The Iranian Government rejected these conditions, and the Russian mission left Teheran in great mortification.

From then on a campaign of threats and abuse was started by the Soviet against Iran, and especially against the Shah whom they considered the principal obstacle to Iran's acceptance of the Russian proposals, and after a time Iran reciprocated, this war of words being daily waged by the press and the radio of the two countries, Khruschev adding menacing personal declarations openly inviting the Iranian nation to rise and overthrow the monarchy. This cold war lasted from March 1959 until the middle of 1962, and although at the beginning the few opponents of the regime, both among the Russophiles and the Anglophiles, pretended to be concerned about the effect this propaganda might have on the Shah's position, not only the people remained unaffected by it, but the feelings of loyalty to the Sovereign were strengthened and the birth of the Crown Prince Reza produced such general outbursts of rejoicing and loyalist enthusiasm among all classes of the population that the Soviets had to recognise the complete failure of their attacks.

In March 1959, after much negotiation, the U.S. entered into bilateral agreements with Turkey, Iran and Pakistan, the documents being signed simultaneously by the Ambassadors of these countries and by the Turkish Foreign Minister, Fatin Rustu Zorlu, at the Turkish Foreign Ministry.

That same year, after a protracted period of tension, the Turkish, British and Greek delegates entered into a compromise agreement concerning Cyprus at Zurich, which was duly accepted by the leaders of the Greek Cypriots, Archbishop Makarios, and of the Turkish Cypriots, Dr. Kuchuk. The whole population of Cyprus numbers about 500,000; 120,000 of whom are Moslem Turks, the others being Greeks.

This agreement had to be officially signed in London, where Zorlu had gone to hold the last conversations with the British about details. On its way there, the plane of the other Turkish delegates, at the head of which was the Prime Minister Adnan

Menderes, crashed near London, several people being killed, whilst Menderes escaped with minor injuries but suffered a bad shock, necessitating his remaining several weeks in hospital in England. On his return he was met by the Ankara population with such enthusiasm that having come with the other diplomats to meet him at the railway station, I was so crushed by the crowd that for three months afterwards my legs and feet ached.

Up to 1960 the political scene in Turkey was characterised by a fierce struggle between the Democratic Party of Menderes and Jelal Bayar, and the Republican People's Party of Ismet Inönü, the former President. Many reasons have been advanced for this bitter hostility, far surpassing the usual bickering between two rival parties, especially as their political and economic programmes did not differ substantially, both of them considering themselves to be the heirs of Atatürk and bound to continue the revolution started by him. It has been suggested that one of the causes of this strife was the mutual hatred between Inönü and Bayar. In my opinion as the supporters of Menderes were chiefly the peasants and members of the religious and traditional circles, and those hostile to him principally the students, university professors, young army officers (besides many not so young), and generally the intelligentsia, it could be considered as the struggle between the partisans of the revival of Islam in Turkey, and those who considered that Islam, by its fatalistic influence, was hampering the progress of the people, and that it ought to be discarded and a radical westernisation of thought substituted for it. Of course, the great majority of the Turks being believing Moslems, even among the middle and upper classes, they could not say this openly, but put in a nutshell the conflict was practically reduced to this.

After several demonstrations and counter-demonstrations, the Government decided to outlaw the Republican Party as using non-parliamentary and revolutionary methods, and in order to do so appointed a commission of investigation, composed of its followers of the Democratic Party, which was considered by the opposition as a violation of the Constitution and afterwards formed the basis of the accusation against the members of the Government and all the deputies who voted for this proceeding. The Republicans left the Majles in protest after a fight with fists and heavy objects, after which student demonstrations started both in Istanbul and Ankara and led to bloody encounters with the police. Early in May on my way to the Indian Embassy to a party given in honour of Jawaharlal Nehru, who was visiting Turkey and with whom I had a discussion about neutralism, I saw a mass demonstration of the cadets of the Military Academy, marching in an orderly manner without arms and shouting anti-Menderes slogans. They were led by their officers at the head of whom was General Sitki Ulay, the Military Academy Commander. I realised at once that the day of Menderes and the Democrats was over, and telegraphed this to my Government.

Menderes did not dare to take drastic measures against this act of indiscipline on the part of the cadets, as he realised that they were supported by many officers. A meeting which he organised with the members of the Democratic Party did not have the expected results as the number of those who turned up did not exceed three or four thousand, and was opposed by students who shouted adverse slogans.

After a few days Menderes departed to the west of the country where the population was mostly in his favour, to hold rallies which he hoped would impress the people all over Turkey. In effect, at a big meeting in Eski Sehir, scores of thousands of people accorded him an enthusiastic welcome, and full of hope he started towards Afyonkarahisar.

On the 27th May at 4.30 a.m. I was awakened by the sound of several shots which appeared to come from the Presidential Palace, and my Counsellor knocking at my door told me that the Ankara radio had announced the rising of the army, the arrest of the ministers and of the President, Menderes being arrested on his way to Afiun, and the constitution of a military junta which had taken in hand the power of the State. My wireless became busy, and at 5 a.m. my Government was already in possession of my reports about these happenings.

The rest of the story is known; the trial, the condemnation and the hanging of Menderes, Zorlu and of the Finance Minister Hassan Polatkan, the Minister of the Interior, Namik Gedik, killing himself by jumping from a window. Jelal Bayar was also condemned to death but his sentence was reduced on account of his age to life imprisonment, more than 400 other persons including several women deputies being condemned to various terms of imprisonment. Having known these people closely, I was much affected by their fate from a purely human point of view, but being a foreigner it was not for me to take sides in this matter.

Three days after the revolution I was received by General Jemal Gursel, the Chief of the junta, of the State and of the Government, and we discovered that we had been at Harbiye at the same time. He was a dignified and friendly person, and I noticed that from the beginning he nurtured an ambition to become President of the Republic. The new Foreign Minister, Selim Sarper, was a highly cultured, courteous and able diplomat, and became very popular with the foreign envoys. I had the impression that he was sincerely sympathetic to Iran and valued highly our friendship and alliance.

Returning from a journey to Europe, the Shah passed through Turkey in order to show that the change of Government in Turkey did not affect our relations with that country, as our friendship was with the Turkish nation and not with any special ruling group, this move of our Sovereign being duly appreciated by the Turks.

Ankara being the Headquarters of CENTO, I was a member of the Council of Deputies, who represented permanently the Foreign Ministers, together with the Ambassadors of the U.K., the U.S.A. and Pakistan and the Turkish representatives. In February 1959 we held our Ministerial meeting in Karachi, and in October had to go to Washington. As it was the first time I had been to the U.S.A. I took a few days' leave to visit New York and New Hampshire, where my sister-in-law had a little house in the midst of the forest which enabled us to admire the world-famous beauty of the autumn foliage there and to make the acquaintance of that charming American animal, the raccoon. My sister-in-law, who led a hermit-like existence, was on intimate terms with the forest creatures.

Returning from Washington, I resumed my work in Ankara, much of my time being devoted to the business of CENTO.

A military body was attached to the Pact under the name of P.M.D.G. with representatives from the member countries. Our delegate was General Batmanglij, the former Chief of Staff. We worked together in harmony striving to get more military aid from the Western members of the Pact, in close collaboration with the Pakistan delegates.

My sister had come from Montevideo to Monaco, where she

was busy transforming a part of the family villa there into a Persian museum in accordance with the wishes of our father. It was renamed Villa Ispahan and contains interesting collections. I asked her to come for a few days to Ankara, but as a result of a car accident we had while driving to Konya she remained with us for a month.

In September 1961, having nearly completed my four years' term in Turkey, I received from Teheran the notification that His Majesty had been pleased to extend my term of service abroad by one year, for service in Pakistan, and that agreement had already been asked for from Karachi. I was sorry to leave Turkey, of which country I was very fond and where I had made many good friends, but on the other hand I was delighted with the opportunity to visit a new Eastern country.

We left Ankara on the 31st October, flying first to Monaco where we stayed a few days with my sister. Whilst we were there I visited General Polovtzef of the Imperial Russian Army, who was living in Monte Carlo, a famous warrior and poet who had commanded the Native Caucasian Cavalry Division (known as the Wild Division) during the First World War, and had related his campaign in verse. He was eighty-four years old, but remembered vividly his adventures of those days and was much moved when I recited some of his verses. From Monaco we went to Paris where my former friends of the École de Guerre (all of them retired generals or colonels) gave a dinner in my honour with many speeches at the Cercle Militaire, and then to England, where The Iran Society, presided over by Lord Bossom, also arranged a luncheon in my honour at which I was glad to meet General Fraser, Colonel Pybus and other old friends from Teheran days. Before leaving England, we also paid a visit to Sir Reader Bullard at Oxford and to the distinguished orientalist Professor Minorski at Cambridge, whose student my wife had been at the School of Oriental Languages in Paris.

We flew to Teheran and from there to Karachi; arriving after a two-hour flight we were met by the Embassy Staff at the airport and drove to the brand new Embassy—a fine building in a large garden. I presented my Credentials to President Ayub Khan, who received me most cordially, and began my work. I was eager to know the whole country, and for this reason we flew to East Pakistan, visiting Dacca with its jute factories, and Chittagong.

We travelled on a river-boat down the Brahmaputra and Ganges to Khulna and Jessore, flying from there to the Sylhet tea gardens. From East Pakistan we flew to Rangoon, where we were met at the airport by representatives of the Iranian colony which numbers nearly 1000 people, most of whom have been there for several generations, and though they did not speak Persian and had adopted Burmese nationality, still cherished their Iranian connection and considered themselves Iranian.

The Foreign Secretary, James Barrington, on whom I called, is an Anglo-Burmese, and Rashid, the Minister of Trade, Industry and Mines, whom I also visited, was a Moslem. Burma is a tolerant country without prejudices!

We noticed while visiting the numerous Buddhist temples the extraordinary devotion and religious fervour of the crowds praying in front of the thousands of Buddhas, large and small, gilded, wooden, ivory and plaster which adorn them. The Buddhist religion is for the Burmese the embodiment of their nationalism, distinguishing them from the Hindus and Christians, and for this reason has, besides a religious, also a political meaning for them.

After three days we went to Bangkok. People there looked very clean and the town appeared prosperous, the temples and palaces are gorgeous and can be visited, as in Venice, by a complicated system of canals along which on the shores and in boats the life of the city is conducted, whilst smaller canals lead enticingly into the tropical forest.

I called on the Foreign Minister, Thanat Khoman, with whom I had a very enlightening conversation on the political situation in SEATO member countries before leaving.

A strange sight at Bangkok is the snake farm where we assisted at the unpacking of a freshly arrived batch of cobras, whose venom is used for vaccine and was dexterously extracted from them by fearless specialists who seize the snakes, forcing them to disgorge the poison into glass tubes, after which they are thrown into a ditch.

A few days after our return to Karachi the Burmese Chief of Staff, General Ne Win, staged his second *coup d'état* arresting all the ministers, including the elder statesman U Nu.

My daughter came to visit us in Karachi and we went together by car to Lahore, Delhi and Agra to see the Taj Mahal. I was proud to know that this architectural jewel had been built with the help of Iranian artists and craftsmen. It is, I suppose, the first monument to conjugal love in the world. Mumtaz Mahal having presented Shahjehan with fourteen children before her death inspired her bereaved husband to build it.

Our next journey was to Peshawar and the famous Khyber Pass through which India has been invaded so many times.

In April we flew to Quetta, where the region is much like many parts of Iran, and I visited Kelat, the chief town of the Baluch Kelat Khanate, which had belonged to Iran up to the eighteenth century, and New Chaman, on the Afghan frontier. On my way there I halted on the top of the Khojak Pass, from where one could see deep into Afghanistan, and which provides a fine natural defence position facing the west.

In May we abandoned the heat of Karachi for Murree, a hill station some 35 miles from Rawalpindi, the seat of Government, surrounded by forest-covered mountains with a magnificent view to Nanga Parbat and the offshoots of the Himalayas. Here we spent nearly three months and I began to write this book.

The relations between Pakistan and Afghanistan having been broken off on account of the closing of the Afghan Consulates which were accused of indulging in subversive propaganda among the Pathan population of the frontier districts which Afghanistan would like to see become an autonomous State, the Shahinshah decided to mediate between these two Moslem countries which had so much in common, and for this purpose came to Murree to talk with Mohammad Ayub Khan. Then from there he flew to Kabul, returning again to Pindi to confer once more with Ayub Khan. These steps brought about an easing of the tension between the two neighbours, and it is to be hoped that good relations will be restored before long.

This move of the Shah further strengthened the very close spiritual and cultural relations existing between Iran and Pakistan to such an extent that a deputy said in the National Assembly that Iran was the flesh and blood of Pakistan and half its soul, and at the same time contributed to the reinforcing of the ties of friendship between Iran and Afghanistan. These two countries have always been culturally related, as Persian is the literary language of Afghanistan and is spoken or understood by the whole Afghan population.

In September, being accredited to Ceylon as well as to Pakistan, we flew to Colombo, staying a few days in Bombay on our way there. I presented my Credentials to the Governor-General, and we had tea with Mrs. Bandaranaike, the Prime Minister, with whom my wife claimed spiritual cousinship by right of an uncle of hers who when Governor of Ceylon had been godfather to Solomon West Ridgeway Bandaranaike, the Prime Minister's late husband and predecessor as Prime Minister. The U.S. Ambassador on whom I had the pleasure of calling was also a lady. Although everybody, both from the Government side and the opposition, told us that the economic situation was catastrophic, everywhere we went we had the impression of prosperity, the houses being neat and the population clean, well dressed and apparently well fed. The literacy rating of Ceylon is the highest in the East, being about 85 per cent.

We visited Kandi, in the middle of the island, near which are the famous botanical gardens ranking second only to Kew, and I bathed at the Mont Lavinia beach several times, enjoying the Indian Ocean's surf in a landscape of blue sea, green coconut trees and golden sand.

A short time after our return to Karachi, we were on the move again, this time to Kashmir. The direct road from Rawalpindi and Murree was closed after the fighting between Pakistan and India in Kashmir, as a provisional cease-fire line had been fixed and communication between the two sides of that line interrupted, so we had to fly to Delhi and then to Srinagar by this roundabout way. In the paradisiac setting of Srinagar we rented a house-boat on the lake and spent our days sailing in a gondola-like rowing-boat called a *shikara* on the several lakes which communicate with one another through canals. Talking with the local population I had the impression that they were dissatisfied with the situation and wished to be united with Pakistan, but at the same time were much afraid of the Indians.

Back in Karachi we began to prepare for our return to Teheran. My term as Ambassador was running out, but before leaving I wished to assist at the emergency session of the National Assembly in Rawalpindi, where the question of the American and British arms-lift to India to help her against China's aggression in the Ladakh district of Indian-occupied Kashmir as well as in the North-East Frontier Area (N.E.F.A.) was to be discussed.

The Pakistanis had already been displeased with the American and British non-committal attitude to the Kashmir question, and the opposition in particular had been clamouring during the Summer Session for Pakistan to denounce the CENTO and SEATO Pacts which, according to them, caused Pakistan to be on bad terms with the Communist countries without giving her the support she felt to be her due as an ally. When the military help being given by the Western members of the Pacts to India, which the Pakistanis considered to be their declared enemy, became known, not only the opposition but the great majority of the nation clamoured for the immediate withdrawal of Pakistan from the Pacts and the reorientation of her policy.

Besides assisting at these momentous debates we went for one day to Swat, a tiny autonomous State some 250 miles to the north of Pindi, visiting Taxila on our way there. The Vali or Sovereign of Swat, with whom we had the pleasure of lunching, is an intelligent and progressive ruler who has created there a model State and is much interested in the excavations of Buddhist sites on his territory, which are being made by an Italian group headed by Professor Tucci.

On returning to Rawalpindi I assisted at the memorable Session of the National Assembly, at which the opposition leaders, Sardar Bahadur, President Ayub Khan's brother, and Farid Ahmed, a staunch supporter of the Islamic State and of a closer collaboration of Pakistan with Communist China and the U.S.S.R., fiercely attacked Pakistan's policy of Alliances with the Western Powers, although approving friendship with Iran and Turkey.

My term of office in Pakistan coming to its close I took leave of President Ayub Khan and of the Foreign Minister Mohammad Ali of Boghra who was already ailing and who died two months later, and on 6th December 1962 I left Pakistan for Teheran.

Mohammad Reza Shah

What are the prospects for Iran after the upheavals which have characterised the country's history as a consequence of the Second World War?

The dominant figure in Iran during these years has been Mohammad Reza Shah Pahlavi, the heir to some 500 kings belonging to 40 dynasties who had reigned and governed Iran during 2500 years, and whose personality burgeoning under his formidable father's rule has developed according to his very different nature under the influence of ordeals and vicissitudes chiefly due to the war.

At first timidly groping to find the way for his country's survival in the face of odds which might have broken the strongest leader, bending but not breaking under the storm which swept away the most powerful States, little by little, through deceptions and disappointments, he asserted his personality, learning the rules of Government and acquainting himself with the often unreliable nature of those who surrounded him and with whom he had to work.

If he was able to survive and succeed it was due to an unflinching faith in the ideals he had inherited from his dedicated father: his unbounded patriotism, love of the common people and desire to raise their condition by the application of social justice, bringing the country out of its backwardness through adequate reforms. An uncommon intelligence and a natural suppleness helped him to surmount many obstacles, sometimes finding a way around them and sometimes forcefully removing them, his objective remaining always the same, although short-sighted people misunderstanding his purpose sometimes failed to discern the pattern of his actions.

As in the case of Reza Shah, the Shah's main support, especially in difficult periods, was the army, and even on the crucial day of the 19th August 1953, although not actively participating in the national rising of the people, the army refused to be used against it and though not as an organised body, joined the loyalists in overwhelming numbers as individuals, leaving the half-dozen Mosaddeq commanders high and dry after the first couple of hours.

Apart from the ingrained discipline of the officers and men accustomed to obey their Supreme Commander, it must be taken into consideration that no military chief's prestige in the army equals that of the Shah who is cherished by the rank and file, and is particularly popular among the younger officers, who form a conscious and critical body.

The Shah's popularity with the people was at the beginning based chiefly on the traditional feeling of loyalty to the Sovereign, the Shahinshah. Then, gradually it became personal as the result of his actions and of the irradiation of his personality. The care he took to secure the well-being of the young officers and N.C.O.s, the natural kindness he displayed on all occasions, his interest in promoting social justice for the working classes and especially the distribution of his personal estates and his insistence on the implementation of the agrarian reforms which he had initiated, won him the hearts of the common people both in towns and in the villages.

This popularity increased with the Shah's third marriage, the grace, ease of manner and sympathy with everybody of Empress Farah winning her the hearts of even the most prejudiced, and her careful observance of what was considered a proper behaviour for a queen in an Islamic country silenced the most devout and even bigoted clericals. The birth of a son to this already deeply loved and respected couple transformed this popularity into adoration, and today the Iranian Imperial couple is the model for the country, and for the first time in Iran's history the Shahbanu (Empress) and the Valiahd share with the Shahinshah the affections of their people.

Confident of the support of the nation, the Shah took a momentous decision.

On the 9th January 1963 a Congress of rural corporations opened in Teheran and in his inaugural address the Shah announced to 4000 delegates that it was the intention of the Government to implement six basic reforms, two of which had already been started.

They were:

    1. A land-reform law, aiming at the division of the estates belonging to the State, to pious foundations and to private persons among the peasants who are at present cultivating them as share-croppers, the ex-landowners receiving compensation.

    2. The sharing of profits by the workers in the industries in which they are employed.

    3. The nationalisation of forests—with compensation to the former owners.

    4. An electoral reform including the right of women to vote and be elected.

    5. The eradication of illiteracy by supplementing the

normal educational institutions by the employment of conscripts having the necessary qualifications to teach in improvised classrooms in the rural districts.

6. The transformation of State-owned industries into shareholding companies in which the public can invest.

At the end of the month, consent of the Iranian nation was ascertained by a referendum.

The implementation of this programme will bring about a radical transformation in the economic and social life of the nation, which will now rank among the most progressive, and this result will have been attained without bloodshed or violent upheaval through the will and determination of Iran's great and enlightened Sovereign.

The Last Two Years

The first and most important of the six basic reforms of January 1963 was certainly the Land-Reform. It was announced that this reform would be implemented in two phases. In the first phase, the landowners possessing more than one village were to sell their surplus villages to the State, which divided them among the share-croppers in full possession, the latter repaying the State by means of annuities. This phase, started in 1963, was practically terminated at the end of 1964 and was also applied to crown lands and estates belonging to religious foundations. These being usually administered by the clergy, who derived substantial profits out of them, great dissatisfaction was felt by the influential Molla class. Of course, many landowners and people related to them were also critical of the Land-Reform, which could never have been applied without the unflinching determination of the Shah.

By contrast, this law gave profound satisfaction to the peasants and workers, although, no longer receiving guidance or financial assistance in times of need by their former landlords, they had difficulty in adjusting themselves to the new conditions. In order to obviate these difficulties, the Government organised cooperative societies composed of representatives of the cultivators and directed by members of the Ministry of Agriculture. These cooperatives, which number some 4500 today, will certainly, after one or two years, gain the necessary experience and authority to guide the new small holders towards the spirit of cooperation necessary for the distribution of water for irrigation, repairing of rural roads and bridges, etc.

In the tribal regions of the South, some landlords who were at the same time chiefs of tribes, being opposed to the Land-Reform, agitated against it among their tribesmen, leading them to believe that their traditional way of life was threatened by the new law. As a result of these provocations, a few clans and groups of tribesmen under their chieftains revolted in the Fars province and took to the mountains. They were pursued by the security forces and forced to surrender in the summer of 1963. Several of the ring-leaders among the chieftains were tried for rebellion and shot.

Another important reform was the right given to women to elect and be elected to the Chamber of Representatives and the Senate. In the new legislature there are now six women deputies out of 200 and two women senators out of 60. If this laudable reform was greeted favourably by the intellectuals and the pro-gressives, it must be acknowledged that the majority of the lower and part of the middle class were hostile to it for religious reasons, believing that women must only look after their homes and have nothing to do with politics or even with the economic life of the country. These reactionary sentiments were openly supported by some Mollas and when a prominent cleric named Khomeīni was arrested in Qom after a particularly provocative speech inciting the people to revolt, disturbances occured in Mashad, Shiraz and Tabriz. In Teheran they took the shape of mob violence, fanatics roaming in the streets adjoining the Bazar, destroying telephone booths, wrecking and burning buses and private cars and even brutally murdering two officers who were driving in their car. Army units were summoned to support the police, martial law was proclaimed and, according to official sources, some 120 people were killed and many others wounded. This strong action broke at once the back of the rebellion and prevented the country from foundering into chaos and anarchy.

A village is the normal unit of estate. It consists of a cluster of houses belonging to the landlord and inhabited by share-cropping peasants. The land surrounding the village is divided into plots assigned by the landlord to these peasants, together with one or more water channels used for artificial irrigation in the dry regions of the country.

The Melliyoun and Mardom parties, organised in 1956, did not succeed in attracting the masses, and a new party was organised under the name Iran Novin (New Iran), and was lead by a young and capable politician, Hassan 'Ali Mansur, the son of 'Ali Mansur who had been twice Prime Minister and was my predecessor at the Embassy in Ankara. This party obtained, in the 1963 elections, the majority of seats both in the Majles (Chamber of Representa-tives) and in the Senate, and soon thereafter Assadellah 'Alam resigned and was replaced by Hassan 'Ali Mansur, who came to power with a cabinet of technocrats and started to work with eagerness and enthusiasm. His task was not easy, as he had to overcome the peasants, workers, and artisans opposed to the voting of women.

Then, in order to satisfy the desire of the United States which enjoyed such privileges in certain other countries, the Government submitted to the Majles a bill placing the members of the American Military Mission outside the jurisdiction of the Iranian courts. This bill was approved by the Majles out of party discipline, but provoked widespread dissatisfaction, people of all classes considering this measure a revival of the abhorred Capitulations, which had been suppressed in 1928 by Reza Shah.

Meanwhile the Government, under the inspiration of the Shah, started a new series of measures destined to bring Iran to the forefront of the progressive nations of Asia. One of these, the Literacy Corps (see pp. 437-38), has showed very good results, many of the young conscript-teachers applying to remain as regular teachers in the villages in which they taught. Some even helped the peasants build schoolrooms. This success encouraged the Shah to start a new campaign for the general rehabilitation of the rural districts, and besides the Literacy Corps a Health Corps was organised in which the conscripted medical students and dentists, after four months military training, were sent to remote villages, where they had to look after the health of the population until the end of their regular term of service.

Another success of the Government was the granting of a concession for offshore oil extraction to two companies on favourable terms (75% to the Government and 25% to the companies), and this success was very favourably received by the public.

In the autumn of 1964, the Government announced the start of the second phase of the Land-Reform. During this phase, the landowners were to come to terms with their tenant sharecroppers for the sale or long-term renting of the lands of their remaining villages, the fruit and vegetable gardens, and also plots which were cultivated directly by the landowners (because of the exclusion of hired labour). Large tracts up to 500 hectares (1250 acres), not previously cultivated by share-croppers, could also be retained by landowners using mechanized implements. This phase is now in the process of application and will probably be terminated in 1966.

Prime Minister Mansur used to say that the country was undergoing a revolution, and if one considers the profound changes in the social, economic and political life of the country, one cannot deny the truth of this statement. Unfortunately revolution provokes struggle and momentary upheavals, and Mansur was the first to fall victim to one of these. On the 21st of January, 1965, while entering the Majles, he was shot by a youth and died of his wounds a few days later. The murderer, who was a member of a fanatical reactionary group, was arrested with his accomplices and brought to trial. This murder provoked general indignation, as Mansur was known as an honest, hardworking and progressive statesman. His friend the Minister of Finance, Amir 'Abbas Hoveida, succeeded him as Prime Minister in order to continue his work according to the program of reforms set forth by the Shah. Hoveïda—who had been my counsellor at the Ankara Embassy—is as progressive and hardworking as Mansur, but somewhat milder and more receptive to constructive criticism and has inherited the confidence the Sovereign had towards the late Mansur.

In spite of the murder of Mansur, all seemed again to be calm and settled, when an event which profoundly shook the country took place on the 10th of April, 1965.

That day, when the Shah was entering his working study, a conscript soldier of the Guards rushed behind the Sovereign, firing wildly with his sub-machine gun. He was attacked and killed by the other Guards, but fatally wounded two of them who fell victims to their courage and loyalty to the Shah. It was first thought that the murderer had run amok, but after inquiries it was discovered that he had belonged to an extreme-left communist group which had helped to start a reign of terror and partisan warfare to bring about the collapse of the regime and subsequent communization of the country on Chinese lines. All the members of this terrorist gang, consisting of young engineers trained in British universities, were arrested and an important amount of subversive literature was seized at their homes. All confessed to belonging to that group, but only two had actually instructed the criminal soldier to attempt to take the life of the Sovereign.

As after the first attempt on his life in 1949, the Shah showed remarkable composure. The afternoon after the attempt, driving his car himself, he went without escort to the populous districts of the city, where he was enthusiastically greeted by the people. A few days later he flew to Shiraz and, to the great anxiety of the security agents, walked on foot in the streets, mingling with the population.

The attempt on the Shah's life stirred profoundly the Iranian nation, everybody realising what a tragedy the disappearance of the Monarch would have been for the country. Spontaneous manifestations of thanksgiving were organised by all classes of the population and a spirit of national union could be felt throughout the Empire. Without doubt, this event strengthened the feelings of loyalty and affection of the nation towards the Sovereign and confirmed him in his determination to persevere in the accomplishment of his task of regenerating the country and leading the Iranian nation along the path of prosperity and progress.

Situation in the Tribal Regions and Zones Outside the Central Government's Control in 1921

1. Starting from Teheran to the North-West, and then rotating to the West, South, East and North-East, there were first the two Shahsevan Turki-speaking tribes of Inanlu and Baghdadi, the first one, under its chief Zaafer Nizam, extending its depredations up to the western gates of Teheran, was located roughly between Qazvin and Saveh.

2. In Gilan, Mirza Kuchik Khan now supported by the Bolshevik forces was roaming in the forests of that region and had proclaimed in Rasht the Persian Soviet Republic.

3. In Iranian Azerbaijan, the Khalkhal district was in the hands of a local chief, Amir Ashair, openly in rebellion against Teheran.

4. Further to the north, the many Turki-speaking Shahsevan tribes in the Ardabil and Khiyav (Meshkin) region, up to the Aras river, were not only rebellious, but used to cross the Bozgush range to attack and pillage the sedentary population and travellers on the Zanjan–Tabriz road.

5. To the west of the Shahsevan, in the region of Karajadagh (today called Arasbaran), a local chief named Amir Arshad held power. After the Azerbaijan Republic's armed forces retreating before the Red Army had crossed into Iran he had had them disarmed, and keeping their arms and many of the former Russian officers as instructors, had organised a private army of 2500 men which was later reinforced by the arms and war equipment of the Armenian Republic's Army, when it also crossed into Iran in December 1920 pursued by Soviet forces, and was disarmed by him. In this way Amir Arshad came into possession of three mountain guns and some thirty Lewis and heavy machine-guns. Although not in open rebellion, this man entertained towards the Central Government relations of 'benevolent neutrality', without allowing any officials or security

forces to enter his realm nor paying any taxes, his residence being at Ahar.

6. In the Maku district, which was unofficially termed Maku Khanate, the Sardar Eqbal-os-Saltaneh was the hereditary Khan according to himself, and the Governor according to the Central Government. His influence extended as far as the district of Khoi, the governor of which was traditionally appointed by the Sardar of Maku from among his relatives. His attitude *vis-à-vis* the Central Government was approximately the same as that of Amir Arshad of Karajadagh, but he had a more important position, living as he did on the frontiers of both Russia and Turkey. The population of this district was partly Kurdish- and partly Turki-speaking, the Sardar himself belonging to the latter category.

7. To the west of Urmia, the chief of the Kurdish Shakkak tribe, Esma'il Aqa Simko, had proclaimed an independent Kurdish State. He was in contact with the Kurdish independent organisation in Paris, called Khaibun. Simko was considered the War Minister in the shadow cabinet of the prospective Republic of Kordestan, the existence of which had been foreshadowed in the Treaty of Sèvres dismembering the Ottoman Empire.

The Shakkak tribe had always been in dissidence, but after its chief Ja'far Aqa, summoned to Tabriz by the Governor, had been murdered there, his younger brother Simko had openly rebelled and occupied the towns of Urmia, Dilman and all the region between the lake and the Turkish frontier, subjecting the Shia Moslem Turki-speaking population of these districts to every kind of exaction, and massacring a great number of Christian Assyrians living around Urmia and Dilman.

Simko had with him about 10,000 well-armed Kurdish warriors from different allied Kurdish tribes besides the Shakkak, and some 400 Turkish deserters manning three mountain guns left over by the Russian Army in Urmia. At that time (1920) he had already defeated several attempts of Government forces to penetrate into the region occupied by him, inflicting on them severe casualties, thereby raising the morale of the Kurds and his prestige among them.

8. The Khamseh province around Zanjan, between Qazvin and Tabriz, was in its greater part subject to the Afshar tribal chief Jan Shah Khan Amir Afshar, who was quite independent and refused to pay any taxes.

9. Other Afshar chiefs were equally rebellious in the Sain Qal'eh (now Shahin Dezh) district of southern Azerbaijan, the most prominent among them being Bahador-os-Saltaneh.

10. In the Kordestan province, all the tribes were at that time armed to the teeth and in open rebellion against the Government, which had only a precarious hold on Sanandaj and a few other places.

11. The rural districts of the Kermanshah province were mostly in the hands of the local Kurdish tribes, some of them, like the Qobadi, Babajani, Valadbegi, Avromi and Javanrudi, in complete dissidence, while others, like the Goran, Sanjabi, Kalhor and Hamavand, although also quite independent and well armed, refrained from overt action against the Government unless interfered with by its security forces.

12. The Lorestan region is formed by two provinces divided by the chain of Kabir Kuh, parallel to the frontier, one of the branches of the Zagros mountains which start at Ararat and continue uninterruptedly towards the Persian Gulf and the Arabian Sea. The inner part of Lorestan to the east of Kabir Kuh called Pish Kuh was inhabited by numerous Lor tribes, the Lors being pure Iranians little affected by the different invasions of Greeks, Arabs, Turks and Mongols, and speaking a Persian dialect nearly devoid of any foreign borrowed words. These tribes had no union among themselves, but had been from time immemorial in permanent revolt against any organised State, and were renowned for their wild and indomitable nature. All these tribes were nomads.

In the outer part of Lorestan called Posht-e-Kuh between the Kabir Kuh and the frontier, the Lor tribes, called Posht-e-Kuhis, this meaning 'from behind the mountains', were subject to the Vali of Posht-e-Kuh, Abu Qaddareh, who was the hereditary Governor of this region, and up to then recognised as Warden of the Marches by the Iranian Government. During the First World War, unwilling to provoke him, the Russians, British and Turks took care not to impinge on his territory, and he managed to keep himself aloof from the struggle until the end. He was practically independent and did not pay taxes nor accept any liabilities towards the Central Government.

13. In Khuzestan, the Sheikh of Mohammarah, who had become Sheikh after having murdered his brother, had carved out

for himself a kind of kingdom comprising the whole south and central part of the province, the only Iranian functionary allowed in his realm being the Belgian customs official at Moham-marah (now Khorramshahr). Sheikh Khazal had concluded in 1910 an agreement with the British Resident in the Persian Gulf, at that time Sir Percy Cox, representing the British Government, authorising the construction of a pipe-line from the oilfields of Mesjed Soleyman to Abadan island on the Shatt-al-Arab, and conceding to them a site for the construction of an oil-refinery. The British Government guaranteed his autonomy and undertook to prevent any interference by the Central Government with his rule. This agreement had not been officially published, and the Iranian Government had never recognised it, but at the time it gave to the Sheikh a sense of security, and he put no obstacles in the way of the Anglo-Persian Oil Company's activities on what he considered to be his territory.

14. The west and south-west of Isfahan was the country of the Bakhtiari tribes of whom there were two groups:

The north-western group, called Bakhtiari Chahar Lang, whose chiefs had held in the middle of the nineteenth century the leadership of all the Bakhtiari tribes, numbering approxi-mately 30,000 tents (all were nomads), amounting like the Qashqai to 150,000 souls, but lost it when Nasr-ed-Din Shah fearing their strength executed their chief, and constituted a great number of separate sub-tribes and clans, who had in common only the desire to prevent any interference of the Central Government in their affairs. They nomadised between Aligodarz and Dezful.

The south-western group, called the Bakhtiari Haft Lang, were under the Bakhtiari Ilkhan family, whose chief Sardar Assad had marched against Teheran in 1909 to help re-establish the Constitution and chase away the autocratic Mohammad Ali Shah. Since then, they had gained considerably in importance and influence, and members of this family were often appointed governors of Isfahan, Yazd and even Kerman. They were traditionally pro-British, being subsidised by the A.P.O.C. for assuring the security of the region of the oilfields, and were more often than not in opposition to their southern neighbours the Qashqai. They were on good terms with Sheikh Khazal of

Mohammarah and at the time not openly hostile to the Central Government, but were jealous of their independent position and not inclined to allow any interference and extension of the central administration to their region. They occupied a vast region between the line Isfahan to Daran in the north and that of Masjed Soleyman–Ram Hormoz–Dehdiz on the south-west, passing the summer in the northern mountainous regions and the winter in the plains of Eastern Khuzistan.

15. To the south of the Bakhtiaris, in the rugged and wild region of the Kuhgelu where many peaks reach altitudes of above 14,000 feet, live the different clans of the Boveir-Ahmad tribes, wild like their country, brave and warlike, who up to this date had never been subjected to a central administration. They were Lors like the Bakhtiaris, but much more unruly and did not have chiefs representing all the clans in an effective way with whom the Government could negotiate and come to terms.

16. In the Fars province, which was chiefly inhabited by tribes, the Qashqai were united under a single chief and as disciplined as wild tribesmen can be. They were also nomadic, staying in winter in the Firuzabad–Farrashband region and moving with all their flocks to the cool mountains in the Semirom region in the summer. They were about six months on the move, having to travel more than 200 miles in spring to reach their summer grazing tracts and 200 miles again to go back to their winter quarters. They were all armed and presented a formidable tribal force, comparable to the Pathans of the former north-west frontier of India, but more dangerous, because recognising but one chief. The Qashqai are supposed to have been brought to Iran by Chengiz Khan from Turkestan. Their Turki dialect is close to that of Azerbaijan.

The tribes of the Khamseh confederation lacked that union, and were consequently less dangerous, but were dispersed over a very extensive region, their winter quarters between Lar, Jahrom and Darab and their summer grazing grounds near Abadeh being at a distance of 350 miles from each other. As their name indicates—Khamseh meaning five in Arabic—they are composed of five big tribes: two Lori-speaking—the Nafar and the Basseri—two Turki-speaking—the Inanlu and the Baharlu—and one Arab. This last one is subdivided into two sub-tribes, the Sheibani and the Jabbara. They used to be under the influence of the Qavam family of Shiraz, but the Qavams have never been their chiefs, but only their representatives and go-betweens with the Governor-General in Shiraz. They were usually not on too good terms with the Qashqai, but occasionally allied themselves with them when menaced from outside the Fars province. This happened once in 1918, when the British were organising the S.P.R., and later when the Central Government forces began pacifying the province.

Apart from the tribes Fars was renowned as the haunt of robbers and highwaymen, mostly outcasts from their tribes, or former road guards and dismissed gendarmes. The rugged and mountainous terrain rendered the pursuit of these robbers a very difficult task, and the proximity of the coast helped in gun-running, which was quite a flourishing trade for the Arabs of the Oman Sheikhdoms.

17. The region south of Kerman had the same characteristics as Fars, but the tribes there were less important and the region suffered chiefly from the depredations of robbers and the raids of Baluchis on the eastern districts of the province.

18. The extensive province of Iranian Baluchistan and Mak-ran is entirely peopled by Baluch tribes. The province of Baluchistan is composed of four natural geographical regions, in each of which the tribes had a special relationship with the Central Government.

The Makran, from Jask to Chah Bahar and Gwatar, was under the chief of the Sadozai, Sardar Said Khan, who lived in Chah Bahar and Gey (now Nikshahr). He did not accept any Central Government officials, and had, as well as several other chieftains of that region, a special relationship with the British Indo-European Telegraph Co.'s agents who paid them subsidies in order to prevent the line from being interfered with, these payments being effected through the British Consular agent at Bandar Abbas. Abdi Khan in Bahu Kelat was in the same position.

Around Bampur and Fahraj (now Iranshahr), in the region known as Garmsir, a Baluch Sardar called Bahram Khan had established his rule in 1915, and had been succeeded by his nephew Dost Mohammad, who defied the Government and tried to subdue the other parts of Baluchistan. He succeeded in taking Magas (now Zaboli), and part of Saravan.

The Saravan region contained several small tribes which were holding their own against everybody.

To the north was the region of the Sarhad, bordering on the Chagai district of British (now Pakistan) Baluchistan. This district contained three important tribes resolutely hostile to the Central Government: the Yarahmadzai under the old Jiand and Shahsavar and their confederates the Gomshadzai to the east of Khash, near the Chagai frontier, and the Esma'ilzai in the Shuru mountains, whose chief was Joma Khan.

To the north of these tribes, as also in some other parts of Baluchistan and in Sistan, were the Narui, who were better disposed to the Central Government.

19. The whole of Qayenat with Birjand and Sistan were subject to Amir Showkat-ol-Molk, hereditary Governor and Warden of the Eastern Marches, who was an enlightened and patriotic man and had a great influence in all the southern part of Khorasan.

20. In Khorasan, in 1921, Colonel Mohammad Taqi Khan held sway against the Government, but he was challenged by certain tribes which were induced by the Government to attack the rebel officers and weaken him until the Government forces were in a position to intervene.

To the south of Mashad the Teimuri, Hazara, Bakherzi and others did not present a security problem to the Government, but to the north, the Darragazi, Zafaranlu and Shadlu were practically independent, although the Zafaranlu were hostile to Mohammad Taqi Khan.

21. The Turkomans formed two groups:

The eastern group, called Goklans, were subject to the Khan of Bojnurd, Sardar Moazzez, who was the chief of the Shadlu Kurds. These Kurds, together with the Zafaranlu and the Keivanlu of Quchan and Chanaran, had been transferred from Kordestan by the Safavi Shahs in the sixteenth and seventeenth centuries in order to form a defence against the depredations of the Turkomans from Khiva and Merv (now Mary).

The western group, called Yomout, comprising Atabay, Aq Atabay and Ja'farbay Turkomans, were nomadising in the Gorgan plain between Maravah Tappeh, Gonbad-e-Kavus and the Caspian Sea, up to the Russian frontier. These tribes used to cross the frontiers into Russia, but after the revolution the frontier was closed and part of the Atabay Turkomans remained on the Russian side, and for many years to come were to try, sometimes not without success, to join their co-tribesmen in Iran. The tribes of the western group were completely lawless, not acknowledging any authority, and raiding periodically the neighbouring districts of Khorasan. The total number of Turkomans was about 200,000.

22. In Mazanderan, Amir Moayyid was still engaging in hostilities against the Government in alliance with the Reds who reappeared, coming from Gilan.

Index